FAMILY LAW

FAMILY LAW
Second Edition

By

HARRY D. KRAUSE
Max L. Rowe Professor of Law
University of Illinois College of Law

BLACK LETTER SERIES®

WEST GROUP

Bancroft-Whitney • Clark Boardman Callaghan
Lawyers Cooperative Publishing • WESTLAW® • West Publishing

For Customer Assistance Call 1-800-328-4880

Black Letter Series and Black Letter Series design appearing on the front cover are registered trademarks of West Publishing Co. Registered in the U.S. Patent and Trademark office.

COPYRIGHT © 1988 WEST PUBLISHING CO.

COPYRIGHT © 1996 By WEST PUBLISHING CO.
    610 Opperman Drive
    P.O. Box 64526
    St. Paul, MN 55164–0526
    1–800–328–9352

Library of Congress Cataloging-in-Publication Data

Krause, Harry D., 1932–
  Family law / Harry D. Krause. — 2nd ed.
    p. cm. — (Black letter series)
  Includes index.
  ISBN 0–314–09709–0 (soft cover)
  1. Domestic relations—United States—Outlines, syllabi, etc.
 I. Title. II. Series.
KF505.Z9K68 1996
346.7301 ' 5—dc20
[347.30615]
             96–22682
             CIP

ISBN 0–314–09709–0

TEXT IS PRINTED ON 10°₀ POST CONSUMER RECYCLED PAPER

1st Reprint–1997

AUTHOR'S PREFACE

ABOUT "STUDY AIDS"

Having authored this Black Letter, it must seem near the height of hypocrisy to repeat the customary pious caution against over-reliance on "study aids." Well, I'll do it anyway. You know as well as I do that the one way of becoming an effective lawyer is to *think* along with the development of the subject matter by studying the cases themselves—or in any event their edited remains—in the *assigned* "study aid," your casebook. But you also find yourself under time pressures that make anything that abstracts the "black letter law" seem inevitably attractive. WEST established this "Black Letter" series to assure a level of quality that some more hastily prepared "outlines" lack. If it is to be done, it should be done well. Consistently with the need for brevity, I have tried to be reasonably accurate in synthesizing this fast-evolving area of law, even if some of the finer points have had to be compromised.

The advice of several students helped me better to understand the needs of students from their own perspective. In varying degrees and various years, Susan Frank, Dawn Ehrenberg, Michelle Gilbert, Cameron DeLong, Carol McCrehan Parker, Chris Sundlof, Robert Felber, Earl Erland, Don Vilim, Robert (Matt) Molash, Linda Freisler, Scott Shiplett and Susan Stitt contributed to this—we hope—successful outcome. In this edition, particular reference must be made to Mary Palumbo, whose valuable effort in printing out innumerable "candidate cases" from WESTLAW, helping to identify good "examples", and abstracting them was a great help. Many thanks as well to Carrie May who skillfully prepared not only the final version, but who patiently typed and retyped the many drafts and redrafts that underlie this product.

ORGANIZATION

The detailed organization of this Black Letter is traced in the Table of Contents. To summarize: A "capsule summary" for last-minute, final review broadly mirrors the organization of the main part. (While major headings are the same, some of the subheadings have been combined or altered to achieve greater brevity and clarity. The included word-processing disk will help you prepare your own course outline.) The "Capsule" is followed by more detailed exposition where the text is supported with summaries of illustrative cases. Quotation of original language is emphasized in order to maintain accuracy and to give "live" flavor to the law. True/false questions follow each substantive chapter. These questions— and even more, the answers—are to be taken with a grain of caution. As you well know, few things are wholly true or wholly false, especially in law. Most of the challenges presented there are "more true than false" or "more false than true." The questions should be reviewed in those terms. At the end, a practice essay examination is provided. A cross reference chart correlates coverage of subject matter in this volume and in leading casebooks. A Glossary, appropriately based on Black's Law Dictionary, and a detailed Index conclude this Black Letter.

AND STILL ANOTHER WORD ABOUT EXAMINATIONS

By now you have had so much advice on how to write a law examination that you have discovered that there is no universal rule, but you probably have a pretty good idea what works best for you. If it works, stick with that. A model answer has not been provided for the practice essay because quite different responses to the same question may merit (or receive) the same grade. Each person has to tailor his or her approach to her or his own style and (if only more were known about that) to the grader's personality and preferences. I would, however, discount the oft-repeated morsel that you should first prepare an elaborate outline of your answer on scrap paper. If there are time limitations— and on the typical law school examination there are—anyone who can, after brief reflection, find the proper starting point from which to develop the answer logically while going along, should do just that. This will leave more time to answer the question where it counts—in the bluebook, pursuing additional issues or elaborating on a basically correct answer. Those who think they are helped if they draw up an outline before answering the question, should re-examine their mental resources whether they cannot train themselves to avoid the time-consuming duplication of thought and writing. Of course, if there is no significant time limit, by all means prepare an outline and even write drafts. It probably will improve your product.

Another variant (intended by the examiner to make you feel more flustered or more comfortable?) is the open book examination. With time constraints, an "open book" examination will tempt you to waste precious time on looking up things you do (or should) know. Again, this typically will be time you would be better off using to *write* your answer.

There is one universal rule. That rule mandates the fair (not necessarily equal) allocation of time and effort to *each* question, to each part of a multi-part examination. The marginal grade-boosting value of a few extra sentences (or even "issues") on one question will rarely come close to the return on getting at least a basic answer worked out to the next question. Do not "borrow" time. If you can't organize, simply stop answering one question and begin answering the next when your watch says so.

Beyond that, clear organization (or at least giving the impression thereof) is as good an indicator of clear thinking as you can provide the grader—and law examination grading is supposed to reward clear thinking. Here is where the value of a structured outline of your answer may come in. A structured response (with numbered subheadings, if appropriate) should begin at a logical starting point, the "core issue", and evolve logically, issue by issue. It will look *and very likely be* more "organized" than a rambling discussion that wanders panic-stricken from issue to issue, back and forth, even if you ultimately "hit" them all.

I'll say nothing about handwriting other than that the sheer physical legibility of your answer is much more important than is generally admitted. Remember that you are in law school, not medical school. Lawyers communicate in language, not in illegible code. Typed or printed answers have the attribute of being more transparent. A good answer will look more obviously good (*i.e.*, perhaps a little better than it really is), and a bad answer will look more obviously bad (*i.e.*, worse than it may actually be). *But there is the uncomfortable fact that the fast typist can add a considerable amount of vol-*

ume to his or her answer! Volume is worthless if it is mere verbiage—but if slow handwriting speed prevents you from putting down all the relevant information and analysis you have ready to pour out of your head, typing will put you ahead of the game. Today, of course, word processing computers have caused the near extinction of conventional typewriters—along with the skill needed to type without opportunity for instant and traceless erasure. Since many law schools do not allow the use in examinations of computers with memory, the typing option is no longer much of an issue. Anachronistically, most students have been turned back to handwritten examinations—thus leveling the playing field.

Good Luck! Remember it was you who decided to study law. All inevitable aggravations aside, "law" should be perceived by you as fun, and examinations as competitive games. Otherwise, the competitive life that follows law school will not be fun. If all else fails, think of Mr. Bumble's lawyer who mused: "The law may be a ass, but it sure is giving me a good ride!"

*

PUBLISHER'S PREFACE

This "Black Letter" is designed to help a law student recognize and understand the basic principles and issues of law covered in the family law course. It can be used as a study aid when preparing for classes and to review the subject matter when studying for an examination.

Each "Black Letter" is written by experienced law school teachers who are recognized national authorities in the subject covered.

The law is succinctly stated by the author of this "Black Letter." In addition, the exceptions to the rules are stated in the text. The rules and exceptions have purposely been condensed to facilitate quick review and easy recollection. A **Text Correlation Chart** provides a convenient means of relating material contained in the Black Letter to appropriate sections of the casebook the student is using in his or her law school course.

FORMAT

The format of this "Black Letter" is specially designed for review. (1) **Text.** First, it is recommended that the entire text be studied, and, if deemed necessary, supplemented by the student texts cited. (2) **Capsule Summary.** The Capsule Summary is an abbreviated review of the subject matter which can be used both before and after studying the main body of the text. The headings in the Capsule Summary follow the main text of the "Black Letter." (3) **Table of Contents.** The Table of Contents is in outline form to help you organize the details of the subject and the Summary of Contents gives you a final overview of the materials. (4) **Practice Examination.** The Practice Examination in Appendix B gives you the opportunity of testing yourself with the type of question asked on an exam.

A number of additional features are included to help you understand the subject matter and prepare for examinations:

Short Questions and Answers: This feature is designed to help you spot and recognize issues in the examination. We feel that issue recognition is a major ingredient in successfully writing an examination.

Author's Preface: In this feature, the author discusses his approach to the topic, the approach used in preparing the materials, and any tips on studying for and writing examinations.

Analysis: This feature, at the beginning of each section, is designed to give a quick summary of a particular section to help you recall the subject matter and to help you determine which areas need the most extensive review.

Examples: This feature is designed to illustrate, through fact situations, the law just stated. This will help you analytically approach a question on the examination.

Glossary: This feature is designed to refamiliarize you with the meaning of a particular legal term. We believe that the recognition of words of art used in an examination helps you to better analyze the question. In addition, when writing an examination you should know the precise definition of a word of art you intend to use.

Index: The Index will get you a quick reference to a specific issue.

The materials in this "Black Letter" will facilitate your study of the family law course and assure success in writing examinations not only for the course but when you take the bar examination. We wish you success.

THE PUBLISHER

SUMMARY OF CONTENTS

*

TABLE OF CONTENTS

CAPSULE SUMMARY

I. THE NATURE OF MARRIAGE

A. RELIGIOUS INFLUENCE
The common law has been greatly affected by the jurisprudence of ecclesiastical courts. In England, these courts had exclusive jurisdiction over marriage, divorce and other family matters until the mid-nineteenth century.

B. CONTRACT OR STATUS
Marriage is a status which is entered into by contract. While the state defines the rights and obligations due each party, the parties are allowed some variation by means of an antenuptial agreement.

C. CONTROLLING FACTORS AFFECTING THE MARRIAGE CONTRACT
1. State Power
States may modify marriage and divorce laws. Even if that results in seemingly "retroactive" application, court challenges on constitutional grounds have not succeeded.

1

2. Change of Residence
Validity of a marriage generally is determined by the law of the place of celebration, whereas the law of the place of marital domicile governs the legal incidents of the relationship as well as divorce.

D. MARRIAGE AND THE SUPREME COURT OF THE UNITED STATES
Numerous aspects of family law have raised constitutional issues. The following concepts have been principal vehicles: equal protection; due process (substantive and procedural); marital and sexual privacy; religious freedom.

E. THE MARITAL RELATIONSHIP AT COMMON LAW
Husband and wife were regarded as one person in law. The legal existence of the married woman was essentially incorporated into that of the husband.

F. "MARRIED WOMEN'S PROPERTY ACTS"
Derogating from the common law, statutes were enacted in the 19th century to allow married women the right to own and convey property, make contracts, sue or be sued, and more.

G. ANTENUPTIAL (PREMARITAL) AGREEMENTS
Today's great interest in antenuptial agreements is due primarily to dual career marriages, easy divorce and the desire of many couples to individualize the marital relationship. Traditionally, antenuptial agreements were used principally by wealthy or older persons, typically with children from a prior marriage, in order to regulate the financial consequences of marriage or upon death.

1. Individualizing Marriage by Contract
A valid antenuptial agreement alters the marital rights and obligations that would otherwise be imposed on the parties by law.

2. Validity of Antenuptial Agreements
Requirements of contract law must be met. In addition, the agreement will be subject to special scrutiny based on the parties' close relationship and public policy.

a. Contract Requirements
1) Statute of Frauds
   Antenuptial agreements generally are required to be in writing. An exception may be made if there has been sufficient part performance, if enforcement would perpetrate a fraud, or if there has been reliance.

2) Consideration

Mutual promises to marry traditionally serve as contractual consideration. Some modern legislation, such as the UPAA, does away with the consideration requirement.

3) Risk of Overreaching

Because of the intimate relationship between the parties, courts scrutinize antenuptial agreements for overreaching. Courts usually require full disclosure by each party (or at least a conscious waiver of disclosure), prefer independent legal advice for both parties, and often insist that the agreement's provisions be fair and reasonable—at the time when executed and/or at the time sought to be enforced.

b. Subject Matter

1) Disposition at Death

If the agreement meets the contractual requirements for validity, it may include provisions for disposing of a party's property at death.

2) Providing for Divorce

Agreements which contemplate divorce traditionally have been held invalid based on the policy against encouraging divorce. A better rationale lies in the difficulty of providing for unforeseen and unforeseeable circumstances. Where statutory regulation (*e.g.*, UPAA) does not prescribe the outcome, many courts feel freer to uphold antenuptial agreements, (a) if a second marriage is involved, (b) if the agreement settles property division upon divorce rather than support obligations, and/or (c) if the agreement does not expressly refer to divorce, but merely has the effect of providing for a disposition upon divorce. If a divorce or separation does occur and the agreement is not expressly limited to a continuing marriage, courts may decide that (a) the agreement is also terminated, (b) the losing (breaching) party cannot enforce the agreement, or (c) absent a specific provision, divorce or separation has no effect on the agreement.

3) Regulating the Ongoing Marriage

Courts typically will not enforce agreements dealing with the day to day aspects of married life such as support *during* marriage, sexual behavior, family religion and child rearing. Such agreements may nevertheless be useful in causing prospective couples to discuss their future plans, thereby reducing uncertainties and possible disappointments.

c–e. Divorce, UPAA, UMPA

Provided all the requirements for contractual validity are met, today's trend is to give effect to antenuptial agreements. The UPAA (24 states) and the UMPA (1 state) broadly favor such agreements. The UMDA makes no detailed provision for antenuptial agreements, and provides only that they may be considered on divorce.

f. Gift Tax Treatment of Antenuptial Agreements
Property transfers prior to marriage are taxable as gifts between unrelated persons. For tax purposes, mutual promises to marry are not adequate consideration in money or money's worth.

H. AGREEMENTS DURING MARRIAGE
Agreements during marriage fall into the following three categories:

1. Agreements Concerning Marital Relationship
Potential problems include lack of consideration (contracted obligations may be covered by the obligations of marriage), statutory limitations, overreaching, and public policy. An agreement that does not deal with day to day aspects of the marriage and is limited to dollars or property has a fair chance of being enforced.

2. Reconciliation Agreements
An agreement to resume cohabitation or to abandon legal proceedings furnishes requisite consideration for the partner's promises.

3. Separation Agreements
In the interest of amicable settlement of marital dissolution, separation agreements dealing with the consequences of divorce are generally upheld, if they are entered into when divorce or separation is imminent and if they are not unconscionable. (Covered in more detail below).

I. CONFLICT OF LAWS ASPECTS OF MARITAL AGREEMENTS
Absent specific (and valid) contractual agreement, conflicts of laws issues are resolved by balancing the interests of each jurisdiction that may be involved, relevant public policies, and the parties' personal interests.

J. BREACH OF PROMISE TO MARRY
See "Heartbalm Actions"

K. GIFTS IN CONTEMPLATION OF MARRIAGE
1–2. Gifts to One Another
A premarital gift (such as an engagement ring) that is conditional on the marriage generally is returnable if the marriage does not occur. The circumstances of each

gift must be examined relative to the donor's intent. For instance, a gift for a special occasion (*e.g.*, birthday) that is not related to marriage may generally be retained.

3. Gifts From Third Parties
Gifts to a couple by a third party usually are considered conditional on marriage and, if the marriage does not take place, may be recovered by the third party.

II. MARRIAGE REQUISITES

A. FORMAL REQUIREMENTS
Consent and solemnization create a legally effective marriage.

1. Consent
The parties must intend to marry each other. At the time of solemnization the parties must be capable of understanding the nature of the act. Some incompetents may be allowed to marry with the consent of a guardian.

2. Solemnization
a. Marriage License
A license must be obtained prior to solemnization. For policy reasons, some courts may hold that a valid marriage was created if there was an attempt to comply, even if license requirements were not complied with fully.

b. Ceremony
A ceremony may be performed by clergy or state officials. A ceremony performed by an unauthorized person may result in a valid or partially valid marriage, if at least one party is unaware of the disqualification.

c. Public Record
The completed license must be recorded at the appropriate state office.

d. Purposes of Solemnization
Aside from religious tradition, secular purposes of solemnization are (1) to give public notice, (2) to create a permanent record, (3) to allow the parties to be impressed with the serious nature of the act, and (4) to aid in the collection of vital statistics.

e. Proxy Marriages
Some states allow marriage by proxy, if one party is unable to attend the ceremony.

3. Common Law Marriage
Approximately one fourth of the states recognize "common law marriage." Common law marriage is a valid marriage entered into by the parties' agreement, but without formal solemnization.

a. Traditional Form
Traditional ways of entering into a common law marriage were:

    (1) Exchange by the parties of vows in the present tense, expressing their intent to be married, or

    (2) Words in the future tense (engagement) followed by consummation.

b. American Law
Most states require (1) an express agreement to be married, (2) actual cohabitation, and (3) that the parties "hold themselves out" to the public as husband and wife. "Holding out" may be shown by joint residence, by representations to friends, neighbors, creditors, and the public, by a common surname, by jointly filed tax returns, and so forth. Arguments against and for common law marriage are that formal marriage provides more certainty, both to the couple and to third parties dealing with one or both of them in reliance on their marital status, whereas common law marriage often protects the parties' reasonable expectations and helps to alleviate possible inequities.

4. Marital Presumptions
When more than one marriage is shown and there is no showing of the dissolution of a former marriage, an evidential presumption favors the validity of the last marriage. Many courts also apply a presumption in favor of the continuation of the first, undissolved, marriage. Where these presumptions conflict, the presumption that on the facts is more probably correct controls.

5. Putative Spouse Doctrine
A "putative spouse" is one whose marriage is legally invalid, but who has participated in a marriage ceremony or solemnization in the reasonable, *bona fide* belief that the marriage was valid. A putative spouse accrues the rights of a legal spouse so long as the good faith belief continues.

6. Cohabitation Without Marriage

In several states, "quasi-marital" property and possibly support obligations may arise from non-marital cohabitation, when there is a cohabitation contract between the parties, and even if there is no express agreement to evoke such consequences ("*Marvin* doctrine"). Many states refuse to follow the *Marvin* doctrine, finding it uncomfortably close to a revival of common law marriage (if abolished in the state), or in derogation of and conflict with ceremonial marriage. Other states follow the *Marvin* doctrine, as it provides a means to protect reliance interests. There remains general agreement that adults, even cohabitants, are free to enter into contracts involving money and other matters, but that contracts are invalid if they are based on sexual services or if other public policies apply. The line separating a valid from a "meretricious" consideration often is thin.

B. SUBSTANTIVE REQUIREMENTS FOR VALID MARRIAGE

The constitutional validity of substantive requirements for marriage depends on a balance between the individual's right to marry when and whom he or she wishes, and the importance of the state's interest in the specific regulation.

1. Same–Sex Marriage Not Recognized

So far, no court in the United States has recognized a *federal* constitutional right of same-sex couples to marry that would override state regulation to the contrary. In 1993, Hawaii's Supreme Court provisionally recognized such a right under Hawaii's constitution, unless, on remand, the state can show that the prohibition "furthers compelling state interests and is narrowly drawn to avoid unnecessary abridgments of constitutional rights." By early 1996, no decision had been reached on remand. (Note that in 1986 the U.S. Supreme Court upheld the constitutionality of a state statute criminalizing homosexual conduct (*Bowers v. Hardwick*), and that numerous states still have such statutes).

2. Consanguinity

Marriages are prohibited between persons related by blood within certain degrees of kinship. Civil incest statutes are justified on the basis of the genetic risks to the offspring of incestuous matings, to maintaining family harmony, and to cultural and religious conceptions of the family. Relationships by the half-blood, or "illegitimate" relationships are not distinguished. Criminal incest statutes may be less extensive or may express parallel prohibitions.

3. Affinity, Step–Relationships, Adoption

Relationship by adoption typically is not distinguished from biological relationship. A minority of states continues the traditional prohibition on marriage between persons related by affinity or between persons standing in a stepparent-child relationship to each other. The justification for such statutes is the protection of family harmony.

4. Age Requirements
a. Regulation
States usually set three minimum ages for marriage: (1) at one age, typically majority, parties are allowed to marry freely; (2) parties below that age and above the minimum age (often 16) may marry if they obtain parental consent; and (3) a court order may authorize marriage at a still lower age in special circumstances, traditionally pregnancy of the bride, but no longer exclusively that.

b–c. Justification and Constitutionality of Age Requirement
Age requirements are justified by the need to protect immature minors from entering into marriage, to promote marital stability, and to assure potential children of mature and responsible parents who are able to provide for their children materially and emotionally. Under modern equality reasoning, as embraced by the U.S. Supreme Court, age requirements must be the same for males and females.

d. Effect of Non–Compliance
If one of the parties is below the age requirement, the marriage is void or voidable. Only the underaged party has standing to attack the marriage. The marriage is validated if the underaged party reaches majority and manifests an intent to ratify the marriage.

5. Monogamy
A marriage attempted while one of the parties is married to another is invalid.

a. Justification
Restrictions on bigamy and polygamy are based on religious, moral and cultural traditions as well as on the desire to promote family stability and prevent exploitation.

b. Criminal Sanctions
As bigamy or as adultery, marriage to more than one partner at the same time is subject to criminal sanctions. (Note that statutes criminalizing bigamy and adultery are rarely enforced).

c. Civil Effects
Although void, a bigamous marriage may have certain legal effects. Children may be deemed legitimate, the protection offered a putative spouse may be triggered, a statute may provide alimony, or, under the UMDA, the declaration of invalidity may be granted non-retroactively, resulting in consequences similar to a divorce.

6. Mental Capacity
Along with having contractual capacity, the parties must be of sound mind at the time of the marriage.

7. Physical Requirements
A health examination, typically but not always limited to a test for venereal disease, is a traditional prerequisite to a marriage license. Test requirements are in decline, even while the HIV infection problem has revived discussion and interest. Epileptics once were but are no longer prevented from marrying.

8. "Miscegenation"
In 1967, the U.S. Supreme Court declared unconstitutional a statute that prohibited marriage between members of different races (*Loving v. Virginia*).

9. Financial Responsibility
In 1972, the U.S. Supreme Court declared unconstitutional a statute that required proof of compliance with prior support obligations as a prerequisite to issuance of a marriage license (*Zablocki v. Redhail*).

10. Waiting Period
Most states impose a waiting period after issuance of a license and before the marriage may be solemnized. The waiting period may be waived by a court.

C. CONFLICT OF LAWS—VALIDITY
1. Law of Celebration
The law of the place of celebration usually governs the validity of the marriage, unless recognition would violate a strong public policy of the state in which recognition is sought.

2. Restatement (Second) of Conflicts
Aside from the law of the place of celebration, the validity of a marriage may be determined by the law of the state that has the most significant relationship to the spouses and the marriage with respect to the particular issue.

3. Uniform Marriage Evasion Act
The Act provides that a party cannot contract a valid marriage in another state if the marriage could not be entered in his/her state of residence. The Commissioners on Uniform State Laws withdrew this Act in 1943, but several states retain it.

D. ANNULMENT

Annulment is a retroactive judicial declaration that, by reason of some defect existing at its inception, a purported marriage does not exist and never has existed.

1. History

Annulment was of great importance when full divorce with the right to remarry did not exist.

2. Impediments

Traditional impediments sufficient to warrant annulment include underage, fraud, duress, impotency, bigamy, religious orders, consanguinity, and affinity. The impediment must have existed at the time of the attempted marriage.

3. Defenses

Ratification or estoppel provide effective defenses to an attack on a marriage alleged to be voidable.

4. The Void/Voidable Distinction

a. Void Marriage

A void marriage is one that violates a strong public policy (such as incest or bigamy). It is void as it stands and does not require a judicial declaration of invalidity. It may nevertheless be useful to obtain such a declaration.

b. Voidable Marriage

A voidable marriage is valid until annulled. It involves a violation of a lesser state concern, but one that is very important (decisive) to one party, *e.g.*, material fraud, going to the "essence" of marriage. The offended party must petition the court to have the marriage declared void.

c. Significance of the Distinction

Proper classification may be important to determine what impact there will be on other legal interests. For example, if the marriage is void, a "spouse" may not elect against a "spouse's" will that leaves her out, whereas the spouse will take if the marriage merely is voidable and was not annulled.

d. UMDA

The UMDA has reduced the traditional distinction between void and voidable marriages and between both and divorce. If the marriage is void or voidable, the court has discretion whether to enter a retroactive decree. If the holding is non-retroactive, the legal rights of the spouse and children will be the same as if a dissolution (divorce) had been granted.

5. Annulment for Fraud
A fraudulent representation must be material, relied on by the other party, and go to the "essence" of the marriage contract. Courts often determine the "essence" of marriage narrowly. To illustrate, fraud as to ability to have children goes to the "essence," whereas fraud as to wealth does not.

6. Annulment for Duress
The duress must have been subjectively perceived by the complaining individual at the time of marriage and have been sufficient to prevent him or her from acting freely.

7. Annulment of Marriage Entered in Jest
Most courts will annul a marriage entered in jest. Consummation traditionally posed an obstacle, and may still cause hesitation in some courts.

8. Annulment of Sham Marriage
The treatment of a sham marriage entered for an ulterior motive (*e.g.,* immigration preference or tax advantage) depends on the parties' intent at the time of marriage and who is challenging the marriage, *i.e.,* the parties, the third party sought to be defrauded, or an outsider.

9. Legal Incidents of Annulment
Despite an annulment, courts may recognize the parties' relationship to some extent, especially if children or property are involved. Annulment usually does not revive a former spouse's duty of support. A court may, instead, impose a support duty on the "annulled" spouse. Some courts seem more willing to allow revival of rights accrued from a former marriage, if the burden falls on a third party such as an employer or on a federal or state social program. (See also 4.d., above).

III. HUSBAND AND WIFE

A. SUPPORT OBLIGATIONS DURING MARRIAGE
1. Historical Basis
Historically, the wife's legal identity merged with her husband's. Since he had control of her property and she typically had no opportunity to earn money, her

husband was obligated to support her. This obligation was carried into the **modern** role-divided marriage.

2. Changing Status

Statutes or courts may equalize the support obligation or impose a support **duty on** the wife if her husband is in need.

3. Constitutional Limitations

Statutes which require only the husband to render support may violate **the equal** protection clause. Statutes which seek to compensate women for past discrimination must be carefully tailored.

4. "Necessaries"

Traditionally, the husband was legally liable only for "necessaries" during **the** marriage. These included all items essential to the family's well-being. **What** courts would consider "necessaries" varied with the husband's financial **status.**

5. Agency Between Husband and Wife

Although there is no flat presumption of agency, actual authority **may be implied,** or it may arise through ratification or estoppel.

6. Justification for Limited Support Obligation

To avoid interfering in an ongoing marriage, courts generally assume that the support obligation is satisfied as long as the parties are cohabiting.

7. Support After Separation or Pending Divorce

Courts typically have statutory authority to enter a temporary or long-term **support** order after separation or pending divorce.

B. PROPERTY RIGHTS

1. Common Law

At common law the husband gained possession of any property owned or **acquired** by the wife. If he predeceased her, she received her property back. If she predeceased him leaving no children, he kept her property. The wife had **a dower** interest in real property her husband owned during the marriage.

2. "Married Women's Property Acts"

Statutes were enacted at the end of the 19th century that gave married women the right to own and manage their property. These statutes also removed numerous other legal disabilities from married women.

3. Separate Property States

The majority of states (41 in 1996) have separate property regimes.

a. Separate Property

During marriage each spouse is entitled to sole ownership and control of his or her property, however acquired and whether acquired before or during the marriage.

b. *Pros* and *Cons* of Separate Property

By providing relief from the old common law, the separate property concept benefits married women who become wage earners. However, the separate property concept has not eliminated inequity because even today the typical married woman with children finds less opportunity than her husband to earn income.

c. Joint Ownership in Separate Property States

In separate property states, spouses may take title by tenancy in common, joint tenancy or tenancy by the entirety. The traditional distinction between presumptions of gift (applying when a husband transferred title to his wife) and advancement (applying when a wife transferred title to her husband) has been generally abandoned. Today, if either spouse transfers his/her separate property to the other spouse as a joint tenant, a rebuttable presumption arises that the interest transferred was intended as a gift to the other or to the marital estate.

d. Devolution of Separate Property Upon Death

A spouse's separate property passes by will or, if there is no will, by intestacy.

1) Election Against the Will

If a spouse is not provided for in a will or is dissatisfied with provisions made, statutes commonly allow the spouse to elect against the will and take a "statutory share," typically one-third, of the deceased spouse's estate. The right of election is effective upon marriage and is not dependent on the duration of the marriage. In many states this right can be defeated with relative ease by depleting the estate through unconditional *inter vivos* transfer of assets, outright or by means of trusts.

2) Uniform Probate Code

To prevent the defeasance of a spouse's share, the Uniform Probate Code provides for "augmenting" the transferor's estate with the value of certain types of transferred property. The spouse's share then is based on this augmented estate. In an interesting departure from tradition, a 1993 change in the UPC would gradually accrue the spouse's share, until after 15 years it has reached 50% of the deceased spouse's estate.

3) Intestacy
If a spouse dies without a will, intestacy statutes set forth the percentage of the estate that goes to the decedent's spouse, children and/or parents.

4. Community Property States
There are nine community property states: Arizona, California, Idaho, Louisiana, New Mexico, Nevada, Texas, Washington, and Wisconsin.

a. Historical Note
The first eight community property states base their regime on civil law sources. Wisconsin's Uniform Marital Property Act espouses a form of community property and was developed to alleviate perceived unfairness of the traditional separate property laws.

b. The Concept of Community Property
Generally each spouse owns a present one-half interest in what a state defines as community property. The definitions of separate and community property, the rights (especially of management and disposition) of each spouse regarding the community property, and the manner of distribution at divorce vary among the community property states.

1) Definition of Separate and Community Property
Separate property typically is property owned before the marriage, as well as property acquired by one spouse during the marriage by inheritance or gift, but states differ in their definitions. (For example, post-marriage income from separate property may be considered separate or community, and treatment of income may differ from treatment of appreciation or capital gain.) Commingled separate property may become community property. Joint property is jointly owned. Community property generally is everything that is not separate or joint.

2) Management and Control
The right to manage and control community property varies among the community property states. Texas gives each spouse sole management and control of community property he/she would have held if single. Commingled community property becomes subject to joint management and control. Other states give each spouse equal, independent management, or require that both spouses consent to community property transfers in excess of a statutory limit.

c. Community Property on Death
At the death of one spouse, the decedent's one-half of the community property passes by will or, if there is no will, by intestacy.

1) Election Against the Will
Since the surviving spouse already owns one-half of the community property, a disinherited or dissatisfied spouse does not have the right to elect against the decedent's will.

2) Intestacy
Intestate succession in community property states is similar to that in separate property jurisdictions.

d. Presumptions
Community property states have adopted presumptions concerning property acquired by spouses as joint tenants. Typically, jointly held property is presumed to be community property.

5. Marital Property and the Conflict of Laws
Choice of law questions arise when a couple lives in a separate property state and moves to a community property state (or *vice versa*). Several states have enacted statutes to determine how this property will be treated on divorce and/or death. (A typical solution is to find a "quasi-community" in separate property acquired in a separate property state, if that property would have been community property if acquired in the forum state.) In other states the outcome is left to the courts.

C. TORTS AND THE FAMILY
1. Torts Between Spouses
Carried forward in the original Married Women's Property Acts, the traditional prohibition against one spouse maintaining a tort action against the other has now been eroded by legislation or in the courts.

a. Justification of Interspousal Immunity
The common law immunity was justified on the logic that any recovery by the wife for a tort committed by her husband—and vice versa—would be both for and against the husband. More recently, the immunity was thought useful (1) to preserve family harmony and (2) to prevent possible collusion, especially on liability insurance claims.

b. Arguments Against Retention
Many interspousal *contract* actions have long been allowed under the Married Women's Property Acts. The family harmony argument is rejected on the

basis that a tort action will not disrupt family harmony any more than will a contract action. If one spouse resorts to suing the other, family harmony already is disrupted. If there is insurance, a judgment will not disrupt family peace. Courts and juries should and can protect against collusion.

c. Limitation of the Immunity

Some courts, while unwilling to abolish the immunity entirely, have refused to recognize it in cases where the arguments in favor do not apply, for example, where the marriage has been terminated by divorce or where one spouse is deceased.

d. Intentional and Negligent Torts Distinguished

Some jurisdictions apply the immunity when dealing with intentional torts, but do not apply it when the case involves negligence, especially when liability insurance is involved. Others do the opposite.

2. Recovery for Loss of Consortium

Today the traditional right of a husband to recover for loss of his wife's consortium generally has been extended to both spouses. A few courts deny recovery to both the husband and wife, seeing the concept of consortium as outmoded.

3. Tortious Interference With Family Relationships ("Heartbalm Actions")

Various tort actions compensate for interference with family relationships.

a. Breach of Promise to Marry

This is generally regarded as a tort rather than a contract action. Because of the difficulty of proof, many courts are willing to imply a contract to marry from circumstantial evidence. Damages allowed vary by state and may range from actual damages to punitive damages.

b. Criminal Conversation

This common law tort allows a spouse recovery against a third party for the latter's adulterous conduct with the plaintiff's spouse. The participating spouse's consent to the relationship is irrelevant. Recently, defendants have been allowed to present evidence concerning the plaintiff's own conduct and the (lack of) quality of the plaintiff's marriage.

c. Alienation of Affections

A spouse may be allowed recovery for a third party's conduct that has caused plaintiff's spouse to transfer his or her affections to another, not necessarily the defendant. In contrast to criminal conversation, alienation of affections does not require that sexual intercourse have occurred. The conduct of both spouses and the quality of their marriage are at issue. Recovery is for defendant's wrongful interference with the spouse's emotions.

d. Modern Treatment of "Heartbalm" Actions
Because of the belief that these actions were being abused and that monetary recovery did not adequately compensate the wronged party, many states have either eliminated "heartbalm" actions or severely restricted recovery.

D. MARRIAGE AND CRIMINAL LAW
The modern trend is to reduce or abolish traditional immunities between spouses that barred certain criminal prosecutions.

1. No Immunity for "Conspiracy"
Today, their marital status generally does not provide a husband and wife immunity from prosecution for conspiracy, even if they are the only conspirators.

2. Reduced Testimonial Privilege
The traditional rule against accepting testimony from a spouse has been changed in varying degrees, depending on the jurisdiction. In the federal courts today, only the witness-spouse has a privilege to refuse to testify. Disclosures between husband and wife that fall within the marital relationship remain protected.

3. Rape
At common law a husband could not be guilty of raping his wife. Today most states allow criminal prosecution of a husband for rape. In some states prosecution depends on whether the couple were living together or were separated at the time of the incident.

4. Marital Violence
Many states have enacted special statutes that deal with domestic violence and provide aid to victims, especially by way of injunctive relief (domestic protection order) that permits quick and decisive police and judicial intervention.

5. The "Battered Wife Syndrome"
States differ on the admissibility of testimony on the "battered wife syndrome" asserted on behalf of a wife who has retaliated against an abusive husband. Some courts have found there to be a sufficient scientific basis for such evidence, while

others claim that the validity and relevance of such evidence has not yet been adequately established.

E. FAMILY NAMES

It has been held that, tradition and custom to the contrary notwithstanding, the common law has never required a married woman to adopt her husband's surname. If the wife has assumed her husband's name by usage, she may have her original name restored after a divorce. Courts today hold that the parents may give their children any name they wish. Most marital children still take the father's surname and some courts have found that to be a common law rule. Other courts have abrogated this rule—if there ever was one. The child's best interests will determine the outcome of a dispute between the parents concerning their child's name. On divorce, the custodial parent's name may carry the greater weight, depending on how the court sees the child's best interest.

IV. DIVORCE—STATUS

A. ACCESS TO AND JURISDICTION OF COURTS
1. Residency Requirements

A state may constitutionally require a divorce plaintiff to have been a resident of the state for a specified period of time prior to bringing the divorce action. (In *Sosna v. Iowa,* the U.S. Supreme Court approved a one year residence requirement.)

2. Personal Jurisdiction

A plaintiff who is a *bona fide* domiciliary of a state may be granted a valid ("*ex parte*") divorce, even though the court has no personal jurisdiction over the defendant. Such a decree is entitled to full faith and credit in other states with respect to the status issue, but not with respect to support, property, child custody and related issues for the adjudication of which personal jurisdiction is required (*Williams; Estin*). If both parties appear before the court (which thus obtains personal jurisdiction) and a divorce is decreed, the decree is entitled to Full Faith and Credit even if neither party was a *bona fide* domiciliary of the forum state (*Sherrer*). While Full Faith and Credit is not due a foreign judgment, states usually enforce foreign divorce decrees by comity, unless that would violate an important state policy.

3. "Long–Arm" Jurisdiction

State statutes assert personal "long-arm" jurisdiction over out-of-state defendants who are, in some way permissible under the Due Process Clause, connected with the forum. In the divorce context, the maintenance of a marital domicile in the forum state is a typical basis for "long-arm" jurisdiction. Other acts or events may provide "long-arm" jurisdiction in support matters. In *Kulko*, the U.S. Supreme Court held that California could *not* exercise "long-arm" jurisdiction over a father who resided in New York and had had only very brief contacts with California in the past. The father's act in allowing his daughter to live with her mother in California was held not to be a sufficient contact to allow California to exercise jurisdiction. In *Burnham*, the U.S. Supreme Court reaffirmed that personal service confers valid *in personam* jurisdiction over a divorce defendant when he was temporarily present in California for unrelated litigation and to visit his children.

B. TRADITIONAL GROUNDS AND DEFENSES
1. Historical Development
a. English Origins
Traditionally in England, ecclesiastical courts had jurisdiction over marital cases. Marriage was indissoluble. The only remedies were "divorce *a vinculo matrimonii*" (annulment) which allowed the parties to remarry because the annulled marriage had never existed, and *"divorce a mensa et thoro"* (legal separation) which did not allow the parties to remarry, but required them to separate. When the common law courts obtained jurisdiction over divorce, divorce *a mensa et thoro* was expanded to allow the parties to remarry.

b. Application in America
The English divorce-for-fault system was applied in the American colonies and was taken over into the law of the states.

2. Divorce for Marital Fault
Today no state retains fault as the sole basis for divorce. The fault system eroded due to strong popular demand for divorce which had produced collusion and increasingly loose practices in the courts. The seemingly strict laws had been permitted to be evaded almost at will. The enactment of no-fault laws was the logical last step. A majority of states, however, have retained fault as an alternative ground for divorce actions. In contrast to the typical no-fault divorce, a fault-based action requires no period of separation, thus allowing a divorce to be obtained more quickly. In some states, fault still has a bearing on alimony, property division, and possibly even child custody.

3. Traditional Fault Grounds
a. Adultery
Adultery is voluntary sexual intercourse between a married person and someone other than that person's spouse.

b. Physical Cruelty
A showing of "extreme and repeated" cruelty is usually required, unless a single act has endangered life and repetition may be expected.

c. Desertion
Desertion requires cessation of cohabitation for the statutory period, intent on the part of the deserting party not to resume cohabitation, and absence of the deserted party's consent.

d. Mental Cruelty
Statutes often speak in terms of "extreme and repeated" mental cruelty, but provide no definite guidelines or an objective standard. What constitutes mental cruelty will often be defined in terms of the effect the conduct had on the particular parties involved.

e. Habitual Drunkenness and Drug Addiction
Alcohol or drug abuse must be "gross" or "continuous" or "habitual" to justify divorce. In some states such habits may provide evidence of cruelty.

f. Impotence and Bigamy
Some states allow divorce on the grounds of impotence and bigamy, although when present at the time of marriage both are more typically grounds for an annulment.

g. Insanity
Insanity may be a ground for divorce or a defense to divorce, depending on the state and the specific facts. What constitutes insanity typically is left open to judicial interpretation. Jurisdictions differ on how an incompetent spouse may obtain a divorce; the appointment of a guardian being typical.

4. Traditional Bars and Defenses
Collusion and recrimination are traditional bars to a fault-based divorce action. Defenses are provocation, connivance, condonation, and insanity. Even where fault grounds are retained as an alternative to no-fault divorce, the traditional bars and defenses have often been modified or abolished.

a. Collusion
Collusion is an agreement between the spouses to procure a divorce and/or to do an act that constitutes a fault ground.

b. Recrimination
The bar of recrimination applies when both spouses have committed marital offenses, and either offense would be ground for a divorce. Some states would bar a divorce only if both offenses were of a similar nature or if both parties

had committed adultery. Recrimination does not require a causal link between the actions of both spouses. Where it survives at all, recrimination typically is a defense, not a bar, to fault divorce.

c. Provocation
If defendant proves that plaintiff has provoked the defendant's marital offense, the divorce will be denied. Defendant must show that his or her marital offense was not excessive in relation to the plaintiff's provocation, and there must be a causal link between the provocation and the marital offense.

d. Provocation and Recrimination Distinguished
Provocation requires a causal connection, recrimination does not. Provocation need not, but may, involve a ground for divorce; recrimination must. Provocation is a defense, whereas recrimination (traditionally) is a bar.

e. Connivance
The defense of connivance requires proof that plaintiff has actively created an opportunity for defendant to commit the marital offense which plaintiff seeks to use as ground for a divorce.

f. Condonation
Condonation is the intentional and voluntary forgiveness of a prior marital offense. The intent to forgive may be implied, especially from sexual intercourse with knowledge of the marital offense.

g. Insanity
Insanity may be a statutory ground for divorce. It also may be a defense, in that insanity negates fault.

C. DIVORCE REFORM
1. Social Trends
The desire to preserve marital privacy, reduce the amount of collusion, and preserve judicial integrity led to dissatisfaction with the fault-based system and to basic reform of the law of divorce.

2. Available Alternatives
Reform proposals included (a) a modification of the fault-based system, (b) consent divorce, and (c) a no-fault system. All states now have enacted some form of no-fault divorce while a majority retain fault grounds as an alternative basis for divorce.

3. No–Fault Grounds

a. Living Separate and Apart

Many no-fault statutes allow divorce where the couple has been consensually separated for a specified period of time, such as six months or a year. Depending on the jurisdiction, the separation may be required to be pursuant to a separation agreement or court order.

b. Marriage Breakdown

Marriage breakdown is proved by showing that the parties' differences are irreconcilable and that a meaningful marriage no longer exists, *i.e.,* that the marriage is "dead." Proof typically is by allegation or affidavit of one or both parties, and/or by proof of separation.

c. Incompatibility

The parties must show marital disharmony "so deep and intense as to be irremediable" or that the "marriage has in fact ended as a result of hopeless disagreement and discord."

D. SEPARATION

Some statutes allow divorce from "bed and board" (limited divorce, divorce *a mensa et thoro*) which provides for adjudication of support and property rights similar to that in ordinary divorce proceedings, but which leaves the marriage bond intact. The latter may have value for tax purposes and under various benefit laws and plans. Remarriage is not available to either party. Under specific statutes or by later use of a no-fault divorce statute, conversion of a limited divorce into full divorce may be accomplished easily. "Separate maintenance," by contrast, does not involve a division of property, but may allow a needy spouse to receive court-ordered support from the other spouse while the separation continues. In that event, most of the legal attributes of the marriage status remain intact.

V. DIVORCE—FINANCIAL CONSEQUENCES

A. ALIMONY ON DIVORCE

Alimony may be awarded on divorce in all states but Texas.

1. Traditional Standards for Awarding Alimony

Alimony developed out of limited divorce (*a mensa et thoro*) which only terminated cohabitation, but not marriage. Alimony represented the continuation of the husband's marital support obligation.

2. **Alimony Today**
   Because property transfers on divorce are now the rule and work opportunities are available to a formerly dependent spouse, alimony is awarded less often, for shorter periods, and in lower amounts than in the past. Many courts award "rehabilitative alimony" which is intended to allow a dependent spouse to become self-supporting. In *Orr v. Orr*, the U.S. Supreme Court has held a state statute unconstitutional that imposed liability for alimony only on husbands.

3. **Determining the Amount of Alimony**
   The amount awarded is typically in the court's discretion, based on factors such as the recipient's need, the payor's ability to pay, and the economic status of the parties during the marriage, with considerable regard to the recipient's own earning capacity and assets, especially from a marital property division.

4. **Fault as a Factor in Alimony Awards**
   Traditionally a guilty party was not awarded any alimony. Today many statutes prohibit consideration of fault when determining an alimony award.

5. **Modification of Alimony**
   An alimony award may be modified due to significantly changed circumstances occurring after the initial decree. Courts may refuse to modify the award if the change in circumstances is voluntary, and, especially, if made for the purpose of making a case for reduction or increase of the alimony award. The recipient's remarriage or cohabitation may be grounds for modification or termination. The obligor's bankruptcy does not discharge an alimony obligation, but may constitute a change in circumstances warranting modification.

6. **Termination of Alimony**
   a. **Death of Either Ex–Spouse**
      Generally the alimony obligation terminates at the death of either payee or payor. If the separation agreement expressly so provides, it may continue after the payor's death.

   b. **Recipient Spouse's Remarriage**
      The recipient's remarriage usually terminates an alimony obligation either (1) by operation of law, (2) pursuant to the divorce decree or separation agreement, or (3) pursuant to a new court order based on changed circumstances.
      "Rehabilitative" alimony may not terminate automatically because the specific purpose for which it is paid is not necessarily superseded by remarriage.

c. **Recipient Spouse's Cohabitation**

Cohabitation with a "lover" may be, but is not necessarily, ground for terminating or reducing the recipient's alimony. When the cohabitation has ceased, some cases have revived an alimony obligation that was terminated by cohabitation.

7. **Enforcement of Alimony by Contempt**

Enforcement of alimony may be by contempt proceedings or by other remedies available to enforce support or money obligations.

8. **Tax Treatment of Alimony**

Generally alimony is deductible by the payor and must be included in the recipient's taxable income. The definition of alimony for federal income tax purposes has undergone considerable change since 1984. The principal effect of these changes is to make it much more difficult to "disguise" a (non-deductible) child support payment or (non-deductible) property transfer as a (deductible) alimony payment.

9. **Alimony and Property Award Distinguished**

The settlement agreement or divorce decree may classify the payments, but the labels used will not necessarily be controlling.

B. **PROPERTY DIVISION ON DIVORCE**

1. **Separate Property States**

Under the "Married Women's Property Acts", separate property states held that each spouse continues to own the property he or she owned before the marriage, as well as any property he or she acquired during the marriage in any manner, including personal earnings, gifts, inheritance, and interest and dividends on, and appreciation of, investments. This usually left the non-earning spouse (wife) without property on divorce. Property could and would be transferred to her as "lump sum alimony" or "in lieu of alimony." Today most states provide for "equitable distribution" of property on divorce. The objective is to achieve a fair distribution of marital property accumulation, and fault is usually not a consideration in the property division. Several traditionally separate property states have adopted a system of (deferred) "marital property" that applies only on divorce. This resembles a community property regime the imposition of which is deferred until divorce. Generally a spouse has an absolute right to dispose of separate property during marriage. Courts, however, may take transactions not in furtherance of a marital purpose into account when deciding on post-divorce distribution. Contempt is not available for the enforcement of a property award, but the usual remedies for the enforcement of judgments are.

2. Community Property States

All property acquired by either spouse during marriage other than by gift or inheritance generally is community property and is owned by *both* spouses. Each spouse's pre-marital property and property acquired during marriage by gift or inheritance remains separate property. On divorce, the court assigns separate property to the respective owners and divides community property.

3. Conflicts Aspects of Property Division

The law of the matrimonial domicile at the time of the acquisition of property generally determines the character of ownership, *i.e.,* whether the property will be considered separate or community. Several states make exceptions where unfairness would result.

4. Property Awards and Bankruptcy

Bankruptcy discharges most (but no longer all) obligations arising from a property settlement incident to divorce, whereas alimony and child support are not dischargeable. What constitutes alimony or child support from a non-dischargeable property obligation is determined under the bankruptcy laws rather than state law.

5. Tax Treatment of Property Awards

Since the 1984 tax reform, the recipient of property in a divorce settlement takes over the transferor's adjusted basis in that property. Previously, the transfer of property incident to divorce had been a taxable event.

6. Treatment of Professional Licenses Upon Divorce

Some courts "divide" the capitalized value of a professional license on divorce, if the couple has no other significant assets and/or if the other spouse has made significant contributions in cash or services to the earning of the license. Other courts allow some form of reimbursement to a spouse who has contributed to his or her partner's earning of the license. Most states, however, continue to consider a spouse's contribution toward the other spouse's education as merely a factor influencing an award of alimony or property.

7. Pensions

In community property states, pensions purchased out of community funds are community property and subject to division on divorce. In separate property states, most courts today define a pension as divisible marital property to the extent the pension was earned during the marriage.

8. The Employee Retirement Income Security Act
A "qualified domestic relations order" (QDRO) under ERISA allows the benefits provided under a pension plan to be assigned or alienated to a spouse without immediate tax consequences.

C. SEPARATION AGREEMENTS
A separation agreement is made during marriage in contemplation of divorce and specifies the parties' wishes as to the settlement of their affairs.

1. Validity of Separation Agreement
Contracts made in contemplation of divorce traditionally were void as contrary to public policy. The public interest in having the parties amicably settle their own affairs has long persuaded courts to uphold separation agreements.

2. Traditional Requirements for Enforceability
The separation must be accomplished or about to occur. The agreement must be fair, there should be full disclosure by both parties, and the agreement must be supported by consideration.

3. The Divorce Decree and the Separation Agreement
Generally, the separation agreement is incorporated into the divorce decree by expressly setting forth its terms or by reference.

a. Specific Incorporation
If the terms of the separation agreement are expressly set forth in the decree, the agreement obtains the status of a judgment and can only be modified in accordance with the rules for modifying a judgment. Failure to comply will be contempt of court.

b. Incorporation by Reference
If the agreement is appropriately referenced by, but not made part of the decree, the agreement does not obtain the status of a judgment, but its validity is *res judicata* between parties.

c. No Incorporation
Courts disagree whether a separation agreement voluntarily entered into by the parties, but not incorporated into the decree, may later be modified by a court.

    d. Court's Discretion
    Courts have considerable discretion whether to accept or reject a separation agreement. The UMDA holds the interspousal provisions of a separation agreement "binding" on the court, unless the agreement is unconscionable. Provisions regarding children (support, custody) are not binding on the court.

    e. Reconciliation
    Reconciliation generally terminates a separation agreement, except to the extent that the provisions have already been executed.

VI. THE PARENTAL CHILD SUPPORT OBLIGATION

A. HISTORICAL DEVELOPMENT
Traditionally the family support obligation was imposed exclusively upon the father. Today's trend is to impose the duty equally upon both parents, depending on their respective ability to pay or render services.

B. DURATION OF THE OBLIGATION
The support obligation continues until the child reaches majority or becomes emancipated, or parental rights are legally terminated or the parent or child dies. The duty continues even where the child has been removed from the home.

C. CRITERIA FOR AWARDING SUPPORT
The UPA and UMDA list common-sense factors that courts should consider in setting the support obligation, including the child's needs, educational needs, the standard of living, financial resources and circumstances of both parents, and the standard of living the child would have enjoyed had the marriage not been dissolved. Today, federal legislation has caused all states to legislate specific, usually mathematical, "guidelines" that determine the support obligation, with the primary or sole reference point being the absent parent's income.

D. STEPPARENTS' DUTY TO SUPPORT
A few states impose a (limited) support obligation upon a stepparent, if the stepchild lives in the same home.

E. MODIFICATION
Child support obligations are modifiable if there is a change in the circumstances of either parent or of the child.

F. CHILD SUPPORT ENFORCEMENT SANCTIONS

A parent who is able to pay but has failed to do so may be held in civil contempt and may be jailed until the specified payment is made. If there is a willful default, the parent may be held in criminal contempt and receive a specific sentence. Under specific statutes, a criminal prosecution for nonsupport, based on the mere existence of the support obligation or on a specific judgment, may also be available. A 1992 federal law makes willful failure to support a child living in another state a federal crime.

G. CONFLICTS ASPECTS OF CHILD SUPPORT: URESA AND UIFSA

Under the Uniform Reciprocal Enforcement of Support Act and the Uniform Interstate Family Support Act, a support action may be filed in the jurisdiction where the dependent lives. The action will be heard where the obligor resides. All states had adopted URESA or its equivalent, and a majority have now replaced URESA with UIFSA.

H. FEDERAL CHILD SUPPORT ENFORCEMENT LEGISLATION

The federal child support enforcement legislation of 1975, as variously amended and strengthened, provides for federal parent locator and collection facilities. It has resulted in a great improvement in state and interstate enforcement procedures. Originally aimed at reducing the cost of the AFDC (welfare) program, the enforcement process is available for a modest fee to persons not receiving public aid. States who fail to comply with federal directives imposed under the legislation may lose some of their federal AFDC funding.

I. RECIPROCITY: THE CHILD'S DUTY TO SUPPORT PARENTS

The traditional rule that children must contribute to the support of their indigent parents remains law in many states, but is rarely enforced.

VII. CHILD CUSTODY

A. CHILD CUSTODY DURING MARRIAGE

During marriage both parents jointly have custody of their child. Within certain limits, they have discretion to make all decisions related to their child's welfare until it reaches majority. If one parent dies, the surviving parent has custody. If both parents die, the court will appoint a guardian for the child.

B. CHILD CUSTODY UPON DIVORCE

Upon divorce, a court may issue temporary and permanent orders awarding child custody to one parent, with or without visitation rights by the other, or jointly to both parents.

1. **Legal Custody Defined**
    The parent with physical custody usually also is awarded legal custody. Legal custody encompasses the right to make all decisions concerning the child's welfare, education, religion, growth and development.

2. **"Best Interest" Standard**
    Courts exercise broad discretion in determining the best interests of the child in custody matters. The UMDA lists criteria to consider, including the parents' and the child's wishes, the child's adjustment to home, school, community and the child's interaction with others. Testimony from a psychiatrist or social work professional may be offered by the parties or requested by the court on its own motion, but the ultimate criterion is what the court considers to be in the child's best interests. In appropriate circumstances, a court may appoint an attorney for the child. The costs will be borne by one or both parents or an appropriate state agency.

3. **"Tender Years" and "Primary Caretaker" Presumptions**
    Historically, the father was primarily entitled to custody. More recently, the custody of a pre-teen child used to be awarded almost automatically to the mother. Today's trend is away from this so-called "tender years presumption," but many courts expressly or subconsciously still consider it when awarding custody. A new "primary caretaker" presumption is gaining ground in many courts, with the practical result that mothers are still favored as the custodial parent of young children.

4. **Religion**
    A parent's religion or lack thereof may be taken into consideration by a court if it determines that the child has actual religious needs or that the parent's religious practices would threaten the health or well-being of the child.

5. **Race**
    The U.S. Supreme Court has held that courts may not consider race as the *sole* factor in determining the best interests of the child (*Palmore v. Sidoti*).

6. **Parents' Morality**
    Traditionally courts have placed great emphasis on the custodial parent's morality. The prevailing view now is that, unless the (immoral) activities of the custodial parent have a direct effect on the child, they are irrelevant.

7. **Parent or "Third Party"**
    There is a strong presumption that it is in the child's best interests to award custody to the parent. This is buttressed by the constitutional right of parents to

the custody and upbringing of their children, as expressed in numerous U.S. Supreme Court cases. Accordingly, courts usually prefer a parent to a third party, unless there is a showing that the parent is unfit or has abandoned the child.

C. RIGHTS OF NONCUSTODIAL PARENT

1. Visitation Rights

The noncustodial parent usually is awarded visitation rights. Visitation may be denied or restricted if it would adversely affect the child. Any such decision will bring into play the noncustodial parent's constitutional (due process) right to a relationship with his or her child.

2. Restriction on Interstate Travel of Custodial Parent

An order preventing the custodial parent from taking the child out of the court's jurisdiction protects the noncustodial parent, but may be challenged as a restriction of the custodial parent's right to travel. Courts generally grant the custodial parent permission to move if he or she has *bona fide* reasons. However, changes in the terms of visitation may be made to protect the noncustodial parent's rights.

3. Enforcement of Visitation Rights

Custody orders are enforceable by the court's contempt power. While courts may uphold the suspension of alimony in retaliation for the recipient spouse's interference with visitation rights, the withholding of child support is not permissible.

4. Joint Custody

An increasing number of states provide for joint custody, involving shared legal and physical custody of the child. A few states impose a rebuttable presumption that joint custody is in the child's best interest.

D. STANDARDS FOR MODIFICATION

Custody orders may be modified upon proof of changed circumstances and a showing that change is in the best interest of the child. The UMDA has tightened the traditional test and substantially increased the importance of the original custody adjudication by providing that modification is indicated only where the child's physical, mental, moral, or emotional health is seriously endangered.

E. VISITATION OPPORTUNITIES OF THIRD PARTIES

Nearly all jurisdictions now provide for the possibility of court-ordered visitation by non-parents. Statutes and cases typically involve grandparents, but may include stepparents, foster parents, and siblings.

F. INTERSTATE RECOGNITION OF CUSTODY DECREES

The federal Parental Kidnapping Prevention Act of 1980 extends Full Faith and Credit protection to (modifiable and therefore nonfinal) child custody decrees and provides assistance in cases of interstate child snatching. The Hague Convention on Civil Aspects of International Child Abduction applies (more or less analogously) to international child abduction to the territory of a country that is party to the treaty. In addition, all states have adopted the Uniform Child Custody Jurisdiction Act or an equivalent. That Act provides that jurisdiction over custody matters remains in the court of original adjudication—with a few necessary exceptions. Together, the state and federal enactments have significantly reduced the incidence of parental child snatching in search of a redetermination of legal custody.

VIII. PARENTAL OBLIGATION OF CARE AND CONTROL AND THE JUVENILE COURT SYSTEM

A. CHILD DEPENDENCY

A dependent child is one who either has no parent or guardian or whose present home conditions are not fit for the care of the child.

B. CHILD NEGLECT

Definitions of neglect vary from state to state and often allow courts broad discretion in finding neglect. Among many others, typical factors indicating neglect are abandonment, refusal or neglect to provide care (especially medical care or support), abuse, and "unfitness" on a variety of grounds including, for instance, drug abuse. Criminal sanctions may also apply to a neglecting or abusive parent.

C. CONSTITUTIONAL RIGHTS

Statutes terminating parental rights have been subjected to constitutional attack—generally unsuccessfully—on the ground of vagueness, due process issues (*e.g.,* lack of notice), and allegedly arbitrary and discriminatory standards. The U.S. Supreme Court has held that, in a termination of parental rights case, allegations as to a parent's unfitness must be supported by "clear and convincing" evidence (*Santosky v. Kramer*), and that indigent parents are *not* constitutionally entitled to the appointment of counsel (*Lassiter v. Department*). In certain contexts, investigatory home visits by welfare workers may be permitted (*Wyman v. James*).

D. PARENTAL CONTROL OVER MEDICAL CARE RENDERED THEIR CHILD

Except in an emergency, parental consent generally is required for any medical treatment given a minor child. A court may appoint a guardian for a child whose parents refuse to consent to needed treatment. Where the refusal is based on religious grounds, the court will step in when the parent's exercise of his or her religion becomes life-threatening to the child. Under modern statutes and recent constitutional adjudications, a (mature) minor may obtain certain kinds of medical treatment without a parent's consent or notification, such as treatment for venereal disease or an abortion.

E. CHILD ABUSE

Physical child abuse is easily defined, but often difficult to prove. To facilitate detection and proof, statutes commonly require health professionals and others, such as teachers, to report cases of suspected abuse. In some courts, evidence of "battered child syndrome" has been used to support a finding of abuse.

F. DISPOSITION OF THE JUVENILE COURT

After a finding of dependency, neglect, or abuse, a court may place a child in foster care, appoint a guardian, institutionalize the child, and/or terminate parental rights.

G. CRIMINAL PROCEDURE

The juvenile court system was developed to protect "delinquent" children against the procedures and punishments applicable to adults. The theme is the best interest of the minor. In the last three decades, the U.S. Supreme Court has granted minors increased protection in terms of procedural rights. In essence, these seek to assure that minors will not fare worse than adults, while retaining special protections offered by the juvenile court system. At the same time, current concern with violent juvenile crime is resulting in legislation lowering the age at which a child may be tried as an adult, thus altogether pulling the "juvenile rug" out from under the feet of some children.

IX. CHILDREN'S RIGHTS

A–B. HISTORY OF PARENTAL CONTROL AND CONSTITUTIONAL RIGHTS

Historically, the father had nearly absolute control over his child. Today, a parent's power is limited by a variety of laws, including the neglect, dependency and abuse laws, school attendance laws and increasing statutory and constitutional recognition of a minor's gradually growing legal independence in a variety of areas, especially in matters relating to procreation, school, and delinquency (criminal) procedure.

C. EMANCIPATION

Emancipation generally occurs when a minor acts independently of his or her parents in a manner associated with adulthood. Emancipation terminates parental support obligations and eliminates minority as a defense to contracts.

D. MINOR'S CAPACITY TO CONTRACT

A contractual obligation incurred by an unemancipated minor generally is voidable, unless ratified when the minor reaches majority. If a parent is unable to provide the minor with "necessaries," the minor is liable on his or her own contract under which he or she has received the necessaries.

E. CHILDREN AND TORT LAW
1. "Wrongful Life"

Considerable litigation has involved professional negligence in birth control, sterilization, *etc.*, that has resulted in an unwanted birth. On the basis of public policy, most courts deny "damages" for the birth of an unwanted *healthy* child, although recovery for direct expenses associated with the pregnancy often is granted. Courts, however, generally allow recovery where a baby has suffered birth defects or lasting damage due to a third party's negligence.

2–6. Wrongful Death, Immunities, "Heartbalm" Actions, Vicarious Liability

A child may recover for the wrongful death of its parent, and parents may recover for the wrongful death of a child. Most states have abolished or eroded the traditional tort immunities between parents and children. Most states do not allow either parent or child to maintain a "heartbalm" action involving the other. Parents may be liable for damages arising out of failure to supervise a child. Under specific statutes, they may also be vicariously liable in limited amounts for their children's torts against third parties, but they are not criminally liable for their children's criminal acts.

F. EDUCATION: STATE AND PARENTS

State laws require children to attend school for a designated period of time. Under long-standing constitutional doctrine, attendance may not be required at a public as opposed to a private school. Constitutional objections to obligatory schooling, classroom content (especially sex education), school prayer and school discipline have been upheld in an increasing number of cases.

X. LEGITIMACY, ILLEGITIMACY AND PATERNITY

A. LEGITIMACY

Legitimacy denotes the status of a child who enjoys a full legal relationship with both parents by virtue of its parents' marriage to each other at the time of its birth or conception. A child born to a married woman is presumed to be her husband's child.

B. ILLEGITIMACY

Illegitimacy denotes the legal status of the child born outside of marriage, or of one born to a married mother whose husband has been found not to be the father. Since the late 1960s, using an intermediate standard of equal protection and due process review, the U.S. Supreme Court has invalidated nearly all forms of legal discrimination against illegitimate children that previously existed in terms of wrongful death recovery, intestate succession, paternal support, paternal custodial interest, eligibility for government benefits and more.

C. ESTABLISHING PATERNITY

All states provide for the judicial ascertainment of paternity. In 1987, the U.S. Supreme Court held that a preponderance of the evidence, the usual civil standard of proof, is constitutionally acceptable in the establishment of paternity (*Rivera v. Minnich*).

D. CONFLICT OF LAWS

Only a judicial determination of legitimate status or of paternity is entitled to Full Faith and Credit. Status created under state law at the place of the child's birth, or where an act of legitimation occurred, is accorded deference.

XI. ADOPTION

A. HISTORY AND DEVELOPMENT

Adoption is a statutory device which did not exist at common law.

B. SOCIAL FUNCTION

Adoption provides would-be parents with a child and furthers the child's best interests by providing it with a stable home environment.

C. THE ADOPTION PROCESS

Adoption terminates the rights and duties of natural parents and creates corresponding rights and duties in adoptive parents. In many states, adoptions involving adoptive parents who are not related to the child must be accomplished through state agencies or state-regulated private agencies. In other states, the natural parent may contract directly with unrelated adoptive parents to place the child. However, "black market" adoptions that involve the "sale" of children are prohibited and criminalized. Many states provide for "subsidized" adoption for children who are difficult to place by reason of some handicap. States that permit adoptions of adults generally impose less supervision on those adoptions, although same-sex couples have encountered judicial reluctance where they sought to create a legal relationship through adoption. In some probate cases, courts have found "equitable adoption" where legal formalities had not been complied with, but where the adoptive relationship had existed for all practical purposes.

D. QUALIFICATIONS OF ADOPTIVE PARENTS

The best interests of the child control who is permitted to adopt. Prospective adoptive parents are evaluated as to marital status, age, religion, ethnic origin, race, physical defects, emotional problems, residency and economic status. The relinquishing mother's wishes are frequently honored, as to general characteristics (*e.g.,* religion) that the adoptive parents should meet.

E. CONSENT TO ADOPTION

Formal consent to an adoption must be obtained from both parents or, if parental rights have been terminated, the agency or guardian in charge of the child. In rare cases, the consent of a noncustodial parent may be dispensed with, although the parent is entitled to notice and an opportunity to be heard. Children above a certain age may be required to consent. The U.S. Supreme Court has held that unmarried fathers have a significant and constitutionally protected (due process) interest in the custody and adoption of a nonmarital child, especially one with whom they have lived in a common household.

F–H. ANONYMITY, REVOCATION AND LEGAL EFFECT OF ADOPTION

Despite attempts by adult adoptees and natural mothers to challenge the anonymity of adoption, adoptions generally have remained anonymous. Some states provide for a voluntary "matching" process through which a biological parent and an adopted child may meet. Statutes usually set a time limit after which an adoption may no longer be challenged by anyone. Courts rarely allow the adoptive parents to request revocation. The legal relationship created between the adoptive parents and child generally is identical to that between a natural parent and child.

XII. PROCREATION

A. CONTRACEPTION AND THE U.S. SUPREME COURT

The U.S. Supreme Court has recognized a protected privacy interest in the use of contraceptives by married couples (*Griswold*). *Eisenstadt* guaranteed *unmarried* persons access to birth control devices. In *Carey,* the Court struck down legislation criminalizing the distribution of contraceptives to minors under the age of 16 years.

B. ABORTION

Since 1973, the U.S. Supreme Court has recognized the woman's right to abortion on many occasions and in numerous settings. A succession of decisions emphasizes that abortion is the *woman's* right. Neither husband (nor an unmarried would-be father), nor parents of a pregnant minor may be required to consent or even to be notified and thus be put in a position to prevent the exercise of the pregnant female's right to abort. With respect to minors, the U.S. Supreme Court has complicated the picture by limiting autonomy to "mature" minors, without clearly defining a "mature" minor, leaving that to individualized judicial determination.

C. STERILIZATION
1. Compulsory Sterilization
In 1927, the U.S. Supreme Court allowed compulsory sterilization of an insane or retarded person, provided there is notice and a hearing, and the action is not arbitrary or in punishment of a crime. (*Buck v. Bell*). If *Buck* were challenged today, change should be expected, but attempts to litigate such a challenge into the U.S. Supreme Court have not yet succeeded.

2. Voluntary Sterilization
Courts have held that a state may not deny elective sterilization.

D. ARTIFICIAL CONCEPTION
New techniques for noncoital reproduction encompass artificial insemination, ovum donation, *in vitro* fertilization, embryo transfer, and "surrogate motherhood."

1. Artificial Insemination
The general rule, espoused by the Uniform Parentage Act, is that "if, under the supervision of a licensed physician and with the consent of her husband, a wife is inseminated artificially with semen donated by a man not her husband, the husband is treated in law as if he were the natural father of a child thereby conceived [and] the donor of semen is treated in law as if he were not the natural father of a child thereby conceived." Similar legislation now is in effect in the majority of states. Decades ago, courts disagreed as to whether a child conceived by way of artificial insemination was legitimate. Vis-à-vis the sperm donor, the legal situation of the offspring of an unmarried woman who was artificially inseminated at her request and for her own purposes, remains largely unclear. If the sperm donor can be identified, a paternity action may lie.

2. *In Vitro* Fertilization and Ovum Transplantation
Legal problems with *in vitro* fertilization extend to the legality of using the technique itself. Some potentially applicable laws include restrictions on fetal research, laws forbidding the sale or donation of ova, or prohibitions on experimentation on embryos or discarded fetal material. The legality of *in vitro* fertilization, even as a medical procedure to overcome infertility, may thus be in doubt in some states. It seems clear that if *in vitro* fertilization involves the

husband's sperm and the wife's ovum and reimplantation of the ovum into the wife, the resulting child is their legitimate child. If actors other than husband and wife are involved, current law does not clearly answer many questions regarding the status of offspring conceived by *in vitro* fertilization. Working rules may be the following: (a) Donor's Sperm—Wife's Ovum: The child should be the wife's and her husband's legitimate child, provided proper procedures were followed. (b) Donor's Ovum—Husband's or Donor's Sperm: The child should be the husband and wife's legitimate child and the donor should be out of the picture, if proper procedures were followed. (c) Surrogate Mother—Husband's Sperm and Wife's Ovum: The child should legally become the husband and wife's child, after appropriate procedures terminate the potential interests of the surrogate mother and her husband, if she is married.

3. Surrogate Motherhood for Pay

Distinguish the "surrogate mother" who is artificially inseminated with the sperm of a man who has contracted with her to have her surrender her rights to the child upon birth, from the "surrogate mother" who carries to birth a child that is not genetically hers, *i.e.*, a fertilized ovum was transplanted into her for "carriage and delivery." California's Supreme Court has decided this second scenario in favor of the genetic parents. Most litigation has centered on the question of the enforceability by the sperm supplier of a so-called surrogacy contract that involves the "surrogate's" (genetically) own child. Some cases have compelled the surrogate mother to surrender her child to the father. Several states have enacted specific statutes outlawing surrogacy for pay. In others, statutes against "baby selling" have been drawn upon to strike down such bargains. Note, however, that the latter type of statute may not apply where the father himself "purchases" his own biological child.

Several cases have struggled with the question how the child created by one or another method of "artificial conception" may be brought into a legal relationship with its father and his wife (or with its unrelated "instigators.") Paternity and adoption statutes have sometimes been drawn upon to establish the desired legal relationships.

*

I

THE NATURE OF MARRIAGE AND MARITAL CONTRACTS

Analysis

A. RELIGIOUS INFLUENCE

In England, the ecclesiastical courts' exclusive jurisdiction in matters of marriage and divorce lasted until the 1850s. *Holy* matrimony served as the setting for the procreation and rearing of children, as a haven from and defense against sin and crime (*i.e.,* fornication) and afforded spouses mutual society, help and comfort. Much of the law created by English church doctrine and religious courts entered into the common law of the United States.

B. CONTRACT OR STATUS

"Marriage is a personal relationship between a man and a woman arising out of a civil contract to which the consent of the parties is essential." UMDA § 201. Entered into by contract, *marriage is a status*. Rights and obligations are delineated by the state, not by the parties. *Maynard v. Hill,* 125 U.S. 190, 8 S.Ct. 723, 31 L.Ed. 654 (1888) pronounced: "Other contracts may be modified, restricted, or enlarged, or entirely released upon the consent of the parties. Not so with marriage. The relation once formed, the law steps in and holds the parties to various obligations and liabilities."

C. CONTROLLING FACTORS AFFECTING THE MARRIAGE CONTRACT

1. STATE POWER
The states have "reserve power" to modify the law of marriage and divorce, even when such a legislative change may interfere with the reasonable expectations of married parties. This has been upheld on the following rationales:

a. Contract Clause Inapplicable
U.S. Const. art. I, § 10 provides: "No State shall * * * pass any * * * ex post facto Law, or Law impairing the Obligation of Contracts * * *." Marriage, however, has been held not to be a contract within the meaning of that article of the Constitution, because "[marriage] is an institution in the maintenance of which in its purity, the public is deeply interested * * *." *Maynard v. Hill, supra.*

b. State Reserve Power
Because marriage involves the public interest, marriage regulation incorporates the reserve power of the state to amend existing laws or enact additional laws.

Example: H and W married when a fault-based divorce statute was in effect. Much later, the state enacted no-fault divorce, and H filed for divorce. W contended that the state's implementation of no-fault divorce constituted an unconstitutional impairment of her contract rights because H would not have been able to divorce her under the fault-based statute in effect at the time they were married.

(Result: Divorce granted. The marriage contract includes the reserve power of the state to amend the law.) *In re Walton's Marriage,* 28 Cal.App.3d 108, 104 Cal.Rptr. 472 (1972).

c. Due Process Clause Inapplicable

"Status" as a married person is *not property* within the purview of the Due Process Clause. Even if that "status" were "property," a retroactive change in divorce laws would not deprive a person of that status *without due process of law.*

Example: W had prevailed in a separation action under fault-based New York divorce law. After the enactment of no-fault (living apart) divorce legislation in 1966, H claimed that the separation under the earlier decree was the basis for a no-fault divorce. This would deprive W of certain economic benefits and rights relating to her relationship with H that she had retained under the separation decree. (Result: Divorce granted. W did not have a vested right that was adversely affected as her "prospective right of inheritance is inchoate and expectant." "In short, the State, having the power directly to limit or abolish rights of accession to the property of a living person, may undoubtedly do so indirectly by providing a new ground for divorce. Since, then, no vested rights of the defendants have been adversely affected, there has been no denial of due process.") *Gleason v. Gleason,* 26 N.Y.2d 28, 308 N.Y.S.2d 347, 256 N.E.2d 513 (1970). In response to *Gleason,* New York *legislated* limited relief for such cases. D. R. L. § 170a.

2. CHANGE OF RESIDENCE

The parties' reasonable expectations as to the incidents of their marriage may be altered by their move from one jurisdiction to another. While the *validity* of marriage generally is determined in accordance with the law of the place of celebration, the law of the parties' domicile generally governs the legal incidents of the *marital relationship* as well as requirements for and consequences of *divorce.*

Example: H and W, both Russian domiciliaries, were married in Moscow. During at least part of their marriage they resided in England. After five years of marriage H was granted an *ex parte* divorce at the Consulate General of the U.S.S.R. in Paris. W later petitioned in England for legal separation. In the court's view, the issue was whether there had initially been a legal marriage which England would recognize. (Result: Yes. While the existence or non-existence of the marriage was governed by the laws of Russia—the place of celebration—the legal incidents and the requirements for divorce were governed by the laws of England—the marital domicile.) *Nachimson v. Nachimson,* All E.R. Rep. 414 (1930).

3. PRIVATE MARRIAGE CONTRACT
An antenuptial agreement, or to a lesser extent a post nuptial agreement, between the parties may affect and alter the terms of the marriage relationship. (See G, below).

D. MARRIAGE AND THE CONSTITUTION

Although marital relationships traditionally are defined and controlled by state law, the U.S. Supreme Court has applied constitutional interpretation to a host of family law issues. In this manner, numerous aspects of family law have been federalized and, incidentally but very importantly, unified throughout the United States. Occasionally, state courts have interpreted a state constitution to expand certain rights (*e.g., Baehr v. Lewin*, 74 Hawaii 530, 852 P.2d 44 (1993)).

1. RELIGIOUS FREEDOM
The state's right to regulate marriage is balanced against the individual's right to practice religion.

> *Example:* H was granted a divorce from W. Both were citizens of India and Hindus of high caste. W contended that the divorce violated her First Amendment (free exercise of religion) rights as the Hindu religion does not recognize divorce. She alleged that if she ever returned to India divorced, her family and friends would treat her as if she were dead. (Result: For H. The order dissolved only the civil contract of marriage and did not dissolve it ecclesiastically. "The wife here may take such view of their relationship after the decree as her religion requires, but as a matter of law the civil contract has been dissolved.") *Sharma v. Sharma*, 8 Kan.App.2d 726, 667 P.2d 395 (1983).

2. MONOGAMY
Marriage to more than one spouse at the same time (bigamy, polygamy) is invalid and subject to criminal sanctions. Aside from intentional bigamy for whatever— often fraudulent, sometimes religious—purpose, much "unintended" bigamy occurred in the days of difficult divorce, when a person remarried whose prior marriage had been divorced by ineffective legal process (*e.g.*, an invalid migratory divorce) or not at all. Note that the practice of polygamy is not yet extinct in the United States; some 20,000–30,000 polygamous families are reported, chiefly among Mormons.

a. Justification for Regulation
1) Religion and Tradition
   Restrictions on bigamy and polygamy are founded in religious beliefs, moral taboos, and Western cultural tradition.

2) Constitutionality

In 1878, the U.S. Supreme Court upheld a statute prohibiting bigamy against attack under the First Amendment. The court held that the public interest in preventing polygamy outweighed the interest of Mormons in practicing that aspect of their religion. Reynolds, a member of the Church of Jesus Christ of Latter–Day Saints, was convicted of bigamy. At that time members believed in and actively practiced bigamy. "[I]t is impossible to believe that the constitutional guarantee of religious freedom was intended to prohibit legislation in respect to this most important feature of social life. * * * [T]he only question which remains is, whether those who make polygamy a part of their religion are excepted from the operation of the statute. If they are, then those who do not make polygamy a part of their religious belief may be found guilty and punished, while those who do, must be acquitted and go free. This would be introducing a new element into criminal law. Laws are made for the government of actions, and while they cannot interfere with mere religious belief and opinions, they may with practices." *Reynolds v. United States,* 98 U.S. (8 Otto) 145, 25 L.Ed. 244 (1878).

3) Modern Rationale

Today, restrictions on polygamy are commonly justified as promoting morality, stability of the family and avoiding sexual and economic exploitation of the spouses and children of the polygamist.

Examples: (1) P's employment as a police officer was terminated when it was learned that he practiced plural marriage. Utah's Constitution prohibits polygamy. P brought suit alleging that his termination violated his right to the free exercise of religion and his right to privacy. (Result: P loses. "Monogamy is inextricably woven into the fabric of our society. It is the bedrock upon which our culture is built. * * * In light of these fundamental values, the state is justified, by a compelling interest, in upholding and enforcing its ban on plural marriage to protect the monogamous marriage relationship." On the constitutional issue of privacy, the court went on to say, "[W]e find no authority for extending the constitutional right of privacy so far that it would protect polygamous marriages. We decline to do so.") *Potter v. Murray City,* 760 F.2d 1065 (10th Cir.1985), cert. denied 474 U.S. 849, 106 S.Ct. 145, 88 L.Ed.2d 120 (1985).

(2) H and W_1 were legally married and had 4 children. In accordance with his religious belief, H later "married" W_2, who lived with H and W_1 and with whom H had 2 more children. Still later H "married" W_3, who had been the plural wife of another man and had had 6 children with him. Two weeks after H and W_3 "married," H and W_1 petitioned to adopt W_3's children. W_3 and the children's father gave their written

consents. Six weeks later, W₃ died. W₃'s father and two sisters intervened and moved to dismiss the adoption petition. The trial court granted the motion and ruled as a matter of law that petitioners' criminal conduct in teaching and practicing polygamous marriage made them ineligible to adopt the children. (Result: The trial court may not disqualify all bigamists or polygamists as potential adopters, and petitioners are entitled to a hearing and specific factual findings on their fitness to adopt. "The fact that the petitioning prospective parents engage or have engaged in activities prohibited by statute or the constitution is one factor the court must consider when determining whether the specific placement at issue would promote the interest of the child to be adopted. Prospective adoptive parents' illegal or unconstitutional conduct, however, is not properly considered as a threshold determination in an adoption petition; rather, such conduct is subsumed by the interest of the child standard.") *Johanson v. Fischer*, 808 P.2d 1083 (Utah 1991).

b. Criminal Sanctions

1) Enforcement Practice
Criminal bigamy and adultery statutes are rarely enforced.

2) "Enoch Arden" Defense
When an individual's spouse has been missing for a specified period of time (such as seven or five years) and if he or she believed that his or her marriage had ended in divorce or through the partner's death, typical statutes provide a defense to criminal bigamy prosecution of a remarried individual. Based on a Tennyson poem, these statutes are commonly referred to as *"Enoch Arden"* statutes. They do *not* have civil effects, such as validating the later marriage.

c. Civil Effects of Bigamous Marriage
A marriage is void if entered while a previous marriage is still in force. Nevertheless, in many states even a bigamous marriage may have certain legal effects: (1) Statutes may declare the offspring of such marriages "legitimate"; (2) Statutes may authorize alimony to be paid to the "victim" of a void marriage; (3) The putative spouse doctrine (p. 76) may protect the interests of the partner who, in good faith, believed his or her partner to be eligible to marry; (4) A subsequent end of the first marriage through divorce or the other spouse's death may validate the previously void marriage in states recognizing common law marriage; (5) A "presumption" may in certain cases uphold a marriage of dubious validity (p. 75); (6) UMDA § 207(b) expressly validates a previously invalid marriage as of the time the impediment is removed; (7) A declaration of invalidity may be granted *non*-retroactively under UMDA § 208(e) Alternative B: "Unless the court finds * * * that the interests of justice would be served by making the decree not retroactive, it shall declare the marriage invalid as of the date of the marriage" (p. 89).

3. THE RIGHT TO MARRY

The most basic historical understanding of marriage—that it involve a heterosexual couple—has been attacked in many courts. This is discussed at p. 100.

In 1967, Virginia was one of sixteen states that still prohibited interracial marriage. Two Virginia residents, a black woman and a white man, had married in the District of Columbia in 1958. After returning to Virginia, they were indicted for violating the statutory prohibition. The sentence was one year in jail which was suspended on condition that they leave Virginia and not return together for twenty-five years. In *Loving v. Virginia*, 388 U.S. 1, 87 S.Ct. 1817, 18 L.Ed.2d 1010 (1967), the United States Supreme Court invalidated the state law. Very importantly, the court classified the right to marry as "fundamental": "The freedom to marry has long been recognized as one of the vital personal rights essential to the orderly pursuit of happiness by free men. * * * Marriage is one of the 'basic civil rights of man,' fundamental to our very existence and survival." Given its facts, *Loving might have been,* but was not, interpreted to be limited to the particularly odious *racial* classification there involved. Instead, the concept of marriage as a fundamental right under the Equal Protection Clause has been used to attack and invalidate a broad variety of marriage restrictions, such as a Wisconsin statute conditioning the issuance of a marriage license on compliance with prior support obligations. *Zablocki v. Redhail*, 434 U.S. 374, 98 S.Ct. 673, 54 L.Ed.2d 618 (1978).

Examples: (1) Missouri prison regulation permitted an inmate to marry only with the permission of the superintendent, and provided that such approval should be given only "when there are compelling reasons to do so." The term "compelling" was not defined, but officials testified that generally only a pregnancy or the birth of an illegitimate child would be considered a compelling reason. (Result: The U.S. Supreme Court held: "We disagree * * * that *Zablocki* [*v. Redhail, supra*], does not apply to inmates. It is settled that a prison inmate 'retains those (constitutional) rights that are not inconsistent with his status as a prisoner or with the legitimate penological objectives of the corrections system.' * * * [T]he almost complete ban on the decision to marry is not reasonably related to legitimate penological objectives. We conclude, therefore, that the * * * regulation is facially invalid.") *Turner v. Safley,* 482 U.S. 78, 107 S.Ct. 2254, 96 L.Ed.2d 64 (1987).

(2) State law required males to be 21 years of age to obtain a marriage license without parental consent (18 with consent; 16 with court order) and females to be 18 without parental consent (16 with consent; 15 with court order). (Result: Statute unconstitutionally denies equal protection on account of sex, and *mandamus* may be used to compel issuance of marriage license to 20–year-old plaintiff.) *Phelps v. Bing,* 58 Ill.2d 32, 316 N.E.2d 775 (1974). Note: More recently, gender-related age discrimination was ruled out by the U.S. Supreme Court's *Stanton* cases. See p. 81.

(3) A debtor who had married while under protection of the U.S. bankruptcy code sought to modify his repayment plan. The trustee in bankruptcy characterized the debtor's marriage as a voluntary change in circumstances that should weigh against the proposed modification. (Result: Modification allowed. Referring to *Loving v. Virginia*, the bankruptcy court held: "Clearly there is no provision of the Code which is intended to inhibit the right to marry while in bankruptcy. Any such interpretation would turn public policy on its ear by requiring payments to creditors under a confirmed plan at the expense of the debtor's support of his family. * * * The obligation of financial support as it flows from the decision, albeit perhaps untimely, to marry or procreate, is not intended to be superseded by the creditor's rights under the Code. * * * Accordingly, the monthly payments will be reduced from $215.00 to $140.00, and the Plan will be extended to sixty months. The dividend to unsecured creditors will be reduced from 100% to 34%.") *In re Walker*, 114 B.R. 847 (Bkrtcy.N.D.N.Y.1990).

4. MARITAL PRIVACY

Griswold v. Connecticut, 381 U.S. 479, 85 S.Ct. 1678, 14 L.Ed.2d 510 (1965), discovered a right to marital privacy in "emanations from" and the "penumbras of" numerous constitutional amendments. On that—subsequently much disputed—basis, the court struck down a Connecticut statute prohibiting—even by married couples—the use of birth control drugs or devices. *Griswold* was followed by *Eisenstadt v. Baird*, 405 U.S. 438, 92 S.Ct. 1029, 31 L.Ed.2d 349 (1972), which invalidated a similar law applied to unmarried persons. *Eisenstadt* cast doubt on whether the right of privacy referred to in *Griswold* is based on the *marital* relationship: "Yet the marital couple is not an independent entity with a mind and heart of its own, but an association of two individuals each with a separate intellectual and emotional makeup. If the right of privacy means anything, it is the right of the individual, married or single, to be free from unwarranted governmental intrusion into matters so fundamentally affecting a person as the decision whether to bear or beget a child."

Caveats. (1) The presence of a third party may dissolve the right to privacy. *Lovisi v. Slayton*, 539 F.2d 349 (4th Cir.1976)(sodomy convictions upheld against H and W when they knew that a third party was present.) (2) The right of privacy figures importantly in the abortion cases, but the U.S. Supreme Court did not extend it to protect homosexual conduct. *Bowers v. Hardwick*, 478 U.S. 186, 106 S.Ct. 2841, 92 L.Ed.2d 140 (1986). Several state courts, however, have done so. *Commonwealth v. Wasson*, 842 S.W.2d 487 (Ky.1992).

E. THE MARITAL RELATIONSHIP AT COMMON LAW

Traditionally, the marital relationship was dominated by the husband. Blackstone's classic phrase was: "By marriage, the husband and wife are one person in law; that is, the very being or legal existence of the woman is suspended during the marriage, or at least is incorporated and consolidated into that of the husband.'' During marriage, all of the *married* woman's real and personal property was controlled by the husband. While the *single* woman had legal capacity at common law, a *wife* could not contract, neither with her husband nor with others, nor could she sue or be sued.

F. MARRIED WOMEN'S PROPERTY ACTS

Trust devices were developed to keep married women's property out of their husbands' control. In the late 1800's, some of the legal disabilities imposed on women were eliminated directly by so-called ''Married Women's Property Acts.'' These typically allowed married women to own and convey property, make contracts, sue or be sued and much more, but they did not end all disabilities imposed on the wife by marriage. Tort immunities continue into the present, although they are disappearing or being limited in state after state. See Ch. IV, p. 118.

G. THE ANTENUPTIAL AGREEMENT

Traditionally, antenuptial (or prenuptial or premarital) contracts have been used by people who are wealthy, are elderly and/or are parents of children from a previous marriage in order to protect their estates. Today, increasing use of such contracts by intending spouses is due to the entirely different economic relationship between H and W in a dual career (or two-job) marriage, the ease with which divorce may be obtained, and the desire of many modern couples to shape the content of their marital relationship. Traditional antenuptial agreements typically dealt only with property division upon death. So limited, they were enforceable. More recently, antenuptial agreements dealing with support and property settlements upon divorce as well as contracts dealing with aspects of the ongoing marriage have become permissible.

1. INDIVIDUALIZING MARRIAGE BY CONTRACT
An antenuptial agreement seeks to individualize aspects of the parties' marriage by altering marital rights and obligations, personal or financial, that otherwise would be imposed by law.

2. VALIDITY OF ANTENUPTIAL AGREEMENTS
Valid antenuptial agreements must meet all requirements of contract law. Beyond that, antenuptial agreements have been subject to special scrutiny based on public policies relating to marriage, the parties' confidential and intimate relationship and, so it sometimes seems, even the court's hindsight.

a. Contract Requirements
1) Statute of Frauds
   Most states require antenuptial agreements to be in writing, as did the original Statute of Frauds. Appropriate exceptions may be made if there was

sufficient part performance, or enforcement would cause a fraud to be perpetrated, or one party's representations coupled with the other's reliance have led to a detrimental change in position. Some statutes require compliance with further formalities, such as requiring the agreement to be witnessed formally.

Example: H and W orally agreed that if she would marry him, he would treat the child, with whom she was pregnant, "as if it were his own." At the time of the agreement, both H and W knew that he was not the biological father of the child. H had his name listed as father on the birth certificate. During the four years of the marriage, he never denied being the child's father. Upon separation H contended that as the agreement was oral, it was not enforceable under the Statute of Frauds and he had no further duty to support the child. (Result: For W. W acted in reliance on H's promises when she agreed not to put up the child for adoption at birth. Therefore, H is estopped from raising the Statute of Frauds.) *T. v. T.*, 216 Va. 867, 224 S.E.2d 148 (1976).

2) Consideration

The mutual promises to marry traditionally have served as consideration. The Uniform Premarital Agreements Act—enacted by about one-half of the states—purports to do without consideration: "It [a premarital agreement] is enforceable without consideration." UPAA § 2. However, that bold step is implicitly limited by UPAA § 4 which provides that "[a] premarital agreement becomes effective upon marriage." Accordingly, not much, if anything, has changed with respect to premarital agreements. The UPAA clause is significant in respect of post-marriage modification of agreements, where consideration had typically been more difficult to find, because married parties already have broad legal duties to each other.

3) Risk of Overreaching

The intimate relationship between intending marriage partners has caused courts to scrutinize antenuptial agreements for signs of overreaching. Many courts speak in terms of a fiduciary duty between the parties. Historically, courts have been more sensitive to wives' complaints about antenuptial agreements than to complaints of husbands, because the traditional wife was (or would through marriage become) economically dependent and was financially less knowledgeable. Moreover, usually it was the wife who relinquished rights in the antenuptial agreement. Recent improvements in the legal and economic status of women have made it less important that courts stretch to protect wives, and newer cases are interpreting premarital agreements in accordance with their terms, even if the terms are harsh and the circumstances of execution less than "squeaky clean."

Example: H and W's antenuptial agreement limited W to support payments of $200 per week in the event of separation or divorce, subject to a maximum of $25,000. H's attorney presented the agreement to W on the eve of the wedding, and she signed the agreement without benefit of independent counsel, nor did H's attorney advise her regarding any legal rights that she surrendered. When they married, H was a 39–year-old neurosurgeon with an income of approximately $90,000 per year and assets worth approximately $300,000. W was a 23–year-old unemployed nurse. The couple separated after 7 years of marriage and commenced divorce proceedings 2 years later. During the two years of separation, H paid W $25,000 for support. On divorce, W claimed rehabilitative alimony. (Result: W's claim denied. The court reviewed earlier cases that had required *either* a reasonable provision for the spouse *or* full and fair disclosure of both the parties' finances as well as of the statutory rights being relinquished. "[E]arlier decisions * * * rested upon a belief that spouses are of unequal status and that women are not knowledgeable enough to understand the nature of contracts that they enter. Society has advanced, however, to the point where women are no longer regarded as the 'weaker' party in marriage, or in society generally. Indeed, the stereotype that women serve as homemakers while men work as breadwinners is no longer viable. Quite often today both spouses are income earners. Nor is there viability in the presumption that women are uninformed, uneducated, and readily subjected to unfair advantage in marital agreements. Indeed, women nowadays quite often have substantial education, financial awareness, income, and assets. * * * By invoking inquiries into reasonableness, * * * the functioning and reliability of prenuptial agreements is severely undermined. * * * Further, everyone who enters a long-term agreement knows that circumstances can change during its term, so that what initially appeared desirable might prove to be an unfavorable bargain. Such are the risks that contracting parties routinely assume. Certainly, the possibilities of illness, birth of children, reliance upon a spouse, career change, financial gain or loss, and numerous other events that can occur in the course of a marriage cannot be regarded as unforeseeable. If parties choose not to address such matters in their prenuptial agreements, they must be regarded as having contracted to bear the risk of events that alter the value of their bargains.") *Simeone v. Simeone*, 525 Pa. 392, 581 A.2d 162 (1990).

a) Full Disclosure
Each party—traditionally the focus was primarily on the future husband—must make full disclosure of all material facts relating to the quantity, character, and value of property. Alternatively, a conscious

waiver of full disclosure, especially when combined with adequate knowledge of the partner's financial situation may be upheld.

Examples: (1) UPAA § 6(a) holds a premarital agreement unenforceable "if the party against whom enforcement is sought proves that: (1) that party did not execute the agreement voluntarily; or (2) the agreement was unconscionable when it was executed and, before execution of the agreement, that party: (i) was not provided fair and reasonable disclosure of the property or financial obligations of the other party; (ii) did not voluntarily and expressly waive, in writing, any right to disclosure of the property or financial obligations of the other party beyond the disclosure provided; and (iii) did not have, or reasonably could not have had, an adequate knowledge of the property or financial obligations of the other party."

(2) H and W executed a home-made antenuptial agreement, neither party being represented by counsel. Under the agreement, W relinquished her rights to all property owned or later acquired by H. The agreement did not mention alimony or attorney's fees. At the time the agreement was entered into, W was keeping the books of H's businesses, and it was conceded that she knew as much about his financial circumstances as he did. (Result: Agreement valid. The fact that this agreement was "basically unfair and inequitable to the wife" was not sufficient to vacate or modify the agreement. "[O]nce it is established that the agreement is unreasonable, 'a presumption arises that there was either concealment by the defending spouse or a presumed lack of knowledge by the challenging spouse of the defending spouse's finances at the time the agreement was reached.' Here * * * the wife had full and complete knowledge of the husband's finances. Thus this presumption was rebutted." The court added a *caveat*: "[W]hile the wife here may be awarded lump sum alimony in the discretion of the trial court, she may not be awarded lump sum alimony in order to accomplish equitable distribution of the husband's property because to do so would be violative of the terms and spirit of the antenuptial agreement.") *Cladis v. Cladis*, 512 So.2d 271 (Fla.App.1987).

b) Fair and Reasonable Provision—*What* Is "Unconscionable?" *When* Is the Deal to Be Evaluated—At Time of Execution or Enforcement?
Fair and reasonable economic provision for the wife may save the agreement even if disclosure was incomplete. Some courts will uphold

antenuptial agreements if *either* full disclosure *or* appropriate economic provision is made. As a practical rule, however, contracts involving *both* full disclosure *and* fair provision are much less likely to be upset.

Examples: (1) UPAA § 6(c) provides: "an issue of unconscionability of a premarital agreement shall be decided by the court as a matter of law." What that may mean in practice is illustrated by UPAA § 6(b): "if a provision of a premarital agreement modifies or eliminates spousal support and that modification or elimination causes one party to the agreement to be eligible for support under a program of public assistance at the time of separation or marital dissolution, a court, notwithstanding the terms of the agreement, may require the other party to provide support to the extent necessary to avoid that eligibility." See UPAA § 6(a), p. 51.

(2) (Not decided under UPAA). H and W executed an antenuptial agreement under which W relinquished her interest in any property owned by H, whether acquired before or after the marriage. At the time of the marriage, H was an attorney and real estate investor with assets of approximately $1,400,000. W, with assets of approximately $100,000, directed nursing programs at two community colleges. Each party had children from their prior marriages and they had one child together. There was full and complete disclosure of earnings, property, and financial condition, and W was found to have waived her opportunity to seek advice from independent counsel. (Result: Remanded for a determination of the agreement's *fairness at both the time of execution and the time of enforcement.* "[T]he court should review the substantive fairness of the agreement in light of the circumstances existing at the inception. This will require appropriate inquiry into facts bearing upon the reasonable expectations of each signatory as to the scope and ultimate effect of the contract in the event the marriage should terminate by dissolution. The court should also review * * * whether in light of [the birth of the parties' child] enforcement would be oppressive and unconscionable. * * * Trial courts engaging in such a review must strike a balance between the law's policy favoring freedom of contract between informed consenting adults, and substantive fairness—admittedly a difficult task.") *McKee-Johnson v. Johnson,* 444 N.W.2d 259 (Minn.1989).

(3) (Not decided under UPAA). When H and W married, H was vice chairman of the board of an advertising

agency. W was his secretary. H's annual income was $285,000 and his net worth was approximately $1,800,000. W had no assets other than some jewelry. The day before the wedding, W signed an antenuptial agreement under which she waived her right to spousal support in excess of $1,000 per month. During their 15–year marriage, W did not work outside the home. On divorce, the parties agreed that she was to retain primary physical custody of their child. (Result: Remanded for a determination of whether the antenuptial agreement was *unconscionable at the time of divorce.* "To enforce a spousal support provision of a premarital agreement because it was reasonable at the time of execution of the agreement can result in unforeseen economic hardship to a spouse that may shock the conscience of the court due to relevant changes in the circumstances of the marriage by the time of the divorce. Public policy mandates against the enforcement of unconscionable support payments.") *Lewis v. Lewis,* 69 Hawaii 497, 748 P.2d 1362 (1988).

c) Opportunity For Advice by Independent Counsel

To eliminate all suspicion of overreaching, it is advisable that both parties—traditionally especially the wife—be represented by independent counsel. However, typical state statutes, the Uniform Marital Property Act, and the Uniform Premarital Agreements Act do *not* specifically *require* counsel.

Example: On the eve of their wedding, H and W executed an antenuptial agreement under which W relinquished all rights to past, present, and future support, division of property, and any other property rights accruing because of the marriage. It was undisputed that there was adequate disclosure of H's assets. Although H's attorney had suggested that W consult with independent counsel, she had declined to do so. (Result: Agreement valid, because W was not denied a meaningful opportunity to consult counsel. The reviewing court added the *caveat*: "When an antenuptial agreement provides disproportionately less than the party challenging it would have received under an equitable distribution, the party financially disadvantaged must have a meaningful opportunity to consult with counsel. The presentation of an agreement a very short time before the wedding ceremony will create a presumption of overreaching or coercion if, in contrast to this case, the postponement of the wedding would cause significant hardship, embarrassment or emotional stress.") *Fletcher v. Fletcher,* 68 Ohio St.3d 464, 628 N.E.2d 1343 (Ohio 1994).

b. Subject Matter

1) Disposition at Death

Antenuptial agreements dealing with the disposition of property on either or both parties' *death* are valid, assuming that the contract requirements for validity are met.

2) Providing for Divorce

Antenuptial agreements seeking to secure the financial consequences of *divorce* have traditionally been held invalid. The courts have seen such agreements as encouraging divorce in violation of public policy against divorce. Since the existence of an antenuptial agreement may actually deter divorce by making the parties aware of the cost of divorce in advance, the traditional rationale has always been weak. Moreover, modern liberal divorce statutes negate any strong state policy against divorce. A sounder policy argument against allowing parties to settle divorce consequences in advance is that divorce may lie so far in the future that it will involve unforeseen and unforeseeable circumstances that render an antenuptial agreement invalid.

> *Example:* An antenuptial agreement provided that, upon a legal separation or dissolution of the marriage, W would receive health insurance coverage and $75.00 per week as alimony but would have no further claim for support or H's property. (Result: Agreement not invalid *per se*. The court overturned its 75–year-old ruling that "the law will not permit parties contemplating marriage to enter into a contract providing for, and looking to, future separation after marriage," and rejected the "notion that divorce is promoted by an antenuptial agreement which contemplates such a possibility." The court upheld "the right of parties to enter into appropriate agreements." It recognized antenuptial agreements in contemplation of divorce, subject to (1) the requirement of full disclosure, and (2) the restriction that the agreement must not be *unconscionable at the time enforcement is sought*. The case was remanded for further proceedings on the issues of disclosure and unconscionability.) *Edwardson v. Edwardson*, 798 S.W.2d 941 (Ky.1990).

a) Second Marriages

If older parties or second marriages are involved, courts have more readily upheld antenuptial agreements making provision for divorce.

b) Property Rights vs. Support Obligations and Other "Essentials" of Marriage

An antenuptial agreement settling the division of *property* upon divorce will be upheld more readily than one affecting *support* obligations. As a matter of public policy, the duty of support is seen as more "essential" to marriage than is the distribution of accumulated marital property. Other explanations are that: (1) parties should not predetermine a maintenance award at a time when the factors which should go into the determination of the award cannot be foreseen, and (2) the public has a direct stake in persons not becoming public charges due to loss of spousal support. UPAA § 3(a)(4) allows provisions negating support, but § 6(b) would enforce such a provision only to the extent a party is not thereby made eligible for public aid. It should be noted that the distinction between support and property is in many cases neither clear nor very useful, because modern divorce often involves parties with limited assets and incomes and their divorce settlements often involve trade-offs between property and support.

> ***Example:*** H and W had entered into an antenuptial agreement which entitled W to a maximum of $200 alimony per month for 10 years if the couple should separate or divorce. W also was to receive one-half of the price received for the marital home, the personal property and possessions in their home, and one car. Attached to the antenuptial agreement was a statement of assets owned by each party. H's assets were valued at $550,000, W's at $5,000. The marriage lasted for 14 years. Upon divorce, H owned assets worth $8,000,000 and had an annual income of approximately $250,000. The trial court found the antenuptial agreement to be valid. The appellate court reversed, holding that such agreements were not enforceable by the party found to be at fault in a divorce proceeding. H appealed to Ohio's Supreme Court. (Result: (1) Marital misconduct does not abrogate an antenuptial agreement. (2) To determine the validity of the agreement, the court held that provisions covering the division of property are to be tested for unconscionability as of the time of execution, while public policy requires that provisions covering maintenance are to be tested as of the time of divorce.) *Gross v. Gross,* 11 Ohio St.3d 99, 464 N.E.2d 500 (1984). (Note: This case was *not* decided under UPAA).

c) Terminology
Specific language used in drafting an antenuptial agreement may make the difference between enforceability and unenforceability. Traditionally, courts were more likely to invalidate a contract that refers to divorce expressly than one that sets up a property regime between the parties that will have the *effect* of leaving each party with certain property upon divorce. With increasing recognition of antenuptial contracts expressly preparing for divorce, however, this precaution has lost much of its value.

3) Regulating the Ongoing Marriage
Today, some intending marriage partners enter into comprehensive agreements that seek to deal with any number of aspects of every day marital life.

      a) Judicial Policy of Noninterference in Marriage

         Courts typically will *not* enforce agreements purporting to deal with
         support obligations *during* marriage, sexual behavior, family religion,
         promises not to defend a divorce action or not to seek a divorce, child
         rearing and other day-to-day aspects of married life.

      b) UPAA

         UPAA § 3(a) increases the range of permissible subject matter:
         "Parties to a premarital agreement may contract with respect to: * * *
         (8) any other matter, including their personal rights and obligations,
         not in violation of public policy or a statute imposing a criminal
         penalty."

      c) Usefulness of Unenforceable Provisions

         Even if an agreement concerning the ongoing marriage is not
         enforceable, it may serve a purpose if the "negotiation" causes a
         prospective couple to make plans for their future and thereby clarify
         their individual and marital expectations. *Caveat*: Given current
         trends, an antenuptial agreement that is unenforceable or of doubtful
         enforceability when made may ultimately turn out to be enforceable, by
         the time an issue arises.

  c. **Effect of Divorce or Separation on Antenuptial Agreement**

     If an antenuptial agreement—for the reasons just outlined—fails to refer to
     divorce or separation, courts must decide what effect divorce or separation is to
     have. Three solutions have been offered: (1) Divorce terminating marriage
     also terminates any agreement made in contemplation of that marriage. (2)
     The party at fault in the divorce action may be barred from enforcing the
     agreement since he/she has breached the marital contract. (3) Absent a
     provision in the agreement, divorce or separation has no effect on the
     agreement.

 d. **UMDA**

    The UMDA makes no detailed provision for antenuptial agreements, but
    provides that agreements concerning *property* may be *considered* on divorce
    (UMDA § 307(a), Alternative A): "In making apportionment [of property and
    assets belonging to either or both spouses] the court shall *consider* the duration
    of the marriage, any prior marriage of either party, *any antenuptial agreement
    of the parties, * * *.*"

 e. **UPAA and UMPA**

    The Uniform Premarital Agreement Act (enacted in one-half of the states) and
    the Uniform Marital Property Act (enacted in Wisconsin) broadly favor
    antenuptial agreements. They would allow almost all such agreements to
    stand unless "unconscionable" when "made" or "executed." (UPAA § 6(a),
    UMPA § 10(g)). Neither Act provides relief if the agreement has become
    "unconscionable" at the time it is sought to be enforced. (See above, p. 51).

f. Gift Tax Treatment of Antenuptial Agreements
Property transfers to a spouse prior to marriage are taxable as *gifts*. Even if the antenuptial agreement is otherwise valid, the exchange of mutual promises to marry has not been deemed adequate and full consideration in money or money's worth within the meaning of the Internal Revenue Code. Rev. Rul. 69–347, 1969–1 Cum. Bull. 227. Since property transfers between spouses are not subject to gift tax, property transfers should be deferred until after the parties are married.

H. AGREEMENTS DURING MARRIAGE

Agreements made *during* marriage fall into three categories: (1) agreements seeking to define the relationship during the marriage or to amend an antenuptial agreement; (2) agreements in anticipation of separation; and (3) agreements effecting a reconciliation between estranged spouses.

1. MARITAL RELATIONSHIP
An agreement made by a couple while married that seeks to define or redefine personal **and** financial details of their relationship may present more serious legal problems than an antenuptial agreement.

a. Consideration
Lack of consideration may defeat a postnuptial agreement because—in contrast to an antenuptial agreement—the mutual promises to marry no longer serve as consideration. Mutual promises of support, housekeeping, or a promise to do or not do something implicit in the marriage relationship cannot serve as consideration because the promisor already is obligated by law to do or not do the same. A *reconciliation* agreement, however, is a common form of postnuptial contract and typically meets the consideration test, in that one or the other or both parties gives up a legal right, such as the right to seek a divorce or separation. (Note that UMPA and UPAA do not require consideration for marital agreements or for modification of premarital agreements.)

b. Statutory Limitations (Married Women's Property Acts)
In the past, further difficulty sprang from traditional prohibitions against contracts between spouses for services or labor. Today, courts typically do not hesitate to enforce agreements between spouses relating to a business relationship that is not inherently dependent on the marriage. Another exception involves marital contracts for services that are extraordinary and beyond the usual obligations implicit in marriage.

Example: H, a recipient of public funds, contracted with W for her services as an attendant and aiding him in activities he was unable to perform. (Result: Contract upheld. Although a husband is entitled to receive the domestic services of his wife, this right does not extend to "all services which she is capable of rendering that he may require," such as the personal care services rendered here. "To say that such is her duty is to say that the wife of a totally disabled man may not leave her home to seek employment without her husband's permission. It is law in Georgia that a husband is not entitled to the salary or wages of his wife, and shall not receive them without her consent. In the shadow of this statute, if nowhere else, stands the right of a married woman to the employment that will give her salary or wages. Her surrendering of this legal right to become a personal attendant to her husband is sufficient consideration for the express contract of employment, as she has suffered a legal detriment.") *Department of Human Resources v. Williams,* 130 Ga.App. 149, 202 S.E.2d 504 (1973).

c. Overreaching

Obviously, postnuptial agreements present even greater potential for overreaching and undue influence than antenuptial agreements. Courts therefore go to considerable lengths to scrutinize such agreements. Moreover, where consideration is still required, there is greater difficulty in finding consideration for a postnuptial agreement.

d. Public Policy

As in the case of antenuptial agreements, traditional public policy invalidated postnuptial agreements (other than separation agreements) that looked to divorce. With limited exceptions involving reconciliation agreements, postnuptial agreements attempting to deal with day-to-day aspects of marital life usually are not enforced. The policy reasons against involving the judiciary in day-to-day management of a marriage are the same as in the case of antenuptial agreements.

e. Gift Tax Consequences

Gift tax generally is not due in connection with property transfers under postnuptial agreements because an unlimited marital deduction applies to transfers between spouses.

2. RECONCILIATION AGREEMENTS

When parties *reconcile* by way of a formal agreement, consideration usually is found in their agreement to continue or to resume cohabitation or in their agreement not to sue or to abandon pending legal proceedings. The risk of overreaching is of less concern here because the marital conflict reduces the probability of undue influence. Another factor in favor of such agreements is that the courts traditionally favor resumption of marriage. Nevertheless, if such an agreement deals with rights upon a future divorce or separation, or seeks to alter an "essential" of marriage, public policy limitations may apply.

3. SEPARATION AGREEMENTS

Even though they do precisely what courts used to hold antenuptial and ordinary postnuptial agreements may *not* do (*i.e.*, define the consequences of divorce), separation agreements entered *when separation or divorce is imminent*, have long been viewed as useful. If "fair," they have long been upheld. UMDA § 306(a) favors separation agreements concerning support, disposition of property and custody of children "to promote amicable settlement of disputes between parties to a marriage attendant upon their separation or the dissolution of their marriage." Such agreements, *except terms affecting children*, "are binding upon the court unless it finds * * * that the separation agreement is unconscionable." UMDA § 306(b). (See further discussion of separation agreements at p. 173).

I. CONFLICTS ASPECTS OF MARITAL AGREEMENTS

Marital agreements may present conflicts of laws questions. Does the law of (1) the state where the agreement was entered, (2) the state where the couple was married, (3) the state where the couple had its usual marital domicile, or (4) the state where the couple is now domiciled, control the enforceability of a marital agreement? To answer this question, courts look to conflicts "policies," the relative weight of the interests of the jurisdictions with potentially applicable laws, and the intent of the parties, especially if expressed in the agreement.

Example: Hours before they married, H and W entered into an antenuptial agreement. H was a senior executive at General Motors Corporation and 25 years older than W, who had been a model but had little business experience. At the end of their 13–year marriage, assets approximated 20 million dollars and almost all were in the sole name of H. The couple had two children. H and W had executed the premarital agreement and married in California, but lived in New Jersey at the time they divorced. (Result: (1) California law applies. "[W]hen an agreement is silent as to which law should be applied, the validity and construction of a contract shall be determined by the law of the place of contracting. But this agreement is not silent and expressly provides that it: 'shall be construed under the laws of the State of California and enforceable in the proper courts of jurisdiction of the State of California.' When the agreement was executed the parties had substantial contracts with California and reasonably expected to retain many of them which, indeed, has been the case. For these reasons the law of California must be applied in this case." (2) Antenuptial agreement is valid and enforceable. In New Jersey, a party to an antenuptial agreement is treated as a fiduciary on the theory that "parties who are not yet married are not presumed to share a confidential relationship." Not so in California. "So long as the spouse seeking to set aside such an agreement has a general idea of the character and extent of the financial assets and income of the other, that apparently is sufficient in California. * * * Accordingly, the court is satisfied that under California law there was a sufficient disclosure by the husband.") *DeLorean v. DeLorean*, 211 N.J.Super. 432, 511 A.2d 1257 (1986).

J.   BREACH OF PROMISE TO MARRY

The cause of action for breaching a promise to marry is classified as a tort.   It is one of the so-called "heartbalm" actions, discussed at pp. 122–126.

K.   GIFTS IN CONTEMPLATION OF MARRIAGE

Termination of an engagement may affect gifts made during the engagement by the prospective husband and wife to each other, as well as wedding gifts made to the couple by third parties during the engagement.

1.   GIFTS BEFORE ENGAGEMENT

Gifts exchanged by a couple *before* engagement generally are considered unconditional and usually need not be returned when the engagement is terminated.   Today, when formal engagements are less common and extended periods of premarital cohabitation more common, this rule can no longer be regarded as very useful.   The individual circumstances of each case (focusing on the donor's intent) should govern the outcome.

2.   GIFTS DURING AN ENGAGEMENT

Courts assume that most gifts made by one partner to the other during engagement are conditional on marriage.   If the marriage does not occur, such gifts (the most obvious example being the engagement diamond) must be returned.   In any particular case, whether a gift must be returned depends upon how the engagement ended, who ended it, and the purpose for which the gift was made.   If the gift was made on a birthday or holiday, it will more readily be held not to have been conditional on marriage and may thus not be returnable.

3.   GIFTS FROM THIRD PARTIES

Wedding gifts made to a couple by third parties usually are considered conditional upon the marriage taking place.   They may thus be recovered when the engagement is terminated.

L.   REVIEW QUESTIONS

1.   **T   or   F**   Most of the rights and obligations of marriage remain defined by common law rather than by statute.

2.   **T   or   F**   Under the Contract Clause of the U.S. Constitution, statutes governing the parties' rights and obligations in marriage and upon divorce may be applied only prospectively.

3. **T or F**   The validity and legal incidents of a marriage are determined by the place of the marriage.

4. **T or F**   An antenuptial agreement between consenting adults will generally be upheld even if it materially changes the parties' economic position from one that would be imposed by the law of divorce.

5. **T or F**   Courts generally will not enforce antenuptial agreements that regulate the parties' finances and personal activities during the ongoing marriage.

6. **T or F**   The fairness of financial provisions in an antenuptial agreement is judged as it appears at the time of the divorce.

7. **T or F**   In the case of an *ante*nuptial agreement, contractual consideration is supplied by the change in legal position effected by marriage.

8. **T or F**   When the parties are already married and thus owe broad obligations to each other, their *post*nuptial agreements may be held invalid for lack of consideration.

9. **T or F**   Antenuptial gifts remain the property of the donee, even if the marriage never takes place or is followed quickly by divorce.

10. **T or F**   The so-called "Married Women's Property Acts" allow married women to own and convey property.

11. **T or F**   The UMDA validates H's bigamous second marriage to W_2 as of the time H's first marriage ends by divorce or by the death of W_1.

12. **T or F**   The UPAA requires invalidation of an antenuptial agreement if its consequences are unconscionable at the time of divorce.

13. **T or F**   The court is bound by a provision in H's and W's separation agreement that specifies that W will have custody of their children.

14. **T or F**   The court is bound by a provision in H's and W's separation agreement that specifies how much property and alimony is to be provided upon divorce.

*

II

MARRIAGE REQUISITES AND COMMON LAW MARRIAGE

Analysis

To create a legally effective marriage, three requirements must be met: There must be (1) consent to the contract; (2) solemnization of the marriage (or in a minority of states, compliance with the rules of "common law marriage"); and (3) compliance with certain substantive prerequisites.

A. FORMAL REQUIREMENTS

1. CONSENT

Valid marriage requires the free and voluntary consent of both parties who must (1) be competent and (2) intend to enter into marriage with each other at that time.

a. Capacity

Capacity to enter the marriage exists if, at the time of solemnization, the parties were capable of understanding the nature of the act. The wisdom of the parties' decision and their capacity to be adequate spouses or parents are *not* at issue.

Lack of capacity, more than eugenic considerations, is the basis for statutory prohibitions against issuing marriage licenses to the mentally infirm, sometimes labeled as "insane," "feebleminded," "mentally incompetent," or those under the influence of liquor or drugs. A person who is mentally retarded may be capable of entering into a valid marriage so long as he or she satisfies the legal definition of capacity. UMDA § 208(a)(1) provides that a marriage shall be invalidated if "a party lacked capacity to consent to the marriage at the time the marriage was solemnized, either because of mental incapacity or infirmity or because of the influence of alcohol, drugs, or other incapacitating substances, or a party was induced to enter into a marriage by force or duress, or by fraud involving the essentials of marriage."

Examples: (1) Both H and W were mentally retarded. After being released from the Beatrice State Home, H lived and worked in Omaha under the auspices of Eastern Nebraska Community of Retardation. H and W were married five years later. After they had been married for two years, H's guardian petitioned to have H's marriage to W declared void. At issue was whether H had sufficient mental capacity to marry. (Result: Marriage valid. H had mental capacity to enter into a marriage contract as he was not mentally retarded to such a degree as to render him mentally incompetent to enter into the marriage relation. H had sufficient capacity to understand the nature of the marriage contract and the duties and responsibilities incident to it at the time of marriage.) *Edmunds v. Edwards,* 205 Neb. 255, 287 N.W.2d 420 (1980).

(2) Five years prior to her marriage, W had been adjudicated to be mentally incompetent. Two days before her marriage, W had unsuccessfully sought restoration of her competency. The

guardian of her estate sought a determination of the validity or invalidity of her marriage. (Result: Marriage void. Under the relevant statute, a person "who has been adjudged insane, feeble-minded or an imbecile" may not marry without filing a certificate from two licensed physicians that he or she has been cured "of such insanity, imbecility, or feeble-mindedness." W had not filed such a certificate. "Since the Legislature intended to bar one found to be suffering from the least severe grade of mental deficiency, an adjudged feeble-minded person, from marriage, it is reasonable to conclude that they intended to bar those suffering from more severe grades of mental deficiency from marriage. * * * Accordingly, we hold that an adjudication of mental incompetency is a bar to a subsequent marriage.") *May v. Leneair*, 99 Mich.App. 209, 297 N.W.2d 882 (1980).

(3) H had been diagnosed as a chronic paranoid schizophrenic and had been in various mental institutions for much of his adult life. In 1975 he was released from a mental hospital pursuant to a judicial finding that he was not imminently dangerous to himself or others. As a condition of his release, H moved to a structured home environment where he was cared for by attendants who did his cooking, cleaning and driving. His guardian, a bank that managed the approximately $900,000 estate H had inherited from his father, paid for the home and services. H's only surviving relatives were an elderly aunt and several cousins, one of whom was chairman of the board of the guardian bank. In 1980 H met W at an outpatient mental health facility. W did not suffer from a mental disability but was confined to a wheelchair. They married and moved into H's home. Several months later, the guardian bank initiated an annulment action. A jury found that H had sufficient mental capacity and understanding on the day of his marriage to enter into a marriage contract. H's guardian appealed. (Result: No annulment. "A marriage of a person incapable of contracting for want of understanding is not void, but voidable. We find that prior adjudication of incompetency is not conclusive on the issue of later capacity to marry and does not bar a party from entering a contract to marry. The mental capacity of a party at the precise time when the marriage is celebrated controls its validity or invalidity. * * * 'The general rule is that the test is the capacity of the person to understand the special nature of the contract of marriage, and the duties and responsibilities which it entails, which is to be determined from the facts and circumstances of each case' ".) *Geitner v. Townsend*, 67 N.C.App. 159, 312 S.E.2d 236 (1984).

1) Practical Relevance of Capacity Issue
Although capacity is a prerequisite for the issuance of a marriage license, the issue of capacity is litigated most often when one of the parties brings an

annulment action. At that time the objecting party must prove that he or she or the other party had lacked the requisite mental capacity to consent to marriage *at the time of the marriage.*

2) Consent of Guardian

An incompetent may be allowed to marry or divorce with the consent of a guardian.

Examples: (1) (Marriage). H was struck by an automobile in 1972 and suffered severe brain damage. One year later H was divorced from the woman to whom he had been married at the time of the accident. Five years after the accident, H became romantically involved with his psychologist, W. That year W and her first husband were divorced, and H's father was appointed as H's guardian. H and W then married without H's guardian's approval. (Result: Guardian's petition to annul marriage is granted. State legislation required the guardian's approval before a ward may marry.) *Knight v. Radomski,* 414 A.2d 1211 (Me.1980).

(2) (Divorce). H sustained a permanently disabling head injury as a result of an automobile accident. W cared for H for six months after the accident but then abandoned her husband to his parents' care. H's mother was granted plenary guardianship over H and his person, and she filed for dissolution of H's marriage to W. W moved to dismiss on the ground that a guardian does not have standing to bring an action for dissolution of a ward's marriage. (Result: No dissolution. "Research reveals a strong majority rule that, absent statutory authorization, a guardian cannot maintain an action, on behalf of a ward, for the dissolution of a ward's marriage. * * * Illinois follows the majority rule.") *In re Marriage of Drews,* 115 Ill.2d 201, 104 Ill.Dec. 782, 503 N.E.2d 339 (1986).

b. Intent

Both parties must intend to marry each other. The intent to marry may be vitiated by fraud, duress, jest, sham or ulterior purposes. (See discussion of annulment, pp. ___–___).

2. SOLEMNIZATION

a. Marriage License

Prospective marriage partners must obtain a marriage license in advance of solemnization. Such a license is issued routinely if the parties' application indicates that there exist no impediments to their marriage, based on the state's prerequisites for marriage.

1) **Waiting Period**

To prevent hasty and impulsive marriages, many states impose a brief waiting period between the time of issuance of the license and the time of the marriage ceremony. Under UMDA § 204, a marriage license becomes effective three days after issuance and expires after 180 days.

2) **Solemnization Without License**

The policy in favor of upholding parties' expectations and protecting existing relationships—even in states not recognizing common law marriage—may in some states lead to a holding that a marriage solemnized without a license is valid. Similarly, a valid marriage may result even if the parties failed to solemnize a marriage after they had obtained a license, or if solemnization was performed by one not legally authorized to perform marriages.

> ***Example:*** Twenty-five years ago, H and W were married in the Roman Catholic church without obtaining a license. (Result: Valid marriage. "Most such cases arise long after the parties have acted upon the assumption that they are married, and no useful purpose is served by avoiding the long-standing relationship.") *Carabetta v. Carabetta,* 182 Conn. 344, 438 A.2d 109 (1980).

b. Ceremony

Except where common law marriage is recognized, marriage must be solemnized by a person authorized by the state, such as a designated civil official or a religious minister. A marriage solemnized by a person not authorized to do so often is upheld if at least one party was unaware of the disqualification. Consummation is not a condition to the validity of a properly solemnized marriage but may help shore up one with defects. UMDA § 206(a) provides, "[a] marriage may be solemnized by a judge of a court of record, by a public official whose powers include solemnization of marriages, or in accordance with any mode of solemnization recognized by any religious denomination, Indian Nation or Tribe, or Native Group."

c. Public Record

The marriage license must be completed by the person solemnizing the marriage and returned to the appropriate state office to be recorded.

d. Purposes of Solemnization

Solemnization gives public notice of the marriage; it provides a permanent record of the marriage; it impresses upon the parties the seriousness of their act; it satisfies religious tradition; and it aids in the collection of vital statistics.

e. Proxy Marriages

If one party is unable to attend the marriage ceremony, a number of states permit marriage to be performed by proxy. Proxy marriage has been employed in times of war to enable a soldier while overseas to marry his (perhaps pregnant) bride who had stayed at home. UMDA § 206(b) gives the person solemnizing a marriage the power to marry a couple when the party unable to be present has authorized in writing a third person to act as his or her proxy.

Federal law limits recognition of proxy marriages for immigration purposes: "The term 'spouse', 'wife', or 'husband' does not include a spouse, wife, or husband by reason of any marriage ceremony where the contracting parties thereto are not physically present in the presence of each other, unless the marriage shall have been consummated." 8 U.S.C.A. § 1101(a)(35).

f. "Confidential" Marriages

California Fam. Code § 500 allows persons "living together as husband and wife" to enter into a confidential marriage.

3. COMMON LAW MARRIAGE

Common law marriage is also referred to as informal marriage. It is a valid marriage entered into by the parties' agreement, but without formal solemnization. All substantive perquisites for marriage must be met (no prior marriage, not within forbidden degrees of relationship, etc.). Today, approximately one fourth of the states continue to recognize common law marriages. Since the law of conflicts recognizes a policy in favor of the validity of marriage, a common law marriage generally is recognized as valid if it was valid where and when celebrated. Accordingly, if the parties have or have had an adequate connection with a state recognizing common law marriage, a common law marriage may be found to be valid even in states that have abolished it.

a. Traditional Form

Older law knew two ways of entering into common law marriage: (1) by exchange of vows by the parties with words expressing their intent to be married in the present tense; and (2) by words in the future tense (engagement), followed by consummation. The chief difference between common law and ceremonial marriage is the absence of a public ceremony and record, and it is the difficulty of proof that has persuaded the legislatures of many states to abolish common law marriage.

b. American Law

Brought to the United States, common law marriage underwent various modifications. Specific requirements vary somewhat among the jurisdictions. In addition to, and as proof of, their express, present agreement to marry, most states now require that the parties actually cohabit as husband and wife and "hold themselves out" to the public as husband and wife. Common law marriage does *not* require that the parties cohabit for any specific period of time. The marriage takes effect at the time of the contract.

Examples: (1) After H's divorce from Gertrude, W (with whom H had long had a sexual relationship) moved into H's house. W took H's surname and lived with him for 24 years. Five children were born to them; the birth certificates of the last three stated that they were married. The community considered them married.

In 1954, H deserted W and went through a marriage ceremony with Betty. H died. Alleging herself to be H's widow, Betty challenged H's will, arguing that H's will had been revoked by H's marriage to her. (Result: H's marriage to Betty was invalid because of H's pre-existing common law marriage to W. The court took a paternalistic view favoring W whom they found to be" illiterate, uneducated, and of childlike simplicity. * * * [T]here was ample evidence, to which we have already referred, to support the conclusion that after the barrier to their marriage had been removed by [H's] divorce from Gertrude, he and [W] entered into a new mutual agreement whereby their previously illicit relationship was terminated and a valid common-law marriage established. That [H] some twenty-five years thereafter declared, in his application for a license to marry Betty, that he was not married, is of no legal consequence; for once his marriage to [W] became complete, as the trial judge held it to be, no act or disavowal of it on his part could invalidate it.") *Campbell v. Christian*, 235 S.C. 102, 110 S.E.2d 1 (1959).

(2) H and W were divorced in July, and H died in December. Despite their divorce, they continued to live together. Though W was observed with H in his home on numerous occasions, it was general knowledge in the community that they had been divorced. W had told a close friend that they would remarry on Christmas. W had bought a new car, but had it registered in her maiden name and at her home address rather than at H's address. During that same period she had signed a bail bond for H, again using her maiden name and home address. (Result: No common law marriage. "* * * [W] and [H] * * * did not have a present intention to again become man and wife since they had already previously agreed to ceremoniously remarry in the future. Furthermore, cohabitation standing alone is not sufficient to supply the requisite mutual assent required for the common-law marriage; there must be words of present assent.") *Humphrey v. Humphrey*, 293 Ala. 118, 300 So.2d 376 (1974).

(3) H and W were married in 1960 and divorced in 1965. Shortly thereafter, they reconciled and lived together until H's death in 1976. During this time they filed separate income tax returns as single persons, and kept separate bank accounts. They purchased insurance as married persons. People in town considered them married. They planned to undergo a second marriage ceremony later in 1976. (Result: Common law marriage. The court found that their agreement to remarry did not negate "present agreement" which was inferred from their cohabitation and from public recognition.) *Skipworth v. Skipworth*, 360 So.2d 975 (Ala.1978).

1) Holding Out

"Holding out as husband and wife" usually is shown by representations made to friends, neighbors, associates, businessmen and creditors, and by use of a common surname, as well as by jointly filed tax returns, and, depending on apparent intent, jointly held bank accounts or realty.

Examples: (1) W worked as H's live-in housekeeper. After three years, she accepted his marriage proposal. Due to opposition from H's children, they agreed to live together as H and W, but without marrying. Although they attended social events together, W retained her surname, they filed separate tax returns as single persons, and W registered herself as a single person when she was hospitalized following a miscarriage. (Result: No common law marriage. " 'Holding out' or open declaration to the public has been said to be the acid test. * * * In other words, there can be no secret common-law marriage.") *In re Dallman's Estate,* 228 N.W.2d 187 (Iowa 1975).

(2) Decedent (H) lived with appellee (W) from 1944 until his death. In 1962, H was divorced from his first wife. H showed W a copy of the divorce decree and said "Now we're legally married." W replied "It's about time. That's just what we were waiting for." W began to wear a wedding ring given to her by H, she used H's surname at times, and they took out life insurance policies naming each other as spouse-beneficiaries. They were known in their community as being married at common law. W filed for a spouse's share in H's intestate estate. (Result: Common law marriage. W was entitled to a spouse's intestate share. "The court could properly infer from the statements and the surrounding circumstances an agreement to alter the former relationship of decedent and appellee—that is, to become married now that decedent's former marriage had been dissolved. The court also relied on corroborating evidence that decedent and appellee agreed to be married. They continued cohabiting after the quoted exchange, and their reputation as husband and wife was unchanged. They took out the life insurance policies, each designating the other as spouse, and [W] began to wear the ring decedent had given her.") *In re Garges' Estate,* 474 Pa. 237, 378 A.2d 307 (1977).

(3) After dating on and off for nine years, during which time W married and divorced two different men, H and W entered into an antenuptial agreement. They never married. For a few months, W resumed living with her first husband. She later returned to H, became engaged to him, and reaffirmed the antenuptial agreement. From a trip to Las Vegas, W

returned wearing a wedding ring and using H's surname, although they had not participated in a wedding ceremony. H and W cohabited and sent out Christmas cards together, with W using H's surname. W filed for divorce. (Result: Common law marriage. "[I]t is well established [that] circumstantial evidence may be relied upon to demonstrate a common law marriage * * *. The record herein regarding the continuous cohabitation of the parties and the declaration or holding out to the public they were in fact husband and wife constitutes circumstantial evidence which tends to create a fair presumption that a common law marital relationship existed.") *In re Winegard,* 257 N.W.2d 609 (Iowa 1977).

2) Abolition of Common Law Marriage

Abolition of common law marriage began in 1753 in England with Lord Hardwicke's Act which required a ceremony and public record. The purpose was to put marriages on a more certain footing, in the interests of the partners, the children, as well as that of third parties dealing with them. The inevitable consequence of the abolition of common law marriage is that some relationships of long standing will be dealt with inequitably. Today, several states allow some relief by recognition of unmarried cohabitation (see *Marvin v. Marvin,* p. 94) or through the putative spouse doctrine, p. 76.

3) Statutes Regulating Common Law Marriage

A few states have lately enacted statutes dealing with the definition and proof of common law marriages.

Example: H and W were ceremonially married in 1981. From 1964 to 1981, before their ceremonial marriage, H and W lived together intermittently and had five children, all supported and acknowledged by H. (Result: Remanded for a determination of whether or not a common law marriage existed, based on a 1989 amendment to the Texas Family Code. "[T]he existence of a common law marriage in Texas requires proof of each of the three elements of an informal marriage * * * no later than one year after the relationship ended. The elements are (1) an agreement to be married, (2) after the agreement, the couple lived together in this state as husband and wife, and (3) the couple represented to others that they were married." "[The Code] does not require direct evidence of an agreement to be married in order to establish a common law marriage, but * * * the agreement may be proved by circumstantial evidence. * * * [L]egally and/or factually sufficient evidence of cohabitation and public representation will not necessarily constitute legally and/or factually sufficient evidence of an agreement to be married.") *Russell v. Russell,* 865 S.W.2d 929 (Tex.1993).

Utah provides: "A marriage which is not solemnized * * * shall be legal and valid if a court or administrative order establishes that it arises out of a contract between two consenting parties who: (a) are capable of giving consent; (b) are legally capable of entering a solemnized marriage * * *; (c) have cohabited; (d) mutually assume marital rights, duties, and obligations: and (e) who hold themselves out as and have acquired a uniform and general reputation as husband and wife." (Utah C. A. tit. 30, § 1–4.5).

4) Modern Rationale

Many courts seem to regard common law marriage less as a conscious alternative to formal marriage, and more as a means of vindicating the reasonable expectations of the parties, or at least one of them. A common law marriage may be found if a formal marriage proves invalid or when partners have lived together in the honest belief that they were married, when such a finding would alleviate inequities concerning property and support matters that would otherwise arise, especially on the death of one of the parties.

> ***Example:*** H and W were married before a Roman Catholic priest. They divorced and later resumed cohabitation. Their priest told them that they need not remarry as they were "already married in the eyes of God." The couple accepted the priest's explanation, went home to resume cohabitation and assumed that they were married. No civil ceremony was ever performed. H died and W applied for dependency benefits under workmen's compensation legislation. (Result: Common law marriage. The court found that it would fulfill the purposes of the legislation to hold W to be a "dependent" under the Act.) *Parkinson v. J. & S. Tool Company,* 64 N.J. 159, 313 A.2d 609 (1974).

5) Conflict of Laws

A common law marriage validly entered under the laws of one state is generally recognized everywhere, even in states that have abolished common law marriage. Moreover, in states that have abolished common law marriage, courts sometimes strain to protect the reasonable expectations of the parties by "stretching" conflict of laws doctrine—focusing on the parties' sojourn to another state that recognizes common law marriage and holding that a valid marriage was entered there.

> ***Examples:*** (1) Following divorces from other individuals, H and W began living together on July 5, 1958. H gave W a wedding band, W took H's surname, and they told friends and relatives that they had married. Subsequently, they celebrated July 5 as their anniversary, filed joint tax returns, and H listed W as his wife and beneficiary on his life insurance policy. For 20 years the couple had lived in New York which does not recognize common law marriage, and on approximately eight occasions, the partners had stayed at a Pennsylvania motel.

Pennsylvania recognized common law marriage. Following H's death, W sought social security benefits as H's surviving spouse. (Result: Valid common law marriage. "The law to be applied in determining the validity of such a marriage is the law of the state in which the marriage occurred. Since plaintiff claims that she contracted a common-law marriage with her husband in Pennsylvania during their travels through the state, the appropriate law to apply is the law of Pennsylvania. * * * Generally, a common-law marriage may be created by uttering words in the present tense with the intent to establish a marital relationship, but where no such utterance is proved, Pennsylvania law also permits a finding of marriage based on reputation and cohabitation when established by satisfactory proof.") *Renshaw v. Heckler*, 787 F.2d 50 (2d Cir.1986).

(2) H and W_2 lived together from 1961 until H died in 1983. H did not divorce W_1 until 1981. H and W_2 held themselves out as husband and wife, W_2 took H's surname, and W_2's four daughters considered H to be their father. At the time of H's death, the couple was domiciled in Nevada. Nevada does not recognize common law marriage. From 1961 until 1963, however, the couple had lived in Texas which recognizes common law marriage and, between 1981 and H's death, the couple made two or three trips to Texas. W filed for social security death benefits as H's surviving spouse. (Result: Valid common law marriage. "Nevada does not recognize common law marriages contracted within its borders, but does recognize common law marriages that arise in another state so long as that state's legal requirements are met." The court found that under Texas law H and W_2 "entered into a marriage which would have been valid if Mr. Orr had not been previously married." When H and W_1 divorced, H's and W_2's marriage became valid under Tex. Fam. Code Ann. § 2.22: "A marriage is void if either party was previously married and the prior marriage is not dissolved. However, the marriage becomes valid when the prior marriage is dissolved if since that time the parties have lived together as husband and wife and represented themselves to others as being married.") *Orr v. Bowen*, 648 F.Supp. 1510 (D.Nev.1986).

6) Uniform Marriage and Divorce Act

The UMDA does not take a stand for or against common law marriage, but suggests that the issue be re-examined by the states, including those that have abolished common law marriage. It provides two alternate versions, one recognizing common law marriage, one not, to "permit each state to make its decision in accordance with its own view as to policy, and to change its law at any time desired without destroying the effect of its adoption of the Uniform Act." (UMDA § 211, Comment.)

4. PRESUMPTIONS REGARDING VALIDITY OF MARRIAGE

The following presumptions are potentially in conflict: (1) Absent proof of divorce, there is a presumption in favor of the continuation of marriage. (2) When a person enters more than one marriage without dissolving a former marriage, a presumption arises in favor of the validity of the marriage last in time.

Example: Two women (W_1, W_2) married decedent (H) a few months prior to his death and both claimed to be H's widows. There was evidence that H's marriage to W_1 had been for the purpose of facilitating W_1's immigration from Canada, but that marriage had not been terminated when H married W_2. The trial court upheld the first marriage, but ruled that W_1 had waived her rights in an antenuptial agreement. Accordingly, neither W_1's nor W_2's claim was allowed. (Result: Affirmed. While the prior marriage may have been for a limited purpose, it was at most voidable and therefore could not be attacked collaterally. Two presumptions, (1) that the later of successive marriages is valid and (2) that continuation of a prior marriage is favored, may be considered in deciding which of successive marriages is valid. "In evaluating these conflicting presumptions, the court must look to the underlying policies intended to be served by the presumption and the extent to which those policies will actually be served under the facts of a particular case. We acknowledge that some commentators have indicated that the presumption favoring the validity of the later marriage should always prevail over the conflicting presumption that the earlier marriage continues, because the social policies underlying the former are more significant than the policies of probability and convenience which underlie the latter. But we think the better approach is to reserve discretion to weigh the various social policies in light of the facts of a particular case." In this case, policy reasons favoring the later marriage over the previous marriage were so weak that trial court properly found W_1's marriage to be valid.) *Appeal of O'Rourke,* 310 Minn. 373, 246 N.W.2d 461 (1976).

5. VALID COMMON LAW MARRIAGE RESULTING FROM REMOVAL OF IMPEDIMENT

UMDA § 207(b) provides that where there has been a marriage *ceremony,* even though one of the spouses was legally incapable of marrying at that time, the resulting cohabitation will automatically turn into a valid marriage upon removal of the impediment. Where the UMDA does not apply, courts may resolve such circumstances in terms of common law marriage.

Examples: (1) While H was still married to W_1, he went through a marriage ceremony with W_2. The latter "marriage," of course, was void. After being divorced from W_1, H continued to cohabit with W_2 but no new marriage ceremony was performed. After leaving W_2, H ceremonially married W_3 and their relationship continued until H's death. Both W_2 and W_3 filed for workmen's compensation benefits. (Result: No common law marriage to W_2; only W_3 is entitled to benefits. "* * * (T)he removal of an impediment to a marriage contract (the divorce in this case) does not convert an illegal bigamous marriage into a common law legal marriage. After the barrier to marriage has been removed, there must be a new mutual agreement, either by way of civil ceremony or by way of a recognition of the illicit relation and a new agreement to enter into a common law marriage arrangement.") *Byers v. Mount Vernon Mills, Inc.*, 268 S.C. 68, 231 S.E.2d 699 (1977).

(2) W and H_1 were married in 1944 and were never divorced. W and H_2 began living together in 1946. H_1 died in 1983. W and H_2 continued to live together until H_2's death in 1984. During this period W and H_2 held themselves out as married. W filed for her statutory share as a surviving spouse, and the executor of H_2's estate objected. (Result: Valid common law marriage. "[W]hile no ceremony or particular words are necessary, there are common elements which must be present, either explicitly expressed or implicitly inferred from the circumstances, in order for a common-law marriage to exist. Those elements are: 1) capacity; 2) present, mutual agreement to permanently enter the marriage relationship to the exclusion of all other relationships; and 3) public recognition of the relationship as a marriage and public assumption of marital duties and cohabitation." The court held these requirements satisfied by the fact that W and H_2 had continued to live together and held themselves out as married in the year following H_1's death.) *Boswell v. Boswell*, 497 So.2d 479 (Ala.1986).

6. PUTATIVE SPOUSE DOCTRINE

"A putative spouse is one whose marriage is legally invalid but who has engaged in (1) a marriage ceremony or a solemnization, on the (2) good faith belief in the validity of the marriage." *Spearman, infra.* UMDA § 209 elaborates:

"Any person who has cohabited with another to whom he is not legally married in the good faith belief that he was married to that person is a putative spouse until knowledge of the fact that he is not legally married terminates his status and prevents acquisition of further rights. A putative spouse acquires the rights conferred upon a legal spouse, including the right to maintenance following termination of his status, whether or not the marriage is prohibited or declared invalid. If there is a legal spouse or other putative spouses, rights acquired by a putative spouse do not supersede the rights of the legal spouse or those acquired by other putative spouses, but the court shall apportion property, maintenance, and support rights among the claimants as appropriate in the circumstances and in the interests of justice."

Example: While H was married to W, H and X went through a marriage
ceremony. X did not positively know that H was married; however,
among other things, she knew that H had fathered two children by W
whom she knew to be using H's surname, that W had secured a
support decree against H, and that H visited W annually during his
vacation. (Result: Putative spouse doctrine not applicable. X could
not meet her burden of showing a "good faith belief in the existence of
a valid marriage.") *Spearman v. Spearman,* 482 F.2d 1203 (5th
Cir.1973).

B. SUBSTANTIVE REQUIREMENTS FOR VALID MARRIAGE

Universally, societies have imposed substantive requirements upon parties to marriage.
These have varied with time, religion and culture. There is general agreement of a few
basics, such as the incest prohibition. *Today,* the validity of state regulation of marriage
may be tested under the federal and state constitutions and my depend on a balancing of
the individual's interest in marrying whom he wishes and the intensity of the state's
interests in the particular regulation. *Loving v. Virginia,* 388 U.S. 1, 87 S.Ct. 1817, 18
L.Ed.2d 1010 (1967); *Zablocki v. Redhail,* 434 U.S. 374, 98 S.Ct. 673, 54 L.Ed.2d 618
(1978); *Turner v. Safley,* 482 U.S. 78, 107 S.Ct. 2254, 96 L.Ed.2d 64 (1987).

1. CONSANGUINITY
Marriage is prohibited between persons related by blood within certain degrees of
kinship.

a. Scope of Prohibition
The scope of the prohibition varies from state to state. Marriages within the
immediate family, between parent and child or brother and sister, are
prohibited universally. Most states also prohibit marriage between an uncle
and his niece or between an aunt and her nephew. Approximately one-half of
the states prohibit marriage between first cousins.

b. Effect of Attempt to Enter Into Incestuous Marriage
Traditionally, an attempted incestuous marriage is void. Depending on the
intensity of the state's interest, this may hold true even when the marriage was
valid when and where made. Note, however, that under more recent statutes
and cases, even a void marriage may have considerable legal consequences.

Examples: (1) Decedent (D) validly married his niece in Italy. They resided
in Connecticut for two years before his death. She applied for a
widow's allowance from D's estate. (Result: Denied. The
"marriage" was contrary to Connecticut's public policy and was
invalid.) *Catalano v. Catalano,* 148 Conn. 288, 170 A.2d 726
(1961).

(2) Decedent wife (W) and H, Jewish and first cousins, married in Rhode Island. Rhode Island allowed marriage between first cousins *only* if the parties were Jewish. Two weeks after their marriage, they returned to New York where they lived for 32 years. New York did not allow marriage between first cousins. H petitioned to be named administrator of W's estate. (Result: Marriage upheld. The validity of a marriage is determined by the law of the place of celebration unless it is against public policy. The court found the Rhode Island law not to violate New York's public policy.) *In re May's Estate*, 305 N.Y. 486, 114 N.E.2d 4 (1953). *Caveat:* Legislative "discrimination" in favor of adherents to a particular religion may raise equal protection questions that may or may not be balanced by First Amendment considerations. (*Cf. Reynolds v. United States*, 98 U.S. (8 Otto) 145, 25 L.Ed. 244 (1878)—the polygamy-in-Utah case).

c. Criminality

Universally, statutes provide for criminal prosecution of incest involving close blood relationships. The definition of relationship for purposes of criminal "incest" varies in many states from that in marriage prohibitions (typically the criminal prohibition is narrower). In other states the definitions are coterminous.

d. Justification of Prohibition

Cultural and religious conceptions of the family are the origin of incest prohibitions. Today, incest statutes are defended as preventing genetically defective offspring, promoting family harmony, and discouraging sexual imposition on minors.

1) Genetics

The genetic argument has been criticized as insufficient to support the prohibition of marriage between extended relatives, because the probability of a "bad" gene affecting an offspring decreases markedly as the degree of kinship of the parents is extended. If the unfavorable gene is common in the population, consanguineous mating would not significantly increase the probability that the defective gene would be passed on to children. Moreover, the genetic argument only justifies prohibiting related individuals from having children, not from marrying or engaging in sexual relations. The latter point has been recognized in several state statutes allowing first cousins to marry if they are beyond child-bearing age, defined as 55 years old or older.

2) Social Arguments

One social argument focuses on preventing sexual rivalries and jealousies between family members and preventing abuse of family authority. Incest prohibitions have also been defended in terms of the social good resulting from increased cultural diffusion and the broadening of family alliances.

d. Criticism of the Prohibition
The most significant argument against common incest prohibitions is that their reach is too broad. Some may be "over-inclusive" in defining prohibited relationships.

e. Relationships of the Half Blood, through Illegitimacy, or Severed by Adoption
Generally, incest statutes do not distinguish between relationships of the full and half blood, nor on the basis of illegitimacy or adoption.

> *Example:* H and W were half-brother and half-sister by blood. W had been adopted and raised by another family. They were indicted for entering into a prohibited marriage. The couple argued that the prohibition of brother-sister marriage was inapplicable due to W's adoption. (Result: Adoption irrelevant. Half-sibling relationships are included under the prohibition despite not being enumerated. Adoption statutes that legally eliminate the tie between an adopted child and its natural relative do not impliedly change the consanguinity statute. The policy of maintaining secrecy of adoption records does not bar any and all inquiry into the facts of an adoption.) *State v. Sharon H.,* 429 A.2d 1321 (Del.1981).

2. AFFINITY, STEP–RELATIONSHIP, ADOPTION
a. "Affinity" and "Step–Relationships"
Marriages between persons related in various ways by "affinity" (through marriage) used to be widely prohibited. This prohibition has survived particularly with respect to step-relationships (*e.g.,* stepfather-stepdaughter).

b. Adoptive Relationships
Most states continue to prohibit marriage between persons related by adoption.

c. Justification
No genetic arguments exist for marriage prohibitions based on affinity, step-relationships, or adoption, but justification has been drawn from the social, "family harmony" argument. "To authorize and encourage marriages of brothers and sisters by adoption would undermine the fabric of family life and would be the antithesis of the social aims and purposes which the adoption process is intended to serve." *Marriage of Mew and MLB,* 4 Pa.D. & C.3d 51 (1977).

d. Constitutionality
The prohibition on marriage of persons related by adoption has been attacked constitutionally.

> *Example:* X and Y were brother and sister by adoption. They were not related by blood. Their parents had married when X was 18 and Y 13 years of age. Three years later, X and Y were denied a marriage license because of their relationship through adoption. Based on equal protection grounds, X and Y argued that the

statute prohibiting their marriage was unconstitutional. (Result: Statute is unconstitutional as applied to brothers and sisters related through adoption as it does not have a rational relationship to a legitimate state interest.) *Israel v. Allen,* 195 Colo. 263, 577 P.2d 762 (1978). *Caveat:* It is probable that the court was influenced by the fact that the adoptive sibling relationship had been of short duration.

3. AGE REQUIREMENTS
a. Regulation

Typical state regulation consists of setting a minimum age for marriage and a higher age below which marriage requires parental consent.

UMDA § 203: "[T]he [marriage license] clerk shall issue a license to marry and a marriage certificate form upon being furnished: (1) satisfactory proof that each party to the marriage will have attained the age of 18 years at the time the marriage license is effective, or will have attained the age of 16 years and has either the consent to the marriage of both parents or his guardian, or judicial approval; [or, if under the age of 16 years, has both the consent of both parents or his guardian and judicial approval]."

Traditionally, many states allow marriage below the minimum age or without parental consent, if a court order is obtained.

UMDA § 205: "(a) The court, after a reasonable effort has been made to notify the parents or guardian of each underaged party, may order the [marriage license] clerk to issue a marriage license and a marriage certificate form: [(1)] to a party aged 16 or 17 years who has no parent capable of consenting to his marriage, or whose parent or guardian has not consented to his marriage; [or (2) to a party under the age of 16 years who has the consent of both parents to his marriage, if capable of giving consent, or his guardian.]" (Note: Bracketed language in Uniform Acts identifies suggested alternatives.)

The UMDA further provides that the court may approve the marriage of an underaged person "only if the court finds that the underaged party is capable of assuming the responsibilities of marriage and the marriage will serve his or her best interests." Pregnancy is expressly singled out as *not* alone establishing that the party's best interests will be served. This proviso discounts the past when courts typically reserved judicial approval of otherwise invalid under-age marriages for cases involving a pregnant bride-to-be. Marriage then was thought preferable to the social stigma attaching to unwed mothers and illegitimate children.

Examples: (1) A 14–year-old girl, alleging her love, her desire to marry and her physical fitness for marriage, petitioned the court for permission to marry the 22–year-old son of her father's second wife. Her father had consented to the marriage. (Result: Denied. The court held that something more than "the usual, ordinary or the mere urgent desire of the parties" is required before it can give its consent to the marriage.) *In re Barbara Haven,* 86 Pa.D. & C. 141 (Orphans' Ct. 1954).

(2) Plaintiff M was 15 years old. She was cohabiting with the 18–year-old father of her child and they wished to marry. New York law required that female applicants for marriage licenses between the ages of 14 and 18 must obtain written consent from both parents. Females between the ages of 14 and 16 must also obtain judicial approval. When M's mother refused to consent, M sought to have the law declared unconstitutional. (Result: Law upheld." [The statute's] requirement of parental consent is rationally related to the State's legitimate interests in mature decision-making with respect to marriage by minors and preventing unstable marriages. It is also rationally related to the State's legitimate interest in supporting the fundamental privacy right of a parent to act in what the parent perceives to be the best interest of the child free from state court scrutiny. [The statute], therefore, does not offend the constitutional rights of minors but represents a constitutionally valid exercise of state power.") *Moe v. Dinkins,* 533 F.Supp. 623 (S.D.N.Y.1981).

b. Justification of Age Requirements
Age requirements are justified by the state's interest (1) in protecting immature minors from entering into marriage, (2) promoting marital stability and (3) providing children resulting from marriage with the care of mature and responsible parents. Studies indicate a considerably higher divorce rate for teenage marriages than for marriages of older parties.

c. Constitutional Limitation
Traditionally, there was a discrepancy in age limitations for males and females. In 1973, a judge in New York still upheld the constitutionality of this discrimination on the basis of the male's duty to provide for his family and his consequent greater need for time to establish his earning capacity. *Friedrich v. Katz,* 73 Misc.2d 663, 341 N.Y.S.2d 932 (1973). She was overruled on appeal (34 N.Y.2d 987, 360 N.Y.S.2d 415, 318 N.E.2d 606). U.S. Supreme Court cases involving similar age discrimination have solidified the consensus that such discrimination violates equal protection guarantees. *Stanton v. Stanton,* 421 U.S. 7, 95 S.Ct. 1373, 43 L.Ed.2d 688 (1975); *Stanton v. Stanton,* 429 U.S. 501, 97 S.Ct. 717, 50 L.Ed.2d 723 (1977). "[W]e do not find any compelling State interest which justifies treating males and females of the same age differently for the purpose of determining their rights to a marriage license." *Phelps v. Bing,* 58 Ill.2d 32, 316 N.E.2d 775 (1974).

d. Effect of Noncompliance
A marriage in which one party fails to meet state minimum age requirements is void or voidable, depending on the provisions of the particular statute or on the common law of the state.

1) Who Can Attack

The underaged party has standing to have the marriage annulled or to attack the marriage collaterally. A party who is of marriage age may not attack the validity of his or her marriage to an underaged person. In many states, the parents of an underaged person may have their child's marriage annulled. UMDA § 208(b): "A declaration of invalidity * * * may be sought * * * (3) for * * * [underage], by the underaged party, his parent or guardian * * *."

2) Ratification

If intent to ratify the marriage is manifested when a previously underaged marriage partner reaches the required age, the invalid marriage is validated. Generally, marital cohabitation past the required age validates such a marriage. UMDA § 208(b)(3) allows an underage marriage to be declared invalid only "*prior* to the time the underaged party reaches the age at which he could have married without satisfying the omitted requirement." (Emphasis added).

4. PHYSICAL REQUIREMENTS
a. Blood Tests

A health examination is a generally accepted prerequisite for the issuance of a marriage license. Usually this consists of a blood test to determine presence of venereal disease, traditionally syphilis. Less frequently, tests are required for tuberculosis, measles, drug addiction or the Rh factor. The number of states requiring blood tests has been declining. Only a few states have added tests to detect HIV (AIDS) infection. If the HIV or venereal disease test is positive, the information may be provided to the carrier and the other party, or the marriage may be prohibited. A Utah statute prohibiting and holding void marriage between HIV or VD infected parties was held unconstitutional. (*T.E.P. v. Leavitt*, 840 F.Supp. 110 (D.Utah 1993)). A few states test also for other conditions such as tuberculosis, rubella, Rh compatibility, drug addiction and alcoholism.

UMDA § 203(3) has made the requirement for a medical examination optional: "[T]he traditional forms of premarital medical examination, now required by the marriage laws of most of the states, need not be preserved. The premarital medical examination requirement serves either to inform the prospective spouses of health hazards that may have an impact on their marriage, or to warn public health officials of the presence of venereal disease. For the latter purpose, the statutes have been proved to be both avoidable and highly inefficient. Moreover, the cursory blood test which satisfied the requirements of most states provides very little service to the prospective spouses themselves." (Official Comment to UMDA § 203).

b. Physical Capacity

UMDA § 208 (a)(2) mirrors the traditional rule by providing that a marriage may be annulled if "a party lacks the physical capacity to consummate the marriage by sexual intercourse, and at the time the marriage was solemnized the other party did not know of the incapacity''.

> *Example:* H appealed from a judgment granting an annulment to W, based on his impotence. The cause of his impotence was not physical but was psychological. (Result: For W. The court considered it irrelevant that H's impotence resulted from psychological causes and not from physical causes.) *Rickards v. Rickards*, 53 Del. 134, 166 A.2d 425 (1960).

c. Epilepsy
At one time, numerous states prohibited an epileptic from marrying. Medical advances have led to the repeal of such statutes.

C. CONFLICTS OF LAWS

1. LAW OF CELEBRATION
The law of the place of celebration generally governs the validity of a marriage.

> *Example:* H and W₁ were divorced in Nebraska. The divorce decree ordered that neither party remarry within six months of the date of the decree. Before the six months expired, H married W₂ in Iowa. W₂ sought to divorce H in Missouri. H alleged that they were not married, as his first divorce was not final when the ceremony was celebrated. (Result: Marriage to W₂ held valid: "[I]n this case, the application of orthodox principles of conflict of laws leads us to the same conclusion we have reached by applying the presumption that the marriage was valid. The validity of the marriage in the first instance must be determined by looking to the law of the state where it was contracted. If we assume that Iowa would not recognize the marriage because the Nebraska decree had not terminated defendant's marital status, ordinary principles of choice of law would require us to look to Iowa's rules of conflict of laws. * * * When we do so, we find that Iowa clearly holds it is the law of the forum which determines whether a party is estopped to attack the validity of a foreign divorce decree. * * * The parties are domiciled here, and this court would hold the defendant estopped to deny the efficiency of the Nebraska decree even if it were shown that [W₁] was alive and well when the parties were married in Iowa.'') *In re Marriage of Sumners*, 645 S.W.2d 205 (Mo.App.1983).

2. "MOST SIGNIFICANT RELATIONSHIP" TEST
Restatement (Second) of Conflicts: "The validity of a marriage will be determined by the local law of the state which, with respect to the particular issue, has the most significant relationship to the spouses and the marriage * * *.'' A

marriage satisfying requirements of the state where contracted is valid everywhere, "unless it violates the strong public policy of another state which had the most significant relationship to the spouses and the marriage at the time of the marriage." § 283. A state usually gives the same incidents to a valid foreign marriage that it gives to a marriage contracted within its territory. § 284.

3. UNIFORM MARRIAGE EVASION ACT

The Uniform Marriage Evasion Act provides that marriage may not be validly contracted in State B by a resident of State A, if such a marriage would be void in State A. Similarly, a marriage meeting all requirements in State A and contracted there by a nonresident party is void if prohibited in that party's state of residence. Only five states have adopted the UMEA. The Commissioners on Uniform State Laws withdrew (*i.e.*, no longer recommend enactment of) the Act in 1943.

D. ANNULMENT

Annulment (today often referred to as "Declaration of Invalidity", *e.g.*, UMDA § 208) is a judicial declaration that by reason of a defect or impediment that existed at its inception, a purported marriage does not exist. Depending upon the impediment on which the annulment is based, a defective marriage is classified as void or voidable. Traditionally, the declaration is retroactive in both circumstances: The marriage is treated as never having existed.

1. HISTORY

Annulment developed contemporaneously with limited divorce (legal separation) when full divorce with the right to remarry did not exist. Annulment of a prior marriage permitted remarriage, because, void or voidable, an annulled marriage was deemed never to have existed.

2. IMPEDIMENTS

Impediments (defects) sufficient to warrant annulment traditionally included failure of one or both parties to meet age requirements, fraud or duress, impotency, bigamy, religious orders, consanguinity, and affinity. To be the basis of a successful annulment action, the impediment must have existed at the time of the marriage.

3. DEFENSES

Generally, a party to an action seeking annulment of a voidable marriage may raise equitable defenses such as estoppel, ratification, and unclean hands. A void marriage, on the other hand, is not ratifiable and is without legal effect even without an annulment or declaration of invalidity. Nevertheless, a party to a void marriage who has "unclean hands" is often held estopped from asserting the voidness of the "marriage" and thereby gaining an unfair advantage.

4. THE VOID/VOIDABLE DISTINCTION

a. Void Marriage

A *void* marriage typically offends a strong public policy (such as the prohibition of incest or bigamy). It requires no judicial declaration or action to establish its invalidity. Nevertheless, such an action may be entertained by a court to provide certainty and to produce a public record that no valid marriage existed.

b. Voidable Marriage

A voidable marriage typically reflects encroachment upon some matter of lesser concern to the state, but of considerable concern to a party to the marriage (such as "fraud" or "duress"). A voidable marriage typically must be attacked during the life of the parties, attack may be allowed only to the parties, and some voidable marriages may be ratified by the parties' voluntary conduct, such as continued cohabitation after gaining knowledge of a fraud or after reaching marriage age.

c. Significance of the Distinction

The void/voidable classification may have potentially significant impact upon other legal interests. To illustrate, if a marriage is *void* and one partner dies, the surviving partner does not inherit as a spouse. (If the putative spouse doctrine or similar remedy applies, this rule may not hold.) If the marriage was *voidable* and has not been annulled, the surviving partner is considered a widow(er).

> *Example:* Potential heirs of deceased W brought an action to annul W's marriage to H on grounds of mental incompetence and fraud. They alleged that W was of unsound mind at the time of the marriage and that H induced W to marry him in order to inherit from her, knowing that she was about to die. (Result: Annulment denied. Allegations would support only a finding of a voidable marriage. Since the action was not brought during W's lifetime, the marriage can no longer be annulled.) *Patey v. Peaslee,* 99 N.H. 335, 111 A.2d 194 (1955).

d. UMDA

The UMDA reduces traditional distinctions between (1) void and voidable marriages and (2) between annulment and divorce. (See p. 89). UMDA § 208 defines and restricts the persons who may attack a defective marriage and when such an attack may or must be made.

5. ANNULMENT FOR FRAUD

As grounds for annulment of a marriage, a fraudulent misrepresentation (1) must have occurred before the parties' marriage, (2) must be material and must have been relied upon by the other party, and (3) must go to the "essence" of the marriage contract. What constitutes the "essence of marriage" is not defined uniformly. Courts have found fraud going to the essence of marriage when there were false representations regarding fertility, or serious misrepresentations concerning religious beliefs. Misrepresentations concerning wealth, character or past life, however, typically have not sufficed to invalidate a marriage, no matter how important the matter was to the other party.

Examples: (1) Before the marriage, W falsely represented to H that she was pregnant by him. Actually she was not pregnant. (Result: Annulment.) *Masters v. Masters,* 13 Wis.2d 332, 108 N.W.2d 674 (1961). *Contra, Husband v. Wife,* 262 A.2d 656 (Del.1970).

(2) W represented that H was responsible for her pre-marital pregnancy when in fact the pregnancy was by another man. (Result: Annulment.) *Yager v. Yager,* 313 Mich. 300, 21 N.W.2d 138 (1946).

(3) After representing to him that she desired children, W refused to have intercourse with H without the use of contraceptive devices. (Result: Annulment.) *Stegienko v. Stegienko,* 295 Mich. 530, 295 N.W. 252 (1940). Compare *Heup v. Heup,* 45 Wis.2d 71, 172 N.W.2d 334 (1969), where H and W had premarital agreement that W would take contraceptive pills only during the first year of marriage, and W subsequently continued to take pills to prevent conception. (Result: Wisconsin's Supreme Court held that this was not clear and convincing proof of W's intention not to have children. W granted divorce. H's counterclaim for annulment dismissed.)

(4) W represented to H_2 that H_1 was dead. In fact, she was divorced and H_1 was still living. As a practicing Roman Catholic, H_2 credibly alleged that he would not have married W if he had known that H_1 was still alive. (Result: Annulment.) *Wolfe v. Wolfe,* 62 Ill.App.3d 498, 19 Ill.Dec. 306, 378 N.E.2d 1181 (1978), aff'd 76 Ill.2d 92, 27 Ill.Dec. 735, 389 N.E.2d 1143 (1979).

(5) Before marriage, H falsely represented himself to W as a practicing Orthodox Jew. (Result: Annulment. The court found that for this W, religion was an "essential of her marriage.") *Bilowit v. Dolitsky,* 124 N.J.Super. 101, 304 A.2d 774 (1973).

6. ANNULMENT FOR DURESS

To allow annulment of a marriage, duress (1) must have been perceived by the complaining party at the time of marriage and (2) must have been sufficient to prevent him or her from acting freely. Many cases seem to apply this test subjectively and may ask whether *this particular individual* was entering the marriage under duress, regardless of whether the belief was reasonable or not. Duress may be exercised by threats or application of physical force, or by threat of arrest or prosecution, and invalidates consent to marriage. Traditionally, a threat of criminal prosecution for seduction, fornication, or a similar offense was held *not* to invalidate a marriage thus induced, because marriage was a defense to such "crimes."

7. ANNULMENT OF MARRIAGE ENTERED IN JEST

"When two people participate in a mock marriage ceremony as the result of jest, exuberance, hilarity, or dare and harbor no intention to be bound thereby, most cases have allowed the marriage to be annulled, reasoning that the public interest would not be served by compelling these persons to accept the legal consequences of their imprudent conduct." *Mpiliris v. Hellenic Lines, Ltd.*, 323 F.Supp. 865 (S.D.Tex.1969).

8. ANNULMENT OF SHAM MARRIAGE

Occasionally, parties will enter into a marriage for a particular, limited purpose. They may marry to legitimate a child, to gain tax benefits, or to circumvent immigration quotas. Courts have not been consistent in their treatment of such marriages. If, at the time of the marriage, the parties intended to establish a life together or if the parties intended to partake of at least one of the inherent incidents of marriage (such as legitimation of a child), the marriage generally is upheld. Traditionally, courts were less likely to annul a marriage that had been consummated. The outcome may depend on who challenges the marriage. The "clean hands doctrine" may estop the parties, but not the federal government which, under specific provisions of the immigration laws, may challenge a sham marriage (or divorce) intended to take advantage of immigration preferences. U.S. law now imposes a 2–year duration test on marriages that lead to immigration preference, and requires a 2–year "exile" on the part of a would-be immigrant, if he or she enters a marriage with a U.S. citizen while deportation or exclusion proceedings are pending. (*E.g., Escobar v. I.N.S.*, 896 F.2d 564 (D.C.Cir.1990) (withdrawn); *Azizi v. Thornburgh*, 908 F.2d 1130 (2d Cir.1990)). A marriage may be valid between the parties to the marriage or vis-à-vis most third parties, but this will not necessarily bind the immigration authorities. Conversely, if the parties later obtain an annulment or divorce, this does not allow the government to revoke an immigration visa granted on the basis of the marriage, unless the immigration laws specifically cover the situation. Similar situations may arise under federal tax laws.

Example: H divorced W_1 in South Korea and married W_2 who had obtained a visa to immigrate to the United States. Days later, W_2 moved to Georgia to live with her sister and brother-in-law. On the basis of his marriage to W_2, H then entered the United States, flew to Georgia and obtained his "green card." H then initiated divorce proceedings against W_2. The divorce became final and, at about the same time, H departed for South Korea and returned a few months later with W_1 and their daughter. H and W_1 then remarried. Two years later, the INS initiated deportation proceedings against H for entry into the United

States with an immigrant visa procured by fraud on the basis of his sham marriage to W₂. (Result: Deportation affirmed. "Based on the record before us, we are satisfied that substantial evidence supports the determination that [H's] marriage to [W₂] was a sham. We agree with the IJ that the sequence of events demonstrates that [H] married [W₂] solely for the purpose of securing an immigrant visa for himself and eventually for his first wife and their child.") *Roe v. Immigration and Naturalization Service,* 771 F.2d 1328 (9th Cir.1985).

9. LEGAL INCIDENTS OF ANNULMENT
a. Effects Regarding Children and Financial Obligations

Even if annulment declares a marriage never to have existed, many courts today recognize the relationship in some particulars, especially regarding the legitimacy of children and financial obligations.

Examples: (1) In an earlier decision, the state supreme court had held that H's common-law marriage to W was void *ab initio* because H had a wife living at the same time that W claimed to be H's wife. W did not know of the first wife until she filed for divorce. W filed this suit to determine her interest in personal and real property accumulated during the alleged marriage. (Result: Damages granted W. The court applied *Buckley v. Buckley,* 50 Wash. 213, 96 P. 1079 (1908): "Where a woman in good faith enters into a marriage contract with a man, and they assume and enter into the marriage state pursuant to any ceremony or agreement recognized by the law of the place, which marriage would be legal except for the incompetency of the man which he conceals from the woman, a status is created which will justify a court in rendering a decree of annulment of the attempted and assumed marriage contract upon complaint of the innocent party; and where in such a case the facts are as they have been found here, where the woman helped to acquire and very materially to save the property, the court has jurisdiction, as between the parties, to dispose of their property as it would * * * in a case of granting a divorce, awarding to the innocent, injured woman such proportion of the property as, under all the circumstances, would be just and equitable.") *Walker v. Walker,* 330 Mich. 332, 47 N.W.2d 633 (1951).

(2) H and W were married at a time when, unknown to W, H was married to another woman. W filed for divorce on the ground that the marriage was null and void *ab initio.* The trial court granted the divorce and awarded W alimony. H challenged the award of alimony. (Result: Alimony award upheld. "The key to the instant case, as we see it, is the legislative declaration that alimony is allowable whenever there is a decree for divorce. We read 'alimony' not in the technical sense of the word, but as

commensurate with 'support'. The inclusion of prevenient invalidity as a ground for divorce must be ascribed some meaning, and we think it shows a legislative intent to permit an award of alimony in a proper case. * * * In the absence of statute, alimony is generally not allowed in any case where the marriage is declared to be null and void *ab initio*. * * * But by statute in many states, support for the putative wife is allowed in all cases of divorce or annulment. In other states, the same result is reached, by construction of the divorce statutes to permit an award of alimony, even where the ground of divorce is that the marriage is a nullity. * * * We take the same view.") *Clayton v. Clayton*, 231 Md. 74, 188 A.2d 550 (1963).

b. Non–retroactive Annulment Under UMDA § 208(e), With Divorce–Like Consequences

UMDA § 208(e) provides that "unless the court finds, after a consideration of all relevant circumstances, including the effect of a retroactive decree on third parties, that the interests of justice would be served by making the decree not retroactive, it shall declare the marriage invalid as of the date of the marriage. The provisions of this Act relating to property rights of the spouses, maintenance, support, and custody of children on dissolution of marriage are applicable to non-retroactive decrees of invalidity."

c. Revival of Former Spouse's Duty of Support

An annulment usually does not revive a former spouse's duty of support that terminated upon the attempted remarriage.

Examples: (1) H_1 was obligated to pay alimony to W until she remarried. Five years after their divorce, W married H_2. Soon after, W was granted an annulment from H_2, their marriage being void because H_2 was legally married to another woman at the time he purported to marry W. W sued H_1 for alimony for the time after the annulment of her "marriage" to H_2. (Result: H_1's alimony obligation not revived. "[T]he understanding must have been that, upon the wife's remarriage, the husband could regard himself as free of the duty to support her. He could then assume new obligations—he could himself remarry, if he were of a mind to, but his means limited—without remaining forever subject to the possibility that his first wife's remarriage would be annulled and the burden of supporting her shifted back to him. And the wife, too, must have understood that by remarrying she abandoned her rights to support under the agreement, for better or for worse, in favor of whatever support would be furnished her by her second mate.") *Gaines v. Jacobsen*, 308 N.Y. 218, 124 N.E.2d 290 (1954).

(2) W was granted an annulment of her marriage to H_2. She then petitioned for reinstatement of alimony from H_1. (Result: H's alimony obligation not revived. The court held that a wife forfeits

her right to alimony from a first husband when she enters into a subsequent *voidable* marriage. The court expressly refused to decide what the effect of a subsequent *void* marriage would be.) *McConkey v. McConkey*, 216 Va. 106, 215 S.E.2d 640 (1975).

d. Revival of Other Rights Related to Marriage

If the "reconstitution" of the relationship preceding the annulment does not burden the former spouse but falls upon an employer, or on a state or federal program designed to support the spouse of a deceased employee, some courts are willing to disregard a subsequent invalid remarriage and allow revival of a right relating to a prior valid marriage.

Examples: (1) W received monthly death benefits as a widow of H_1, who was killed in the course of his employment. When she remarried, the death benefits terminated and she was awarded a 2–year lump-sum payment. Three years later and following the birth of their child, W learned that H_2 had a prior existing marriage that had never been terminated. The marriage between W and H_2 was annulled, and W filed for reinstatement of the monthly death benefits relating to H_1. Following a hearing, the benefits were reinstated as of the date of the void marriage, and the insurance carrier was credited with the 2–year lump-sum payment. The insurance carrier appealed. (Result: Award upheld. "Since the marriage [to H_2] was annulled, [W] is entitled to all of the benefits she would have received had there been no attempted marriage, subject only to the return of the amount paid in a lump sum. Here, the latter requirement was satisfied by crediting the amount of the lump sum payment to the benefits due.") *United States Fidelity and Guaranty Co. v. The Industrial Commission of Arizona*, 25 Ariz.App. 244, 542 P.2d 825 (1975).

(2) After W's marriage to H_2 was annulled, she filed an application for Social Security survivor's benefits based on H_1's earnings, with whom she had lived until his death. (Result: Benefits denied. "* * * [R]eference to state law is necessary * * * for the narrow purpose of determining whether the widow has entered into a relationship that will entitle her under state law to support from her second husband." The court found that she would be so entitled). *Nott v. Flemming*, 272 F.2d 380 (2d Cir.1959).

E. REVIEW QUESTIONS

1. **T or F** Since a mentally incompetent person lacks capacity to marry, a guardian must consent to his/her marriage.

2. **T or F** A marriage will be annulled on the ground of fraud if the injured party can show his/her detrimental reliance.

3. **T or F** A marriage may be found even though the couple failed to have it solemnized.

4. **T or F** Proxy marriages generally are considered sham marriages and therefore are invalid.

5. M and W have lived together for five years. They have no children. They have told everyone that they are married, but no ceremony was ever performed. W now wants a divorce. In the typical state that recognizes common law marriage, which is the correct answer?

   A. Since M and W have no children, a valid common law marriage did not come into existence. Therefore, there can be no divorce.

   B. W may file for divorce in the same manner as if she had been married ceremonially.

   C. Since M and W have not cohabited for seven years, they do not have a common law marriage.

6. **T or F** The putative spouse doctrine protects a husband and wife who are not actually married, but who hold themselves out as married.

7–10. Questions 7 through 10 should be answered based on the following facts: H and W are married, and S is their 21–year-old son. G is a 16–year-old unrelated female. B is an 18–year-old unrelated male. A is W's 25–year-old sister.

7. **T or F** All states prohibit W from marrying S, but most allow S and A to marry.

8. **T or F** To marry B, G needs parental consent.

9. **T or F** If H and W had adopted G, some states would allow G to marry S.

10. **T or F** If the parties' religion requires a man to have several wives, a state law forbidding H to marry both W and G (if G's parents consent), would be in violation of the constitutional guaranty of religious freedom.

11. **T or F** Sam and Diane enter into a common law marriage in a state that recognizes common law marriage, meeting all the required prerequisites. Their marriage is not recognized in their home state which has abolished common law marriage.

12. **T or F** Richard, age 25, and Liz, age 15, marry. One year later Richard has second thoughts and wants an annulment because Liz was underage at the time of their marriage. He may annul the marriage.

*

III

COHABITATION WITHOUT MARRIAGE—HETEROSEXUAL RELATIONSHIPS AND SAME–SEX UNIONS

Analysis

A.   UNMARRIED COHABITATION

1.   *MARVIN v. MARVIN*
In the landmark *Marvin* case, Michelle Triola Marvin sued actor Lee Marvin to enforce an oral agreement purportedly giving her rights to support and one half of the property accumulated during the seven years the two cohabitated.   The Supreme Court of California held:

a.   Family Law Statutes Do Not Govern a Non–Marital Relationship
"No language in the Family Law Act addresses the property rights of nonmarital partners, and nothing in the legislative history of the act suggests that the Legislature considered that subject.   The delineation of the rights of non-marital partners before 1970 had been fixed entirely by judicial decision; we see no reason to believe that the Legislature, by enacting the Family Law Act, intended to change that state of affairs."

b.   Contracts Between Partners Are Enforceable, Unless the Consideration Is Meretricious
"The decisions in [earlier California] cases thus demonstrate that a contract between nonmarital partners, even if expressly made in contemplation of a common living arrangement, is invalid only if sexual acts form an inseparable part of the consideration for the agreement. In sum, a court will not enforce a contract for the pooling of property and earnings if it is explicitly and inseparably based upon services as a paramour.   [One case] indicates that even if sexual services are part of the contractual consideration, any severable portion of the contract supported by independent consideration will still be enforced."

c.   If There Is No Express Agreement—Other Remedies May Protect the Parties' Expectations
"The courts may inquire into the conduct of the parties to determine whether that conduct demonstrates an implied contract or implied agreement of partnership or joint venture or some other tacit understanding between the parties.   The courts may, when appropriate, employ principles of constructive trust or resulting trust.   Finally, a nonmarital partner may recover in quantum meruit for the reasonable value of household services rendered less the reasonable value of support received if he can show that he rendered services with the expectation of monetary reward."   *Marvin v. Marvin*, 18 Cal.3d 660, 134 Cal.Rptr. 815, 557 P.2d 106 (1976).

d.   Outcome of *Marvin*
The California Supreme Court remanded the *Marvin* case to the trial court which rejected Michelle's contract claim, but awarded her $104,000 for "rehabilitation."   On further appeal, the California Appellate Court denied this recovery on the ground that "no basis whatsoever, either in equity or in law, exists for the challenged rehabilitative award."   *Marvin v. Marvin*, 122 Cal.App.3d 871, 176 Cal.Rptr. 555 (1981).   The California Supreme Court denied further review.

2. APPLICATION OF THE "*MARVIN* DOCTRINE"

Despite the negative outcome of the case and the fact that *Marvin* was not the first such decision, *Marvin* now stands for the proposition that support and property obligations *may* arise from cohabitation without marriage. With the increase in unmarried cohabitation in today's society, the *Marvin* holding has been widely discussed and cited. Courts have allowed recoveries on the basis of express and implied agreements, as well as on the theory of unjust enrichment or quasi-contract and resulting and constructive trusts.

a. Application to Facts Resembling Common Law Marriage

Examples: (1) H and W divorced after 14 years of marriage and the birth of 5 children. Approximately a year later they resumed cohabitation. They had 2 more children and maintained a stable *de facto* family relationship until they separated permanently 20 years later. Both H and W had worked outside the home. While H had earned more than W, W had done the housework. W was granted equitable division of the property the couple had accumulated during the 20 years they had lived together. The trial court found that H's and W's contributions to the family were equal and, excepting the value of an inheritance which went solely to H, divided the property equally. H appealed. (Result: Equitable division upheld. "[T]he legal relationship of husband and wife may be created only in conformity with the procedures authorized by the statute law of the state. * * * Notwithstanding, upon permanent separation, our law authorizes and sanctions an equitable division of property accumulated by two persons as a result of their joint efforts. This would be the case were a common law business partnership breaking up. It is equally the case where a man and woman, who have accumulated property in the course of a non-marital cohabitation, permanently separate. * * * [W]here one party to the relationship acts without compensation to perform work or render services to a business enterprise or performs work or services generally regarded as domestic in nature, these are nevertheless economic contributions. They are to be valued by reference to the cost of similar services in the marketplace. Where, as here, the man accepted the benefit of such services, he will not be heard to argue that he did not need them and that their economic value should not be considered as the woman's economic contributions to the joint accumulation of property between them.") *Pickens v. Pickens*, 490 So.2d 872 (Miss.1986).

(2) P and D lived together for 28 years. They never participated in a formal marriage ceremony or obtained a marriage license, but they held themselves out as married and were regarded by others in the community as husband and wife. On three separate occasions they purchased real property jointly, as though a married couple. When they separated, P sued to establish a

marriage between herself and D in order to become eligible for spousal social security benefits, and to equitably divide the couple's property. (Result: No common law marriage. Equitable division ordered. "[T]he citizens of this state, by way of the legislative process, have expressed a preference for the solemnization of marriage. Due to the presence of this statutory provision, we will not impose an alternative view. * * * We base our opinion on the principle that adults who voluntarily live together and engage in sexual relations are nonetheless as competent as any other persons to contract respecting their earnings and property rights. Of course, they cannot lawfully contract to pay for the performance of sexual services * * *. So long as the agreement does not rest upon illicit meretricious consideration, the parties may order their economic affairs as they choose, and no policy precludes the courts from enforcing such agreements. * * * [W]e hold that a court may order a division of property acquired by a man and woman who are unmarried cohabitants, but who have considered themselves and held themselves out to be husband and wife. Such order may be based upon principles of contract, either express or implied, or upon a constructive trust. Factors to be considered in ordering such a division of property may include: the purpose, duration, and stability of the relationship and the expectations of the parties. Provided, however, that if either the man or woman is validly married to another person during the period of cohabitation, the property rights of the spouse and support rights of the children of such man or woman shall not in any way be adversely affected by such division of property. The expectations of the parties under these circumstances would be equitable treatment by the other party in exchange for engaging in such a cohabiting relationship.") *Goode v. Goode*, 183 W.Va. 468, 396 S.E.2d 430 (W.Va.1990).

(3) P and D lived together for 12 years and had two children. They held themselves out to the public as husband and wife, filed joint income tax returns and maintained joint bank accounts. D insured P as his wife on his medical insurance policy, and P and D purchased real and personal property as though husband and wife. P obligated herself on promissory notes to lending institutions as though D's wife, and she worked as a receptionist in D's business for 3 years. P also took care of the children and the house and contributed personal property. After a bitter separation, P sought an accounting and a share of accumulated property under family law statutes, marriage by estoppel, express or implied in fact contract, constructive trust based upon unjust enrichment, and partition. (Result: (1) Unmarried cohabitants are not a family within the meaning of the statute that authorizes the division of

property in an action affecting the family. (2) The doctrine of marriage by estoppel is inapplicable. (3) P has valid claims for breach of contract, express or implied in fact, unjust enrichment, and partition. "We disagree with the circuit court's implicit conclusion that courts cannot or should not, without express authorization from the legislature, divide property between persons who have engaged in nonmarital cohabitation. Courts traditionally have settled contract and property disputes between unmarried persons, some of whom have cohabited. Nonmarital cohabitation does not render every agreement between the cohabiting parties illegal and does not automatically preclude one of the parties from seeking judicial relief, such as statutory or common law partition, damages for breach of express or implied contract, constructive trust and quantum meruit where the party alleges, and later proves, facts supporting the legal theory.") *Watts v. Watts*, 137 Wis.2d 506, 405 N.W.2d 303 (Wis.1987).

b. Recovery for Services

Examples: (1) P and D had a 13– or 14–year relationship and lived together for 7 of those years. In 1978 they purchased a home in Reading, Massachusetts. On the way to the closing, D told P that he would have to take title in his name alone in order to obtain Veterans' Administration financing, and the deed was so recorded. During the 3 years they lived together in Reading, D (a career army officer) attended law school at night and P (who had given up her career as a flight attendant to maintain a home for D) worked as a waitress. D paid the mortgage, taxes, utilities, and insurance on the house. P paid for food, household supplies, and much of the furniture. P did all of the housework. When D was transferred to Washington, D.C., P moved with him. Their relationship deteriorated and P, who wished to move back to Reading, sued to obtain title to the house as tenant in common with D. (Result: No tenancy in common, but D held one-half of the property in constructive trust in favor of P. "The judge's unchallenged findings of fact demonstrate that there was a fiduciary relationship between the parties and that the defendant violated his fiduciary duty to the plaintiff. Equitable principles impose a constructive trust on property to avoid the unjust enrichment of a party who violates his fiduciary duty and acquires that property at the expense of the person to whom he owed that duty.") *Sullivan v. Rooney*, 404 Mass. 160, 533 N.E.2d 1372 (Mass.1989).

(2) P and D cohabited on and off for eight years. P brought suit for a one-half interest in a house D had built during their cohabitation. (Result: P's claim rejected. (1) D's retention of house constructed during period of cohabitation did not constitute unjust enrichment; (2) D did not hold a part interest in the house

in trust for P (no purchase money resulting trust was created); (3) P was not entitled to constructive trust equal to undivided one-half interest in real estate; (4) evidence did not support finding of oral contract between the parties; and (5) P was not entitled to partition. "We agree with trial court's conclusion that plaintiff has produced no clear and convincing evidence showing defendant has enriched himself inequitably or unconscionably at plaintiff's expense. Plaintiff absented herself for months while much of the construction took place. The record reflects she is a bright, aggressive person who followed her own interests and who was fully capable of legally protecting any right she might have asserted in the real estate. It was only after the house virtually was completed and paid for that she presented defendant with a quitclaim deed to sign, conveying to her a one-half interest. Upon his refusal, she continued to live in the house until her occupancy was terminated, whereupon she commenced this action. There is a clear inference in the evidence that the services and benefits these parties conferred upon each other during the course of their cohabitation were gratuitously rendered and extended. We find nothing in this situation that would invoke the conscience of an equity court.") *Slocum v. Hammond,* 346 N.W.2d 485 (Iowa 1984).

(3) P brought an action for the reasonable value of services rendered and material furnished in the improvement and renovation of D's home. P and D had been cohabiting at the time the services were performed. (Result: P was entitled to recover funds he expended, the reasonable value of work he performed, and services he rendered in renovating and improving D's home, reduced by the reasonable value of benefits received by him. "[W]e cannot agree that the fact of unmarried cohabitation between the parties bars either party from asserting against the other a claim which would otherwise be enforceable under principles of law of general applicability. * * * [W]e regard the position that the courts will not participate in resolving the disputes in accordance with general principles of law and, thus, will leave the parties to their own devices, to be unrealistic and unresponsive to social need.") *Mason v. Rostad,* 476 A.2d 662 (D.C.App.1984).

3. *MARVIN* DOCTRINE REJECTED

In *Hewitt v. Hewitt,* 77 Ill.2d 49, 31 Ill.Dec. 827, 394 N.E.2d 1204 (1979), a man and woman had lived together as husband and wife for fifteen years. They had three children. No marriage ceremony had been performed, but H allegedly had told W that they were married, that no ceremony was necessary and that he would "share his life, his future, his earnings and his property" with her. Because Illinois does not recognize common law marriage and fearing that to allow her recovery would adopt the *Marvin* doctrine in derogation of what should be the legislature's prerogative, the Illinois Supreme Court held that H had no obligation to share any property earned by him throughout their years together or to pay her any support in the future.

4. *MARVIN* DOCTRINE "CODIFIED"

Minnesota Stat. Ann. § 513.075: "If sexual relations between the parties are contemplated, a contract between a man and a woman who are living together in this state out of wedlock, or who are about to commence living together in this state out of wedlock, is enforceable as to terms concerning the property and financial relations of the parties only if: (1) the contract is written and signed by the parties, and (2) enforcement is sought after termination of the relationship." § 513.076: "Unless the individuals have executed a contract complying with [the above] provisions, the courts of this state are without jurisdiction to hear and shall dismiss as contrary to public policy any claim by an individual to the earnings or property of another individual if the claim is based on the fact that the individuals lived together in contemplation of sexual relations and out of wedlock within or without this state."

B.   SAME–SEX RELATIONSHIPS

1. PARTNERSHIPS

The *Marvin* Doctrine has been applied to same-sex cohabitants.

Example: When P and D, both men, began living together, they orally agreed that P would quit school and devote himself full-time to being D's chauffeur, bodyguard, social and business secretary, partner in real estate investments, and spokesman.   In turn, D agreed to give P one-half equity in all real estate thereafter acquired by D or jointly by D and P, to support P for life, and to permit P to withdraw from D's bank accounts and use D's credit cards.   D also agreed to engage in a homosexual relationship with P. The parties further agreed that if any portion of the agreement was found to be unenforceable, that portion would be severable and the remaining provisions would remain in full force and effect.   Seven years later D barred P from his premises.   P sued for property rights based on the oral agreement. D argued that the agreement was unenforceable (1) under the statute of frauds and (2) because it was based upon illicit consideration, *i.e.*, sexual services. (Result: (1) D is estopped from raising a statute of frauds defense in light of P's detrimental reliance.   (2) The agreement is enforceable even though the parties' sexual relationship was an express part of the consideration.   "The issue here is whether the sexual component of the consideration is severable from the remaining portions of the contract. * * * The services which plaintiff alleges he agreed to and did provide included being a chauffeur, bodyguard, secretary, and partner and counselor in real estate investments. If provided, these services are of monetary value, and the type for which one would expect to be compensated unless there is evidence of a contrary intent. Thus, they are properly characterized as consideration independent of the sexual aspect of the relationship.") *Whorton v. Dillingham*, 202 Cal.App.3d 447, 248 Cal.Rptr. 405 (1988).

2. SAME–SEX MARRIAGE

So far, no American jurisdiction has recognized marriage between partners of the same sex. Several states have enacted explicit statutes that recognize marriage only between a man and a woman.

Courts have supported the prohibition against same sex marriage by invoking the state's interest in encouraging procreation. The principal purpose of marriage is seen as providing a stable social and economic environment in which children may be raised. Opponents argue that this reflects an outdated conception of the role of marriage and the family in modern society.

a. Constitutionality

In 1986, the U.S. Supreme Court upheld a Georgia law criminally punishing consensual homosexual acts involving adults in private. *Bowers v. Hardwick*, 478 U.S. 186, 106 S.Ct. 2841, 92 L.Ed.2d 140 (1986). In states that criminalize homosexual conduct, this laid to rest any *constitutional* argument regarding the validity of same-sex marriage. In several states, the same-sex marriage prohibition has been attacked on equal protection, due process, and right to privacy grounds, but courts have not recognized a *federal* constitutional right of same-sex couples to marry, and most have rejected application of state constitutional provisions.

Examples: (1) Two men sought to compel the issuance of a marriage license to them. Plaintiff's claim, *inter alia,* relied on Washington's Equal Rights Amendment. (Result: License denied. "[T]he refusal of the state to authorize same-sex marriage results from * * * impossibility of reproduction rather than from an invidious discrimination 'on account of sex'. Therefore, the definition of marriage as the legal union of one man and one woman is permissible as applied to appellants, notwithstanding the prohibition contained in the ERA, because it is founded upon the unique physical characteristics of the sexes and appellants are not being discriminated against because of their status as males per se. In short, we hold the ERA does not require the state to authorize same-sex marriage.") *Singer v. Hara*, 11 Wash.App. 247, 522 P.2d 1187 (1974).

(2) In a 1993 landmark decision, Hawaii's Supreme Court decided, on *state* constitutional equal protection grounds, that Hawaii's

prohibition of same-sex marriage is presumably unconstitutional, unless the state demonstrates "that it furthers compelling state interests and is narrowly drawn to avoid unnecessary abridgements of constitutional rights." *Baehr v. Lewin*, 74 Hawaii 530, 852 P.2d 44 (1993). Promptly, the legislature reaffirmed heterosexual marriage. In late 1995, a Hawaii state commission recommended legalizing same-sex marriage. By early 1996, the decision on remand had not yet been made. See *Baehr v. Miike*, 1996 WL 22333 (Hawaii). Whatever it is, will be front-page news.

b. "Common Usage" or Dictionary Definition of Marriage

Examples: (1) Two men applied for a marriage license in Minnesota. Their application was denied on the ground that they were of the same sex. They argued that state statutes authorize issuance of a marriage license or, if not, that authorization is compelled constitutionally. (Result: Same sex marriages are prohibited. The court held that, in common usage, the word "marriage" means "the state of union between persons of the opposite sex," and that the statute does not violate the First, Eighth, Ninth, or Fourteenth Amendments. It refused to find a fundamental right to marry without regard to the sex of the parties.) *Baker v. Nelson*, 291 Minn. 310, 191 N.W.2d 185 (1971).

(2) Two females applied for a marriage license, and appealed from a denial. (Result: There is no constitutional protection of a right of marriage between persons of the same sex. Female persons are incapable of marrying one another. The term "marriage" is defined according to common usage, and the proposed relationship is not a marriage.) *Jones v. Hallahan*, 501 S.W.2d 588 (Ky.1973).

3. TRANSSEXUALS

If at one time both parties were of the same sex, and one underwent a successful sex change operation *prior* to marriage, it has been held that no public policy prevents such a marriage from being valid.

Examples: (1) W filed a complaint for maintenance. H defended that W was a male and, therefore, their marriage was void. W testified that she was born a male but had gone through surgery to make her a female before her marriage. (Result: For W. "Successful sex reassignment surgery harmonized W's gender and genitalia so that W became physically and psychologically unified and fully capable of sexual activity as a woman. Absent fraud, husband has a legal obligation to support her as his wife. If such sex reassignment surgery is successful and the postoperative transsexual is, by virtue of medical treatment, thereby possessed of the full capacity to function sexually as a male or female, as the case may be, we perceive no legal barrier, cognizable social taboo, or reason grounded in public policy to prevent that person's identification at least for purposes of marriage to the sex finally indicated.") *M.T. v. J.T.,* 140 N.J.Super. 77, 355 A.2d 204 (1976).

(2) Marriage held not valid where the sex change operation took place *after* marriage. *Anonymous v. Anonymous,* 67 Misc.2d 982, 325 N.Y.S.2d 499 (1971).

C. REVIEW QUESTIONS

1–2. Questions 1 and 2 should be answered based on the following facts: Charles and Camilla lived together for many years but had no children and never married. When they separate, Camilla wants to sue for alimony.

1. **T** **or** **F** She may recover alimony under the state's divorce statute.

2. **T** **or** **F** In several states, she may recover support under the *Marvin* doctrine.

3. **T** **or** **F** Francis has a sex change operation. He changes his name to Francine and marries George. Their marriage is valid.

4. **T** **or** **F** Two men participate in a ceremonial marriage and live together for many years as a married couple. Although the statute in their state restricts marriage to "the union of a man and a woman," they seek to establish a common law marriage based their having spent time as a married couple in Iowa, a state that recognizes common law marriage.

5. **T** **or** **F** Paul and Joanne lived together for two years but never married. Joanne worked in Paul's business without compensation, but relied on Paul's oral promise to pay her once the business began turning a profit. While Paul paid for Joanne's living expenses, he paid her no wages even after the business started turning a profit. When they separate, Joanne has no claim against Paul.

IV

HUSBAND AND WIFE

A. SUPPORT OBLIGATIONS DURING MARRIAGE

Traditional law required the husband to support his wife during the marriage, irrespective of the wife's financial resources. Today, while the facts lag behind, the legal support obligation is mutual. Mutuality may be required by constitutional guarantees of equal protection. (In *Orr v. Orr,* 440 U.S. 268, 99 S.Ct. 1102, 59 L.Ed.2d 306 (1979), the U.S. Supreme Court invalidated a sexually discriminatory *alimony* statute.)

1. HISTORICAL BASIS

At English common law, the wife's legal identity was merged with her husband's. The husband had sole control over his *and her* legal estates in land and other property and any income therefrom. As the typical wife had no opportunity to earn money to support herself, the husband was obligated to support her. This one-sided support obligation survived even after married women were given the right to own and control property. It was carried into modern society as a concomitant of role-divided marriage which, until recently, was the norm.

2. CHANGING STATUS

A number of states had long imposed a conditional support duty on the wife, if her husband was "in need." Today, the mutual legal duty of support is equally applicable to husband and wife and, as women have entered the work force, courts are prone to minimize alimony, the husband's traditional obligation upon divorce.

3. "NECESSARIES"

The husband's legal obligation of support during the ongoing marriage extended only to "necessaries." The "necessaries doctrine" sometimes has been explained as an agency implied in law, resting on the spouse's legal support obligation. Beyond the narrow "necessaries doctrine," however, principles having their roots in the law of express or implied (in fact) agency, apply to hold one spouse liable for the other spouse's expenditures on a considerably broader scale.

a. Necessaries Defined

"Necessaries" purchased for the family by one spouse, for which the other would be held liable, include all things essential to the family's well being, such as food, apparel, medicine and medical care, transportation, housing, and even furniture. What in any given case constitutes "necessaries" varies with the obligated spouse's financial status.

Example: Arguing that she was indigent, W requested appellate review at public expense after her conviction for possession of a controlled substance and possession of marijuana. After her first trial which had been declared a mistrial, but prior to her second trial, W had married H. H had ample resources to pay for the appeal. (Result: Legal expenses are "necessary" when a criminal action is involved and the spouse's liberty is at stake. While related to an antenuptial act, this expense is not an antenuptial debt, for which H would not be responsible. Therefore, H's resources are considered in determining whether W is indigent for this purpose.) *State v. Clark,* 88 Wash.2d 533, 563 P.2d 1253 (1977).

b. Merchant's Recovery

Under the "necessaries doctrine" the creditor had to show that (1) he supplied to the wife an item that was "necessary," and (2) the husband had failed to provide. Some courts have relieved the merchant of showing the latter, requiring the merchant to show only that the item sold was in the "necessaries" category. Continued use of an item in the home may give rise to the conclusion that (1) a disputed item actually is "necessary," or (2) an actual (express or implied) agency relationship existed, or (3) the husband ratified the purchase.

Example: W purchased a sofa from P. There was no evidence that W was acting on H's behalf. The family enjoyed a position of social and economic prominence in the area where they resided. P contended that the necessaries doctrine applied to hold H liable for the purchase. (Result: For P. "[H and W's] socio-economic standing justifies a finding that the sofa at issue here was a suitable and proper item for their household.") *Sharpe Furniture, Inc. v. Buckstaff,* 99 Wis.2d 114, 299 N.W.2d 219 (1980).

c. Gender Neutrality

The necessaries doctrine has come under attack, especially in its traditional form where it imposes the liability on the basis of gender.

Example: Medical provider (MP) sued H and W for medical services rendered to H. The trial court dismissed MP's claim against W on the ground that W had not executed an agreement to pay for the services. The appellate court reversed. (Result: MP does not collect from W. "Because constitutional considerations demand equality between the sexes, it follows that a husband can no longer be held liable for his wife's necessaries. We therefore abrogate the common law doctrine of necessaries, thereby leaving it to the legislature to determine the policy of the state in this area. We do not make a judgment as to which is the better policy for the state to adopt. We merely leave it to the appropriate branch to decide this question." Dissent: "I agree that the common law doctrine of necessaries in its present form violates the equal protection clause * * *. However, unlike the majority, I conclude that this Court, as a matter of policy, should extend the doctrine to apply to both spouses rather than abrogate it entirely. In doing so, I would make the spouse who incurred the debt primarily liable. * * * Under these circumstances, the extension of the doctrine fits like a glove by requiring the more able spouse to care for the needs of the household. I submit that the application of the doctrine is just as necessary in today's society as it was one hundred years ago. It is my strong belief that we should not repeal this doctrine; we should simply refine it to meet equal protection requirements, and, by doing so, strengthen the martial obligation.") *Connor v. Florida Regional Medical Center*, 668 So.2d 175 (Fla.1995).

4. ACTUAL AGENCY BETWEEN HUSBAND AND WIFE

There is no flat presumption that one spouse is an agent for the other. If authority is express, few problems peculiar to the marriage relationship arise. Importantly, however, authority of one marriage partner to act on behalf of both or the other will be readily implied, so that a spouse may become liable on a contract made by his or her partner. Similarly, estoppel may bar the non-purchasing spouse's protest if his or her actions have reasonably indicated to the merchant that the purchasing spouse is acting as his or her agent. Finally, if the non-purchasing spouse fails to disclaim a transaction by the other spouse, liability may be predicated on agency by ratification.

5. JUDICIAL REFUSAL TO INTERFERE IN ONGOING MARRIAGE

The necessaries doctrine and agency principles primarily protect creditors and help the family only indirectly. Reluctant to interfere in an ongoing marriage, courts are unwilling to enforce the spousal support obligation "inside" the home. As long as the home is maintained and the parties are cohabiting, courts assume that any support obligation is being satisfied. Only when the home breaks up, courts have statutory authority to enter a support order pursuant to legal separation or while divorce is pending.

Example: In a 1953 case, H and W had been married for approximately 33 years. During the four years preceding the action, H had not given W money to purchase furniture or other household necessities. The house had electricity but did not have running water. W's children gave W clothes to wear. H owned land valued at $83,960, had bank deposits in the sum of $104,500, and had an annual income of $8,000–9,000. W had a bank account of $5,960. W brought an action to recover suitable maintenance and support money. (Result: For H. The court considered public policy and common law and held "[i]n the light of the cited cases it is clear, especially so in this jurisdiction, that to maintain an action such as the one at bar, the parties must be separated or living apart from each other. The living standards of a family are a matter of concern to the household, and not for the courts to determine, even though the husband's attitude toward his wife, according to his wealth and circumstances, leaves little to be said in his behalf. As long as the home is maintained and the parties are living as husband and wife it may be said that the husband is legally supporting his wife and the purpose of the marriage relation is being carried out.

Public policy requires such a holding.") *McGuire v. McGuire,* 157 Neb. 226, 59 N.W.2d 336 (1953).

6. "NECESSARIES" AFTER SEPARATION OR PENDING DIVORCE

Generally, the support obligation continues so long as the marriage continues. Recently, however, some courts have been willing to loosen the "necessaries" obligation when the parties no longer lived in an active marriage, particularly when high medical expenses were involved.

> *Example:*   H and W had separated more than 4 years prior to H's hospitalization. During this time they did not live together or support each other. They did not have a separation agreement, and neither had filed for divorce or legal separation. After H died, the hospital assigned H's $16,000 debt to P. P sought recovery from W. (Result: W not liable for necessaries supplied to H more than 4 years after separation. "We cannot regard the marriage as viable at the time of Jose's hospitalizations. Certainly the couple was not a financial unit at that time. Thus plaintiff's assignor, when it admitted Jose to its facility, could not have reasonably assumed that Isabel's assets would be available for payment of its bill. In the circumstances liability should not be imposed on her.") *National Account Systems, Inc. v. Mercado,* 196 N.J.Super. 133, 481 A.2d 835 (1984).

7. CONSTITUTIONAL LIMITATIONS

a. Federal Constitution

On equal protection reasoning, the U.S. Supreme Court struck down an Alabama state alimony statute which provided that only husbands, not wives, may be required to pay alimony. *Orr v. Orr,* 440 U.S. 268, 99 S.Ct. 1102, 59 L.Ed.2d 306 (1979): "Legislative classifications which distribute benefits and burdens on the basis of gender carry the inherent risk of reinforcing the stereotypes about the 'proper place' of women and their need for special protection." The Court rejected the argument that the classification was justified by a legislative purpose of providing help for the needier spouse, typically the wife. The Court also rejected the claim that the classification was justifiable as an attempt to compensate women for past discrimination: "Thus, even statutes purportedly designed to compensate for and ameliorate the effects of past discrimination must be carefully tailored. Where, as here, the State's compensatory and ameliorative purposes are as well served by a gender-neutral classification as one that gender-classifies and therefore carries with it the baggage of sexual stereotypes, the State cannot be permitted to classify on the basis of sex." Although *Orr* was concerned specifically with alimony, the Court's language suggests reevaluation of all laws which place greater or different obligations on the husband than on the wife, and *vice versa.*

Example: Hospital sued H and W for hospital bill representing necessary services rendered to W. Under the common law doctrine of necessaries, the lower court held H responsible (along with W). H appealed. (Result: H and W are each responsible for necessaries provided to the other, if the other is unable to pay. "We agree with the husband that equal protection requires that husbands and wives not be treated differently with respect to the responsibility of one spouse for necessaries provided to the other spouse. But we disagree that a husband may not be responsible for necessaries provided to his wife. * * * [W]e conclude that a wife may be responsible for necessaries provided to her husband. * * * [W]e also conclude that one spouse may not be responsible for necessaries provided to the other spouse unless the other spouse is unable to pay therefor.") *Webb v. Hillsborough County Hospital Authority,* 521 So.2d 199 (Fla.App.1988).

b. State Constitutions

Numerous courts have eliminated inequality in support obligations through interpretation of Equal Rights or Equal Protection Clauses in their state constitutions.

Example: A Maryland "necessaries statute" made a husband responsible for his wife's necessaries, but did not obligate the wife for the husband's necessaries. It was argued that this violated the *state* constitution's equal rights amendment. (Result: Statute struck down. The common law doctrine of necessaries and the statute relating to the husband's liability for the wife's necessaries are both invalid under the State's equal rights amendment. Absent contract, express or implied, neither husband nor wife is liable for necessaries supplied to the other.) *Condore v. Prince George's County,* 289 Md. 516, 425 A.2d 1011 (1981). Similarly, *Schilling v. Bedford County Memorial Hospital,* 225 Va. 539, 303 S.E.2d 905 (1983).

B. PROPERTY RIGHTS

1. COMMON LAW

Complex common law rules essentially precluded a wife from owning property in her own name, so long as her husband was alive. The wife's personal property became the husband's upon marriage. Her husband also gained possession of any real property she owned at the time of marriage or obtained subsequently. Conversely, the wife had a "dower" interest in all real property her husband owned during the marriage, which prevented him from alienating it without her concurrence.

a. Scope

If the wife survived her husband, she received back her realty and whatever personal property the husband had not "reduced into possession." If she predeceased her husband and the marriage had produced a child, her real property would stay with him for life.

b. Circumvention of Rules

Equity provided devices to overcome the rigid common law rules of marital property. Properly arranged through a trust, a married woman could have the use (though not legal ownership) of her property, convey it during her lifetime or upon death, make contracts enforceable against her estate, and sue or be sued in matters concerning her property.

2. MARRIED WOMEN'S PROPERTY ACTS

Since the late 19th century, the so-called "Married Women's Property Acts" have granted married women the right to own and manage their property on their own. Out of this, the separate property concept developed.

a. Scope of Statutes

The "Married Women's Property Acts" provided the married woman with a separate legal existence for most purposes. One long-term holdover from the common law was a disability that prevented the spouses from contracting with each other regarding compensation for labor and services. Today, that disability has been eliminated if the contract is not necessarily related to the marital relationship. Based on the common law concept of legal "oneness" of husband and wife, spousal tort immunity also was continued by these statutes, but has recently been largely abandoned. One result is that tort liability may now be litigated either alongside or separately from divorce and sometimes unexpectedly affect the financial outcome of divorce. Contracts between spouses and intending spouses directly affecting the marriage, however, continue to be treated differently.

> ***Example:*** An Alabama law denied W the power of alienating or mortgaging her lands without the assent and concurrence of her husband, whereas H could convey his land without W's signature. W contended that this was unconstitutional under the equal protection clause of the *state* constitution. (Result: For W. "There is no provision of the Constitution which would permit the legislature to deny to married women rights possessed by all other adults.") *Peddy v. Montgomery,* 345 So.2d 631 (Ala.1977).

b. Purpose and Effect of Statutes

The "Married Women's Property Acts" were enacted to remedy inequities of the common law marital property regime. On their face, they did much to improve the married woman's legal status. In practice, however, the statutes fell short. Under the separate property scheme imposed by these acts, the property of each spouse, whether earned or acquired before *or after* marriage, is that spouse's and only that spouse's property during the marriage. Except by gift or inheritance, the non-earning spouse acquires no property interest in the earner's savings. Traditionally, the court's power to order upon divorce a transfer of one spouse's property to the other was severely restricted or non-existent.   Because the husband typically was the sole earner and thus became the sole owner of all property acquired out of his earnings during the marriage, the "equality" provided by these acts remained largely theoretical.

Example: H turned over a weekly household allowance to W, more or less regularly. With savings resulting from W's dismissal of a maid, W purchased securities in her own account. Upon divorce, H claimed the funds. (Result: No valid gift. To constitute a gift, delivery, intent and transfer of absolute power of disposition must be shown. Absent such a showing, the saved funds remained H's.) *Hardy v. Hardy*, 235 F.Supp. 208 (D.D.C.1964).

3.   SEPARATE PROPERTY STATES

The separate property regime applies in 41 states.   The 9 community property states are Arizona, California, Idaho, Louisiana, New Mexico, Nevada, Texas, Washington and Wisconsin.

a.   Separate Property

Under the separate property scheme each spouse is entitled, *during marriage*, to sole ownership and control of his or her property, whether earned or however acquired, before or after the marriage. *On divorce*, courts have become increasingly willing to delve into a spouse's separate property in order to adequately provide for a financially dependent wife. Reforms in the law of divorce now recognize the partnership aspect of marriage in financial terms and have developed the concept of (distributable) "marital property." "Equitable distribution" may extend to all property, marital and separate, of either party. This is discussed in connection with divorce.

b.   Pros and Cons of Separate Property

The traditional separate property regime ignored the fact that a married woman, especially if she had children, typically did not have the same opportunity as her husband to acquire property or earn income. Today, as most married women have become wage earners, social conditions give more meaning to the separate property concept. The "marital property" concept now generally applied on divorce—essentially an "override" of separate property—has proved a useful safety valve. An advantage of a separate property regime *during* marriage is ease of management and disposition.

c.   Joint Ownership in Separate Property States
1) Forms of Joint Ownership

Spouses may avail themselves of various forms of joint ownership: (1) Tenancy in common, (2) joint tenancy, and (3) tenancy by the entirety. Joint tenancy and tenancy by the entirety give both spouses undivided interests in the property with the right of survivorship. Tenancy by the entirety closely resembles joint tenancy, but is a form of joint ownership available only to spouses. In contrast to joint tenancy, a tenancy by the entirety may be terminated only by dissolution of the marriage. Property held "by the entirety" traditionally was subject to the husband's sole control and possession. This historical relic has survived occasional constitutional attack because the parties are free to choose how to hold their jointly owned property.

2) Interspousal Transfers, Joint Ownership and Presumptions of Gift or Advancement

If a husband places his separate property in joint tenancy or in tenancy by the entirety with his wife, a strong but rebuttable presumption arises that he intends to make her a gift of the one-half interest. Traditionally, this presumption covered only gifts from the husband to his wife. By contrast, if the wife acquired separate property and transferred an interest to her husband as a joint tenant, an opposite presumption (of "advancement") held that she did *not* intend a gift, and the husband was seen as holding his interest in the property for the wife's benefit. These divergent presumptions have come under attack.

Examples: (1) H and W held a number of promissory notes relating to the sale of a farm, cattle, and equipment. Three notes were payable to both parties. H testified that the land was owned by H and W jointly, but that the cattle and equipment were owned solely by H. The chancellor divided the note for the farm evenly, but divided the cattle and equipment notes so that H was awarded $20,000 more than W. W appealed. (Result: Reversed. The court applied the presumption that where H "is responsible for the [the note] being taken in both names" a presumption arises "that there was a gift of an interest by the husband to the wife, even though the wife may have no knowledge of the transaction.") *Ramsey v. Ramsey*, 259 Ark. 16, 531 S.W.2d 28 (1975).

(2) While married, H and W took title to a parcel of land as tenants by the entireties and built a house on the land. W filed for divorce and requested the court to determine the property rights in the realty. The Master found that at least $16,000 of the total cost of $22,000 had come from W. The Master held that "as a result of the actions of [H] in taking 'undue advantage' of his wife by having her transfer her assets into their names without consideration, a 'constructive trust' in the amount of $16,000.00 was created in favor of [W]." H appealed. (Result: Reversed. "[I]n a marital relationship a gift to entireties property is presumed for contributions made by either husband or wife. A constructive trust will be imposed only when it appears that the parties are in fact in a confidential relationship with one party enjoying an advantage over the other because of superior knowledge or influence and

that this domination caused a gift to entireties property to arise. Finally, it must appear that it would be manifestly unjust to allow one party to thereby profit at the expense of the other." The "presumption of advancement" was struck down and the "presumption of gift" extended to both parties under the state's ERA.) *Butler v. Butler,* 464 Pa. 522, 347 A.2d 477 (1975).

3) Effect of the "Marital Property" Concept on "Gifts"

To the extent traditional presumptions of "gift" or "advancement" remain in effect, they have been adjusted where a "marital property" regime applies on divorce. To illustrate, a "gift" of non-marital property by one spouse to the other is classified on divorce as marital property, not as the recipient's non-marital property.

d. Devolution of Separate Property Upon Death

At the time of a spouse's death, his or her separate property passes by will, or if there is no will, by the law of intestacy.

1) Election Against the Will

If a spouse is not provided for in a will, or is dissatisfied with the provision made, statutes in separate property states commonly allow the omitted spouse to elect against the will and take a "statutory share," typically one-third (or one-half if the deceased left no descendants) in *all* of the spouse's share, whenever or however acquired. State laws, however, are lax in protecting this "indefeasible" right of inheritance against manipulation. In many states, the decedent may defeat this provision by transferring separate property during his or her life and leaving little or nothing of value in the estate for the surviving spouse to collect.

Examples: (1) W executed an *inter vivos* trust in which she placed substantially all of her assets. The trust provided that H was to receive as much of the income and principal as necessary to meet any emergency situation for his "reasonable support, medical, and burial expenses." This provision was limited by another provision which advised the trustee to consider other sources available to H and the needs of certain of W's family before making any payments to H. After W's death, H asked that the trust be set aside as it deprived him of his marital rights in the property held in trust. (Result: Trust upheld. "We conclude that an *inter vivos* transfer of property is valid as against the marital rights of the surviving spouse unless the transaction is tantamount to a fraud as manifested by the absence of donative intent to make a conveyance of a present interest in the property conveyed.") *Johnson v. La Grange State Bank,* 73 Ill.2d 342, 22 Ill.Dec. 709, 383 N.E.2d 185 (1978).

(2) H made gratuitous transfers of property acquired by the joint efforts of H and W with the intent to deprive W of the property. W did not have knowledge of these transfers. Suit was brought by W for one half of the gifts. (Result: For W. "While we do not agree that a wife has a vested interest in jointly acquired property * * *, a married man cannot make gifts of jointly acquired property during his lifetime without the consent of or knowledge of his wife where the transfer is in fraud of the wife's marital rights.") *Sanditen v. Sanditen,* 496 P.2d 365 (Okl.1972).

2) Uniform Probate Code
To protect the surviving spouse, the Uniform Probate Code provides a detailed statutory scheme of "augmenting" the decedent's estate by disregarding certain *inter vivos* transfers for the purpose of calculating the survivor's statutory share. In an important break with tradition, recent UPC revisions would abandon the traditional, rigid (typically one-third) share in the deceased spouse's estate and provide instead a share that slowly accrues until, after fifteen years, it reaches one-half of the decedent's estate.

3) Intestacy
If a spouse dies without a will, state intestacy laws govern the distribution of his or her separate property. Intestacy statutes typically provide for the surviving spouse to take all if there are no children or parents of the decedent, or a one-half or one-third share if there are children or parents. The remainder goes to the children, or if there are no children, to the parents.

The Uniform Probate Code § 2–102 suggests the following model for separate property states:

"The intestate share of the surviving spouse is: (1) if there is no surviving issue or parent of the decedent, the entire intestate estate; (2) if there is no surviving issue but the decedent is survived by a parent or parents, the first [$50,000], plus one-half of the balance of the intestate estate; (3) if there are surviving issue all of whom are issue of the surviving spouse also, the first [$50,000], plus one-half of the balance of the intestate estate; (4) if there are surviving issue one or more of whom are not issue of the surviving spouse, one-half of the intestate estate."

4. COMMUNITY PROPERTY STATES
Nine states employ a community property system: Arizona, California, Idaho, Louisiana, New Mexico, Nevada, Texas, Washington, and, in a 1984 adaptation, Wisconsin. Traditionally a separate property state, Wisconsin adopted a revised version of the Uniform Marital Property Act in 1984 and 1985 and thereby became the first (and so far only) common law property state to enact a modern version of community property.

a. Historical Note

The traditional community property states—the first eight listed above—derived their marital property regimes from civil law sources. The rest of the United States followed the common law, and separate property reigned until the late 1940's. A number of separate property states then adopted community property schemes to obtain a federal income tax rate advantage arising from the fact that one-half of the husband's earning would be treated as his wife's income. To avert this trend, the 1948 Revenue Act allowed married couples to "split" incomes by filing joint returns. (In effect, each partner would henceforth pay income tax as though he or she had received one-half of the joint income. When tax rates were highly progressive and one partner was a high earner, this translated into potentially huge tax savings). The separate property jurisdictions that had adopted a form of community property subsequently reverted to separate property regimes. At the time of divorce reform in the 1960's and 1970's, the unfairness of the traditional separate property system was reconsidered, and separate property states adopted various regimes of "equitable distribution" on divorce. In 1984, late in the reform discussion, the Commissioners on Uniform State Laws proposed the Uniform Marital Property Act (UMPA) which would impose a modern form of community property. Twelve years later, UMPA had been adopted only in Wisconsin.

b. The Concept of Community Property

American community property regimes differ in detail. Generally, each spouse owns a *present* one-half interest in what is defined as community property. Principal distinctions among states concern (1) the definition of what is separate and what is community property, (2) the rights of each spouse to manage and control the community property, and (3) the distribution on divorce of separate and community property.

1) Definition of Separate and Community Property

In any marriage there may be four types of property: (1) the wife's separate property; (2) the husband's separate property; (3) joint property; and (4) "community" or "marital" property. Typically, separate property includes property owned before the marriage and property acquired during the marriage by inheritance or gift to one spouse or, with exceptions, by a recovery for personal injury by one spouse. Recovery for lost earnings typically is community or marital property, as the earnings would have been. Joint property is titled jointly, as discussed above. Community or marital property (the latter being the term separate property states use for property deemed divisible on divorce), generally is defined as including all property not designated by law as separate or joint property. One significant difference between states—community and separate property—concerns the classification of post-marriage income from a spouse's separate property. The majority of community property states consider such earnings separate property, in contrast to Texas and Louisiana which consider them community property. In defining marital property on divorce, the common law property states also have split on this issue. A further distinction is made in a few states (and by UMPA § 4(d) and (g)(3)) between (1) income on and (2) appreciation of separate property. "Income" becomes community or marital property and "appreciation" stays separate. *Caveat*: In classifying an item as income or appreciation, the courts will *not* necessarily look to federal income tax definitions of "interest," "dividends" or "capital gains."

2) Management and Control
A spouse's right to manage and control community property varies among the community property regimes. Several models have emerged:

a) Louisiana
A Louisiana statute gave the husband exclusive control over the disposition of property jointly owned with his wife. This statute was struck down in *Kirchberg v. Feenstra,* 450 U.S. 455, 101 S.Ct. 1195, 67 L.Ed.2d 428 (1981). In *Kirchberg,* H had executed a mortgage on a house he owned jointly with W as security for a promissory note. Under the statute, W was not required to be informed and, in fact, she was not informed. W learned about the mortgage when the mortgagee threatened to foreclose if W did not pay off the outstanding balance on H's promissory note. W did not pay and the attorney foreclosed on the mortgage. The U.S. Supreme Court held that the statute imposed gender-based discrimination and was in violation of the Equal Protection Clause.

b) Texas
Under the Texas model, each spouse has sole management and control of the community property that he or she would have owned if single. Any community property that is commingled, however, becomes subject to the joint management and control of the spouses, unless the spouses provide otherwise.

c) Equal Management and Control
With certain important restrictions, California and Arizona allow each spouse, equally and independently, to manage and even dispose of community property.

d) Modified Joint Control
In several community property states, both spouses must consent to community property transactions in excess of a statutory limit. Remedies such as restitution and temporary restraining orders are available if one spouse transfers or attempts to transfer community property without the other's consent.

e) Relative Merits of These Models
Under the Texas model, the non-earning spouse's situation *during* marriage does not differ materially from that of the non-earning spouse in separate property states. The equal management model better protects the non-earning spouse, but has the disadvantage that one

spouse might spitefully or unwisely dissipate community assets. A modified joint control model sets limits for one-party autonomy.

c. Community Property on Death
At the death of a spouse, one-half of the community property passes by his or her will or, if no will exists, by the law of intestacy.

1) No Election Against a Spouse's Will
In community property states, the surviving spouse already owns his or her half of the community property upon the other's death. In view of that provision, community property states do not allow a dissatisfied spouse to elect a further share against a decedent spouse's disposition by will of his or her one-half interest in community property or all of his or her separate property.

2) Intestacy
Except for the absence of a right to elect against a spouse's will (which is compensated by the surviving spouse's ownership of one-half of the community property upon the partner's death), the intestate succession laws in community property states are similar to those in separate property jurisdictions.

The intestate regime recommended by UPC § 2–102A for adoption in community property states tracks the provision for separate property quoted above (p. 114) and adds: "as to community property (i) the one-half of community property which belongs to the decedent passes to the [surviving spouse]."

d. Presumptions
In community property states, presumptions may help classify property acquired by spouses as joint tenants or in separate names.

Example: H appealed from a judgment that determined H's and W's ownership interests in their residence and in a motor home. Both items had been purchased with a combination of community and separate funds. The home was held in joint tenancy and the motor home title was in W's name. (Result: Residence is community property and motor home is W's separate property. Where the only findings were that neither party intended a gift to the other, the joint tenancy title makes the residence community property. Where H was aware of W's sole title and did not object, there was evidence that H intended a gift of his community interest in the motor home to W.) *Lucas v. Lucas,* 166 Cal.Rptr. 853, 27 Cal.3d 808, 614 P.2d 285 (1980).

5. MARITAL PROPERTY AND THE CONFLICTS OF LAWS
a. The Problem
H and W live in state X, a separate property state. H owns land in X, and W is protected by her right to elect against H's will and/or inchoate dower rights. H

sells the land, W releases her rights of dower and they move to state Y, a community property state, where H reinvests the proceeds in securities in his name. H dies, leaving nothing to W in his will. W has now lost the protection of the law of state X (dower and the right to elect against H's will), and receives no protection from state Y, because the proceeds used to buy the securities were H's separate funds. A similar scenario may be imagined upon divorce where there would be no community property to divide. See R. Weintraub, Conflict of Laws 441 et seq. (3d ed. 1986) and P. Hay, Conflict of Laws 118–21 (West's Blackletter 2d ed. 1994). The reverse scenario obtains when spouses move from a community property state to a separate property state: On one spouse's death, is the other entitled to a forced share in the decedent's half of the community property they brought along?

b. The Solution

The Uniform Disposition of Community Property at Death Act, enacted in about a dozen (of 41) separate property states, does *not* allow the surviving spouse elective share rights in the decedent's half of community property.

Several community property states have enacted remedial statutes that, in essence, eliminate unfair results by treating property (regardless of its technical classification) in accordance with the attributes it had where it was acquired. Such reclassified property is referred to as "quasi-community property." Statutes differ in detail, some apply only on death, some on divorce and others on both occasions. (See p. 165).

C. TORTS AND THE FAMILY

1. TORTS BETWEEN SPOUSES

Traditionally, one spouse could not maintain a tort action against the other. At first the Married Women's Property Act carried this immunity forward; today the immunity has been almost wholly eliminated by legislation or in the courts, usually with no distinction made between intentional and negligent torts.

a. Justification for Interspousal Immunity

The fact that the common law gave the husband control over his wife's property and disabled the wife from suing in her own name supported interspousal tort immunity: Any recovery against H on W's behalf would be paid out of H's right pocket into his left, quite aside from H having to sue himself! Later, the argument was that the tort immunity helps preserve the peace and harmony of the home and, still later, that it prevents possible collusion to collect on liability insurance. Abrogating the doctrine, *Beaudette v. Frana*, 285 Minn. 366, 173 N.W.2d 416 (1969), nevertheless cautioned: "Interspousal immunity * * * has been * * * firmly rooted in the common law, both historically and ideologically, based upon the unique unity of a husband and wife within the marriage relationship. * * * Collusion in making spurious claims is an undeniable temptation where a member of the family is insured."

Unwilling to abolish the immunity completely, some courts had for some time refused to apply the defense when the family harmony and collusion arguments did not apply. To illustrate, courts refused to allow immunity when the spouse was dead at the hands (or car) of the other, and the action was for wrongful death, or after the marriage had otherwise terminated.

b.   Reintroducing "Fault" into Divorce Settlements?
The abolition of interspousal tort immunity has been criticized for its potential for bringing fault issues back into divorce settlements.

Examples: (1) During their marriage, H berated W in public and in private. H had screamed at her because she could not drive a boat, slammed a door so hard it gouged a hole in the wall, threw a cup of coffee at the wall, and pulled food from the refrigerator onto the floor. He never physically abused her, although H once sprayed beer on W. H tightly limited the money he permitted W to spend. When he (accurately) suspected that W has having an affair, he angrily confronted W and her lover. When he thought she was drinking too much, he went through her garbage looking for evidence. In the divorce action, W sought damages for H's intentional infliction of emotional distress and the jury awarded W $362,000 in distress damages. H appealed. (Result: Award upheld. "[I]n a divorce proceeding a spouse may recover for intentional (but not negligent) infliction of emotional distress.") *Massey v. Massey,* 867 S.W.2d 766 (Tex.1993).

(2) After 10 years of marriage, H and W separated and H filed to dissolve the marriage. W countered alleging intentional infliction of emotional distress. The trial court found that during the marriage, H had assaulted and battered W, had insulted and screamed at her at home and in the presence of others, had once locked W out of the residence overnight in winter when she wore nothing but a robe, had made repeated demeaning remarks about W's sexuality, and had refused to allow W to pursue schooling and hobbies. The trial court also found that W had been legally incompetent during the last 4 years of the marriage, and medical experts agreed that W was temporarily emotionally disabled at the time of the hearing. The trial court awarded damages to W. H appealed. (Result: Reversed. W's claim can be disposed of summarily, because H's "insults and outbursts" fail to meet the legal standard of outrageousness. The court reasoned: "Conduct intentionally or recklessly causing emotional distress to one's spouse is prevalent in our society. This is unfortunate but perhaps not surprising, given the length and intensity of the marital relationship. * * * Not only should intramarital activity ordinarily not be the basis for tort liability, it should also be protected against disclosure in tort litigation. Although the spouse who raises a claim has no right to complain of the exposure

of matters relevant to the claim, the courts must be sensitive to the privacy interests of the defending spouse. Any litigation of a claim is certain to require exposure of the intimacies of married life. This feature of the tort distinguishes it from intramarital torts already recognized in New Mexico. For example, a suit by one spouse against the other arising out of an automobile accident poses no such risk. Nor does one ordinarily think of exposure of an incident of battery as implicating legitimate privacy interests. * * * A cautious approach to the tort of intramarital outrage also finds support in the public policy of New Mexico to avoid inquiry into what went wrong in a marriage. * * * [I]n determining when the tort of outrage should be recognized in the marital setting, the threshold of outrageousness should be set high enough—or the circumstances in which the tort is recognized should be described precisely enough, *e.g.*, child snatching, that the social good from recognizing the tort will not be outweighed by unseemly and invasive litigation of meritless claims.") *Hakkila v. Hakkila*, 112 N.M. 172, 812 P.2d 1320 (N.M.App.1991).

c. Arguments Against Immunity

Rejecting the family harmony argument, courts reason that (1) a personal injury action is not likely to disrupt family peace more than a property or contract action that now is universally allowed; (2) one spouse being willing to sue the other signals such a lack of "harmony" that to disallow the action would hardly mend the rift; (3) if insurance is present, a judgment against a spouse will have no impact on intra-family peace, since outside (insurance) money will compensate for the injury; (4) although the presence of insurance offers opportunity for fraud and collusion, courts and juries provide adequate protection.

Example: H allegedly assaulted and battered W. W sued H to recover for her injuries. The trial court dismissed W's complaint. W appealed. (Result: Doctrine of interspousal tort immunity is abrogated. "A survey of all states and the District of Columbia reveals that at present 31 states have fully abrogated the doctrine of interspousal immunity. Eight states have abrogated the rule for vehicular torts, four states have abrogated the rule for intentional torts; one state for all personal injury actions; and one state where death of either spouse intervenes between tortuous [sic] act and commencement of suit. One state has immunity imposed by statute while five states plus the District of Columbia continue to acknowledge and sustain the doctrine. One state has a cause of action but no remedy to enforce it. * * * The idea that maintenance of interspousal immunity will promote the public interest in domestic tranquillity is wholly illusory. If one spouse commits against the other an act which, but for the immunity, would constitute a tort, the desired state of matrimonial tranquillity is necessarily destroyed. But common sense suggests the peace is destroyed by the act of the offending spouse, not the lawsuit filed by the other. Beyond that, maintenance of the immunity surely cannot prevent injured spouses from harboring ill will and anger. Seen in this light, our traditional rule of interspousal immunity appears incapable of achieving the end claimed for it. Instead it leaves injured spouses without adequate or complete remedies. It is also noted that remedies incident to divorce and criminal prosecution are not adequate of the protection sought in this type of intentional tort.") *Burns v. Burns,* 518 So.2d 1205 (Miss.1988).

d. Is the Immunity Unconstitutional?

Moran v. Beyer, 734 F.2d 1245 (7th Cir.1984), held that the interspousal tort immunity denies the spouses equal protection.

e. Intentional and Negligent Torts Distinguished

In terms of the interspousal immunity, somewhat different policy arguments apply to intentional and negligent interspousal torts. Some jurisdictions continue to make such a distinction.

> ***Example:*** After separation, H and W developed a contentious relationship concerning the custody of their child. H succeeded in having W involuntarily committed for one day for mental illness. W sued H for malicious prosecution, false imprisonment, and abuse of process. Based on the interspousal immunity doctrine, the trial court granted summary judgment for H. (Result: For H. The Supreme Court of Florida held: "[T]he protection of the family unit and family resources, including the needs of minor children, merits a continuation of the interspousal immunity doctrine for intentional torts. In reaffirming the doctrine, we have taken into consideration and emphasize the authority of the trial judge in a dissolution proceeding to direct the offending spouse to pay the necessary medical expenses not covered by insurance and the judge's authority to consider any permanent injury, disfigurement, or loss of earning capacity caused by an intentional tort in establishing appropriate alimony * * *.") *Hill v. Hill,* 415 So.2d 20 (1982).

2. RECOVERY FOR LOSS OF CONSORTIUM

At common law, a husband could recover for loss of his wife's consortium (companionship and services) caused by injury to her. Today, the cause of action generally is available to both spouses. The cause of action has *not* been extended to cohabitants—even in California, the home of the *Marvin* doctrine. *Elden v. Sheldon,* 46 Cal.3d 267, 250 Cal.Rptr. 254, 758 P.2d 582 (Cal.1988).

> ***Example:*** H was seriously injured at work when a 600 pound pipe fell and struck his head, causing "severe spinal cord damage which left him totally paralyzed in both legs, totally paralyzed in his body below the midpoint

of the chest, and partially paralyzed in one of his arms." H was unable to care for himself, and W quit her job to devote her full energies to him. H and W filed suit against H's employer for H's physical injuries as well as for the consequences to W. The lower court denied W's cause of action and W appealed. (Result: Reversed. "We * * * declare that * * * each spouse has a cause of action for loss of consortium * * * caused by a negligent or intentional injury to the other spouse by a third party.") *Rodriguez v. Bethlehem Steel Corp.,* 12 Cal.3d 382, 115 Cal.Rptr. 765, 525 P.2d 669 (1974). *Caveat:* A few courts have used the sex discrimination argument to *deny* recovery to both the husband and the wife.

3. TORTIOUS INTERFERENCE WITH FAMILY RELATIONSHIPS ("HEARTBALM ACTIONS")

Although declining in number, numerous states still recognize tort actions for wrongful interference with family relations, collectively known as heartbalm actions.

a. Breach of Promise to Marry

1) Proof

Short of a formal engagement, difficulty in proving the existence of an express promise to marry has led courts to imply an agreement to marry from circumstances indicating such promises. Evidence may include the gift of an (engagement?) ring, activities undertaken together, expressions of affection, preparations for a wedding, and any other relevant circumstances.

2) Tort Action

Breach of promise to marry is in tort, not contract. This is particularly relevant in determining damages, especially punitive damages.

3) Damages

In a breach of promise action, the plaintiff may seek actual financial damages, such as the cost of a wedding dress, relinquishment of a job and the like, as well as recovery for injury to feelings, health and reputation. An Illinois statute limits recovery to *actual* damages. Other states exclude recovery for loss of expected benefits, such as social and financial position. Since these injuries "to the heart" are incapable of precise measurement, awards of damages are unpredictable and sometimes may seem excessive. Beyond that, if the defendant is shown to have acted maliciously, punitive damages may be awarded. Of late, heartbalm awards have been more readily reversed or reduced on appeal than have other tort awards.

Examples: (1) During their courtship, D told P that he was worth over $2 million, that he planned to retire in two years after which they would travel, that P would never have to work again, and that D would support P's children. After their engagement, P placed her house for sale, sold most of the furniture, reserved a church, engaged a minister, ordered a wedding dress and a dress for the matron of honor, and arranged the reception. Two months after the engagement, D broke it off. This caused P medical problems, expense in ordering new furniture, and considerable embarrassment. P sought damages to compensate for these losses and to compensate for her loss of expected security. (Result: For P on direct damages, against P on loss of expectancies. "[W]e have decided that the breach-of-promise-to-marry action should be retained as a quasi-contract, quasi-tort action for the recovery of the foreseeable special and general damages which are caused by a defendant's breach of promise to marry. However, the action is modified to the extent that a plaintiff cannot recover for loss of expected financial and social position, because marriage is no longer considered to be a property transaction.") *Stanard v. Bolin,* 88 Wash.2d 614, 565 P.2d 94 (1977).

(2) P, a Chicago attorney, and D, an Oregon cattle rancher, met in January of 1992 and became engaged in March of 1992. D began having second thoughts, and broke off the engagement in April of 1992. P sued D under the Illinois Breach of Promise Act. A jury awarded P $178,000 ($25,000 for past and future medical costs, $93,000 for pain and suffering, and $60,000 for lost business profits). The court remitted the award to $118,000, concluding that the lost business profits were not attributable to the broken engagement. D appealed. (Result: Award reversed on the technical point that P had failed to provide the date of the engagement in the notice of intent to sue. "Because the fact of the engagement was not in issue in this case, Sharon insists that her omission of the engagement date was insignificant. This argument overlooks the fact that the date of the engagement may be important for reasons other than determining whether or not a defendant proposed. Here, for instance, the date of the engagement was potentially dispositive. An admission concerning the date of the engagement would have unequivocally established the place of the engagement—a fact that was quite important for reasons noted in our choice-of-law analysis.") *Wildey v. Springs,* 47 F.3d 1475 (7th Cir.1995).

b. Criminal Conversation

The common law tort of "criminal conversation" allows a spouse to recover damages against a third party for adulterous conduct with the plaintiff's spouse.

1) Elements of Cause of Action

To prosecute an action for criminal conversation successfully, the plaintiff must only prove sexual intercourse between the defendant and his or her spouse. The plaintiff does not have to prove that defendant was aware of the spouse's marital status. Actionable sexual intercourse includes rape. Damages are presumed.

> ***Example:*** H brought a criminal conversation action against D. D admitted that he had had sexual relations with W while H and W were married. Based on D's admission, the lower court granted judgment for H. D appealed. (Result: The Supreme Court of Pennsylvania abolished the tort of criminal conversation, holding that in today's society it is unreasonable to impose such harsh results upon a defendant without looking to the role of the plaintiff's spouse and the quality of the plaintiff's marriage. "[T]he Court in 1959 * * * laudably rejected the fictitious notion that a wife, like a servant, was the personal property (chattel as it were) of the husband and that an action in criminal conversation was a right sacrosanct to none but the master. Still, the Court's extension to married women of the right to bring such a cause of action only delayed what today demands; that is, the total abolition of a pious yet unrighteous cause of action.") *Fadgen v. Lenkner,* 469 Pa. 272, 365 A.2d 147 (1976).

2) Defenses
Traditionally, the only defense available to the defendant is proof of the *plaintiff's* consent. It is not a defense that the plaintiff's spouse consented or was the aggressor or seducer.

c. Alienation of Affections
1) Elements of Cause of Action
The tort of "alienation of affections" allows a spouse to recover for a third party's conduct that has caused the plaintiff's spouse to transfer his or her affections to another, not necessarily to the defendant. Most states have abolished the cause of action, and many have restricted it.

> ***Example:*** H developed a sexual relationship with D. H moved out of the marital home and W filed for divorce. One day before the divorce was granted, W filed a civil complaint against D, alleging alienation of affections. A jury awarded W $10,000, and the appellate court affirmed. D moved for review whether the cause of action for alienation of affections should be abolished. (Result: Reversed. "We conclude that the tort of intentional interference with the marital relation should be abolished because foundation of this action is based on the misperception that spousal affection is capable of theft by a third party.") *Hoye v. Hoye,* 824 S.W.2d 422 (Ky.1992).

2) Criminal Conversation and Alienation of Affections Distinguished
The tort action of "criminal conversation" allows recovery for the defendant's wrongful interference with the plaintiff's right to an exclusive

sexual relationship with his or her spouse. Traditionally, proof of actual loss of affection or marital breakup was *not* required. By contrast, "alienation of affections" allows recovery for the defendant's wrongful interference with the spouse's emotions. Sexual intercourse is not a prerequisite, although it may be an element of proof and may aggravate damages.

d. Modern Treatment of Heartbalm Actions

In most states, heartbalm actions have been abolished or limited. The preamble to an Illinois statute that limits recovery to actual damages sums up the case against heartbalm actions:

"[T]he remedy heretofore provided by law for the enforcement of the action for criminal conversation has been subjected to grave abuses and has been used as an instrument for blackmail by unscrupulous persons for their unjust enrichment, due to the indefiniteness of the damages recoverable in such actions and the consequent fear of persons threatened with such actions that exorbitant damages might be assessed against them. * * * [T]he award of monetary damages in such actions is ineffective as a recompense for genuine mental or emotional distress." 740 ILCS 50/1.

The ingenuity of lawyers has sought to revive heartbalm actions in many disguises. Some "cohabitation cases" fit into this context. Modern "retreads" also may include cases seeking damages for the infection of a sexual partner with venereal disease, or for intentional infliction of emotional distress, or for certain types of "professional malpractice."

Examples: (1) W had an affair with D, who supervised both H and W at work. D arranged for W to accompany him on business trips. H learned of the affair and suffered from severe depression, requiring hospitalization and counseling. H sued D for intentional infliction of emotional distress, but his claim was dismissed. H appealed. (Result: No cause of action. Nothing in H's allegations distinguished his claims from those of alienation of affections or criminal conversation, both of which were abolished by statute.) *Speer v. Dealy*, 242 Neb. 542, 495 N.W.2d 911 (Neb.1993).

(2) H and W began marriage counseling with D, a licensed psychologist. Most sessions were joint, but on some occasions D met only with W. A sexual relationship developed between D and W. In counseling sessions, D advised H to be distant from W and not to engage in sexual contact with her. On D's advice, H ultimately separated from W. H's suit against D for intentional infliction of emotional distress and professional negligence was dismissed. H appealed. (Held: The gravamen of P's claims was not merely the sexual act or the alienation of his wife's affections. Instead, it was the entire course of conduct engaged in by his *therapist*, D. Therefore H's claims

were not barred by the abolition of actions for criminal
conversation and alienation of affections.) *Figueiredo-Torres
v. Nickel*, 321 Md. 642, 584 A.2d 69 (Md.1991).

D. MARRIAGE AND CRIMINAL LAW

1. IMMUNITIES

Immunities traditionally granted to spouses (or more usually wives) served to bar
criminal prosecutions in certain circumstances, particularly when the charge
involved conspiracy or alleged that the wife was an accessory in her husband's
crime.   Modern reality has supplanted the common law, and the trend is to abolish
criminal immunities: "[E]ven when a husband and wife conspire only between
themselves, they cannot claim immunity from prosecution for conspiracy on the
basis of their marital status." *People v. Pierce,* 61 Cal.2d 879, 40 Cal.Rptr. 845, 395
P.2d 893 (1964).

2. TESTIMONIAL PRIVILEGE

The common law disqualified a person from testifying against his or her spouse.
This rule has undergone substantial modification.   In the context of a federal
prosecution, the U.S. Supreme Court held: "[T]he witness-spouse alone has a
privilege to refuse to testify adversely; the witness may be neither compelled to
testify nor foreclosed from testifying."   Information "privately disclosed between
husband and wife in the confidence of the marital relationship" remains protected.
Trammel v. United States, 445 U.S. 40, 100 S.Ct. 906, 63 L.Ed.2d 186 (1980).   The
testimonial privilege has no application in cases of spousal or child abuse.

3. RAPE

At common law and under typical criminal statutes, a husband could not be guilty
of rape of his wife.   Instead, if force was used, the act was punishable as a criminal
assault.   A 17th century English treatise (1 Hale, History of the Pleas of the Crown
629) stated the rule and rationale: "But the husband cannot be guilty of a rape
committed by himself upon his lawful wife, for by their mutual matrimonial
consent and contract the wife hath given up herself in this kind unto her husband,
which she cannot retract."   Today, few states continue exemptions or exceptions
for marital rape.   Most states allow criminal prosecution of a husband for the rape
of his wife, with varying emphasis on the question whether the spouses were living
together or were separated at the time of the incident.

Examples: (1) H broke into the apartment of his estranged W and raped her. At
that time, they had been legally married for seven years and had lived
separately for one year. H was charged with and convicted of rape.
(Result: Conviction upheld. "A man separated from his wife—and
perhaps one not separated—could not invoke an outdated and

doubtful rule to avoid prosecution for rape simply because he was still legally married to his victim.") *State v. Smith,* 85 N.J. 193, 426 A.2d 38 (1981).

(2) H and W were living apart pursuant to a family court order of protection. In the presence of their 2–year-old son, H forcibly raped and sodomized W. (Result: H's conviction upheld. The Court of Appeals of New York held the "marital exemption" from the criminal rape statute unconstitutional. "We find that there is no rational basis for distinguishing between marital rape and nonmarital rape. The various rationales which have been asserted in defense of the exemption are either based upon archaic notions about the consent and property rights incident to marriage or are simply unable to withstand even the slightest scrutiny. We therefore declare the marital exemption for rape in the New York statute to be unconstitutional.") *People v. Liberta,* 64 N.Y.2d 152, 485 N.Y.S.2d 207, 474 N.E.2d 567 (1984).

4. MARITAL VIOLENCE
Traditionally, the law has been reluctant to intervene in domestic matters. Recently, many states have addressed the significant incidence of domestic violence by specific legislation and by instituting programs to aid victims.

a. Order of Protection and "No Contact" Orders
Orders of "protection" or "no contact" orders now are widely available. The key element of this new remedy is that may cover a potentially very wide list of conduct that in itself would not (necessarily) amount to a crime or even a tort. A *criminal* contempt citation follows a violation. *Caveat:* A conviction for criminal contempt (with possibly lesser sanction) may bar a later criminal protection for the same act. *United States v. Foster/Dixon*, 509 U.S. 688, 113 S.Ct. 2849, 125 L.Ed.2d 556 (1993).

b. Police Protection
In the absence of very special circumstances, the police are not liable for failure to protect one spouse from the other.

Example: W and H were separated. W had obtained a permanent order of protection because H had punched and threatened to kill her. W notified the local police department that H had attempted to run her car off the road, again had threatened to kill her, and had purchased a gun. Upon recommendation by the police, W recorded H's threats and delivered a tape to the police. The police took no action. H was arrested for attempting to break into W's apartment but was released on bail. During his arrest, he had asked for several friends who were police officers. After H's release, W again called the police and requested action based on the tapes, but the police took no action. Less than a week after his release, H shot into W's car and killed their son. W brought civil rights and negligence claims against the municipality (D). The civil rights claims were dismissed, but a jury awarded $250,000 for the son's wrongful death. D appealed. (Result: Evidence sufficient to establish a special relationship, imposing a duty on D to provide police protection. "Generally, a municipality is not liable under New York law for failing to provide an individual with police protection. '[I]n order for liability to be imposed upon a municipality . . . there must be proof of a "special relationship" between that person and the municipality.' The 'special duty' imposed by that relationship is recognized only in a 'narrow class of cases.' The reason for limiting this exception is that a municipality's duty to provide police protection is owed to the public at large rather than to any individual or class of citizens, and questions of resource allocation, such as how much protection a municipality must provide to an individual or class, are left to the discretion of the municipal policy makers. The elements of the special relationship are (1) an assumption by the municipality, through promises or actions, of an affirmative duty to act on behalf of the party who was injured; (2) knowledge on the part of the municipality's agents that inaction could lead to harm; (3) some form of direct contact between the municipality's agents and the injured party; and (4) that party's justifiable reliance on the municipality's affirmative undertaking. Once the special relationship is found to exist between the municipality and the injured person, the actions of the municipality's agents will be subject to a reasonableness standard.") *Raucci v. Town of Rotterdam*, 902 F.2d 1050 (2d Cir.1990).

5. THE "BATTERED WIFE SYNDROME"

The existence of a battered wife syndrome has been asserted to defend a wife who has retaliated against an abusive husband. This defense differs from the usual definition of self-defense in that the threat is not immediate. The theory underlying the syndrome is "that it is not unusual for a battered woman who has been abused over a long period of time to remain in such a situation, that a battered woman's self-respect is usually very low and she believes she is a worthless person, that a battered woman typically believes that the man is not going to repeat the abuse when he promises not to do it again, that the battered woman becomes increasingly afraid for her own well-being, and that the primary emotion of a battered woman is fear." *Smith v. State,* 247 Ga. 612, 277 S.E.2d 678 (1981). Not all courts admit psychiatric or other expert testimony on this syndrome, but some states have passed statutes defining and favoring the defense.

Examples: (1) During the seven years that H and W were married, H had periodically attacked W. When W fatally stabbed H with a pair of scissors, W claimed that H had attacked her on the same afternoon. At her trial, W claimed that she had acted in self-defense. The trial court ruled that expert testimony about the battered women's syndrome was inadmissible. W appealed from her conviction. (Result: Reversed and remanded for new trial. "[T]he battered woman's syndrome has a sufficient scientific basis to produce uniform and reasonably reliable results.") *State v. Kelly*, 97 N.J. 178, 478 A.2d 364 (1984).

(2) During a 15–year marriage, W was repeated abused by H. H had kicked W until she required hospitalization, held a shotgun to her head and threatened to kill her, and beat her with a baseball bat. Allegedly H also sexually abused W's 12–year-old daughter from a previous marriage. When H ordered W to kill and bury her daughter W filed for divorce and voluntarily left H for the first time. Shortly thereafter, W was hospitalized following an overdose of psychiatric medication and agreed to move back in with H. On the evening of her return, H insinuated that he planned to take W's life. When H had fallen asleep, W shot and killed H. The judge instructed the jury on self-defense, and W was found not guilty. (Result: The self-defense instruction was erroneous. A battered woman cannot reasonably fear imminent life-threatening danger from her sleeping spouse. "Where self-defense is asserted, evidence of the deceased's long-term cruelty and violence towards the defendant is admissible. In cases involving battered spouses, expert evidence of the battered woman syndrome is relevant to the determination of the reasonableness of the defendant's perception of danger. Other courts which have allowed such evidence to be introduced include those in Florida, Georgia, Illinois, Maine, New Jersey, New York, Pennsylvania, Washington, and Wisconsin. However, no jurisdictions have held that the existence of the battered woman syndrome in and of itself operates as a defense to murder. In order to instruct a jury on self-defense, there must be some showing of an imminent threat or a confrontational circumstance involving an overt act by an aggressor. There is no exception to this requirement where the defendant has suffered long-term domestic abuse and the victim is the abuser. In such cases, the issue is not whether the defendant believes homicide is the solution to past or future problems with the batterer, but rather whether circumstances surrounding the killing were sufficient to create a reasonable belief in the defendant that the use of deadly force was necessary.") *State v. Stewart*, 243 Kan. 639, 763 P.2d 572 (Kan.1988).

E. FAMILY NAMES

1. HUSBAND AND WIFE

Tradition, custom and common understanding to the contrary, the Wisconsin Supreme Court found that the common law has never *required* a married woman to adopt the surname of her husband. Instead, she acquires the husband's name by express choice or usage. On divorce, a wife who has assumed her husband's surname may request the court to legally restore her original surname.

Example: W had never used H's surname as her own. Her employer insisted that, for group insurance purposes, she either use H's surname or "legally" change her surname back to her maiden name. When W petitioned the court for a name change, the trial court refused her request on the basis of "well settled * * * common-law principles and immemorial custom that a woman upon marriage abandons her maiden name and assumes the husband's surname." W appealed. (Result: Reversed. "[W] was never compelled to change her name, nor did she ever in fact adopt the surname [of H] by usage.") *Kruzel v. Podell,* 67 Wis.2d 138, 226 N.W.2d 458 (1975).

2. CHILD

Traditionally, the child of a marriage has taken the husband's surname. This is no longer assumed. Many courts have held that parents have the right to give their child any surname they wish, whether that is the name of either or both parents or a hybrid or combination name. On divorce or remarriage, litigation over a child's name often results when a mother having custody of a child who bears the father's name wishes to change the child's name to her own maiden name or to her new married name. Few courts still think in terms of the husband's common law right to have his child bear his surname. Instead, they look to the child's best interests when deciding such cases.

Examples: (1) H and W sued after the state refused to let them give their son the surname of "Jebef," which was a contracted combination of their surnames. The state would have allowed them to use either H's last name or a hyphenated combination of both of their last names. (Result: For Jebef. "Plaintiffs have a constitutionally protected right to give their own child any surname they choose.") *Jech v. Burch,* 466 F.Supp. 714 (D.C.Hawaii 1979).

(2) H and W separated when W was four months pregnant. When their child (C) was born, W registered C's name on the birth certificate under her maiden name. The divorce decree awarded custody of C to W, but ruled that W must change C's surname to that of H. W appealed. (Result: Reversed. "[W] had the right to a determination of surname, based on the legal standard of the child's best interest.") *In re Marriage of Schiffman,* 28 Cal.3d 640, 169 Cal.Rptr. 918, 620 P.2d 579 (1980).

F. REVIEW QUESTIONS

1. **T or F** Statutes that hold only the husband liable for alimony have withstood constitutional challenge. The reasoning is that the reasonable and legitimate

purpose of such statutes is to compensate women for past discrimination and to adjust for the current economic reality that wives, as a class, are far more often economically dependent on their husbands than husbands are dependent on their wives.

2. **T or F** On a "no-returns" sale, W bought a dining room set. H has returned the set to the store and refuses to pay for it. W has no funds. The creditor's best course of action is to seek payment from H under the "necessaries" doctrine.

Questions 3 through 6 should be answered on the assumption that H and W are married and live in a separate property state.

3. **T or F** Property owned by each spouse *prior* to marriage is their separate property, while property acquired *during* marriage belongs to both.

4. **T or F** If H and W divorce, their separate property is not subject to being distributed to the other spouse.

5. **T or F** H and W can take title to property as tenants by the entirety, but not by tenancy in common or as joint tenants.

6. **T or F** By making lifetime transfers of her property, W can assure that H inherits none of her separate property, including savings from her earnings during the marriage.

7–9. Questions 7 through 9 should be answered on the assumption that H and W are married and live in a community property state.

7. **T or F** Separate property is limited to what each spouse acquired *prior* to marriage; community property is everything acquired by either spouse *after* marriage from any source, including earnings.

8. **T or F** The amount of control H has over the portion of community property earned by him varies, depending on the specific community property state in which the parties reside.

9. **T or F** If W dies, her will only can distribute her separate property, because the community property automatically passes to the survivor.

10. **T or F** So-called "heartbalm" actions have been abolished universally, because of the difficulty of proof, the uncertainty of damages, the possibility of blackmail, and/or the notion that—in our liberated society—these "torts" are outdated.

11. **T or F** In a criminal prosecution, one spouse may testify against the other only if the defendant spouse consents.

12. **T or F** Neither a wife nor her children are required to take the husband's surname.

13. **T or F** Courts will intervene in an ongoing marriage to ensure that a financially dependent spouse receives suitable maintenance and support.

14. **T** **or** **F** All of the community property states derive their property regime from civil law sources.

15. **T** **or** **F** Many states have extended recovery for loss of consortium to cohabitants.

16. **T** **or** **F** Most states have abolished the traditional exemption for marital (spousal) rape.

17. **T** **or** **F** H and W are married and live in a separate property state. W gives H a house during their marriage. If they should divorce, the gift is H's separate property.

18. **T** **or** **F** H and W are married and live in a separate property state. If the recent Uniform Probate Code revisions are in effect when H dies with a will disinheriting W, the amount of W's statutory forced share will depend on how long W and H were married.

V

DIVORCE—STATUS ISSUES

Analysis

A. ACCESS TO AND JURISDICTION OF COURTS

1. RESIDENCY REQUIREMENTS

State statutes conferring jurisdiction over divorce actions typically require the plaintiff to have been a resident of the state for a specified period of time prior to commencement of the divorce action, such as 90 days or a year.

Example: UMDA § 302 provides that a court has jurisdiction over the action if *either party* was domiciled in the state for 90 days prior to commencement of the divorce action.

a. Constitutionality of Residency Requirement

The Supreme Court has upheld Iowa's one year residence requirement against a challenge that the statute violated the divorce seeker's constitutional right to interstate travel and due process. A state has sufficient interest in the incidents of marriage to require persons seeking divorce to show "attachment to the state." Iowa's reasonable (one year) residency requirement is justified by the state interest in avoiding interference with the interest of other states in their residents' marital status and in having its own decrees respected elsewhere, *i.e.,* avoiding the increased risk that divorce decrees not based on adequate jurisdictional facts may be subject to collateral attack in other states. *Sosna v. Iowa,* 419 U.S. 393, 95 S.Ct. 553, 42 L.Ed.2d 532 (1975). (*Cf. Shapiro v. Thompson,* 394 U.S. 618, 89 S.Ct. 1322, 22 L.Ed.2d 600 (1969) the interstate-travel/welfare-eligibility case, and *Boddie v. Connecticut,* 401 U.S. 371, 91 S.Ct. 780, 28 L.Ed.2d 113 (1971), the no-fee-for-indigent's-divorce decision).

2. PERSONAL JURISDICTION
a. Full Faith and Credit
1) *Ex parte* Divorce

If plaintiff is a domiciliary of the state, a state court may grant him or her a divorce decree whether or not there is personal jurisdiction over the defendant. A divorce decree thus obtained is valid in the state issued and is entitled to Full Faith and Credit in other states. *Williams v. North Carolina,* 317 U.S. 287, 63 S.Ct. 207, 87 L.Ed. 279 (1942)("Williams I"); *Williams v. North Carolina,* 325 U.S. 226, 65 S.Ct. 1092, 89 L.Ed. 1577 (1945)("Williams II"). The full faith and credit effect of an *ex parte* decree, however, does not extend to the incidents of divorce, especially financial dispositions. *Estin v. Estin,* 334 U.S. 541, 68 S.Ct. 1213, 92 L.Ed. 1561 (1948); *Vanderbilt v. Vanderbilt,* 354 U.S. 416, 77 S.Ct. 1360, 1 L.Ed.2d 1456 (1957).

2) Rule in *Sherrer*

If plaintiff and defendant made personal appearances and thus were subject to the court's jurisdiction and had an opportunity to contest the issue of the plaintiff's domicile, neither party may later collaterally attack the decree on the ground that the court lacked jurisdiction. The effect of a "migratory" decree thus obtained extends to all matters properly adjudicated, *including incidents of divorce. Sherrer v. Sherrer,* 334 U.S. 343, 68 S.Ct. 1087, 92 L.Ed. 1429 (1948). The effect of such a decree may extend to third parties, such as children (*Johnson v. Muelberger,* 340 U.S. 581, 71 S.Ct. 474, 95 L.Ed. 552 (1951)) or a second spouse (*Cook v. Cook,* 342 U.S. 126, 72 S.Ct. 157, 96 L.Ed. 146 (1951)).

b. Comity

Recognition of a divorce decree obtained in a foreign, non-U.S. jurisdiction is not constitutionally compelled. However, unless an important state policy is violated (for instance, the divorcing parties are domiciliaries of the state and could not have obtained their divorce locally) such decrees will ordinarily be recognized and enforced on the basis of comity.

c. Federal Jurisdiction Over Divorce Actions

Under specific legislation, federal courts exercise jurisdiction over certain matters ancillary to domestic relations disputes, such as interstate child custody and child support enforcement. Despite the theoretical applicability of diversity jurisdiction to domestic relations actions in which the spouses are citizens of different states and the amount in controversy meets the federal standard, federal courts—following century-old dicta—decline to take jurisdiction over domestic relations matters. For a time, some federal courts tended to discount the traditional rule, though most continued to refuse to involve themselves in any family law matters. In 1992, the U.S. Supreme Court reaffirmed the continued existence of the abstention rule. *Ankenbrandt v. Richards,* 504 U.S. 689, 112 S.Ct. 2206, 119 L.Ed.2d 468 (1992).

3. "LONG–ARM" JURISDICTION
a. Divorce

Many state "long-arm statutes" contain provisions subjecting both parties to personal jurisdiction in the state of "marital domicile." Additional, specific jurisdictional bases vary considerably and, of course, must meet the test of procedural due process. *Lieb v. Lieb,* 53 A.D.2d 67, 385 N.Y.S.2d 569 (1976). In 1990, the U.S. Supreme Court reaffirmed the traditional rule that "jurisdiction based on physical presence alone constitutes due process." The context was a divorce action a wife had brought in California where personal service was had on the out-of-state father when he visited the children in California. Aside from physical presence, no additional "minimum contacts" were needed. *Burnham v. Superior Court of California,* 495 U.S. 604, 110 S.Ct. 2105, 109 L.Ed.2d 631 (1990).

b. Child Support

In *Kulko v. Superior Court,* 436 U.S. 84, 98 S.Ct. 1690, 56 L.Ed.2d 132 (1978), the father resided in New York. The mother (who resided in California) sued him in California for child support. The father's only contacts with California included (1) two brief transit visits to the state while in the military years ago and (2) recently allowing his daughter of whom he had custody to reside with her mother in California. The U.S. Supreme Court held that these contacts with California were insufficient to give the California court personal jurisdiction over the father. The court noted that California's interest in securing support for its residents is protected by the Uniform Reciprocal Enforcement of Support Act.

B. TRADITIONAL GROUNDS AND DEFENSES

1. HISTORICAL DEVELOPMENT
Traditional American divorce laws allowed divorce only upon proof of marital fault, as defined by statute.

a. English Origins
The American fault-based divorce system derived from English divorce laws, which, in turn, derived from ecclesiastical (canon) law.

1) Early English Law
Until the mid-nineteenth century, ecclesiastical courts had jurisdiction over marital cases in England. Marriage was viewed as an indissoluble union. Even after other countries began to recognize divorce and the right to remarry, England continued to allow only two exceptions:

a) Divorce *a vinculo matrimonii*
Where impediments to marriage existed at the time of marriage or the marriage was not validly entered, any attempted marriage was a nullity. Divorce *a vinculo* (annulment) allowed the parties to "re"marry.

b) Divorce *a mensa et thoro*
Based on marital fault, the courts would grant a divorce *a mensa et thoro* (from bed and board). This remedy gave the parties permission to live apart (indeed it required them to do so) and provided for alimony, but did not allow them to remarry. This remedy has evolved into modern law governing legal separation or separate maintenance.

2) English Reform
In the mid–1850s, the English common law courts obtained jurisdiction over marital actions. The body of law concerning "divorce *a mensa et thoro*" was extended to a type of divorce that included the right to remarry. As it had for divorce *a mensa et thoro,* the law required proof of marital fault.

b. Application in America
The English divorce-for-fault system was applied in the American colonies and was taken over into the law of the states.

2. DIVORCE FOR MARITAL FAULT

a. Decline of Fault–Based Divorce Laws

Today, no state retains fault as the sole basis for divorce. The fault system eroded in stages. Arcane complexity and evasionary tactics contributed to its decline.

1) Bars and Defenses

To illustrate, "collusion" between the parties—perhaps as little as acquiescence—was a bar to divorce. "Recrimination" barred a divorce if both parties were "guilty" of a marital offense. Defenses included provocation, connivance, condonation and insanity. As matters developed, courts silently acquiesced in the parties' collusion or overlooked recrimination and, by granting divorces in uncontested actions without serious insistence on proof of allegations of marital fault became participants in evading the strict divorce-for-fault laws. See detailed treatment of bars and defenses at p. 141.

2) Loose Standards

The requisite degree of marital fault was diminished when "looser" grounds, such as "mental cruelty," were added to the list of fault grounds. Judicial definition of mental cruelty often seemed to include more or less "normal" marital conflicts.

3) No–Fault Laws

Today, all states offer no-fault divorce. More or less token proof of the "breakdown" of the marital relationship, typically by showing a period of separation, is the current standard. The no-fault laws go beyond the collusive (consent) divorces that had long been procured under the fault system in that they allow "unilateral divorce"—divorce at the will of one party.

b. Modern Relevance of the Fault System

The fault-based system remains relevant because a majority of states have retained fault as an alternative ground for divorce actions, along with more recently enacted no-fault standards. Whether a divorce is obtained on a fault or a no-fault ground may, in some jurisdictions, affect property division, alimony, and child custody, as well as how quickly a party can procure a divorce. (No-fault divorce typically requires a period of living apart, whereas a fault-based divorce carries no such requirement.)

3. TRADITIONAL FAULT GROUNDS

The most important fault grounds for divorce are adultery, physical cruelty, mental cruelty, desertion or abandonment, impotency, habitual drunkenness and, less commonly, "indignities," and "insanity." (Note that "insanity" may in a fault-based system also function as a defense as it negates "fault.")

a. Adultery

For purposes of divorce law, adultery is defined as voluntary sexual intercourse between a married person and someone other than that person's spouse.

Disputes rarely go to the definition and more often involve proof. Circumstantial evidence, including evidence of mutual affection, an adulterous inclination, and an opportunity to commit adultery, typically is sufficient.

Examples: (1) W's adulterous conduct was established by evidence given by a private investigator that W's alleged paramour was in W's home almost daily from early evening until one or two hours after midnight, that when seen together in public W had her arm around the alleged paramour, and that certain entries by W in her diary constituted confessions of adultery. *Leonard v. Leonard*, 259 So.2d 529 (Fla.App.1972).

(2) W filed for divorce. H counterclaimed, alleging that W's lesbian relationship constituted adultery. W argued that a non-heterosexual relationship cannot constitute adultery. The trial court ruled for H, and W appealed. (Result: For H. "It is not the intent of this court to either condone or condemn homosexuality; that is a social issue best left to a more appropriate forum. What is important is to define, in human terms, those acts which constitute adultery so as to give rise to a termination of the marriage. Accordingly this court finds that adultery exists when one spouse rejects the other by entering into a personal intimate sexual relationship with any other person, irrespective of the specific sexual acts performed, the marital status, or the gender of the third party. It is the rejection of the spouse coupled with out-of-marriage intimacy that constitutes adultery.") *S.B. v. S.J.B.*, 258 N.J.Super. 151, 609 A.2d 124 (1992).

b. Physical Cruelty

Divorce based on physical cruelty traditionally required a showing of "extreme and repeated" cruelty. A single act may suffice if it endangers life, limb or health.

Examples: (1) W was denied a divorce when she relied on a *single* instance of physical abuse by H to support her claim of cruelty. H's claim for a divorce on grounds of W's desertion was also denied, because he had provoked her desertion when he struck her. *Capps v. Capps*, 216 Va. 382, 219 S.E.2d 898 (1975).

(2) After 26 years of marriage, H sought a divorce alleging cruel and inhuman treatment. H alleged that W struck him with objects, including a lamp and a vase, threatened him with a knife, attempted to choke him, and frequently berated him. The trial court granted H a divorce on the grounds of cruel and inhuman treatment. The appellate court reversed. H appealed. (Result: No divorce. Given the length of the marriage, H made an insufficient showing of cruelty. "[W]hether a plaintiff has established a cause of action for a cruelty divorce will depend, in part, on the duration of the marriage in issue. The existence of a long-term marriage does not, of course, serve as an absolute bar to

the granting of a divorce for cruel and inhuman treatment, and even in such a marriage 'substantial misconduct' might consist of one violent episode such as a severe beating.") *Brady v. Brady,* 64 N.Y.2d 339, 486 N.Y.S.2d 891, 476 N.E.2d 290 (N.Y.1985).

c. Desertion

Required elements of desertion include the absent party's intent not to resume cohabitation, separation for the statutory period, no consent to the separation by the opposing party and absence of provocation. (The latter two "ingredients" may also be seen in terms of defenses.)

1) Time Period

The statutory time period for desertion commences when the parties separate or when the intent to desert is formed, if the latter is later. The time period must run without interruption. If a temporary reconciliation is followed by a second desertion, the time periods may not be added together.

2) Constructive Desertion

Courts may find "constructive desertion" in misconduct of the "deserting" spouse. In an appropriate setting it may be held that the spouse who physically departed was actually the one deserted—if the absence was provoked.

> ***Examples:*** (1) The refusal to fulfill a basic obligation of marriage (such as permanent and inexcusable denial of sexual intercourse) constitutes abandonment. *Diemer v. Diemer,* 8 N.Y.2d 206, 203 N.Y.S.2d 829, 168 N.E.2d 654 (1960).
>
> (2) A wife's refusal to have uncontracepted intercourse with her husband was held not to constitute desertion where the husband consented, albeit reluctantly. *Zagarow v. Zagarow,* 105 Misc.2d 1054, 430 N.Y.S.2d 247 (1980).
>
> (3) Deliberate attempts to force a spouse from the marital home, such as removal of the husband's clothes from the marital dwelling and a change of locks, constitute constructive desertion. *Fort v. Fort,* 270 S.C. 255, 241 S.E.2d 891 (1978).

4) Reconciliation Offers

An offer to reconcile, made by the absent spouse in good faith and rejected by the non-deserting spouse without justification, may stop the running of the period of desertion. The (formerly innocent) spouse who refuses such an offer may then become the "deserter."

d. Mental Cruelty

1) Requirements

Statutes providing for divorce based on mental cruelty often require "extreme and repeated" mental cruelty, but provide no definite guideline. Courts have construed these statutes to include anything from inexcusable denial of sexual intercourse over an extended period to humiliating and degrading treatment of a spouse. Some courts have refused to find mental cruelty based on false accusations of infidelity, unwillingness to have children, or occasional strife and disharmony.

2) Subjective Standard
What constitutes mental cruelty may depend upon the particular parties involved rather than on objective criteria. Relevant considerations may include family tradition, ethnic and religious backgrounds, local customs and standards, and other cultural differences. Moreover, the definition of "mental cruelty" seems to differ in contested cases and in uncontested cases. In uncontested cases, standards often are considerably less stringent, and standards may be at their strongest when a marriage of long duration is at issue.

3) Opportunity for Collusive Divorce
Because mental cruelty is such a vague standard, it was (ab)used in obtaining what amounted to consent divorces, before the spread of the no-fault option made this approach less attractive.

e. Habitual Drunkenness and Drug Addiction
In some states, habitual drunkenness and drug addiction specifically are fault grounds for divorce. Under one such statute, alcohol or drug abuse must be "gross" or "continuous" or "habitual" or continued "for the space of 2 years" to justify divorce. Elsewhere, these habits may provide evidence of (mental) cruelty.

f. Impotence and Bigamy
Though traditionally grounds for annulment when present at the time of marriage, some states allow impotence and bigamy as grounds for divorce.

g. Insanity
1) Plaintiff's
Courts disagree as to how an incompetent spouse may obtain a divorce. A court-appointed guardian generally may act on behalf of the ward; however, some courts hold that an action for divorce may not be maintained by the incompetent spouse's guardian without express statutory authorization or that due process requires a case-by-case determination of the issue.

2) Defendant's
A spouse's insanity constitutes a ground for divorce in some states, but in other states may be a defense to fault-based divorce. Divorce statutes seldom provide a definition of insanity, leaving the matter to judicial interpretation. Some statutes require that the insanity have existed for some specified time period, or that it be permanent or incurable, or that there have been confinement to a mental institution for a stated period or a formal adjudication of insanity.

> ***Example:*** H's unusually bizarre sexual fixations were held to be "indignities" sufficient as W's *ground* for divorce, but *not* sufficient as H's (insanity) *defense* to divorce. *Steinke v. Steinke*, 238 Pa.Super. 74, 357 A.2d 674 (1975).

4. TRADITIONAL BARS AND DEFENSES
Collusion and recrimination are traditional *bars* to a divorce action based on fault grounds. Traditional *defenses* include provocation, connivance, condonation, and insanity. In traditional fault-based practice, the bars and defenses provided an often effective (if sometimes unsavory) negotiating tool to "facilitate" settlement of property and alimony claims.

a. Collusion
Collusion is an agreement between the spouses to procure a divorce. The traditional rule was that evidence of an agreement between the spouses to get a divorce may bar a divorce even if the marital offense did in fact occur. More recently, the view was that collusion bars the divorce only if the alleged marital offense did not actually occur or when, pursuant to agreement between the spouses, one spouse committed a marital offense to provide the other a ground for divorce.

Quite at odds with the law on the books, the vast majority of divorce actions in fault-based jurisdictions had long been uncontested. These divorces typically were based on thoroughly collusive agreements negotiated between the parties, with careful attention to financial and child custody consequences. Generally, the courts did not question such agreements, unless the parties were too flagrant about their consent and collusion.

b. Recrimination
Traditionally, recrimination barred a divorce when *both* spouses had committed a marital offense. The theory was that "the law is for the relief of an oppressed party, and the courts will not interfere in quarrels where both parties commit reciprocal excesses and outrages." *Mogged v. Mogged,* 55 Ill.2d 221, 302 N.E.2d 293 (1973). Some states limited the operation of the bar to offenses of a similar nature or to adultery on both sides. Even before the demise of for-fault-only divorce, many courts and legislatures had either abolished recrimination outright or had eroded the operation of recrimination by making application of the bar discretionary with the court, or transforming the bar into an affirmative defense, *i.e.,* by requiring it to be specifically raised by defendant in the pleadings.

c. Provocation
The defendant in the divorce action proves provocation by showing that the plaintiff provoked the defendant's marital offense. Defendant must show that the marital offense was not excessive in relation to the provocation. If defendant succeeds, the plaintiff is denied a divorce.

d. Provocation and Recrimination Distinguished
a) Causal Connection
"Provocation" requires a causal connection between the marital offense and the other spouse's provoking conduct. "Recrimination" does not require a causal connection between both parties' grounds for divorce.

b) Defense vs. Bar

Provocation is a *defense* which is waived if it is not raised by the party whereas recrimination traditionally was a *bar* to a divorce and would be raised by the court if relevant evidence came to light. It could not be waived by the parties.

c) Misconduct vs. Ground for Divorce

To constitute the valid defense of "provocation," the plaintiff's misconduct need not itself constitute a ground for divorce. "Recrimination," however, applies only when both parties have been guilty of marital offenses that constitute grounds for divorce.

d) Rationale

Both provocation and recrimination rest on the "clean hands" theory that, under the fault system, only an innocent and injured spouse is entitled to a divorce.

e. Connivance

The defense of connivance derives from the maxim that one who has consented to misconduct is not injured by it. Connivance, however, is more than the plaintiff's consent to the defendant's misconduct. Plaintiff must have actively created an opportunity for the other to commit the marital offense of which he now complains. If the plaintiff has merely acquiesced in the opportunity rather than helped to create it, the defense of connivance is not available. (In such a situation, the defense of "condonation" may apply.)

Examples: (1) H was granted a divorce on grounds of W's habitual drunkenness. Although H knew of W's weakness for alcohol, H was not guilty of connivance when he had brought liquor into the home and had taken W to places where liquor was served. Said the court, "I do not believe that the plaintiff was obliged to forego his own proper and ordinary recreation at the risk of being charged with the corrupt intent to make his wife an habitual drunkard." *Muir v. Muir,* 46 Del. 578, 86 A.2d 857 (1952).

(2) H hired a private detective to employ a number of persons to entice W to engage in immoral conduct, for the purpose of giving H grounds for a divorce. Although W ultimately succumbed, H was denied a divorce because of his connivance. *Greene v. Greene,* 15 N.C.App. 314, 190 S.E.2d 258 (1972).

f. Condonation

Condonation is the intentional and voluntary forgiveness of a marital offense. Because the defense turns on the mental state of the offended party (who is resisting the defense), problems of proof may be serious.

1) Proof of Intent

Intent to condone may be inferred from the spouse's conduct. Courts have divided on the question whether condonation occurs when the offended spouse, with knowledge of the marital offense, engages in sexual intercourse with the guilty spouse. Generally, continued cohabitation after obtaining knowledge of the offense is sufficient to prove condonation, unless the cohabitation is the result of necessity.

> *Example:* W's petition for divorce was dismissed on grounds of W's condonation of H's physical cruelty. (Result: Reversed. "We do not believe [W's] conduct in this case is sufficient to prove her full, free and voluntary forgiveness of [H's] misconduct. [W] did continue to occupy the same house as [H] after his acts of cruelty, for two months prior to the auto accident and for over a year between two of [W's] hospitalizations. However, the sole fact that the parties lived together after the matrimonial offense does not, in and of itself, establish condonation. Even the continuation of sexual relations between the parties would not be sufficient in itself to prove condonation. Continued cohabitation is a factor to be considered in determining whether a matrimonial offense has been condoned, but it is not conclusive evidence of condonation, and if the facts of the particular case indicate the cohabitation was the result of necessity, rather than forgiveness, the defense of condonation must be rejected. That necessity, rather than forgiveness, caused [W] to live with and care for [H] between his hospitalizations, was evinced by [W's] compelling testimony. [W] testified that [H] was totally incapable of caring for himself, and this conclusion was supported by [H's] medical records and the fact he was found legally incompetent by the circuit court.") *In re Marriage of Rogers,* 74 Ill.App.3d 351, 30 Ill.Dec. 131, 392 N.E.2d 786 (1979).

2) Conditional Condonation

Jurisdictions were divided on whether condonation was conditional on the offending spouse's future good behavior. If conditional, a later act of misconduct would revive the original (condoned) marital offense and reconstitute it as a ground for divorce. Conditional condonation was criticized as a blackmail tool in the hands of the offended spouse. Proponents argued that conditional condonation facilitated reconciliation because it afforded an opportunity to attempt reconciliation without jeopardizing a ground for divorce. Some statutes provided that under certain circumstances reconciliation attempts do not constitute condonation. Since all states now offer no-fault divorce, the "preservation" of a ground for divorce has become unnecessary, and the issue is largely irrelevant. (Note that if a jurisdiction still correlates financial consequences with divorce-for-fault, the revival of a fault ground may be worth pursuing.)

g. **Insanity**

In traditional usage, insanity constituted a defense to a fault ground for divorce in the sense that insanity negates fault. (*Anonymous v. Anonymous,* 37 Misc.2d 773, 236 N.Y.S.2d 288 (1962)).

C. DIVORCE REFORM

1. SOCIAL TRENDS

Dissatisfaction with the fault-based divorce system provided impetus for reform of the divorce laws. In theory too restrictive, the fault system also had become too "wide open," as demonstrated by the overwhelming majority of collusive consent divorces. Disgust with the airing of the couples' private life in a judicial proceeding combined with the view that even if "fault" manifests itself in a statutorily recognized marital offense, the offense may be more a symptom than the cause of marital disharmony. For many reformers, it was persuasive that the legal system had effectively lost control over divorce. Concern with the integrity of a legal system that fostered collusion and perjury ran deep.

2. AVAILABLE ALTERNATIVES

Alternatives available to the reformers included 1) modernization of the fault-based system, 2) consent divorce, 3) a solely no-fault system, and 4) adding a "no-fault option" to the traditional fault system. Today, while all states offer no-fault divorce, only a minority of states have opted for a pure no-fault approach. The majority of states have retained traditional fault grounds and added some form of "no-fault" as an alternative basis for divorce. A few states have updated their catalogue of marital fault. No state has adopted consent divorce in the sense of explicitly *requiring* both parties' consent to divorce. Of course, collusive consent divorce remains available under the fault option, and as a practical matter, the uncontested "irretrievable breakdown" ground in no-fault divorce also typically involves a consent divorce.

a. Fault–Based Systems

The arguments in favor of abandoning fault-based divorce have been summarized. Traditional defenders of the fault-based system contended that it promotes stability of marriages and that society has too great an interest in the institution of marriage to let it be terminated at the will of the parties or one of them. One pragmatic argument for *retaining* some sort of fault-based system was that the power to block a divorce provides the "innocent" spouse with a bargaining tool to facilitate settlement of issues collateral to divorce (*e.g.,* spousal and child support, property, and child custody).

b. No–Fault Systems

The advantages of no-fault divorce are obvious. The major argument *against* no-fault divorce focuses on the notion that the decision to terminate a marriage should not be allowed to rest with the party who is in the "wrong," and should not be allowed to be made against the will of an "innocent" party. Critics of no-fault divorce argue that it allows a divorce to be obtained too easily, while proponents counter that this is in accord with modern social reality.

3. **NO–FAULT GROUNDS**

Common no-fault grounds for divorce include "living separate and apart," "irretrievable breakdown" of the marital relationship, and "incompatibility." For most practical purposes, no-fault divorce is "irresistible."

a. **Living Separate and Apart**

A common no-fault ground requires separation for a specified period of time. Statutes vary and range from six months to two years. A statute may require separation pursuant to a separation agreement or a court order; others are satisfied if the parties have voluntarily lived apart for the statutory period, regardless of the reason for or method of separation. (The element of consent distinguishes such separation from the fault ground of desertion.) Delaware regards separation "under the same roof" as effective "provided * * * the parties occupy separate bedrooms and do not have sexual relations with each other." Illinois counts six months' separation as sufficient if the partners agree, but requires two years of separation if one party objects.

Example: (1) H was sleeping at his mother's home and had not had sexual relations with W for the statutory period of separation. Except for this change, the couple had continued their relationship substantially the same as it had been prior to H's moving from the marital domicile. When H was not working or attending classes, he spent basically all of his waking hours with W at the former marital home. (Result: The parties had not lived separate and apart. The mere finding that their relationship was bereft of positive qualities is insufficient to support a divorce on ground of separation.) *Ellam v. Ellam,* 132 N.J.Super. 358, 333 A.2d 577 (1975).

b. **Marriage Breakdown**

Breakdown is proved by a showing that the marriage is "broken" or "dead", or that the parties' differences are irreconcilable and that a meaningful marriage no longer exists. Typically, the statutes require some objective proof (usually separation for a specific period of time) beyond the mere assertion by one party or both parties that the marriage is dead, but courts do not require an elaborate (or even any) investigation.

Examples: (1) H and W married in 1947 and had 5 children whose ages ranged from 17 to 28 years at the time of the 1978 dissolution proceedings. H was an alcoholic and the 3 youngest children had serious drug and behavioral problems, all of which contributed to the couple's marital discord. After H moved out of the marital home in 1976, he made several unsuccessful attempts at reconciliation. By the time of these proceedings H believed that no hope of reconciliation remained. W claimed the marriage could be saved if H were treated for alcoholism and sought a court order dismissing H's dissolution petition unless H completed a treatment program. The trial court dissolved the marriage. W appealed. (Result: Upheld. (1) Record supports the trial court's

findings of serious marital discord and irretrievable breakdown.
(2) Evidence of H's untreated alcoholism does not defeat findings
of serious marital discord and irretrievable breakdown warranting
dissolution.) *Hagerty v. Hagerty*, 281 N.W.2d 386 (Minn.1979).

(2) Twenty-one years after H and W married, H left W and moved
in with X, another woman. (Also living with X were her teenage
daughter as well as the father of her daughter, to whom X was not
married.) Efforts at reconciliation were futile, H sought
dissolution, and the trial court dissolved the marriage. W
appealed, arguing that the marriage could be saved if H were
removed from X's influence. (Result: Affirmed. "Respondent's
appeal borders on the frivolous. Her contentions merit little
discussion. It is sufficient to say the record discloses a reasonable
effort to effect reconciliation has been made and it is obvious the
petitioner has no desire to continue the marriage relationship.
The evidence clearly supports the trial court's finding, the
marriage was irretrievably broken.") *Roberts v. Roberts*, 200 Neb.
256, 263 N.W.2d 449 (Neb.1978).

(3) A hearing on all pending matters regarding the dissolution of
H and W's marriage was held. Neither party appeared personally.
The court declared the marriage dissolved, reserving division of
marital property for a later hearing. W moved to vacate the
decree. (Result: Decree vacated. Statute specifically requires a
hearing on whether the marriage is irretrievably broken and a
specific finding to that effect. Short of that, judgment was entered
prematurely.) *Marlenee v. District Court* , 181 Mont. 59, 592 P.2d
153 (Mont. 1979).

D. SEPARATION

1. DIVORCE FROM BED AND BOARD
Traditional statutes that provide limited divorces (divorce *a mensa et thoro*—from
bed and board) allow for adjudication of the parties' rights similar to that which
would occur in an ordinary divorce proceeding. The major points of distinction are
that remarriage is not available to parties to a limited divorce, and that limited
divorce may preserve certain entitlements (*e.g.*, inheritance rights, pension rights
or tax or social benefits) that may be lost by divorced spouses. Many states have
abandoned "limited divorce" and provide only for full divorce and (temporary) legal
separation, in the sense of separate maintenance. Some states allow the latter as
an option to limited or full divorce.

2. SEPARATE MAINTENANCE
Most states allow a spouse to obtain spousal support by bringing an action for
separate maintenance. Typical statutes allow a "needy" spouse, sometimes only if

"innocent," to obtain court ordered support from the other spouse while the parties are separated. Separate maintenance does not involve the division of property that is available in limited divorce.

3. CONVERSION INTO FULL DIVORCE

Some statutes provide for conversion of a separation or limited divorce into full divorce at the request of either party. This is no longer a serious issue because the same result may be achieved if a "living-apart" no-fault ground is later used to obtain a full divorce. Questions may arise regarding the relitigation of financial consequences that were previously fixed on the occasion of a limited divorce. (Following *Gleason v. Gleason*, 26 N.Y.2d 28, 308 N.Y.S.2d 347, 256 N.E.2d 513 (1970), New York enacted a statute allowing compensation for financial loss upon conversion of an earlier limited divorce into a later full divorce. N.Y. Dom. Rel. Law. Art. 10 § 170.)

E.   REVIEW QUESTIONS

1. **T or F** H left W in their marital home in Iowa, moved to Wisconsin, established domicile and obtained a divorce which denied W any alimony. Although notified by registered mail, W refused to appear. Because Wisconsin did not have personal jurisdiction over W, Iowa need not recognize the Wisconsin decree.

2. **T or F** Same facts as in Question # 1, but W brings the divorce action against H in Iowa, H refuses to appear, and W obtains the divorce along with a substantial alimony award. The alimony award is unenforceable in Wisconsin.

3–4. For questions 3 and 4, choose the correct terms to fill in the blanks: A = Divorce *a vinculo matrimonii;* B = Divorce *a mensa et thoro.*

3. _____ was the rough equivalent of today's annulment. Traditionally it was the only form of "divorce" that allowed the parties to remarry. It was granted where an impediment to marriage existed at the time of the marriage or where the marriage was not validly entered.

4. _____ was the rough equivalent of today's legal separation or limited divorce. It did not allow the parties to remarry. Traditionally, this remedy was based on marital fault and gave the parties permission to live apart.

5. **T or F** H wants a divorce from W. Neither party is guilty of any "fault". Today all states allow H to obtain the divorce against W's opposition.

6. **T or F** Even before no-fault divorce, divorce was widely available by consent of the parties.

7. **T or F** No-fault divorce typically is granted on the basis of at least one of the parties' assertion that the marriage has broken down.

8. **T   or   F**   With the universal acceptance of no-fault divorce, fault grounds and defenses to fault grounds have become irrelevant.

9. **T   or   F**   Provocation and recrimination are really the same defense.

10. **T   or   F**   "Desertion" under a fault-based divorce system is really the same as "living apart" under a no-fault system.

11. **T   or   F**   Despite the abstention rule, federal courts have increasingly heard cases involving family law.

12. **T   or   F**   W leaves H and moves to Maine, a state neither H nor W had visited before, taking along H's beloved cat.   W initiates divorce proceedings against H in Maine.   H travels to Maine solely to retrieve his cat.   While H is there, he is served with process.   The Maine court does not obtain jurisdiction over H because H lacks the requisite minimum contacts with Maine.

13. **T   or   F**   Under a divorce-for-fault regime, H provokes W to leave him.   W has deserted H.

14. **T   or   F**   Under a divorce-for-fault regime, H helped create the opportunity for W's adultery.   W can claim the defense of collusion.

VI

DIVORCE—FINANCIAL CONSEQUENCES

Analysis

A. ALIMONY ON DIVORCE

1. TRADITIONAL STANDARDS FOR AWARDING ALIMONY

a. Historical Development

When full divorce with the right to remarry was not available and limited divorce (*a mensa et thoro*) did not dissolve marriage but only terminated cohabitation, alimony represented the continuation of the husband's marital support obligation. When full divorce became available, the obligation to pay alimony was carried forward. Critics argue that, when divorce terminates the marriage, the continuation of the marital support obligation does not make sense.

b. Mutuality of Alimony Obligation

Based on the husband's one-sided legal obligation to support his wife, the traditional right to alimony extended only to the wife. The U.S. Supreme Court has held that such discrimination violates equal protection. *Orr v. Orr,* 440 U.S. 268, 99 S.Ct. 1102, 59 L.Ed.2d 306 (1979). Accordingly, in today's divorces, either spouse may be entitled to alimony, although, as a practical matter, relatively few husbands are awarded alimony.

> *Example:* At W's request, H quit his job as a toy salesman after one and a half years of marriage. For the remaining seven and a half years of marriage, W supported H with contributions from her father and from her own separate estate. H was now 37 years old. The trial court awarded H $30,000 in lump-sum alimony, $5,000 a month rehabilitative alimony for 18 months, and $30,000 for H's attorneys. (Result: Affirmed.) *Pfohl v. Pfohl,* 345 So.2d 371 (Fla.App.1977).

2. ALIMONY TODAY

Due to the radical divorce reforms of the 1970s as well as greatly improved employment opportunities for women, courts now award alimony less often, for shorter periods and typically less generously than in the past. Another reason is that property transfers incident to divorce are now common, in contrast to the recent past when the traditional separate property systems did not allow the non-earning spouse (typically the wife) to share. Reinforcing this trend, the UMDA is phrased so as to make an award of alimony seem to be an exceptional case. (See especially 3.b., below).

Where a pre-divorce separation agreement or an antenuptial agreement does not provide otherwise, the trend is away from awarding large amounts of alimony for extended periods of time, even to a dependent spouse who does not receive or have much property. Courts emphasize the concept of "rehabilitative alimony" which is intended to allow a dependent spouse to become self-supporting.

> *Example:* At the time of the parties' marriage in 1954, W was a skilled executive secretary. After the birth of a child, W never returned to the job

market. H became executive vice president of a major corporation and ultimately earned in excess of $120,000 per year. At the time of the divorce, W was 45 years old. The trial court found that with some additional training, W could earn from $12,000 to $18,000 per year and awarded W rehabilitative alimony for a period of four years, in addition to property valued at $225,000. (Result: Affirmed, based on a statute patterned after the UMDA.) *Otis v. Otis,* 299 N.W.2d 114 (Minn.1980).

Because of their limited duration and potentially harsh effect, awards of rehabilitative alimony often receive close scrutiny by appellate courts. Although most courts feel that marriage should not be a "ticket to a perpetual pension," the earner-spouse's support responsibility remains long-term—and may extend for life—when the dependent spouse has no realistic employment opportunities and the marriage was of considerable duration.

Examples: (1) H and W were married for 26 years. During the last six years, W was employed for only three months. Beyond a high school education, W had no formal training. The trial court awarded W rehabilitative alimony for nine months. (Result: Reversed. "* * * (I)t is not likely that she (W) will be able to obtain a job paying more than one-quarter of what her husband now earns. In view of this, the husband should be required to assist her in her support on a permanent basis subject always to the right of obtaining relief under changed circumstances.") *Lash v. Lash,* 307 So.2d 241 (Fla.App.1975).

(2) When H and W divorced after 27 years of marriage, H was a commercial airline pilot earning $75,000 per year and W was a reading specialist earning $43,000 per year. H and W did not have children. During the marriage W had worked continuously and had supported H while he obtained a private pilot's license and flight instructor's license, studied architecture for 2 years, and earned two degrees. The couple moved at least six times during the marriage because of H's educational, military, and employment commitments, and W lost seniority and retirement benefits with each move. Upon divorce, H was ordered to pay W temporary monthly alimony of $1,300 for the first year and $1,000 for a second year. Both parties appealed. (Result: Alimony awarded to W held inadequate and unfair. Court extended alimony of $1,000 per month for an additional 10 years. "The magnitude of Ruth's contribution to the community over many years is not fairly recognized by the two-year alimony award she received when the marriage was terminated.") *Gardner v. Gardner,* 110 Nev. 1053, 881 P.2d 645 (Nev.1994).

3. DETERMINING THE AMOUNT OF ALIMONY

Statutes typically leave the amount of the alimony award to the court's discretion, limited by stated factors. UMDA § 308(b) sums up a modern approach:

"The maintenance order shall be in amounts and for periods of time the court deems just, without regard to marital misconduct, and after considering all relevant factors including: (1) the financial resources of the party seeking maintenance, including marital property apportioned to him, his ability to meet his needs independently, and the extent to which a provision for support of a child living with the party includes a sum for that party as custodian; (2) the time necessary to acquire sufficient education or training to enable the party seeking maintenance to find appropriate employment; (3) the standard of living established during the marriage; (4) the duration of the marriage; (5) the age and the physical and emotional condition of the spouse seeking maintenance; and (6) the ability of the spouse from whom maintenance is sought to meet his needs while meeting those of the spouse seeking maintenance."

a. Standard of Living Maintained During Marriage, Need and Ability to Pay

Traditionally, the amount of the alimony award was based on the receiving spouse's needs and the paying spouse's ability to pay, as reflected by the pre-divorce standard of living. (See factors (1), (3), (6) in the UMDA excerpt above.)

b. Recipient's Earning Potential and Assets

Employment opportunities for women have improved dramatically and the ability of a spouse to be self-supporting now is a major consideration in awarding alimony. Today's question is not so much whether the typical ex-spouse *can* go to work, but whether she or he *must* and if so, in what position. Factors against forcing an ex-spouse into paid employment are (1) the presence of young children of whom the spouse has custody, and (2) long-term dependency with attendant loss of job skills. Earning *capacity* and assets, especially marital assets distributed on divorce, have become another major factor. UMDA § 308(a) explicitly *conditions* spousal maintenance on these elements, before looking at any other factors related to ability to pay or need: "[T]he court may grant a maintenance order for either spouse, only if it finds that the spouse seeking maintenance: (1) lacks sufficient property to provide for his reasonable needs; and (2) is unable to support himself through appropriate employment or is the custodian of a child whose condition or circumstances make it appropriate that the custodian not be required to seek employment outside the home."

Examples: (1) W and H agreed that W would work to put H through law school instead of completing her biology degree. During that part of the marriage W became proficient as a secretary. H later became an attorney in a prominent law firm. After their separation, W returned to college in a pre-medical course. The trial court awarded her $200 weekly as alimony and child support, to allow her to obtain her medical education. (Result: Reversed. The wife can be self-supporting as a secretary and her "goal in medicine * * * was never in the contemplation of the parties during marriage.") *Morgan v. Morgan,* 52 A.D.2d 804, 383 N.Y.S.2d 343 (1976).

(2) H and W's marriage lasted 22 years before they separated in May of 1987. W had a college degree in business, did not work outside the home during the marriage and had difficulty obtaining employment following the separation. H was a self-employed businessman who had founded a software company that was acquired by a large company. H regularly engaged in stock transactions, and his average gross monthly income in 1987 was more than $40,000. By March of 1988 it was "only" about $16,000. The couple owned more than $3,000,000 in assets, and these were equitably divided by the trial court upon divorce, with each party receiving in excess of $1,000,000. The trial court also awarded W permanent monthly alimony of $4,000 per month. Neither party appealed the property division, but H appealed the alimony award, the district court of appeal reversed, and W appealed. (Result: Alimony reinstated. The trial court had authority to award permanent alimony even though the recipient had also received a substantial distribution of marital assets.) *Hamlet v. Hamlet*, 583 So.2d 654 (Fla.1991).

(3) H and W had been married for 15 years. H was a pathologist. For the first seven and a half years of marriage, W had worked as a qualified medical technician. The youngest of their four minor children was five years old. The trial court awarded child support, made a property division and awarded $1,000 per month alimony for a period not to exceed 144 months. (Result: Affirmed. "The contention [that W is employable] ignores the interests of the children, and the desire of the wife to continue to care for them properly.") *Morris v. Morris*, 201 Neb. 479, 268 N.W.2d 431 (1978).

4. FAULT AS A FACTOR IN ALIMONY AWARDS

Traditionally, if the wife was at fault in the divorce (especially if she was guilty of adultery), she could not obtain alimony. Worse, in a separate property state, there was no right to share in property earned by H. Conversely, H's fault was a prerequisite to an alimony award (as it was, of course, a prerequisite for the divorce itself), and some courts gave increased awards of alimony to an innocent wife, if the husband was guilty of a serious matrimonial offense. Along with acceptance of no-fault grounds for divorce, today's statutes often expressly prohibit the courts from considering the parties' marital misconduct when awarding alimony, dividing property or deciding on child custody. UMDA § 308(b) provides that "the maintenance order shall be in amounts and for periods of time the court deems just, without regard to marital misconduct * * *." In jurisdictions where fault grounds continue in effect as an *alternative* to no-fault divorce, fault usually remains relevant if the divorce is granted on a fault ground. However, some such states will now disregard marital fault even where the divorce itself is granted for fault. Conversely, in a few no-fault states, fault (not necessarily defined by traditional grounds for divorce) may be considered even when the divorce is awarded on a no-fault ground.

Examples: (1) W ran a beauty salon and H worked for the postal service. They divorced after 18 years of marriage. During the trial W established that H was having an affair, and the trial court took H's fault into account when it awarded W alimony of $500 per month for 100 months. H appealed. (Result: Reversed and remanded for a determination of alimony without regard to marital fault. "We conclude that in domestic relations actions it was the legislative intent that, in all but extremely gross and rare situations, financial penalties are not to be imposed by a trial court on a party on the basis of fault.") *Marriage of Sommers*, 246 Kan. 652, 792 P.2d 1005 (1990).

(2) H was president of an insurance firm, and W did not work outside the home during their 9–year marriage. W admitted to post-separation adultery, and H was granted a divorce on that ground. The trial court found that to deny W alimony would create manifest injustice and awarded her $1,200 per month. H appealed. (Result: Alimony award upheld. "Even though one party may have been the major force in creating the 'fault during the marriage' which led to its dissolution and the other spouse may have been relatively blameless, those conditions constitute but one of the factors the court must weigh. The court must also weigh and consider the parties' relative economic positions in deciding whether it would be manifestly unjust to deny a spousal support award. * * * The judge expressly noted and considered that the wife had committed adultery. The adultery, however, occurred after the parties were separated and, according to the finding of the trial judge, after the marriage had been irretrievably lost * * * due to gradual dissolution caused by mutual inattention and fault from both parties. * * * The evidence supports the trial judge's conclusion that, based on the parties' respective degrees of fault during the marriage and their relative economic circumstances, a denial of spousal support to the wife would be manifestly unjust.") *Barnes v. Barnes*, 16 Va.App. 98, 428 S.E.2d 294 (1993).

(3) W and H were granted a divorce after 18 years of marriage. The trial court reserved the issues of alimony, property division, and child support. Several weeks later, W sought to have H murdered, but the man with whom she contracted was an undercover agent for the Wisconsin Dept. of Justice. After W's arrest, W and H agreed on property division and child custody (to H), and H agreed to pay her $230 per month in temporary alimony. W pleaded guilty to solicitation in connection with first degree murder and was incarcerated for 10 months. Upon her release, she moved for increased alimony. The relevant statute listed 10 factors to be considered in determining eligibility for monthly alimony. Under

factors 1–9, W was eligible, but the court denied alimony altogether based on factor 10, "[S]uch other factors as the court may in each individual case determine to be relevant." W appealed. (Result: Denial of alimony affirmed. Unlike adultery, which is *marital* misconduct, solicitation to kill one's spouse is not in that sense conduct against the marital relationship. "Requiring [H] to pay maintenance to the person who tried to have him killed is fundamentally unfair. Additionally, the trial court did not punish [W] by refusing her maintenance, it merely refused to reward her for her failure; if [W] had been successful in having [H] killed, she would receive no maintenance.") *Brabec v. Brabec*, 181 Wis.2d 270, 510 N.W.2d 762 (1993).

5. MODIFICATION OF ALIMONY

When (1) alimony (even a nominal amount) is awarded in the original divorce decree, or (2) jurisdiction is reserved to consider the issue of alimony at a later date, or (3) a statute so provides, an alimony award may be modified upon a showing of changed circumstances. Any such change must occur after the alimony decree.

a. Recipient Spouse's Changing Need

A significant change of circumstances in the dependent spouse's needs may allow modification of alimony.

Example: Ex–H brought proceedings against ex-W to have his alimony obligation of $350 per month terminated because she had become employed as a school teacher. (Result: Alimony reduced to $100 per month, rather than terminated. "[I]t should be the policy of the law to encourage one receiving alimony to seek employment. This purpose would not be served if a wife who manifests sufficient initiative and industry to get a job is penalized by having her alimony cut off entirely.") *Carter v. Carter,* 584 P.2d 904 (Utah 1978).

b. Change in Obligated Spouse's Ability to Pay

When ascertaining the obligor's ability to pay, courts may consider not only the actual earnings of the obligor, but also his or her *potential* earning capabilities. Thus, courts will not necessarily decrease alimony payments when earnings are lowered through a change in employment or retirement, and will deny modification if circumstances show that the change was voluntary and for the purpose of reducing alimony payable. Many courts refuse to consider changes in employment made for *bona fide*, but non-essential reasons. It is disputed whether an ex-spouse's remarriage, resulting in decreased ability to pay or decreased need, warrants a change in alimony payments.

Examples: (1) H and W separated after 12 years of marriage but did not divorce. Under a written separation agreement, H paid W $160 per week for 6 years until he retired. H had worked continuously for 45 years. Prior to retirement H had earned approximately

$50,000 per year, but one year after retirement his net income was only $193 per week. H moved for a reduction of his support obligation, the trial court reduced it to $123 per week. H appealed. (Result: Remanded. "If the evidence demonstrates that he retired solely to extinguish or reduce his earning for the purpose of avoiding support payments to his wife the lower court would then be justified in setting a support order based on his pre-retirement income. * * * The entire circumstances of his retirement must be examined to determine the extent of the husband's responsibility to support his estranged wife." On remand the trial court should consider medical evidence that H suffered from duodenal ulcers, mild hypertension, diabetes, diverticulosis, emphysema, and other medical problems.) *Burns v. Burns*, 232 Pa.Super. 295, 331 A.2d 768 (1974).

(2) Following 42 years of marriage, H and W divorced and W was awarded $2,000 monthly alimony. When H won $20 million in the Wisconsin "Megabucks" lottery, W moved to modify alimony. The trial court granted the motion, increasing W's monthly maintenance to $5,333. H appealed, claiming the increase was unjustified. W appealed, claiming the amount was too low. (Result: Lottery winnings could be considered a change in H's financial circumstances justifying an increase in alimony. W, however, was entitled only to an amount that would afford her the same standard of living she enjoyed during the marriage. Case remanded to determine the increase that would achieve this goal.) *Gerrits v. Gerrits*, 167 Wis.2d 429, 482 N.W.2d 134 (1992).

c. Obligated Spouse's Bankruptcy

The obligor's bankruptcy does not discharge alimony or child support obligations. (Obligations based on property settlements, on the other hand, are dischargeable unless the debtor has the ability to pay them and the detriment to the non-debtor spouse outweighs the benefit to the debtor of discharging the debt. See p. 166).

6. TERMINATION OF ALIMONY
a. Death of Either Ex–Spouse

Generally, the alimony obligation terminates at the death of either the payee or the payor. When the premarital or separation agreement expressly so specifies, the alimony obligation may continue after the payor's death as a charge against his estate. If the obligation is to continue beyond death, the agreement should provide for a method to determine a present value, or specify a lump sum payment at the obligor's death, to facilitate administration of the estate. In practice, protection for the recipient spouse often is achieved by the maintenance in her favor of a life insurance policy on the obligor's life. When this is accomplished in a separation agreement, no issue arises. When, at the time of divorce, a court orders an obligor to maintain a life insurance policy in favor of his or her spouse, the order may be attacked as inappropriately continuing the alimony obligation beyond death. Some courts have rationalized such orders as being in the nature of current alimony, as premiums are paid during the obligor's lifetime.

Example: Ex–W sought continued payment of alimony against the estate of her deceased ex-H. A separation agreement incorporated into their divorce decree provided that alimony would terminate upon ex-W's remarriage. Ex–W contended that this should be interpreted to mean that remarriage was the exclusive factor to terminate the obligation. (Result: Ex–W loses. "The failure to expressly provide for continuation of alimony payments after death should be viewed as evidence of a contrary intent.") *Estate of Kuhns v. Kuhns,* 550 P.2d 816 (Alaska 1976).

b. Recipient Spouse's Remarriage

If the premarital or separation agreement does not provide otherwise, the receiving spouse's remarriage usually terminates an alimony obligation relating to a prior marriage. This may occur either (1) automatically (by operation of a statute or under the terms of the divorce decree), or (2) pursuant to a new court order based on changed circumstances. Depending on the purpose and circumstance of the award (*e.g.*, is it in lieu of property?), alimony specifically ordered for a defined period may not terminate. Similarly, "rehabilitative" alimony may be held not to terminate upon the recipient's remarriage because rehabilitative alimony is paid for a specific purpose that is not necessarily superseded by remarriage.

Example: Prior to entry of a decree of divorce, H and W entered into a property settlement agreement. In the agreement H agreed to pay "W for her maintenance and support during her lifetime * * *." A payment schedule was set out for the first twenty years. This agreement was incorporated into their divorce decree. Two months after the divorce decree, W remarried. H made payments for over five years before bringing suit for modification or termination of the payments. (Result: Modification denied. The court found that H had a duty to continue making the payments "because the payments were for 'contractual support' and not alimony.") *In re Marriage of Mass,* 102 Ill.App.3d 984, 58 Ill.Dec. 941, 431 N.E.2d 1 (1981).

c. Recipient Spouse's Cohabitation

The alimony recipient's unmarried cohabitation with another person typically is a circumstance sufficient to justify reconsideration of an alimony award. Many courts have held that unmarried cohabitation does not necessarily require termination of alimony. Interpreting separation agreements, some courts have construed the word "remarriage" to include cohabitation, but most have not. By statute, several states provide for automatic termination of an alimony obligation, if the party receiving the alimony cohabits with another person on a resident or longer-term basis. New York speaks in terms of termination of alimony if the recipient is "habitually living with another man and holding herself out as his wife". California employs a presumption of "decreased need" if "the supported party is cohabiting with a person of the opposite sex". Illinois looks to termination "if the party receiving maintenance cohabits with another person on a resident, continuing conjugal basis." It is disputed whether an alimony obligation that was once terminated by cohabitation revives when cohabitation ends.

Examples: (1) Ex–H petitioned for modification of an alimony award. Ex–W had cohabited four nights a week from December 1 to March 15 and one night in four between April and July 29, the date of the hearing. (Result: Modification denied. Cohabitation may constitute changed circumstances, but the test for modification is whether the relationship has reduced the financial needs of the recipient. "The extent of actual economic dependency, not one's conduct as a cohabitant, must determine the duration of support as well as its amount.") *Gayet v. Gayet,* 92 N.J. 149, 456 A.2d 102 (1983).

(2) Ex–W filed a contempt complaint against ex–H for his failure to make support payments. The decree of divorce incorporated a separation agreement which provided for alimony to end upon, *inter alia,* "the wife's living together with a member of the opposite sex, so as to give the outward appearance of marriage * * *." Ex–W cohabited on a regular basis with a man in his apartment, sharing the bedroom. She did not use her lover's surname, nor did she represent that she and her lover were married. (Result: Contempt denied, alimony terminated. Evidence was sufficient to support conclusion that divorced wife lived "together with a member of the opposite sex, so as to give the outward appearance of marriage" within meaning of the contingency in the parties' incorporated separation agreement. Alimony terminated despite lack of evidence that her lover financially supported ex-W.) *Bell v. Bell,* 393 Mass. 20, 468 N.E.2d 859 (1984).

(3) When H and W divorced after 30 years of marriage, H was ordered to pay W monthly alimony of $750. Several years later, H moved to terminate the alimony payments under the applicable statute, alleging that W was cohabitating with a man (A) "on a resident, continuing conjugal basis." W and A went out together socially, traveled together, and exchanged birthday and Christmas gifts. They did not sleep in the same bedroom, and A alleged that he was impotent. The circuit court and the appellate court held that a *sexual* relationship was an essential element of a conjugal relationship under the statute. H appealed. (Result: Reversed; W's alimony terminated. "We believe that a relationship can have a conjugal basis even though there is an absence of any sexual

relationship.'') *Marriage of Sappington*, 106 Ill.2d 456, 88 Ill.Dec. 61, 478 N.E.2d 376 (1985).

7. ENFORCEMENT OF ALIMONY BY CONTEMPT

Along with the usual remedies for the enforcement of money obligations, alimony has the additional advantage—to the recipient—that it is enforceable by contempt. This means that the sanctions may include jail.

8. FEDERAL TAX TREATMENT OF ALIMONY

Generally, alimony is deductible by the payor and included in the recipient's federal taxable income. The definition of alimony was substantially changed in the 1980s. Rules for alimony under pre–1985 decrees and separation instruments continue in effect for pre–1985 obligations. For current divorces, the definition of "alimony" guards against disguising as alimony a non-deductible payment, such as child support or an installment property settlement. The following rules apply: (1) The payment must be in cash or its equivalent. (2) The parties must not designate that the payment is not alimony. (3) If the parties are separated under a decree of divorce or separate maintenance, the parties must not be members of the same household when the payment is made. (4) There must be no liability to make payments after the death of the recipient spouse. (5) The payment must not be described or treated as child support. (6) If amounts exceeding $10,000 per calendar year are to be paid, they must be payable in each of the first three post-separation years. Generally, if annual payments decrease by more than $15,000 during the three-year period, there will be a "recapture" of excess alimony deductions.

9. ALIMONY AND PROPERTY AWARD DISTINGUISHED

The terms of the settlement agreement or of the divorce decree may help assure the classification and thereby the legal consequences of post-marital payments. The parties or court's designation, however, is not necessarily controlling for all purposes. Specific payments may be classified differently under different laws and for different purposes (*e.g.*, bankruptcy, or taxation, or enforcement).

B. PROPERTY DIVISION ON DIVORCE

1. SEPARATE PROPERTY STATES

With some variations, separate property states hold that each marital partner owns and controls property he or she owned before marriage, plus property acquired by him or her during the marriage through personal earnings, gift, inheritance, interest and dividends on investments or their appreciation, or separately acquired in any other manner.

a. Property Transfers on Divorce

In traditional separate property states, courts would order a transfer of property between divorcing spouses only for the purpose of sorting out the spouses' commingled separate property. Jointly titled property was subject to the presumptions of gift or advancement, discussed at pp. 112–113. Any other transfer of separate property would be labeled "in lieu of alimony" or "lump sum alimony" or "alimony in gross."

b. Equitable Distribution

Adherence to the pure separate property scheme left the non-earning spouse (typically the wife) without assets, despite vital services she or he may have contributed to the marriage. Largely in the 1970s, courts and legislatures adopted various schemes to rectify this state of affairs. Today, statutes in separate property states commonly provide, or are interpreted by the courts to provide, for an "equitable distribution" of property acquired during marriage. The current theory is that marriage is a shared enterprise, and equitable distribution is the division of the assets of the shared enterprise, based on the partners' presumably equal contributions and other equities.

c. "Marital Property"

Several separate property states have adopted detailed definitions of "marital property." In its technical concern for distinguishing between separate property and marital property, this approach closely resembles a community property scheme. However, in contrast to community property which vests in both parties when it is acquired by one party to a marriage, this scheme comes into effect only upon divorce. It then deals with distribution of property as if a community property regime had been in effect all along. This approach has been unsuccessfully attacked as a "retroactive impairment of contract"*(Kujawinski*, below), or a deprivation of "vested rights" (*Fournier*, below).

> ***Example:*** (1) An Illinois statute presumed all property acquired by either spouse during the marriage to be marital property upon divorce. Exceptions included property acquired by gift or devise. H sought a judgment that retroactive application of that statute was unconstitutional, arguing that transfer of an interest in his property to W impaired his contractual relations with third parties. (Result: Application of the statute is *not* unconstitutional. "Had the legislature chosen to apply the concept of equitable distribution of property only to property acquired after the Act became effective, the full impact and purposes of the new Act would not have been felt for at least a generation. Such prospective application would continue the very inequity which the legislature sought to remedy and would place the present generation of married couples at a decided disadvantage in comparison with subsequent generations of married couples. Moreover, in each dissolution proceeding involving property, courts would be presented with the impracticable dilemma of applying,

depending upon the acquisition date of any disputed property, differing sets of laws and policies. * * * [W]e conclude that the State interest to be promoted by applying the section retrospectively greatly outweighs the asserted property interest, which is only slightly more impaired by such application.'') *Kujawinski v. Kujawinski*, 71 Ill.2d 563, 17 Ill.Dec. 801, 376 N.E.2d 1382 (1978).

(2) A Maine statute classified as marital property all property acquired by either spouse during the marriage. Statutory exceptions included property acquired by gift, devise, or descent. During the marriage, W acquired by intestate succession a 33% interest in beach property and shortly thereafter obtained full title by purchasing the similarly acquired interests of her father and sister. Upon divorce, the trial court ruled that the beach property was marital property, with the exception of W's 33% interest acquired by descent. W appealed, arguing that the statute deprived her of vested property rights. (Result: Statute is constitutional. ''In enacting [the statute], the legislative purpose was to provide a more equitable method of distributing property upon the termination of a marriage and not to affect property titles retrospectively. * * * [T]he Act becomes operative when a divorce or separation proceeding is involved [and] limits the definition of 'marital property' to the 'purposes of this section only.' The Act does not prevent married persons from owning property separately during marriage and disposing of it in any fashion either of them may choose, assuming neither a separation nor a divorce intervenes. Viewed in this light, the defendant's claim that [the Act] deprived her of vested property rights without due process of law is without merit.'') *Fournier v. Fournier*, 376 A.2d 100 (Me.1977).

d. The Uniform Marriage and Divorce Act
The UMDA's provisions on the distribution of property on divorce have been influential, even if not followed precisely. § 307 provides:

Alternative A (recommended generally for adoption)

''In a proceeding for dissolution of a marriage, [or] legal separation * * * the court, without regard to marital misconduct, shall, and in a proceeding for legal separation may, finally equitably apportion between the parties the property and assets belonging to either or both however and whenever acquired, and whether the title thereto is in the name of the husband or wife or both. In making apportionment the court shall consider the duration of the marriage, any prior marriage of either party, any antenuptial agreement of the parties, the age, health, station, occupation, amount and sources of income, vocational skills, employability, estate, liabilities, and needs of each of the parties, custodial provisions, whether the apportionment is in lieu of or in addition to maintenance, and the opportunity of each for future acquisition of capital assets and income. The court shall also consider the contribution or dissipation of each party in the acquisition, preservation, depreciation, or appreciation in value of the respective estates, and the contribution of a spouse as a homemaker or to the family unit.''

Alternative B (included for consideration by community property states)

''In a proceeding for dissolution of the marriage [or] legal separation * * * the court shall assign each spouse's separate property to the spouse. It also shall divide community property, without regard to marital misconduct, in just proportions after considering all relevant factors including: (1) contribution of each spouse to acquisition of the marital property, including contribution of a spouse as homemaker; (2) value of the property set apart to each spouse; (3) duration of the marriage; and (4) economic circumstances of each spouse when the division of property is to become effective, including the desirability of awarding the family home or the right to live therein for a reasonable period to the spouse having custody of any children.''

e. Marital Fault and Economic Fault ("Dissipation")
Under most no-fault divorce statutes and some fault statutes, the division of property on divorce is not subject to consideration of marital fault. "Economic fault," by contrast, is increasingly considered in the apportionment of property. Sometimes it is not altogether clear whether marital or economic fault is being punished.

Examples: (1) H and W were married for 30 years and both parties worked continuously throughout the marriage. H had been a department store vice president earning $85,000 per year, but had lost this job as a result of a corporate takeover. During the last year of the marriage H earned $12,000. W was a nurse earning $41,000 per year. The marital property was valued at $500,000, of which $300,000 represented H's pension and IRA. Upon divorce, the trial court awarded 60 percent of the marital property to W upon a finding that H's same-sex relationships may have placed W at risk of acquiring AIDS and therefore affected her future economic circumstances. H appealed. (Result: Reversed and remanded for an equal division of the marital property. "[I]f the husband is also at risk for AIDS to the same (or even greater) extent as the wife, we can conclude as a matter of law that this risk has an identical impact upon the husband's future economic circumstances. Therefore, absent the injection of fault into the analysis, the trial court's division of the marital estate in favor of the wife—based upon the risk that the wife might develop a communicable disease for which the husband shares the same risk—is clearly against the logic and effect of the facts and the reasonable inferences to be drawn therefrom and constitutes an abuse of discretion. We conclude that the trial court's 'health and economic circumstances' justification for an unequal division of marital assets in favor of the wife is based upon insufficient evidence and is implicitly based upon fault.'') *R.E.G. v. L.M.G.*, 571 N.E.2d 298 (Ind.App.1991).

(2) When they married in 1979, W was a college sophomore and H had just been drafted by the New York Jets to play professional football. W had not finished college and did not work during the marriage. H played with the Jets for nine years and his final annual contract salary was $775,000 plus $50,000 in bonuses. The parties had bought a $550,000 resort home and spent much of H's salary on other luxury items, including a power boat, a Rolls Royce and four other cars. In 1988, H met an actress (A), with whom he had an intimate relationship. When A developed cancer, H broke his football contract to accompany A to chemotherapy treatments. H played only six of the 16 games of the 1988 season, forfeiting $484,437 in salary, or $324,573 in net pay after taxes. After H broke his contract, he was unable to sign with a U.S. football team and earned only $20,000 in the Canadian Football League in 1989 before he was cut. Thereafter, he earned no money, and at the time of the divorce the only marital asset of value remaining was $264,000 in equity in the couple's New York home. (Result: Marital assets held to *include* the NFL salary H forfeited, *i.e.*, $324,573. Together with the home equity, the assets thus totaled $591,573, of which W was awarded 33%, or $194,229. Because H owed W $71,707 in past due support, W was awarded the full equity in the New York home plus a judgment for the balance, *i.e.*, $1,936.) *Gastineau v. Gastineau*, 151 Misc.2d 813, 573 N.Y.S.2d 819 (1991). (Note: This was *not* the usual "dissipation of marital assets" case, where the marital community is reimbursed for what one spouse actually has spent for his or her nonmarital purposes.)

f. Post–Divorce Joint Ownership
"Continued joint ownership following divorce is the exceptional case 'reserved for the unusual situation where the economics involved call for such a solution.'" *Hopkins v. Hopkins,* 597 S.W.2d 702, 706 (Mo.App.1980). Upon divorce, a tenancy by the entireties automatically converts into a tenancy in common and is subject to partition, unless the court provides for joint tenancy.

g. Pre–Divorce Transfers of Separate Property
Generally, a spouse has the right to dispose of his or her separate property during marriage without the consent of the other spouse. As discussed above, the notion of "dissipation" of marital property may be applied at the time of divorce to compensate one spouse for losses through the other spouse's wrongful misapplication of marital property.

2. COMMUNITY PROPERTY STATES
Under community property regimes, all property acquired during marriage generally is community property, and is owned by *both* spouses as of the time it is

acquired. Pre-marital properties and properties acquired during marriage by gift or inheritance or, depending on the state, as earnings on or appreciation of separate property, remain separate property unless commingled. On divorce, the court assigns the separate property to the owners and divides the community property equally or, in several states, "equitably."

Examples: (1) Upon their divorce, W was awarded substantially all of the community property which had a net value of about $32,000. H received his separate property which was valued at substantially more than the property distribution to W. (Result: Reversed and remanded. On divorce, separate property *and* community property are before the court for distribution. The court should make a "just and equitable distribution" of the property, considering the following factors: "(1) the respective merits of the parties; (2) the condition in which they will be left by such divorce; and (3) the party through whom the property was acquired." These factors are not exclusive.) *Friedlander v. Friedlander,* 80 Wash.2d 293, 494 P.2d 208 (1972).

(2) In dividing community property, the trial court "rewarded" H for his "successful efforts" in preserving and protecting the community property estate, and "punished" W for destroying any meaningful father-daughter relationship between H and his children. W was awarded land valued at $27,400. H was awarded land estimated to be worth as much as $170,000. W appealed the unequal distribution. At issue was whether the required "equitable" distribution must be "equal." (Result: For W. The court felt that the distribution of community property was "whimsical and arbitrary" and that, in the absence of sound reason, division "must be substantially equal." The lower "court's unequal property distribution was arbitrary, unreasonable and an unconstitutional deprivation of the appellant's vested property interest in the community.") *Hatch v. Hatch,* 113 Ariz. 130, 547 P.2d 1044 (1976).

3. CONFLICTS OF LAWS ASPECTS OF PROPERTY DIVISION

The law of the matrimonial domicile at the time of acquisition generally determines ownership of property acquired by the husband and wife, as well as its characterization as separate or community property. (See p. 117).

Example: H and W lived their marriage in New Jersey, a separate property state. They acquired property in the form of securities and bank accounts. H left W and moved to Idaho, a community property state, taking the property with him. H then obtained a divorce in Idaho. No distribution to W was made of the property. W appealed. (Result: For W. The Idaho court looked to the fact that Idaho's concept of "separate property" differed significantly from New Jersey's and held that the law of the state (New Jersey) where the separate property was acquired should apply to give W the equitable share to which she would have been entitled in New Jersey.) *Berle v. Berle,* 97 Idaho 452, 546 P.2d 407 (1976).

Several other community property states provide for this problem by statutes that create so-called "quasi-community property."

Example: Tex. Fam. Code § 3.63(b) provides: "In a decree of divorce or annulment the court shall also order a division of the following real and personal property, wherever situated, in a manner that the court deems just and right, having due regard for the rights of each party and any children of the marriage: (1) property that was acquired by either spouse while domiciled elsewhere and that would have been community property if the spouse who acquired the property had been domiciled in this state at the time of the acquisition; or (2) property that was acquired by either spouse in exchange for real or personal property, and that would have been community property if the spouse who acquired the property so exchanged had been domiciled in this state at the time of its acquisition."

4. PROPERTY AWARDS AND BANKRUPTCY

Bankruptcy generally discharges obligations arising from a property settlement, whereas alimony and child support are not dischargeable. 11 U.S.C.A. § 523(a)(5). What constitutes alimony, maintenance, or support is determined under the bankruptcy laws, not state law. 11 U.S.C.A. § 523 (a)(15)(B). Courts construe "alimony" as the term is used in the Bankruptcy Act to mean payments in the nature of support for a former spouse. 1994 legislation provided new procedural protections for children and spouse. It also ended dischargeability for certain debts arising out of a division of property incident to divorce, where the debtor has the ability to pay them and the detriment to the nondebtor spouse outweighs the benefit to the debtor of discharging such debts.

Example: When H filed for bankruptcy, he owed W substantial past-due alimony, although the exact amount was disputed. The bankruptcy court held that H's obligation to pay alimony arrearages was dischargeable because W did not need the payments when H filed his bankruptcy petition. The district court reversed, and H appealed. (Result: Affirmed; alimony arrearages are *not* dischargeable. "We conclude that Congress intended that bankruptcy courts make only a simple inquiry into whether or not the obligation at issue is in the nature of support. This inquiry will usually take the form of deciding whether the obligation was in the nature of support as opposed to being in the nature of a property settlement. Thus, there will be no necessity for a precise investigation of the spouse's circumstances to determine the appropriate level of need or support. It will not be relevant that the circumstances of the parties may have changed, *e.g.*, the spouse's need may have been reduced at the time the Chapter VII petition is filed. Thus, limited to its proper role, the bankruptcy court will not duplicate the functions of state domestic relations courts, and its rulings will impinge on state domestic relations issues in the most limited manner possible.'') *Harrell v. Sharp*, 754 F.2d 902 (11th Cir.1985).

5. TAX TREATMENT OF PROPERTY AWARDS

The recipient of property in a divorce settlement takes the transferor's adjusted basis for that property. *Before* 1984, the transfer by one spouse to the other of property was a taxable event, if the fair market value of the property differed from its basis. To illustrate, if the property had appreciated in value, the transferor was liable for capital gains tax to the extent of the appreciation. If the property had lost value, there was a loss for tax purposes. *United States v. Davis*, 370 U.S. 65, 82 S.Ct. 1190, 8 L.Ed.2d 335 (1962).

6. TREATMENT OF PROFESSIONAL LICENSES AND PRACTICES

When a divorce occurs shortly after (or before) one spouse completes advanced education and qualifies for a professional license, an award of generous alimony provides a ready remedy, if (or indeed, whether or not) the other spouse has made a significant contribution either in cash or services to the earning of the license. With antipathy to alimony growing, a few courts have classified a professional license as an "asset" and "divided" it upon divorce, by awarding a specific percentage of the "present value" of the license to the other spouse as property. Other courts have taken the license into account under a variety of theories.

a. The Professional License as a Factor in Determining Alimony

Example: When W and H married in 1976, W had finished 3 years of college and H was entering medical school. During H's first 3 years of medical school, W left college and worked as a department store clerk until the couple's first child was born. After 7 years of marriage, when H had one year left to complete his medical residency, H left W and moved in with another woman. In H and W's divorce, W was awarded child support, rehabilitative maintenance of $500 per month, and restitution of the salary she had earned while H attended medical school. W appealed, seeking a maintenance award reflecting H's increased earning potential resulting from his degree. (Result: Rehabilitative maintenance and restitution awards vacated; remanded to determine appropriate alimony and property division. "[W]hen one spouse obtains a professional degree during the marriage, but the marriage ends before the benefits of the degree can be realized, the future value of the professional degree is a relevant factor to be considered in reaching a just and equitable maintenance award.") *Downs v. Downs*, 154 Vt. 161, 574 A.2d 156 (1990).

b. "Goodwill" Distinguished

A professional degree or license should be distinguished from the actual value of an existing practice, *i.e.*, goodwill.

Example: W supported H while he attended college and law school. H
became the sole shareholder in a professional corporation
specializing in personal injury and medical malpractice cases. W
raised their children and never worked outside the home. When
the couple divorced after 23 years of marriage, H appealed the
distribution of marital assets, arguing that the court improperly
included his professional goodwill. (Result: It is not improper to
divide professional goodwill as a marital asset, if the goodwill has
monetary value over and above the tangible assets and cases in
progress and is separate and distinct from the attorney's
professional reputation. "[T]he courts of at least twenty states
have held that professional goodwill is a marital asset that, if it
exists in a particular case, should be distributed upon dissolution.
* * * Goodwill is property of an intangible nature commonly
defined as the expectation of continued public patronage. * * * It
should be emphasized that such goodwill, to be a marital asset,
must exist separate and apart from the reputation or continued
presence of the marital litigant. * * * Generally, clients come to
an individual professional to receive services from that specific
person. Even so, if a party can produce evidence demonstrating
goodwill as an asset separate and distinct from the other party's
reputation, it should be considered in distributing marital
property.") *Thompson v. Thompson*, 576 So.2d 267 (Fla.1991).

c.   The Professional License as "Marital Property"

The majority of courts continue to consider one spouse's contribution to the
other spouse's education as an important factor influencing the alimony award
or the division of property. Only a few states, prominently New York,
characterize the degree or license as marital property and attempt to "divide"
it.

Examples: (1) H and W were married for nine years. At the time of their
marriage, W had a bachelor's degree. She held a temporary
teaching certificate and needed about 18 months of postgraduate
training to receive permanent certification. During the marriage,
she pursued her education. H had nearly completed college when
they married. During the marriage, he completed his bachelor's
degree and medical school. H initiated divorce proceedings two
months after receiving his medical license. The trial court found
that W had contributed 76% of the household's income, exclusive
of a $10,000 student loan obtained by H. Finding H's medical
degree and license to be marital property with a present value of
$188,800, the court awarded W 40%, to be paid in eleven annual
installments. The appellate court reversed. W appealed (Result:
(1) A license to practice medicine, acquired during marriage, is
marital property subject to equitable distribution; (2) a working
spouse is entitled to equitable portion of the license, not a return
of funds advanced; (3) there was no suggestion that W was guilty

of fault sufficient to shock the conscience of court, to be a proper consideration in equitable distribution of marital property. "Limiting a working spouse to a maintenance award, either general or rehabilitative, not only is contrary to the economic partnership concept underlying the statute but also retains the uncertain and inequitable economic ties of dependence that the Legislature sought to extinguish by equitable distribution.") *O'Brien v. O'Brien*, 66 N.Y.2d 576, 498 N.Y.S.2d 743, 489 N.E.2d 712 (1985).

(2) W postponed her degree in nursing and worked full-time to put H through law school. W also did all of the household work. H blamed the fights he started with W on the stresses of law school. W claimed that by the end of their marriage, her whole life revolved around trying not to agitate H. The parties separated when H admitted that he had occasionally dated another woman while W was working. Upon divorce, the trial court determined that H's law degree was a marital asset, and H appealed. (Result: Remanded for valuation of W's equitable interest in H's law degree. Where an advanced degree is the end product of a concerted family effort, involving the mutual sacrifice, effort, and contribution of both spouses, there arises a marital asset subject to distribution, and the non-student spouse has an equitable claim against this asset. "[T]he goal is to attempt to financially return to the nonstudent spouse what that spouse contributed toward attainment of the degree. Because such an award is not premised upon the notion that a nonstudent spouse possesses an interest in the degree itself, we do not believe the actual value of the degree is a relevant consideration. * * * [T]he focus of an award involving an advanced degree is not to reimburse the nonstudent spouse for 'loss of expectations' over what the degree might potentially have produced, but to reimburse that spouse for unrewarded sacrifices, efforts, and contributions toward attainment of the degree on the ground that it would be equitable to do so in view of the fact that that spouse will not be sharing in the fruits of the degree.") *Postema v. Postema*, 189 Mich.App. 89, 471 N.W.2d 912 (1991).

d. "Career Enhancement"
At least in New York, courts analogize the enhancement of a spouse's career during the marriage to the acquisition/creation of a marital asset and award the "silent" partner a share in the other's "career."

Example: When W and H married, W had just embarked on her career as an opera singer. Seventeen years later, when the marriage was ending, W (Frederica von Stade) had become a celebrated artist with the Metropolitan Opera Company as well as an international recording artist and television performer. During the marriage, H sacrificed his own career as a singer to advance W's career, traveled with W to her performances, cared for the couple's children, photographed W for album covers and magazine articles, and worked as her voice coach for 10 years. Upon divorce, H argued that his efforts would not be sufficiently compensated unless W's career as a performing artist and celebrity would be subject to equitable distribution. (Result: W's career and celebrity status is marital property. "We agree with the courts that have considered the issue, that the enhanced skills of an artist such as the plaintiff, albeit growing from an innate talent, which have enabled her to become an exceptional earner, may be valued as marital property subject to equitable distribution.") *Elkus v. Elkus*, 169 A.D.2d 134, 572 N.Y.S.2d 901 (1991).

e. "Restitution" of Educational Contribution

A number of jurisdictions award the spouse who has financed the other's education a form of restitution. In its most basic form this amounts to a return of funds advanced, plus interest.

Examples: (1) H and W were married for about seven years. Both had undergraduate degrees when they married. With the exception of a one and one-half year period when H earned his M.B.A. degree, they shared household expenses during their marriage. While H was attending school, W contributed $24,000 to the household, and H made no contribution. About $6,500 of H's educational expenses were covered by veterans' benefits and the Air Force. W began a part-time graduate program during the same period. Her educational expenses were paid by her employer, and she continued to work full-time. The Appellate Division held that W was not entitled to reimbursement. W appealed. (Result: Reversed. The court refused to hold H's degree to be property, but held that W had a right to be reimbursed. "Valuing a professional degree in the hands of any particular individual at the start of his or her career would involve a gamut of calculations that reduces to little more than guesswork." Concerning reimbursement the court said: "Where a partner to marriage takes the benefits of his spouse's support in obtaining a professional degree or license with the understanding that future benefits will accrue and inure to both of them, and the marriage is then terminated without the supported spouse giving anything in return, an unfairness has occurred that calls for a remedy.") *Mahoney v. Mahoney,* 91 N.J. 488, 453 A.2d 527 (1982).

(2) In California, a statute prescribes an elaborate version of the reimbursement of expenditures concept, "with interest at the legal rate." Cal. Fam. Code § 2641(b).

(3) In Illinois a statute requires that "contributions * * * to the education, training, career or career potential, or license of the

other spouse" must be considered in the determination of alimony. 750 ILCS 5/504.

7. ALLOCATION OF PENSIONS

In community property states, pensions derived out of community funds are community property and subject to division on divorce. In separate property states, the non-earning spouse had a right to the continuation of alimony after the earner's retirement and thus shared in pension rights. With the general move toward "equitable distribution" or the concept of "marital property," most courts now allocate pensions on divorce to the extent they were earned during the marriage, and the non-earning spouse is awarded a share in the pension. The valuation of pension interests, however, presents great difficulty, especially when a final adjustment at the time of divorce is contemplated, or when the pension is not vested.

Examples: (1) When H and W divorced after 15 years of marriage, W was awarded alimony of $100 per month. The community property was divided evenly, with the exception of H's retirement plan, over which the court retained jurisdiction. Six months following the divorce, H first became eligible to retire. His monthly benefit would then have been $717.18, of which W's interest was $177.14. H did not retire, however, and represented that he intended to work for some years in the future. W moved to require H to pay her share of his pension immediately, retroactive to the date he became eligible to retire. (Result: W is entitled to immediate distribution of her share of H's retirement benefits. "Under the cases and statutory law, H cannot time his retirement to deprive W of an equal share of the community's interest in his pension. It is a settled principle that one spouse cannot, by invoking a condition wholly within his control, defeat the community interests of the other spouse. * * * H would deprive W of the immediate enjoyment of an asset earned by the community during the marriage. In so doing, he would subject W to the risk of losing the asset completely if H were to die while he was still employed. Although H has every right to choose to postpone the receipt of his pension and to run that risk, he should not be able to force W to do so as well. * * * H's claim that he is being forced to retire misses the point. He is free to continue working. However, if he does so, he must reimburse W for the share of the community property that she loses as a result of that decision.") *Gillmore v. Gillmore,* 29 Cal.3d 418, 174 Cal.Rptr. 493, 629 P.2d 1 (1981).

(2) H and W divorced after 20 years of marriage. In dividing the marital property, the trial court awarded H's nonvested pension with a then-present value of $27,000 to H and offsetting assets to W. H appealed, arguing that a nonvested pension is not a marital asset. In the alternative, H argued that the trial court should not have used the present value method to value the pension. (Result: A nonvested

pension is a marital asset, but its valuation should not be determined using the present value method; instead, the court should retain jurisdiction and, upon request of the nonemployee spouse, value and divide the pension after it has vested. "The trend * * * is to consider pensions as marital property regardless of whether they have vested. * * * Supporting this trend is the reasoning that the contingent nature of a nonvested pension presents simply a valuation problem, not bearing on the non-employee spouse' entitlement to a just share of the marital assets. * * * Since [under the present value method] the non-employee spouse receives his or her share in a lump sum at the time of the divorce, the method unfairly places all risk of possible forfeiture on the employee spouse.") *Laing v. Laing*, 741 P.2d 649 (Alaska 1987).

(3) At the time of divorce, H was employed by the United States as a physicist and eligible to retire. At the trial level, W had argued that H's pension should be valued assuming that H would retire immediately. H's expert presented valuations based on four possible retirement dates, at ages 65, 70, 62 and 57. The trial court valued the pension based on a "normal" retirement date of 65. W appealed. (Result: Affirmed. "We are of opinion that a judge determining present value of a pension should not invariably be required to assume the earliest possible retirement age. In general, fair value analysis assumes norms. Rates of return are based on market analysis. Fair rents, fair market prices of real estate or businesses, rates of return, utilities rates, and insurance premiums are based on the facts of the marketplace. As we have seen, the earlier the retirement age chosen, the higher the present value and vice-versa. There is no distortion if a judge chooses a retirement age that is the norm, namely, sixty-five.") *Dewan v. Dewan*, 30 Mass.App.Ct. 133, 566 N.E.2d 1132 (1991).

8. THE "EMPLOYEE RETIREMENT INCOME SECURITY ACT" (ERISA) AND THE "QUALIFIED DOMESTIC RELATIONS ORDER" (QDRO)

ERISA applies to employee benefit plans that are maintained by an employer engaged directly or indirectly in commerce. The Act supersedes state laws on the subject. The Act provides: "Each pension plan shall provide that benefits provided under the plan may not be assigned or alienated." 29 U.S.C.A. § 1056(d)(1). A 1984 amendment expressly applies the restriction to a "domestic relations order," unless it is a "qualified domestic relations order." 29 U.S.C.A. § 1056(d)(3)(A).

"[T]he term 'qualified domestic relations order' means a domestic relations order—(I) which creates or recognizes the existence of an alternate payee's right to, or assigns to an alternate payee the right to, receive all or a portion of the benefits payable with respect to a participant under a plan, and (II) with respect to which the requirements of subparagraphs (C) and (D) are met, and (ii) the term 'domestic relations order' means any judgment, decree, or order (including approval of a property settlement agreement) which—(I) relates to the provision of child support, alimony payments, or marital property rights to a spouse, former spouse, child, or other dependent of a participant, and (II) is made pursuant to a State domestic relations law (including a community property law.)" 29 U.S.C.A. § 1056(d)(3)(B).

A QDRO must specify names and addresses, amounts or percentages to be paid, applicable periods and the plan to which the QDRO applies. A QDRO must *not* require the plan to provide any benefit not otherwise provided under the plan, require the plan to provide increased benefits, or require payment of benefits which have previously been divided in a qualified domestic relations order to another alternative payee. 29 U.S.C.A. § 1056(d)(3)(D). The ordering of payment of benefits to an alternative payee on or after the date the employee attains the earliest retirement age, as if he or she had actually retired on that date, meets these requirements. 29 U.S.C.A. § 1056(d)(3)(E).

C. SEPARATION AGREEMENTS

A separation agreement is made during marriage in contemplation of divorce. The agreement specifies the parties' wishes as to the settlement of their economic affairs and may extend to questions relating to children.

1. VALIDITY OF SEPARATION AGREEMENT
Traditional law governing the validity of separation agreements involved conflicting policies. On the one hand, contracts facilitating divorce were considered void as contrary to the public policy against divorce. On the other hand, it has long been obvious that it is in the public interest for parties to settle their own affairs without unnecessary recourse to the courts. Resolving this conflict on the side of practicality, the courts have upheld separation agreements when the parties' separation or divorce had already occurred or was about to occur, the agreement was supported by consideration, and the agreement was fair.

2. TRADITIONAL REQUIREMENTS FOR ENFORCEABILITY
a. "Facilitating" or "Encouraging" Separation or Divorce
Traditionally, to render the agreement valid, the parties' separation must have been accomplished or about to occur.

> ***Examples:*** (1) While separated, and in contemplation of divorce, H and W executed a separation agreement in which H agreed to pay for upkeep on the marital home where W lived, make one-half of the mortgage payments as long as W did not remarry or either of the couple's children remained at home, and to pay child and spousal support. H argued that the agreement was void on the grounds that it violated public policy by being premised on the consideration of divorce. (Result: Agreement valid. "In line with the policy favoring family settlements, even where made in

contemplation of divorce, in order to render an agreement unenforceable some *overt* manifestation of mutual assent with respect to a bargained for divorce must appear.") *Wife, B.T.L. v. Husband, H.A.L.,* 287 A.2d 413 (Del.Ch.1972).

(2) H was separated from W and living with D. W's attorney informed D that W would not sign a property settlement with H unless D executed a guaranty of payment. D signed. H and W divorced. H married D. H and D divorced. H stopped payments due W under the separation agreement. W sued D and obtained a judgment for nearly $9,000. D contended that her agreement was void on public policy grounds in that it was intended to induce W to divorce H. (Result: Agreement valid. "In determining whether public policy forbids the enforcement of an agreement 'promotive' of the dissolution of a particular marriage, we must look not solely to the terms of the agreement but also to the viability of the marriage in question at the time the contract was entered into. If the marriage had so deteriorated that legitimate grounds for divorce existed and if there was little hope of reconciliation, the dissolution of such a marriage is not contrary to public policy. Divorce is often, in fact, the preferred solution.") *Glickman v. Collins,* 13 Cal.3d 852, 120 Cal.Rptr. 76, 533 P.2d 204 (1975).

b. Consideration

A promise to perform duties imposed by the marital relationship generally is not effective consideration. However, separation agreements rarely founder on the consideration issue. Courts have upheld agreements supported by the wife's promise to take custody of the children, the husband's promise to support his wife, or the release by a spouse of property or support rights which he or she may have.

c. Full Disclosure, Fraud, Fairness and Representation by Attorney

Separation agreements may be invalidated if there was no full disclosure, or if the agreement is unfair. If both partners are represented by separate counsel, a resulting agreement is far more secure than it is when only one or neither party is represented by counsel. Traditionally, it was postulated that the confidential relationship between husband and wife required the dominant partner (H) to bear the burden of proving the fairness of the agreement. The modern view is that whether or not such a relationship exists depends on the facts of the particular case, and courts will invalidate a separation agreement only upon a showing of *actual* fraud, misrepresentation, coercion, or undue influence. Under UMDA § 306 only an "unconscionable" separation agreement is not binding on the court. (Note: Provisions in separation agreements relating to child custody or child support are *not* binding on the court, whether or not they are "conscionable.")

Examples: (1) W's attorney prepared a separation agreement. H made two significant changes (reducing child support from $700 to $300 per month and adding the disposition of eleven houses owned by the couple). H's secretary retyped the agreement. H asked W to come to his office to sign the agreement. When W arrived, H suggested they discuss the agreement in private. He did not mention the changes, but informed W that he knew of her affair with a police lieutenant and that he would go to the newspapers if W did not sign the agreement. W requested that she be able to talk to her attorney and threatened to leave several times. H threatened to "start the ball rolling." W negotiated several changes in the agreement and then signed it. H received $163,000, and W received $45,000 under the agreement. W sued for cancellation of the separation agreement on the grounds that it was obtained by duress or undue influence. (Result: For H. The evidence sustained finding that there was a lack of trust and confidence between parties necessary to the establishment of a confidential relationship between them. "[T]here is no rule of law that precludes a woman from giving away a substantial portion of her property to save her reputation, if it is her voluntary act.") *Bell v. Bell*, 38 Md.App. 10, 379 A.2d 419 (1977).

(2) H owned an interest in a closely held insurance business. When H and W divorced, H assured W that the business furnished him only a salary and that its stock had no market value. H produced financial records to support this representation. Several years after the divorce was final, W learned that the business had been sold just prior to the divorce and that H had received $340,000 for his share; H thus had concealed 99.5 percent of his net worth. W sought to reopen the divorce. The trial court denied her motion because she had failed to exercise due diligence. W appealed. (Result: Judgment reopened and new trial ordered on the property distribution issues. "Of paramount significance * * * is the court's express finding that in concealing his assets, the defendant had perpetrated a fraud on the court. * * * The defendant's conduct was a deliberate, fraudulent and egregious concealment of assets. The record clearly shows that, at the time he filed his affidavit, the defendant knew exactly how much he would be receiving from the sale of his business. If we allow such a deliberate and fraudulent statement of assets to go unchallenged, the role of the financial affidavit will be reduced to a meaningless formality, as will the court's role in reviewing it. We will not permit such a result.") *Greger v. Greger*, 22 Conn.App. 596, 578 A.2d 162 (1990).

(3) H and W negotiated the details of their separation agreement without legal representation. Their divorce was uncontested. The attorney for H's car dealership drew up the agreement, filed the divorce and told the parties that he could represent them only if there were no disagreements regarding the terms of the divorce.

He did not advise W, and nothing in the record indicates that he advised H that their interests might be adverse, or that each should be represented by a separate attorney. Following the divorce, W consulted another attorney and sought to have the judgment set aside. (Result: Judgment affirmed. "[T]here is no evidence that H failed to disclose assets or misrepresented their value. Nor is there an allegation or evidence of active collusion between H and the attorney representing W to deprive W of her rightful share of marital property. W's own evidence demonstrates that she was aware of all of the assets of the marriage and agreed on their division. A party is not entitled to relief from choices freely and deliberately made.") *Kolmosky v. Kolmosky*, 631 A.2d 419 (Me.1993).

3. THE DIVORCE DECREE AND THE SEPARATION AGREEMENT

Generally, courts incorporate separation agreements into divorce decrees. This may be accomplished by specific reference or by expressly setting forth the terms in the decree. Validity, modifiability and enforceability of the separation agreement are affected by the relationship between the agreement and the divorce decree.

a. Specific Incorporation

When the decree expressly sets forth (and orders compliance with) the terms of the separation agreement, the agreement obtains the status and enforceability of a judgment. Among other consequences, failure to comply will be contempt of court. Moreover, the incorporated agreement may be modified only in accordance with the rules for modifying judgments. (UMDA § 306(e) *additionally* allows enforcement as a contract.)

b. Incorporation by Reference

If the terms of the agreement are not expressly set forth in the decree, but the agreement is incorporated by reference, the issue of validity of the agreement is assured (*res judicata*). However, the agreement is not enforceable as a judgment.

Example: While separated, H and W entered into a separation agreement. The agreement provided that it was to be incorporated by reference in the divorce decree, but that it would not merge with it. The divorce decree ordered incorporation by reference. Eight years later, H petitioned to set aside the agreement on the basis that, during negotiations, he had suffered from a mental disease. (Result: The court held that the separation agreement was not merged, but that H was precluded from attacking the agreement. "[W]here, as in the instant case, the agreement provides that it shall be incorporated but not merged in the decree, it is patent that the parties did not intend merger and the agreement survives as a separate and independent contractual arrangement between the parties. * * * [W]here, as in the instant case, the property settlement agreement is presented to the court for approval and is approved by the court and incorporated in the divorce decree, the validity of the agreement is conclusively established and the doctrine of res judicata operates so as to preclude a collateral attack on the agreement.") *Johnston v. Johnston,* 297 Md. 48, 465 A.2d 436 (1983).

c. No Incorporation

A separation agreement entered into by the parties, but not incorporated into the divorce decree, is enforceable as a contract, subject to the various inhibitions applying to marital agreements.

Example: Prior to H and W's divorce in 1986, they entered into a separation agreement providing that, when H retired, W was to receive 50% of H's pension and social security benefits. Their agreement was *not* incorporated into the final divorce decree. After H retired, he paid W these benefits for 2 years. When H stopped paying, W filed suit to enforce the separation agreement. (Result: Summary judgment under a breach of contract theory for W in the amount of H's arrearages up to the date of the judgment. W, however, was *not* entitled to specific performance of the unincorporated agreement, nor could H be held in contempt for breach of the agreement.) *Eickhoff v. Eickhoff,* 263 Ga. 498, 435 S.E.2d 914 (1993).

d. Court's Review of Separation Agreement

Courts usually accept the separation agreement as offered by the parties. Nevertheless, judicial discretion to accept or reject is considerable. Traditionally, scrutiny has run almost exclusively in favor of the wife. UMDA § 306(b) reduces traditional judicial discretion by providing that a separation agreement, except to the extent it provides "for the support, custody, and visitation of children", is "binding upon the court unless it finds, after considering the economic circumstances of the parties and any other relevant evidence produced by the parties * * * that the separation agreement is unconscionable."

Example: H and W executed a separation agreement under which W was to receive the first $60,000 from the proceeds of the sale of their home and H was to receive the difference. The intent of the agreement was to give W enough money to buy a condominium with an affordable mortgage. W, who waived maintenance, also was to have custody of the children and $250 per month in child support. When H realized that the home would sell for much less than he had expected and that he would receive only $10,000, he moved to set aside the agreement. The trial court granted H's motion, the appellate court affirmed, and W appealed. (Result: Separation agreement reinstated. Before a court incorporates a separation agreement into the divorce decree, it must review the agreement for fraud, overreaching, and fairness under the totality of the circumstances. Under that standard, the agreement at issue was not unfair or unreasonable. "Although the terms of the separation agreement relating to property disposition are presumed binding upon the court without a specific finding of unconscionability, the court is not to accept blindly the agreed-upon terms. * * * [W]e conclude that before a court incorporates property division provisions of a separation agreement into a dissolution decree, it should first review the provisions for fraud, overreaching, concealment of assets, or sharp dealing not consistent with the obligations of marital partners to deal fairly with each other, and then look at the economic circumstances of the parties which result from the agreement, including a determination whether under the totality of the circumstances the property disposition is fair, just and reasonable.") *Marriage of Manzo*, 659 P.2d 669 (Colo. 1983).

e. Reconciliation

The parties' reconciliation generally terminates their separation agreement, but does not override a court decree. Executed provisions of the agreement, such as completed property transfers, are not affected. Specific action by the court is needed to vacate a court decree.

1) What Is Reconciliation?

Holdings differ on what constitutes reconciliation. Some courts require renewed cohabitation; others may find that even isolated acts of sexual relations accomplish reconciliation.

2) Effect of Reconciliation on Separation Agreement

It has been argued that, after reconciliation, the separation agreement turns into an invalid post-nuptial agreement since it still contemplates divorce. More reasonably, reconciliation constitutes a change of circumstances that amounts to an implied revocation of prospective, but not of executed, provisions of the separation agreement.

Example: H was obligated to pay W $80,000 under a settlement agreement that was merged into their divorce decree. H paid $30,000 upon execution of the agreement, but never paid the remaining installments. Seven months later the parties remarried, but six years later their second marriage also ended in divorce. The court assigned to divide the marital estate for the second divorce declared the settlement agreement from the first divorce "null and void," and W appealed. (Result: Reversed. "This property settlement was not merged into the second marriage, and according to the record, H still owes for this judgment. Those assets from the judgment are W's separate assets.") *Marriage of Nordberg*, 265 Mont. 352, 877 P.2d 987 (1994).

D. REVIEW QUESTIONS

1. **T or F** Most courts now embrace the idea of short-term or intermediate term "rehabilitative alimony" and no longer award lifetime alimony.

2. **T or F** Even where a fault ground is used for divorce, "fault" no longer is a consideration with regard to alimony or property division.

3. **T or F** Modern "no-fault" statutes dispense with proof of "marital fault" insofar as the divorce itself is concerned, but typically allow consideration of marital fault in determining the financial consequences of divorce.

4–7. Questions 4 through 7 should be answered based on the following facts: H and W divorced after 10 years of marriage. Their separation agreement was incorporated verbatim in the divorce decree. H agreed to pay W "rehabilitative" alimony of $500 per month for 6 years. In addition, W was given a one third interest in stock which H had purchased out of his earnings during the marriage.

4. **T or F** H quits his job, sells his furniture, moves in with his parents, and starts writing a book about divorce. He has no current income. Because of this significant change in circumstances, his alimony payments will be eliminated or modified to a much lower amount.

5. **T or F** Three years after the divorce, H dies of a heart attack. W will not collect any further alimony payments from H's estate.

6. **T or F** Two years after the divorce, W remarries. H petitions to terminate the alimony payments alleging her change in circumstances. H's petition will be granted.

7. **T or F** H goes through bankruptcy with no assets available for his creditors. After discharge, H continues to be liable to pay W alimony, but W has no claim for the value of stock not yet transferred to her.

8. **T or F** Upon a showing of the payor's or the recipient's changed circumstances, an alimony award may generally be modified up or down.

9. **T or F** For federal income tax purposes, alimony is deductible by the payor and is included in the recipient's taxable income.

10. **T or F** For federal income tax purposes, a property settlement upon divorce is treated as a nontaxable event.

11. **T or F** Today, a professional license or academic degree earned during the marriage is treated as marital property upon divorce.

12. **T or F** After the parties' reconciliation, their separation agreement remains in force to govern property rights upon a subsequent divorce.

*

VII

THE PARENTAL CHILD SUPPORT OBLIGATION

Analysis

A. DEFINITION OF THE PARENTAL OBLIGATION

Traditionally, the duty to support the family was imposed primarily on the father and only secondarily on the mother. Today the duty to support children rests equally upon both parents, although the custodial parent (still typically the mother) generally fulfills the obligation by providing care. A child's independent wealth or income normally does not relieve the parents of their support obligation. Because courts are reluctant to intervene in family relationships, litigation concerning child support issues typically is limited to situations where the obligated parent is separated, divorced or not married. The neglect and dependency laws assure a minimum level of child support in the ongoing family. When the parents cannot adequately support the child, the AFDC (Aid to Families with Dependent Children) program has long provided relief, but welfare reform proposals, pending in early 1996, may change that. The child support obligation continues after a child is removed from the home or moves out voluntarily, although, in such cases, enforcement of adequate support is often impossible. Termination of parental rights ends the obligation of support.

B. STEPPARENT'S DUTY TO SUPPORT

A stepparent who has married the custodial parent but who has not adopted the child typically is not legally obligated to support the child. Iowa imposes a support duty on the stepparent while the relationship continues. *Kelley v. Iowa Department of Social Services,* 197 N.W.2d 192 (Iowa 1972). In New York, a stepparent was held not obligated to support a stepchild when the child was receiving AFDC. *Slochowsky v. Shang,* 67 A.D.2d 926, 412 N.Y.S.2d 923 (1979).

C. DURATION OF THE OBLIGATION

The obligation to support a child runs until the child reaches majority or becomes emancipated, or until either the parent or the child dies. Under certain circumstances, a parent may be liable for the cost of higher education. If the child is handicapped and unable to provide for itself, the obligation may be wholly open-ended.

Example: Twenty-three-year-old C suffered from severe mental illness and was incapable of supporting and caring for herself. After reaching age 21, C had moved into her own apartment and held a job for a time, but later moved back in with M because of her disability. M and F were divorced, and M sought support for C from F. The trial court denied support, finding that the duty to support an adult child exists only when the disability precedes majority and that, when she attained the age of majority, C was not disabled. The appellate court reversed. (Result: Support obligation upheld. "[T]he appellant would draw a distinction in the parents' support obligation based upon the time that the child's disability arose. We do not agree. * * * Unlike physical injuries, mental disabilities often develop over time. The evidence in the instant case traced the roots of Janette's mental disability into her childhood. Yet, her mental difficulties, though present all along, did not become disabling, according to the master's finding, until after she passed the age of majority. * * * The arbitrary age chosen for the age of majority should not override the clear policy expressed in plain language by the legislature * * *. We cannot accept the inconsistency and inequity that would follow from applying an emancipation rationale as urged by appellant.") *Sininger v. Sininger*, 300 Md. 604, 479 A.2d 1354 (1984).

1. MAJORITY

Widespread change in the statutory age of majority from 21 to 18 years of age generally has ended parental responsibility for support after age 18. Several states extend parental liability to cover higher education past majority, most often only in post-divorce situations. No clear rule defines the extent to which the support-paying parent may control the adult child's lifestyle or choice of studies; however, in regard of choice of school (private or public) a reasonableness test (measuring the child's ability against the parent's educational background and financial resources) is emerging.

Examples: (1) F was held obligated to finance his 18–year-old son's continuing education because the latter suffered from dyslexia and would need further education in order to support himself and pay future medical bills. *Elkins v. Elkins,* 262 Ark. 63, 553 S.W.2d 34 (1977).

(2) C attacked an Illinois statute allowing courts to order divorced parents to provide for the education of children who have reached the age of majority even though undivorced, married parents do not have the same obligation. (Result: No Equal Protection violation. The statute does not require that divorced parents provide majority age children with education in all cases. The situation of the child of divorced parents differs from that of the intact family. "Unfortunately, it is not the isolated exception that noncustodial divorced parents * * * cannot be relied upon to voluntarily support the children of the earlier marriage to the extent they would have, had they not divorced. * * * If parents could have been expected to provide an education for their child absent divorce, it is not unreasonable for the legislature to furnish a means for providing that they do so after they have been divorced.") *Kujawinski v. Kujawinski,* 71 Ill.2d 563, 17 Ill.Dec. 801, 376 N.E.2d 1382 (1978). (*Contra: Curtis v. Kline*, 666 A.2d 265 (Pa.1995) where divorced F succeeded in ending his child support obligation on the child's majority. The following statute was held *unconstitutional*: "[A] court may order either or both parents who are separated, divorced, unmarried or otherwise subject to an existing support obligation to provide equitably for educational costs of their child whether an application for this support is made before or after the child has reached 18 years of age." The Pennsylvania Supreme Court held:

"In the absence of an entitlement on the part of any individual to post-secondary education, or a generally applicable requirement that parents assist their adult children in obtaining such an education, we perceive no rational basis for the state government to provide only certain adult citizens with legal means to overcome the difficulties they encounter in pursuing that end.")

(3) When his parents separated, C was a senior in high school. C lived with M for 3 months following the separation. Relations between M and C became strained, and C moved in with F. Prior to his departure, C had shoved M and spat at her during a fight. After this C did not communicate with or visit M. F paid all of C's college expenses during C's freshman year, and C continued to live with F when not in school. When C was accepted as a transfer student to a more expensive private college, he commenced an action against M and F to secure financial assistance for his college expenses. The trial court found that the estrangement between M and C was not a bar to support and directed M to pay $3,250 per year to C. M appealed. (Result: Reversed. "Perhaps the single most compelling piece of evidence in this case is [M's] testimony that her son 'spat in my face and shoved me so that I fell over. He never spat but once. He did push me more than once. He struck me at least twice.' That any father would condone, let alone encourage, a son who has so abused his mother in taking legal action against her shocks the sensibilities of this writer. The dissent would add insult to injury by finding that [C] is entitled to exact funds for college from his mother's already strained resources. Such compounding of the tragedy of this family cannot be countenanced. * * * If as an adult, a child repudiates a parent, that parent must be allowed to dictate what effect this will have on his or her contribution to college expenses for that child.") *Milne v. Milne*, 383 Pa.Super. 177, 556 A.2d 854 (1989).

2. EMANCIPATION

Through emancipation, a minor becomes legally independent of his or her parents, ending parental rights and duties, and becomes fully responsible for his or her own acts and contracts. The following acts or events point toward emancipation: marriage, enlistment in the military, providing for self support, or any other circumstance that shows the minor has assumed the position of an adult to the point where the legal rights and obligations of adulthood should go with it.

Examples: (1) F was excused from supporting his 18–year–old daughter (C) who had left home to have a child, when C was supported by public assistance. "[W]e cannot agree with the commissioner that whenever an older child chooses to leave home, for any reason, the parents must pay for the child's separate maintenance, or contribute support, if the child applies for public assistance. The courts must still consider the impact on the family relationship and the possibility of injustice in the particular case. Of course the fact that the child is eligible for public assistance may, as is evident here, permit her to avoid her father's authority and demands however reasonable they may be. But it does not follow that the parent must then finish what has been begun by underwriting the lifestyle which his daughter chose against his reasonable wishes and repeated counsel." *Parker v. Stage,* 43 N.Y.2d 128, 400 N.Y.S.2d 794, 371 N.E.2d 513 (1977).

(2) M and F were divorced. Under their divorce agreement, F was obligated to support C until she married, died, turned 21, or became "otherwise emancipated." After graduating from high school, C continued to live with M, but began working full-time for a hospital at an annual salary of approximately $15,000. F moved to end his support obligation. (Result: F not obligated to pay support. C became "otherwise emancipated" when she began working on a full time basis and earned a liveable salary). *Ware v. Ware,* 10 Va.App. 352, 391 S.E.2d 887 (1990).

(3) At the age of 16½, C refused to enter an in-patient facility for a psychiatric evaluation. F locked her out of the house and refused to continue to support her. C maintained herself with a part-time job and the help of friends and neighbors. C petitioned for support from F. (Result: F's support obligation continues. "The obligations of parents cannot be avoided merely because the child is at odds with her parents or has disobeyed their instructions. Even a child's delinquent behavior will not, of itself, relieve a parent of the obligation to support. * * * Additionally, petitioner's part-time employment since leaving her home is insufficient to sustain her, and therefore, does not result in her emancipation. Inasmuch as respondent has refused to allow petitioner to return to her home, 'there is no injustice in having him provide for her support elsewhere.' ") *Jennifer S. v. Marvin S.,* 150 Misc.2d 300, 568 N.Y.S.2d 515 (1991).

3. REVERSION TO UNEMANCIPATED STATUS
An emancipated minor may revert to unemancipated status if the state of facts that caused the emancipation ceases to exist. In that case, the minor may again be entitled to support from his or her parents until again becoming emancipated or reaching the age of majority.

Examples: (1) Under a divorce decree, F supported his four children. While still a minor, C, his daughter, married, became pregnant, and divorced. C's mother argued that C's emancipation was only temporary and ended with her divorce. (Result: C's divorce did not undo her emancipation. When C married, her spouse assumed legal responsibility for support, and that burden should not be reimposed on her father.) *Meyer v. Meyer,* 493 S.W.2d 42 (Mo.App.1973).

(2) Following his divorce from M, F paid support for C. At age 16, C married, but her marriage was soon annulled. When C was 17, and following the annulment, M sought to have F's child support obligation increased. F claimed that C had become emancipated by marriage, thus extinguishing his child support obligation. Summary judgment for F. M appealed. (Result: Reversed. F must pay child support for C. Annulment of C's marriage during her minority reinstated her status as an unemancipated minor child, for purposes of child support. "An annulment * * * voids the marriage from the beginning; the law treats the parties as never having married. Accordingly, the legal definition of annulment supports the conclusion that the daughter's unemancipated status has been reinstated.") *Eyerman v. Thias*, 760 S.W.2d 187 (Mo.App.1988).

4. DEATH OF PARENT
a. Parents' Not Divorced
The death of parent or child terminates the support obligation. In nearly all jurisdictions a parent may disinherit a minor child. In some states disinheritance must stop short of putting a minor child on welfare. A parent may freely disinherit an adult child. Pretermitted heir laws guard against unintentional disinheritance. Intestacy laws provide children with a portion of the estate when the parent leaves no will. In (civil law) Louisiana, disinheritance of minor and even adult children is restricted.

b. Parents Divorced
UMDA § 316(c) breaks with the traditional rule in the event of divorce: "Unless otherwise agreed [ordered] * * *, provisions for the support of a child are terminated by emancipation of the child *but not by the death of a parent obligated to support a child*. When a parent obligated to pay support dies, the amount of support may be modified, revoked or commuted to a lump sum payment, to the extent just or appropriate in the circumstances." (Emphasis added).

Example: The Supreme Court of Illinois upheld a similar provision against equal protection challenge: "Two reasonable justifications are given by defendant for singling out divorced parents. First, though a nondivorced parent may disinherit a dependent child, he may not disinherit his family. The surviving parent may renounce the will of the deceased parent and demand a statutory forced share of the deceased parent's estate. The forced share then becomes available for the support of the dependent child because the surviving parent remains obligated to support the child. In effect, a child of a nondivorced parent has some indirect security against the possible loss of support due to disinheritance. The dependent child of a divorced parent has no similar protection because a surviving divorced spouse is not entitled to a forced share of a former spouse's estate. * * * In balance, section 510(c) mitigates rather than aggravates inequality. Second, while it is comparatively rare for a nondivorced parent to leave a spouse and their children out of a will, it is not so uncommon for a divorced parent to do so. A divorced parent may establish a new family which may command primary allegiance in a subsequent will." *Kujawinski v. Kujawinski,* 71 Ill.2d 563, 17 Ill.Dec. 801, 376 N.E.2d 1382 (1978).

D. TRADITIONAL CRITERIA FOR AWARDING SUPPORT

In awarding support, courts consider all relevant facts, including the needs of the child, the standard of living and circumstances of the parents, the relative financial means of the parents, the earning ability of the parents, the need and capacity of the child for education, including higher education, the age of the child, the financial resources and the earning ability of the child, the responsibility of the parents for the support of others, and the value of services contributed by the custodial parent. (*Cf.* Uniform Parentage Act (UPA) § 15). The UMDA § 309 lists similar factors and would also consider the standard of living the child would have enjoyed had the marriage not been dissolved. The UMDA, of course, applies in the context of divorce only, whereas the UPA applies primarily in the context of illegitimacy.

E. CHILD SUPPORT GUIDELINES

Prodded by federal legislation, all states now have much more specific, often formulaic, child support guidelines that primarily orient themselves on the obligated (typical the non-custodial) spouse's income, or on the joint income of both parents. All states are mandated to have such guidelines, but they have freedom to experiment. State approaches range from assessing specific percentages (increasing with the number of children) of the non-custodial, absent parent's net or gross income, to extremely complex formulae.

Examples: (1) The divorce decree awarded custody of C to M. F was ordered to pay $275 a month in child support. Five years later, M filed to increase F's child support payments, alleging C's increased needs and F's increased income. At that time, M's net monthly income was $2,046 and F's net monthly income was $1,986. The trial court found that M had sustained her burden of proving C's increased needs and F's increased income. The court increased F's support obligation to $400 per month finding that it was obligated to follow the legislated child support guidelines that state the obligation in terms of specified percentages of the absent parent's income (20% for one child, progressing up to 50% for six children), with little room for discretion. F appealed. (Result: Affirmed. Child support guideline statute (1) did not violate the separation of powers clause requirement of the state Constitution, (2) did not deprive the noncustodial parent of procedural or substantive due process, and (3) did not infringe on the noncustodial parent's right to equal protection under the law.) *Boris v. Blaisdell*, 142 Ill.App.3d 1034, 97 Ill.Dec. 186, 492 N.E.2d 622 (1986).

(2) When C was born, M and F were married to other persons. M's marriage was dissolved. F remained married and had two children from his marriage. M filed for child support. The state child support guideline provided four separate charts based on the number of children. F argued that his obligation to support his two children from his existing marriage, in addition to C, justified use of the chart for three children. The trial court determined F's obligation to C using the chart for one child. (Result: Affirmed. Unable to present evidence of any special circumstances that would make a support obligation based on the one-child chart unjust or inappropriate, F failed to overcome the presumption that the trial court's application of the one-child chart was correct.) *Gilley v. McCarthy*, 469 N.W.2d 666 (Iowa 1991).

(3) M and F had two minor children but were never married. F, an actor, earned in excess of $300,000 per month and had agreed to pay $3,500 per month in child support as well as the children's medical expenses. F and his parents also voluntarily provided child care, a housekeeper, vacations, food, transportation, private schooling, and a 4–bedroom house with beach and tennis facilities. M sought to modify the support order to comply with statutory child support guidelines, and moved for full disclosure of F's assets. F stipulated that he had had a gross income of at least $1.4 million in each of the past three years, and stated that he could pay any reasonable amount the court determined to be necessary for the support of his children. The trial court ordered discovery regarding F's income, expenses and assets. (Result: Reversed, on the basis of *White v. Marciano*, 190 Cal.App. 3d 1026, 235 Cal.Rptr. 779 (1987), where the court determined "evidence of detailed lifestyle and net worth to be relevant only in those situations where the ability of the noncustodial parent to make adequate support payments may be affected by the unwise expenditure of income to the detriment of the supported minor. Where there is no question of the noncustodial parent's ability to pay any reasonable support order, we conclude that evidence of detailed lifestyle [is] irrelevant to the issue of the amount of support to be paid and thus protected from discovery and inadmissible in determining the support order.") *Estevez v. Superior Court*, 22 Cal.App.4th 423, 27 Cal.Rptr.2d 470 (1994).

(4) F had an extramarital affair with M. C was born, and F had no further contact with M or C. Initially, F was ordered to pay $200 per month in child support. When F's income increased dramatically, M petitioned to increase F's child support obligation. The trial court ordered F to pay $3,092 per month, with $1,780 reserved for a trust fund established for C's college education. The appellate court reversed, limiting the support payment to $1,312 per month (based on the first $6,250 of F's monthly income, the top income to which the statutory support guidelines explicitly applied, multiplied by 21 percent, the percentage applicable to one child). The

appellate court disallowed the trust, finding that it improperly extended support beyond majority. (Result: Reversed. (1) The court may take into account income that exceeds the highest amount listed in the child support guidelines, and (2) an educational trust is not an award of post-majority support. "Obviously, to treat the monthly income figure of $6,250.00 as a cap and automatically to limit the award to 21 percent of that amount for a child whose non-custodial parent makes over $6,250.00 may be 'neither appropriate nor equitable.' * * * Rather than adopting either of these diametrically opposed approaches, we conclude that the trial court should retain the discretion to determine—as the guidelines provide, 'on a case-by-case basis'—the appropriate amount of child support to be paid when an obligor's net income exceeds $6,250.00 per month, balancing both the child's need and the parents' means.") *Nash v. Mulle*, 846 S.W.2d 803 (Tenn.1993).

F. MODIFICATION

Child support obligations are modifiable if circumstances change. Typical changes obligors assert are (1) unfavorable income and employment changes, (2) the needs of a subsequent family, or (3) disability. On behalf of the child, assertions for more support include (1) increase in the cost of living (2) a special need, such as medical care, (3) increased need by reason of age, and (4) the obligated parent's increased income.

G. CHILD SUPPORT ENFORCEMENT SANCTIONS

Courts sometimes confuse or fail to distinguish sharply between superficially similar remedies, especially civil and criminal contempt. A century ago, the matter seemed quite clear: "If the contempt consists in the refusal of a party to do something which he is ordered to do for the benefit or advantage of the opposite party, the process is civil, and he stands committed till he complies with the order. The order in such a case is not in the nature of a punishment, but is coercive, to compel him to act in accordance with the order of the court. If, on the other hand, the contempt consists in the doing of a forbidden act, injurious to the opposite party, the process is criminal, and conviction is followed by fine or imprisonment, or both; and this is by way of punishment. In one case the private party is interested in the enforcement of the order, and, the moment he is satisfied, the imprisonment ceases, on the other hand, the state alone is interested in the enforcement of the penalty, it being a punishment which operates in terrorem, and by that means has a tendency to prevent a repetition of the offense in other similar cases." *State v. Knight*, 3 S.D. 509, 54 N.W. 412 (1893).

1. CIVIL CONTEMPT
Civil contempt applies to a parent who has failed to pay, but who is able to meet the obligation. It may involve an open-ended jail sentence, allowing the defaulter to leave jail as soon as the specified payment is made.

2. CRIMINAL CONTEMPT

Criminal contempt applies to a willful default on a support judgment and carries a specific sentence.

3. CIVIL AND CRIMINAL CONTEMPT DISTINGUISHED

The U.S. Supreme Court sees the difference between criminal and civil as follows: "[T]he critical features are the substance of the proceedings and the character of the relief that the proceeding will afford. 'If it is for civil contempt the punishment is remedial, and for the benefit of the complainant. But if it is for criminal contempt the sentence is punitive, to vindicate the authority of the court.' The character of the relief imposed is thus ascertainable by applying a few straightforward rules. If the relief provided is a sentence of imprisonment, it is remedial if 'the defendant stands committed unless and until he performs the affirmative act required by the court's order,' and is punitive if 'the sentence is limited to imprisonment for a definite period.' If the relief provided is a fine, it is remedial when it is paid to the complainant, and punitive when it is paid to the court, though a fine that would be payable to the court is also remedial when the defendant can avoid paying the fine simply by performing the affirmative act required by the court's order. These distinctions lead up to the fundamental proposition that criminal penalties may not be imposed on someone who has not been afforded the protections that the Constitution requires of such criminal proceedings, including the requirement that the offense be proved beyond a reasonable doubt." *Hicks on Behalf of Feiock v. Feiock*, 485 U.S. 624, 108 S.Ct. 1423, 99 L.Ed.2d 721 (1988).

4. CRIMINAL PROSECUTION FOR NON-SUPPORT

A criminal prosecution for non-support may also be available, based on state statutes that focus on the existence of the duty to support or on a specific judgment. A sentence for criminal contempt or for criminal non-support may be suspended on condition that payment is made.

5. FEDERAL CRIME

The Child Support Recovery Act of 1992 makes willful failure to support a child in another state a federal crime. (18 U.S.C.A. § 228). Prosecution is available for arrearages exceeding $5,000 or remaining unpaid for longer than one year. Penalties range from imprisonment to fines. First offenses are misdemeanors. Repeat offenses are felonies. Federal courts may make the payment of spousal and child support a condition of probation. In late 1995, the Act was held unconstitutional as not meeting federal jurisdictional prerequisites of the interstate commerce clause. *U.S. v. Schroeder*, 894 F.Supp. 360 (D.Ariz.1995); *U.S. v. Parker*, 1995 WL 683215(E.D. Pa.1995). Other federal courts have upheld the statute. *U.S. v. Hampshire*, 892 F.Supp. 1327 (D.C.Kan.1995); *U.S. v. Sage*, 22 Fam.L.Rptr. (BNA) 1004 (D.C. Conn. 10/3/95).

H. CONFLICTS OF LAWS ASPECTS OF CHILD SUPPORT: THE UNIFORM RECIPROCAL ENFORCEMENT OF SUPPORT ACT

All states had adopted the Uniform Reciprocal Enforcement of Support Act (URESA) or its equivalent. In 1992, encouraged by federal endorsement, the Uniform Interstate Family Support Act began to replace URESA. UIFSA provides an updated approach to interstate support that runs in tandem with pervasive federal legislation in this field. By early 1996, 26 jurisdictions had enacted UIFSA. For the (soon to be historical) record, URESA allows a support action to be filed in the jurisdiction where the dependent resides. The action is heard where the obligor resides. This avoids the need for travel and overcomes possible difficulties with personal jurisdiction. If the court at the obligor's residence finds the obligor owing, the judgment will be enforced there. The award is then forwarded to the initiating court to be paid to the dependent. UIFSA retains most of URESA's good features. It contains comprehensive long-arm provisions that enable a state to take jurisdiction over an absent party who has a significant connection with the state. When a state has taken jurisdiction and is the state of residence for any party, that state retains exclusive jurisdiction. If simultaneous proceedings are initiated in more than one state, the home state of the child takes priority in adjudicating the dispute.

I. FEDERAL CHILD SUPPORT ENFORCEMENT LEGISLATION

Since 1975, federal legislation has strengthened nationwide enforcement of child support obligations. Washington imposes broad burdens on state AFDC programs if they wish to participate in the federal scheme. The original purpose was to reduce the cost of AFDC programs, and failure to comply results in the state's loss of a portion of federal AFDC funding. For a small fee, the child support enforcement is available to persons not receiving public aid. Principal mechanisms include federal parent locator and collection facilities, and improved state enforcement procedures. Wage withholding is a key weapon and the states are required to apply guidelines to determine the level of child support awards. The federal pressure has resulted in a general strengthening of state child support laws across the United States. It is unclear what effect proposed federal welfare reforms will have, insofar as they may grant much more autonomy to the states.

J. FULL FAITH AND CREDIT

Full faith and credit is due to valid and final sister state judgments. This rule means generally that accrued installments, reduced to a money judgment, are entitled to full faith and credit, whereas accrued installments *not* reduced to judgment are due full faith and credit only if the accrued installments are not modifiable where the judgment was rendered. Under the traditional rule, full faith and credit was not due to modifiable accrued installments nor to future support (which is always modifiable). Since 1994, the "Full Faith and Credit for Child Support Orders Act" (28 U.S.C.A. § 17389B) requires that if a sister-state child support order meets federal standards it may be (1) enforced in any state and (2) modified only in very limited circumstances.   The Act sets jurisdictional requirements substantially similar to those of the Parental Kidnaping Prevention Act. (Note: Full faith and credit does not extend to judgments rendered in a *foreign country*, although such judgments may be and often are accorded ''comity.'')

K.   RECIPROCITY: THE CHILD'S DUTY TO SUPPORT PARENTS

Traditionally, children were required to contribute to the support of their indigent parents.   Many states continue to have such laws on the books, although they are rarely enforced.   Courts have upheld such laws against constitutional challenge on the ground that they further the legitimate state purpose of alleviating some of the burden of caring for the indigent.   In early 1996, welfare reform proposals sought to impose broad reimbursement liability on children of Medicaid recipients, especially children of elderly parents in nursing care.

> ***Example:***   The California Supreme Court held constitutional a civil code provision that required adult children of parents receiving aid to the aged to contribute to their parents' support according to a fixed schedule.   ''Since these children received special benefits from the class of 'parents in need', it is entirely rational that the children bear a special burden with respect to that class.'' *Swoap v. Superior Court of Sacramento County*, 10 Cal.3d 490, 111 Cal.Rptr. 136, 516 P.2d 840 (1973).

L.   REVIEW QUESTIONS

1–3.   Based on the following facts answer Questions 1 through 3: H and W are divorced and have one daughter, D. W has custody of D, and H is obligated to pay D's support.   W is remarried to H_2, and they live in a state in which the age of majority is 18.

1.   **T   or   F**   At age 17, D inherits $500,000 from a paternal aunt.   Since D now has sufficient means to support herself, H is no longer obligated to support her.

2.   **T   or   F** H_2 has no obligation to support D.

3.   **T   or   F**   H moves to Kansas and defaults on his child support obligation.   W must file an action in Kansas to enforce the support obligation.

4.   **T   or   F**   The common law imposed the duty to support the family's children on the father.

5.   **T   or   F**   The parents of a handicapped child have no further duty of support when the child reaches the age of majority.

6.   **T   or   F**   A child of undivorced parents is entitled to enforce support for higher education, if a state statute makes such support available to children of divorced parents.

7. **T or F**   Once emancipated, a minor child cannot revert to unemancipated status.

8. **T or F**   Unlike alimony, child support obligations are not modifiable.

9. **T or F**   It is unconstitutional for a state to require adult children to support their indigent parents.

10. **T or F**   Generally, a parent's child support obligation ends upon the parent's or the child's death or the child's emancipation or reaching the age of majority.

11. **T or F**   Freddie-the-Lout, a famous rock star, earns $50 million a year and must pay child support for one child. The state's statutory child support guideline percentage for one child is 20 percent. Freddie must pay $10 million per year.

*

VIII

CHILD CUSTODY

Analysis

A. CHILD CUSTODY DURING MARRIAGE

Parents are "natural guardians" of their child. During marriage, both parents jointly
have custody. Short of violating the neglect, dependency, abuse, school attendance and
other protective laws, the parents have full discretion to make all decisions related to the
welfare of their child. While this prominently includes medical care, the U.S. Supreme
Court has formulated exceptions for the case of abortion involving a "mature minor."
Under state statutes, various (usually medical) decisions may be made by a minor without
involving the parents.

1. CUSTODY AFTER DEATH OF PARENT(S)
When one parent dies, the survivor takes over custody and guardianship. If the
parents are separated or divorced and the custodial parent dies, the noncustodial
parent is first in line for custody. In special circumstances (especially if the
surviving parent cannot offer a suitable home), custody and guardianship may be
awarded to a third party such as a grandparent or stepparent. If the second parent
dies, the court appoints a guardian for a minor child. The court may designate
separately a guardian of the child's person and a guardian of the child's estate,
although the same person usually serves both functions. If a guardian is
designated in the deceased parents' or last-to-die parent's will, courts usually
approve the appointment of that guardian, although they are not bound by such a
designation.

2. THE CHILD REACHES MAJORITY
Parental control and obligations terminate when a child reaches majority or is
emancipated. If the adult child cannot manage his or her own affairs, a parent
may retain or regain guardianship under statutes providing for judicial
appointment of conservators. In some cases, parents have successfully used these
statutes to "kidnap" their *adult* children away from religious cults in order to have
them "deprogrammed." Unless the parents proceed as judicially appointed
guardians, they may incur civil and criminal liability.

B. CHILD CUSTODY UPON DIVORCE

1. LEGAL CUSTODY DEFINED
On divorce of the child's parents, the court has power to award custody of the child
to one parent, with or without visitation rights to the other, or jointly to both
parents. During the pendency of divorce proceedings, the court may order
temporary custody of children. Legal custody encompasses the right to make all
decisions concerning the child's welfare, education, religion, growth and
development. UMDA § 408(a) provides:

"[T]he custodian may determine the child's upbringing, including his education, health care, and religious training, unless the court after hearing, finds, upon motion by the noncustodial parent, that in the absence of a specific limitation of the custodian's authority, the child's physical health would be endangered or his emotional development significantly impaired."

2. "BEST INTEREST" STANDARD

Most state statutes give the courts broad discretion in awarding custody upon divorce. The child's "best interest" is the governing consideration.

a. Discretion

Because of the inexactness of statutory and common law child custody criteria, as a practical matter the custody decision (at least between two more or less equally fit parents) is in the discretion of the trial judge, whose decision is seldom upset on appeal.

b. Historical Criteria

Prior to the widespread adoption of the "best interests" test, other factors, both statutory and common law, determined who received custody of the child on divorce. Under the old law, the father was entitled to custody. Later, the "tender years" presumption gave a strong preference to the mother of young children. Religion, race, and morality played important roles. Although these criteria have not been retained in full force or at all, they still influence many judges' custody decisions.

c. Modern Criteria

The UMDA § 402 provides that "[t]he court shall not consider conduct of a proposed custodian that does not affect his relationship to the child" and that "[t]he court shall determine custody in accordance with the best interest of the child. The court shall consider all relevant factors including: (1) the wishes of the child's parent or parents as to his custody; (2) the wishes of the child as to his custodian; (3) the interaction and interrelationship of the child with his parent or parents, his siblings, and any other person who may significantly affect the child's best interest; (4) the child's adjustment to his home, school and community; and (5) the mental and physical health of all individuals involved."

1) Preference of Child

The child's preference is considered when the child is of sufficient age to express an intelligent preference. In an exceptional case, this has included a seven year old child. *Flaherty v. Smith,* 87 Mich.App. 561, 274 N.W.2d 72 (1978). More typically, a child's preference will not be considered (or even elicited) until the child is substantially older and more mature. Generally, the child is asked to express its preference in the privacy of the judge's chamber and not in open court. UMDA § 404(a) provides that "[T]he court may interview the child in chambers to ascertain the child's wishes as to his custodian and as to visitation. The court may permit counsel to be present at the interview. The court shall cause a record of the interview to be made and to be part of the record in the case.''

2) Court's Best Interests Findings

A trial court is not required to use the words "best interests of the child" in its findings, but sufficient factual findings must be made to enable a reviewing court to determine whether the award is based on the child's best interest.

3) Reports of Professionals

Psychiatric testimony or the advice of social work professionals often is sought or offered in custody proceedings to aid the court in ascertaining the child's best interests. UMDA § 404(b) provides:

"The court may seek the advice of professional personnel, whether or not employed by the court on a regular basis. The advice given shall be in writing and made available by the court to counsel upon request. Counsel may examine as a witness any professional personnel consulted by the court."

Courts typically place considerable reliance on professional investigative reports. Such reports are often admitted by stipulation. Otherwise, the limits on hearsay evidence may prevent the use of such reports without the preparer and possibly other witnesses being present in court.

4) Counsel for Child

Since there may be a conflict if an attorney representing one of the parents also seeks to act for the child, the child's best interests may require that an attorney be appointed for him or her. UMDA § 310 provides:

"The court may appoint an attorney to represent the interests of a minor or dependent child with respect to his support, custody, and visitation. The court shall enter an order for costs, fees, and disbursements in favor of the child's attorney. The order shall be made against either or both parents, except that, if the responsible party is indigent, the costs, fees and disbursements shall be borne by the [appropriate agency]."

A guideline detailing the child's attorney's duties and responsibilities was provided by the bench and bar of a Wisconsin county and is quoted with approval in *Veazey v. Veazey,* 560 P.2d 382 (Alaska 1977).

3. THE "TENDER YEARS" PRESUMPTION AND THE MATERNAL PREFERENCE RULE

Other things being equal, if the child was of "tender years" (generally pre-teenage), recent tradition all but automatically gave custody to the mother. Once hailed as one of the strongest presumptions in the law, today's trend in courts and legislatures is to eliminate the tender years doctrine, at least nominally. Several states have struck down the doctrine as violative of equal protection or of a state ERA. Others have upheld the doctrine against constitutional challenge. Many courts, expressly or subconsciously, are still influenced by the doctrine, especially where it has been "repackaged" in overtly sex-neutral terms as in the "primary caretaker" preference.   One study found that for each child going to the father, seven go to the mother (Maccoby & Mnookin, 1992).

Examples: (1) The parents divorced after having been involved in an auto accident.   M had been in a coma for 6 weeks.   F alleged that M's mental condition resulting from the accident made her unfit.   The appellate court reversed a custody award to F, stating "[w]hen the child will be equally well cared for by either parent, the mother, in preference to the father, is entitled to its custody. The latter is especially so where the child is of tender years." *Funkhouser v. Funkhouser,* 158 W.Va. 964, 216 S.E.2d 570 (1975).

(2) Divorce ended a marriage during which both parents had taken care of the children.   Most recently the children had lived with M for the 9–months academic year in Germany where M had a job, and had spent the summers with F in the U.S.   The trial court deemed it inappropriate for the children to be raised by only one parent in a foreign country, and awarded custody to F. M appealed.   (Result: Custody to M, who was found to be the primary caretaker of the children for the majority of their lives.   "In addressing the primary caretaker issue * * *, we enumerated several duties which would typically be performed by the primary caretaker.   These include preparation of meals, grooming, medical care, discipline, and education.   It is the parent who assumed these childrearing duties who is to be awarded custody.   Only if neither parent is entitled to the primary caretaker presumption does the court endeavor to determine which placement would be in the best interests of the child.") *Rhodes v. Rhodes,* 192 W.Va. 14, 449 S.E.2d 75 (1994).

4. RELIGION

Courts sometimes take the parents' religion (or lack thereof) into account in their determination of custody.   This risks an award of custody based on the court's approval or disapproval of the parents' religious views, and may raise First Amendment issues.   On solid ground, courts have considered whether a parent's religious beliefs or practices threaten the physical health or well-being of the child. If psychological effects are alleged, the difficulty is more serious.

Examples: (1) The district court awarded custody to F.   The Maine Supreme Court remanded, concluding that the district court had given undue weight to the fact that, as a Jehovah's Witness, M would not consent to a blood transfusion for the son.   "If and only if the court is satisfied that an immediate and substantial threat to the child's well-being is posed by the religious practices in question" need the court proceed to a balancing of interests.   Any order should make the "least possible intrusion upon the constitutionally protected interests of the parent." *Osier v. Osier,* 410 A.2d 1027 (Me.1980).

needs" and whether one parent can better satisfy such needs. The Alaska Supreme Court defined "actual religious needs" to be "an expressed preference of a child mature enough to make a choice" between religions or between religion and no religion. *Bonjour v. Bonjour,* 592 P.2d 1233 (Alaska 1979).

5. RACE

The U.S. Supreme Court has made it clear that courts may not consider race as the *sole* factor in determining the "best interests" of the child. It is not clear whether race or ethnic background may continue to be considered as *one* factor among others in deciding custody.

Example: When M and F were divorced in Florida, M was awarded custody of their 3–year–old daughter. The following year, F filed to modify the custody order alleging changed conditions, specifically that M was then living with an African–American man whom she later married. Without addressing the parental qualifications of F, M, or M's new husband, the trial court reasoned that the daughter would be stigmatized by growing up in a racially mixed household and awarded custody to F. The appellate court affirmed, and M appealed. (Result: Reversed. The U.S. Supreme Court held that race may not be the sole determinant of a custody decision. "The Constitution cannot control such prejudices but neither can it tolerate them. Private biases may be outside the reach of the law, but the law cannot, directly or indirectly, give them effect. * * * The effects of racial prejudice, however real, cannot justify a racial classification removing an infant child from the custody of its natural mother found to be an appropriate person to have such custody.") *Palmore v. Sidoti,* 466 U.S. 429, 104 S.Ct. 1879, 80 L.Ed.2d 421 (1984).

6. PARENT'S SEXUAL MORALITY

Traditionally, courts have placed great emphasis on the custodial parent's sexual morality. An adulterous mother stood a good chance of losing a disputed custody case. Today much less emphasis is placed on the parent's sexual morality. The prevailing view is that unless the (sexual) activities of the custodial parent have a direct effect on the child, they are irrelevant and UMDA § 402 provides specifically: "The court shall not consider conduct of a proposed custodian that does not affect his relationship to the child." As a practical matter, the issue of a parent's sexual morality is most frequently litigated in the context of attempts to obtain modification of a prior custody award.

Examples: (1) M was awarded sole custody. F, attempting to modify the award so as to receive joint custody of the child, charged that M had committed adultery and smoked marijuana in the presence of the child. (Result: For M. "Infidelity per se does not result in a parent being denied custody. Rather, it is necessary to examine whether such behavior was damaging to the child. This determination involves the evaluation of several factors: (1) Is the child aware of the illicit relationship? (2) Has sex play occurred in the presence of the child? (3) Was the sexual misconduct notorious, bringing embarrassment to the child? (4) What effect has this conduct had on the family home life? While there was some testimony that the plaintiff had committed adultery in the presence of the child, at one point the court noted that the testimony was so bizarre that it was unbelievable. * * * Even if plaintiff had committed adultery, it appears that the court found that there was no conclusive evidence that the sexual behavior occurred in the presence of the child or that it was in any way detrimental to the child so as to render plaintiff morally unfit. * * * As the court noted, due to the past relationship between the parties, joint custody may have only served to foster continued disagreement and therefore, would not be in the best interests of the child.") *Wiley v. Wiley,* 459 So.2d 105 (La.App.1984).

(2) When M and F divorced, F was awarded custody of their three daughters ranging in age from 7 to 12. Three years later M sought custody of the two younger daughters. At an evidentiary hearing F testified that his girlfriend occasionally spent the night and that he had had sexual relations with her while his daughters were in the home. The trial court changed custody to M. F appealed. (Result: Reversed and remanded for a new evidentiary hearing before a different judge. The trial court's finding, based on F's admission, that F was morally unfit was clear legal error. "Standing alone, unmarried cohabitation is not enough to constitute immorality under the Child Custody Act.") *Truitt v. Truitt,* 172 Mich.App. 38, 431 N.W.2d 454 (1988).

(3) M and F separated when F informed M that he was gay. F then moved in with his male partner. M and F's divorce decree provided for joint custody of their three children who would reside with M. After the divorce, their twelve-year-old eldest son (S) developed serious academic and behavior problems. M, who suffered from chronic illness requiring frequent hospitalizations, had difficulty handling S and agreed to let him move in with F on a trial basis. F accepted a demotion at work to spend more time with S and monitored S's conduct closely. During the five months S lived with F, his behavior and schoolwork improved noticeably. When S moved back with M, his behavior deteriorated, and F moved to modify the divorce decree to receive custody of S. F did not seek custody of the two younger children. In an *in camera* interview, S expressed his embarrassment

over F's homosexuality and his strong desire to remain with M. (Result: Custody awarded to F. "The court finds that [F] is a caring, worthy father. His homosexuality is not flaunted and has no adverse deleterious effect on his twelve-year-old son. In view of the cases cited, the court finds that it is impermissible as a matter of law to decide the question of custody on the basis of the father's sexual orientation. The guiding consideration must be [S's] best interest. At this time, [S's] needs can best be met by his father.") *M.A.B. v. R.B.*, 134 Misc.2d 317, 510 N.Y.S.2d 960 (1986).

(4) When M and F (who was gay) divorced, M was awarded custody of their daughter (C). M remarried and her new husband was accused of molesting C. C was then placed in foster care. F sought custody, and the juvenile court awarded custody to F, finding that F's homosexuality did not disqualify him. After M divorced her second husband, custody of C was changed back to her, in part because F was HIV-positive and had not been forthright about his health problems with the court. F appealed. (Result: For M. "While neither of these parents can be considered a paradigm of parenthood, nevertheless, from the evidence in the record, the trial court could have easily concluded that the father's present health and lifestyle, coupled with the living arrangements he has provided for the daughter since the last decree, when considered with the actions of the mother to improve her situation to care for the daughter, resulted in a change of circumstances sufficient to warrant a change of custody, and that such a change would materially promote the best interests of the daughter.") *H.J.B. v. P.W.*, 628 So.2d 753 (Ala.Civ.App.1993).

7. PARENT VS. "THIRD PARTY"

A strong presumption holds that it is in the best interest of the child to be in the custody of a parent. Indeed, parents are *prima facie entitled* to have custody, and a statute authorizing courts to award custody to a third party without a finding that the parents are unfit may violate due process. The N.Y. Court of Appeals noted: "Neither the lawyer nor judge in the judicial system nor the experts in psychology or social welfare may displace the primary responsibility of child raising that naturally and legally falls to those who conceive and bear children." *Bennett v. Jeffreys,* 40 N.Y.2d 543, 387 N.Y.S.2d 821, 356 N.E.2d 277 (1976). Accordingly, a court may not award custody to a third person merely because that person can do a "better job" than the parent of raising the child. In late 1995, however, the Pennsylvania Supreme Court seemed to retreat slightly from the parental priority rule, as follows: "We now abandon the presumption that a parent has a prima facie right to custody as against third parties * * *. Thus there is no single overriding factor; rather, courts should consider every fact relevant to a child's physical, emotional, intellectual, moral, and spiritual well-being. Parenthood, though not paramount, will always be a factor of significant weight. In *Ellerbe*, both opinions, representing all seven justices, agreed on several principles: 'the parent-child relationship should be considered to be of importance in determining which custody arrangement is in the child's best interest,''special weight' and 'deference' should be accorded the parent-child relationship, and the relationship should not be disturbed 'without some showing of harm' or unless circumstances 'clearly indicate the appropriateness of awarding custody to a nonparent.' We adhere to these principles, for, in general, parents have a deep, abiding commitment to the well-being of their children." *Rowles v. Rowles*, 668 A.2d 126 (Pa. 1995).

Examples: (1) In June 1974 M voluntarily placed her son (S) in the care of his paternal aunt. At that time S was 1½ years old. M visited S once in the fall of 1974. In November 1974 M was hospitalized for a nervous breakdown and did not visit S again until 1976, when she saw S twice. In November 1976 the aunt petitioned for and was granted sole custody; M failed to appear. Two years later the trial court awarded custody to M. The aunt appealed. S continued to reside with M during the appeal. (Result: The court recognized the aunt as the psychological parent of S and awarded custody to her. "It is now well recognized that there is a serious potential for psychological harm occurring to young children if they are removed from a home where they have lived and been nurtured during their early years by loving and devoted parents, albeit foster parents. * * * Defendant's placement in 1974 and her failure for several years thereafter to seek a return of George Jr. enabled him to develop an attachment to plaintiff which cannot now be ignored or terminated if the best interests of the child are to be protected and advanced.") *Hoy v. Willis*, 165 N.J.Super. 265, 398 A.2d 109 (1978).

(2) When M and F divorced in 1976, M was awarded custody of their daughter (D). In 1982, M and F agreed that D should live with F and his new wife (W₂). When F and W₂ separated 3 years later, D opted to live with W₂ and W₂ was granted interim custody of D. It was undisputed that W₂ had been primarily responsible for providing parental care, discipline, love, guidance and attention to D. M then sought and was awarded custody. W₂ appealed. (Result: Reversed. The evidence established that D's best interests will be served by W₂ retaining D's custody.) *Zuziak v. Zuziak*, 169 Mich.App. 741, 426 N.W.2d 761 (1988).

(3) When M and F divorced, M was awarded custody of their infant son (S). F dropped out of S's life. During the next few months M became involved with several men and then met a female gift shop manager with whom she began a lesbian relationship. M's lover supported M and became a parent figure to S, who called her "Da Da." When M revealed her lesbian relationship, her mother, S's grandmother (G), sought custody of S. The following was put into evidence: S had spent 70% of his time, including every weekend, with G during the 2 years preceding the hearing. On three occasions, M had left S with G without informing G of her whereabouts. M had

neglected to clean S and change his diapers. M's lover had hit S. M had spent welfare checks on manicures before buying food for S. The trial court awarded custody to G; the appellate court reversed. G appealed. (Result: G regained custody. "Although the presumption favoring a parent over a non-parent is strong, it is rebutted when certain factors, such as parental unfitness, are established by clear and convincing evidence. * * * The evidence plainly is sufficient * * * to support the trial court's findings that the parental presumption has been rebutted, that the mother is an unfit custodian at this time, and that the child's best interests would be promoted by awarding custody to the grandmother. Among the factors to be weighed in determining unfitness are the parent's misconduct that affects the child, neglect of the child, and a demonstrated unwillingness and inability to promote the emotional and physical well-being of the child. Other important considerations include the nature of the home environment and moral climate in which the child is to be raised. We have held, however, that a lesbian mother is not *per se* an unfit parent. * * * In the present case, the record shows a mother who, although devoted to her son, refuses to subordinate her own desires and priorities to the child's welfare.") *Bottoms v. Bottoms*, 249 Va. 410, 457 S.E.2d 102 (1995).

(4) In a celebrated case, the deceased M's parents were awarded custody over F's objections. The Supreme Court of Iowa held that the best interests of the seven-year-old boy required that his 60–year-old maternal grandparents, who had been asked by F to take temporary charge of the child after M's death two years before and who had provided a "stable, dependable, conventional, middle-class, middlewest background," be awarded permanent custody as against F who had since remarried. The Court emphasized the likelihood of a seriously disrupting and disturbing effect upon the boy's development that could result from his return to the "unstable, unconventional, arty, Bohemian, and probably intellectually stimulating" household of F. *Painter v. Bannister,* 258 Iowa 1390, 140 N.W.2d 152 (1966). (Note: Don't be too concerned, the boy ultimately ended up in his father's custody.)

C. JOINT CUSTODY

Under "joint custody," both parents share legal and may share physical custody of the child. California provides: "In making an order for custody with respect to both parents, the court may grant joint legal custody without granting joint physical custody." West's Ann. Cal. Fam. Code § 3085 (1995). A majority of the states have enacted legislation providing for joint custody as an alternative disposition. Several states make joint custody the preferred alternative and presume that joint custody is in the child's best interest. By contrast, the Vermont Supreme Court has stated a presumption that joint custody is *not* in the child's best interests, except in extraordinary circumstances.

Lumbra v. Lumbra, 136 Vt. 529, 394 A.2d 1139 (1978). Based on sometimes sad experience, there has been some retreat from the initial enthusiasm that had greeted the new "doctrine."

Examples: (1) *Sua sponte,* the trial court ordered joint custody for the parties' two adopted daughters. On appeal, sole custody was awarded to M with liberal visitation for F. The New Jersey Supreme Court reviewed the record and recognized that joint custody presents practical problems and requires parental cooperation. It nevertheless held the trial judge's *sua sponte* determination proper, but remanded for a review of present circumstances as more than two years had passed since the original decree. *Beck v. Beck,* 86 N.J. 480, 432 A.2d 63 (1981).

(2) A circuit court order made the parents "joint primary physical residential parents" and required the children to move back and forth between their parents. (Result: Reversed. The Florida statute mandating that parental responsibility be shared in absence of a finding that such a disposition would be detrimental to the child, "does not mandate that the physical residence of the children is to be shifted back and forth between the parents as a necessary concomitant of shared parental responsibility." The children's best interests were not well served by alternating their residence.) *Frey v. Wagner,* 433 So.2d 60 (Fla.App.1983).

(3) M and F's divorce decree incorporated a separation agreement that gave physical custody to M. It further provided that F was to have full and equal participation in the education of their son and that M and F were jointly to select his school. Eighteen months later F petitioned the court to enforce the decree, claiming that M planned to enroll the son in a Buddhist school over F's objections. F argued that M's choice of school would isolate their son from mainstream American culture and hamper his social development and requested that the court select the school if M and F could not agree. The trial court denied the motion, the appellate court reversed, and M appealed. (Result: For M. "The agreement at issue required that the parents consult concerning their child's education and jointly select his school. The agreement neither selected a school nor provided a means of resolving deadlocks over school selection. In essence, the parties merely 'agreed to agree,' to negotiate and reach agreement at some future time concerning their child's education. Ordinarily, such agreements are unenforceable because the court has no power to force the parties to reach agreement and cannot grant a remedy. * * * Because no enforceable agreement concerning the child's education exists, the power to control the child's education remains with the mother as custodial parent.") *Griffin v. Griffin,* 699 P.2d 407 (Colo. 1985).

D. RIGHTS OF THE NONCUSTODIAL PARENT

Traditionally, courts have awarded sole custody of a child to one parent. Typically, that parent obtains legal and physical custody. Physical custody is shared through visitation rights. Quite recently, the concept of joint and shared custody has made significant inroads on the traditional sole custody concept. "Joint custody" provides a "decision-participating" role for the parent who does not have physical custody and who, typically, pays support.

1. VISITATION RIGHTS

Courts have held that the right of a parent to the companionship of his or her child is a fundamental constitutional right that may not be restricted without evidence that the parent's activities may tend to impair the child's emotional or physical health. Accordingly, courts usually award visitation rights to the noncustodial parent. If it would affect the child adversely, visitation may be denied or restricted. Jurisdictions differ on the strength of showing that must be made to deny or take away visitation rights. First amendment issues may arise when the custodial parent complains that the noncustodial parent uses visitation to instruct the child in the noncustodial parent's religion. Granting that the custodial parent has the right to make ultimate decisions concerning the child's religious upbringing, the California Appellate Court nevertheless held that a noncustodial parent cannot be enjoined from discussing religion with his child or involving his child in religious activities in absence of a showing that the child would be thereby harmed. *In re Marriage of Murga,* 103 Cal.App.3d 498, 163 Cal.Rptr. 79 (1980).

UMDA § 407 provides:

"(a) A parent not granted custody of the child is entitled to reasonable visitation rights unless the court finds, after a hearing, that visitation would endanger seriously the child's physical, mental, moral, or emotional health. (b) The court may modify an order * * * whenever modification would serve the best interest of the child; but the court shall not restrict a parent's visitation rights unless it finds that the visitation would endanger seriously the child's physical, mental, moral, or emotional health."

2. RESTRICTION ON INTERSTATE TRAVEL BY CUSTODIAL PARENT

To protect the exercise of the noncustodial parent's visitation rights, courts commonly order the custodial parent not to take the child out of the jurisdiction without the court's specific permission. A violation of the court's order may be prosecuted as contempt. Such restrictions have been challenged as unconstitutionally limiting the custodial parent's right to interstate travel.

If the custodial parent's reasons for wishing to move are *bona fide* (*e.g.,* a significantly better professional opportunity beckons), and it appears that defeating the other parent's visitation rights is not an important motive, permission to move usually will be granted. A compensating change in visitation arrangements may then be made. For instance, the noncustodial parent may be granted longer-term summer visitation, instead of frequent weekend visitation.

Examples: (1) The trial court had granted M permission to move her three children to France where her new husband had been transferred. The move was not required by any compelling financial, educational, employment or health considerations and would significantly curtail the frequency and quality of F's regular visitation. (Result: Reversed. "A custodial parent may be properly called upon to make certain sacrifices to ensure the right of the child to the benefits of visitation with the noncustodial parent.") *Daghir v. Daghir,* 82 A.D.2d 191, 441 N.Y.S.2d 494 (1981) aff'd 56 N.Y.2d 938, 453 N.Y.S.2d 609, 439 N.E.2d 324 (1982).

(2) M and F's divorce judgment awarded primary physical custody of their 2–year-old daughter to M and provided that neither M nor F was to remove the child from the state without the court's permission. Five years later, M petitioned for permission to move to California, where she had been offered a better and higher paying job. M claimed that F was behind in his child support payments and that M's father, who lived in California, would provide financial and emotional support to the child. The trial court granted M's petition. The district court reversed, ruling that to allow M to remove the child would be contrary to the state's precedent discouraging removal. M appealed. (Result: M is permitted to move with the child to California, based on application of the following test: "1. Whether the move would be likely to improve the general quality of life for both the primary residential spouse and the children. 2. Whether the motive for seeking the move is for the express purpose of defeating visitation. 3. Whether the custodial parent, once out of the jurisdiction, will be likely to comply with any substitute visitation arrangements. 4. Whether the substitute visitation will be adequate to foster a continuing meaningful relationship between the child or children and the noncustodial parent. 5. Whether the cost of transportation is financially affordable by one or both of the parents. 6. Whether the move is in the best interests of the child.") *Mize v. Mize,* 621 So.2d 417 (Fla.1993).

3. ENFORCEMENT OF VISITATION RIGHTS

If the custodial parent interferes with the non-custodial parent's visitation rights, the proper remedy is judicial enforcement of the custody order, not self-help. Suspending the payment of child support without a specific court order is not a legitimate response, although some courts may consider the obligor's suspension of alimony justified. UMDA § 315 provides: "If a party fails to comply with a provision of a decree or temporary order or injunction, the obligation of the other party to make payments for support of maintenance or to permit visitation is not suspended; but he may move the court to grant an appropriate order."

Custody orders are enforceable by the court's civil or criminal contempt power. Potentially, the custodial parent's protracted denial or frustration of the other parent's visitation rights may be grounds for a change in custody. However, given the overriding importance of the child's sense of security and permanence, a change in custody is rarely if ever ordered solely as "punishment" for the custodian.

Examples: (1) M was held in contempt for interfering with F's visitation rights. She unsuccessfully invoked her right to free speech when she had been specifically ordered "to do everything in her power to create in the [children's] minds a living, caring feeling toward the father * * * and to convince the children that it is the mother's desire that they see and love their father." The Florida Supreme Court found that "[t]he cause of the blind, brainwashed, bigoted belligerence of the children toward the father grew from the soil nurtured and tilled by the mother." *Schutz v. Schutz*, 581 So.2d 1290 (Fla.1991).

(2) The Iowa Supreme Court has allowed a tort action for money damages (potentially including punitive damages) for wrongful interference with one parent's custody of a child by the other. *Wood v. Wood*, 338 N.W.2d 123 (Iowa 1983).

E. STANDARDS FOR MODIFICATION

Once a final (non-temporary) custody order is made, the typical court will modify the award only upon proof of substantially changed circumstances that indicate that modification is in the best interests of the child.

1. STABILITY OF ENVIRONMENT

Judicial reluctance to modify a custody award is based on the perception that "shuffling" a child between parents is harmful to the child's emotional development. Secondly, if access to modification is too easy, the child may become the victim of a continuing legal battle between its parents.

2. CHANGE IN CIRCUMSTANCES

A change of circumstances sufficient to change custody typically involves activities of the custodial parent that are likely to affect the child adversely. A change in circumstances that improves the *non*custodial parent's ability to raise the child rarely suffices to obtain a change in custody, unless combined with a significant deterioration in the custodial parent's ability to function as a parent. To reduce vexatious custody litigation brought by unhappy noncustodial parents, the UMDA significantly raised the hurdles against changes in custody. § 409 allows a change during the first two years after a custody award only if there is "reason to believe the child's present environment may endanger seriously his physical, mental, moral, or emotional health." After two years, UMDA makes modification available only if "the child's present environment endangers seriously his physical, mental or emotional health, and the harm likely to be caused by a change of environment is outweighed by its advantages to him." Is there a significant difference between the two tests?

Examples: (1) "[W]e cannot hold the statute is satisfied where the court finds only that the interests of the children would be 'best served' by a change in custody, and that such a change would be 'to the environmental benefit' of the children. For the court in this case to have jurisdiction to modify a custody decree under [the UMDA], there must be a finding of danger to the physical, mental, moral, or emotional health of the children in their present environment, and a finding that the harm likely to be caused by such a change is outweighed by its advantages to them." *In re Custody of Dallenger,* 173 Mont. 530, 568 P.2d 169 (1977).

(2) M was awarded custody of her two daughters. F sought to gain their custody, alleging a change of circumstances and emphasizing M's open and continuing cohabitation with her boyfriend, in violation of Illinois' fornication statute. (Result: Change in custody granted: "The moral values which Jacqueline currently represents to her children, and those which she may be expected to portray to them in the future, contravene statutorily declared standards of conduct and endanger the children's moral development.") *Jarrett v. Jarrett,* 78 Ill.2d 337, 36 Ill.Dec. 1, 400 N.E.2d 421 (1979), cert. denied 449 U.S. 927, 101 S.Ct. 329, 66 L.Ed.2d 155 (1980).

F. THE UNMARRIED FATHER'S VISITATION RIGHTS

In many states, the fit though unwed father has been expressly granted visitation rights by statute or by courts. A variety of U.S. Supreme Court cases should be read to hold that where the father, the mother and the child have lived in a *de facto* family setting, the fit father has standing to assert appropriate visitation rights. (See p. 254).

G. VISITATION RIGHTS OF THIRD PARTIES

All jurisdictions now authorize visitation to be given to grandparents in some circumstances. Many statutes specifically refer to them; others are phrased more broadly in terms of the child's best interest. As distinguished from the parents' *right* to visitation, some statutes and courts speak in terms of a "privilege" that may be extended to third parties who may include grandparents, stepparents, foster parents, siblings and other persons who are significant to the child. Several states limit grandparental visitation rights to cases where the parent is deceased; others specifically extend the right to the case of divorce, annulment or separation. Very few courts have allowed grandparental visitation over the objections of both parents in an ongoing family and against the argument that parents have the constitutional right to raise their child as they see fit. Most states insist that, if both parents are fit and object, the ongoing family is *not* subject to enforced intrusion by grandparents. The majority holds that adoption preempts visitation with exceptions in the case of stepparent adoption.

Example: M and F fought bitterly with F's parents and eventually severed all ties with them. F's parents sought court-ordered visitation with M and F's two children. The trial court found that visitation with the grandparents would be in the children's best interests, the appellate court affirmed, and M and F appealed. (Result: Reversed. "Tennessee's historically strong protection of parental rights and the reasoning of federal constitutional cases convince us that parental rights constitute a fundamental liberty interest under Article I, Section 8 of the Tennessee Constitution. * * * In this case, the paternal grandparents directly challenge this fundamental privacy interest by seeking court-ordered visitation. * * * They insist that a judicially determined finding that visitation is in the best interests of the children is a sufficiently compelling justification to override the parents' united opposition, regardless of the fact that the parents' fitness is not challenged and that the parents' domestic situation has never been the subject of judicial concern. We find, however, that without a substantial danger of harm to the child, a court may not constitutionally impose its own subjective notions of the 'best interests of the child' when an intact, nuclear family with fit, married parents is involved.") *Hawk v. Hawk,* 855 S.W.2d 573 (Tenn.1993). (Minority *contra*: Grandparental visitation allowed over both parents' objections in an ongoing family setting. *King v. King,* 828 S.W.2d 630 (Ky.1992))

H. INTERSTATE RECOGNITION OF CUSTODY DECREES

1. "FORUM SHOPPING" UNDER THE "OLD" LAW

Because a custody determination remains modifiable if circumstances change, it was not viewed as a final order and was not entitled to Full Faith and Credit in sister states. *May v. Anderson,* 345 U.S. 528, 73 S.Ct. 840, 97 L.Ed. 1221 (1953).

Modifiability of custody awards led to forum shopping. A typical scenario was that the dissatisfied parent "kidnapped" the child and took it to another state where a sympathetic court would be asked for modification of the custody determination on the basis of "changed circumstances." Until relatively recently, if the child was present in the jurisdiction and the petitioning parent alleged conduct by the other parent that was detrimental to the child, many courts were willing to hear such cases and redetermine custody. Note that kidnapping one's own child in violation of a court order was not a crime under state or federal kidnapping laws, although it was punishable by contempt.

2. EARLY JUDICIAL RESPONSES

To reduce abuses, some courts adopted a "clean hands" doctrine under which they would refuse jurisdiction over a custody dispute brought to them by a parent who had obtained custody of the child in violation of an existing custody order. Today, the problem is covered by state (UCCJA) and federal (PKPA) statutes.

3. THE UNIFORM CHILD CUSTODY JURISDICTION ACT

In 1968, the National Conference of Commissioners on Uniform State Laws promulgated the Uniform Child Custody Jurisdiction Act (UCCJA). The Act responded to the then rapidly growing problem of parental "kidnapping." The Act fosters cooperation among states involved in a custody dispute. In 1996, the UCCJA was under review by the Commissioners on Uniform State Laws and an updated version, reconciling it with the federal PKPA (below), may be promulgated soon.

a. Purposes of UCCJA

The UCCJA (1) provides means to avoid jurisdictional competition and conflict between courts of different states in matters of child custody, and (2) assures that litigation concerning custody takes place in the state with which the child and his family have the closest connection.

b. Statutory Provisions

Under the UCCJA one court assumes full and continuing responsibility for the custody of a particular child. Usually this is the court with the best access to relevant information about the child and its family. That court's judgment is to be enforced in other states who "shall not modify" it (UCCJA § 14). All modifications are to be made by the original court, unless the parties and the child no longer have appreciable ties with that court, or that court declines to exercise its jurisdiction.

UCCJA § 8 provides that a court may decline to exercise jurisdiction if the petitioner: (1) "has wrongfully taken the child from another state or has engaged in similar reprehensible conduct", or (2) "without consent of the person entitled to custody, has improperly removed the child from the physical custody of the person entitled to custody or has improperly retained the child after a visit or other temporary relinquishment of physical custody." UCCJA §§ 12, 13, 14 provide that any custody decree rendered pursuant to the Act must be respected and enforced, subject to modification only if the court which rendered the original decree did not have jurisdiction *and* the modifying court has jurisdiction. The Act also provides a procedure for the filing and enforcement of custody orders in other states.

4. THE FEDERAL PARENTAL KIDNAPPING PREVENTION ACT

Since 1980, federal legislation mandates that Full Faith and Credit be given to sister-state custody decrees. Exceptions are (1) where the original forum did not have jurisdiction, or (2) where it declines to exercise jurisdiction, or (3) when an emergency (*e.g.*, abuse, neglect, abandonment) requires intervention to protect the child. The parties must have had notice and an opportunity to be heard. The parent locator facilities developed under the child support enforcement program are made available.

Examples: (1) M and F's North Dakota divorce decree awarded custody to M. Following the divorce, M continued to live in North Dakota with the couple's two sons. F moved to Pennsylvania to live with his parents. Following an extended visit with his sons in Pennsylvania, F refused to return them to M and sought custody in a Pennsylvania court. F was granted custody and M appealed. (Result: Decision vacated. The PKPA required that Pennsylvania relinquish jurisdiction to North Dakota, which had proper subject matter jurisdiction to enter the original decree and had not lost that jurisdiction.) *Barndt v. Barndt*, 397 Pa.Super. 321, 580 A.2d 320 (1990)

(2) M and F divorced when their son (S) was three years old. M was granted custody by a Washington court. Three years later, M accepted a job in Germany and enrolled S in a German boarding school where S lived until he was 10, seeing M irregularly on holidays and weekends. M and S returned to the United States and began living in California, moving 4 times during the next 2 years. During this period, visitation with F in Washington state resumed. When S was twelve years old, M entered law school and S lived with M's former boyfriend, seeing M on weekends and F during school vacations. During his visits with F, S saw a counselor who ultimately recommended that custody be changed to F. F then petitioned a Washington court to modify custody, the court changed custody to F, and M appealed on jurisdictional grounds. The appeals court reversed, and F appealed. (Result: Washington had continuing jurisdiction to modify custody under UCCJA and PKA. "It appears that the majority of appellate courts which have addressed the issue presented here hold that the state in which the initial decree was entered has exclusive continuing jurisdiction to modify the initial decree if: (1) one of the parents continues to reside in the decree state; and (2) the child continues to have some connection with the decree state, such as visitation.") *Greenlaw v. Smith*, 123 Wash.2d 593, 869 P.2d 1024 (1994).

In the case of interstate or international child-snatching, the PKPA invokes FBI assistance under the Fugitive Felon Act, but only if the violation of a judicial custody order is a *felony* under state law. A majority of the states now have enacted such felony statutes. Note: Parental kidnapping of a child remains exempt from criminal prosecution under the federal kidnapping statute (18 U.S.C.A. 1201): "The federal kidnaping statute, enacted initially in 1932, * * * was limited to cases of kidnaping involving interstate commerce in which the victim was held 'for reward or ransom'. * * * The obvious purpose of such restricted scope for that crime ('for reward or ransom') was to eliminate from the statute's coverage the kidnaping, conspiracy to kidnap or aiding and abetting in the kidnaping by a parent of his or her child." *United States v. Boettcher*, 780 F.2d 435 (4th Cir.1985).

5. INTERNATIONAL CUSTODY DISPUTES—HAGUE CONVENTION
In 1985, the U.S. Senate ratified the Hague Convention on the Civil Aspects of International Child Abduction. The Convention facilitates the return of abducted

children and the exercise of visitation rights across international boundaries giving jurisdiction to the court at the place of the child's "habitual residence." By 1996, the treaty was in effect between the United States and some thirty countries. The Hague Convention and U.S. implementing legislation (International Child Abduction Remedies Act, 42 U.S.C.A. § 11601), are powerful weapons in the orderly resolution of international child custody disputes. U.S. courts have not hesitated to return even U.S.–born children abroad, where an American parent had brought his or her child to the United States in violation of a foreign custody order. In the U.S., the "International Parental Kidnapping Crime Act" (18 U.S.C.A. § 1204) has added criminal clout to the Convention's civil sanctions.

Example: F, a German citizen, and M, a U.S. citizen stationed with the U.S. Army in Germany, married and had one son (S) in Germany. After several trial separations, F ordered M to leave their apartment with S and put most of their belongings in the hallway. Four days later, after F had visited with S several times, M took S to the U.S. and filed for divorce in Ohio where she was awarded temporary custody of S. In Germany, F sought and was awarded custody of S by a German court. F also filed a petition in U.S. federal court, alleging that M had wrongfully removed S from Germany in violation of the Hague Convention. The district court denied F's claim, and he appealed. (Result: Reversed and remanded; F's claim reinstated. "Under the Convention, the removal of a child from one country to another is wrongful when: (a) it is in breach of rights of custody attributed to a person, an institution or any other body, either jointly or alone, under the law of the State in which the child was habitually resident immediately before the removal or retention; and (b) at the time of removal or retention those rights were actually exercised, either jointly or alone, or would have been so exercised but for the removal or retention. * * * The district court appears to agree that before the argument of July 27, 1991, Thomas was a habitual resident of Germany. The district court, however, found that Thomas's habitual residence was 'altered' from Germany to the United States when Mr. Friedrich forced Mrs. Friedrich and Thomas to leave the family apartment. Habitual residence cannot be so easily altered. Even if we accept the district court's finding that Mr. Friedrich forced Mrs. Friedrich to leave the family apartment, no evidence supports a finding that Mr. Friedrich forced Mrs. Friedrich to remove Thomas from Germany.") *Friedrich v. Friedrich*, 983 F.2d 1396 (6th Cir.1993).

I. REVIEW QUESTIONS

1. **T or F**   After parents are divorced, and one parent has obtained custody of their children, the custodial parent has discretion to specify in his/her will who will get custody of the children upon his/her death.

2. **T or F**   In their will, parents may specify a guardian for their surviving child.

3. **T or F**   Which of the following criteria are important factors in awarding custody?

   A.   Parent's wishes

   B.   Child's wishes

   C.   Moral/sexual conduct of each proposed custodian

   D.   Child's adjustment to his/her home, school and community

   E.   Parents' premarital agreement

4. **T or F**   If a court awards legal custody to only one parent, the noncustodial parent has a right to visitation.

5. **T or F**   A joint custody arrangement divides physical custody between the parents, but only one parent has ultimate decision-making power, *i.e.*, legal custody.

6. **T or F**   A noncustodial parent's petition for change of custody will not be granted on the sole ground that he or she has experienced a substantial improvement in circumstances.

7. **T or F**   Under the UMDA, once a visitation order is entered it may not be modified for two years.

8. **T or F**   Under the UMDA, a parent's visitation rights may be restricted if it can be shown that this would be in the child's best interest.

9. **T or F**   A court must determine child custody "in the best interests of the child."

10. **T or F**   Natural parents have a constitutional right to the companionship of their child.

11. **T or F**   Joint custody gives both parents legal custody.

12. **T or F**   If in the child's best interest, a court will enforce a grandparent's visitation rights to his or her grandchild against married parents in an ongoing marriage if the parents unreasonably refuse the grandparent access.

13. **T or F**   The "tender years presumption" favoring the mother as custodian of young children has all but disappeared.

14. **T or F**   There is a strong presumption that it is in the "best interest" of a child to be in the custody of a parent, even if a foster parent or third party could seemingly do a better job.

15. **T or F**   The court may award custody *sua sponte*, even if the decision resolves the dispute against the wishes of both parents.

16. **T or F** M blocks F from visiting their children. F is entitled to refuse to make child support payments.

17. **T or F** When M and F divorce, F (who is unemployed) is awarded custody of the children. M is ordered to pay child support from her modest income as a lawyer. F wins the "Powerball" lottery. M may have the support order terminated based on F's enormously improved ability to provide for the children.

18. **T or F** Although modifiable, judicial child custody determinations are entitled to Full Faith and Credit.

IX

THE PARENTAL OBLIGATION OF CARE AND CONTROL, AND THE JUVENILE COURT SYSTEM

Analysis

Juvenile courts hear three types of proceedings: (1) Child neglect and dependency, including child abuse, that may result in the appointment of a guardian and/or the termination of parental rights; (2) Status offenses; and (3) Delinquency. Only the first category directly involves "family law" and will be dealt with here. The other two categories are referred to briefly.

Through the juvenile court, the state may intervene to protect young children from parental absence, neglect or abuse. Inadequate parents may lose (1) custody of or (2) all rights (and obligations) to their children. The parental obligation of care and control is most poignantly at issue in actions to terminate parental rights.

A. CHILD DEPENDENCY

A "dependent" child is one who either has no parent or guardian or whose present home conditions are not fit for the proper care of the child. In short, the child *depends* upon the state for its support and well-being. The actual conditions supporting a finding of "dependency" closely resemble those spelling "neglect", but in "dependency" there is less or no emphasis on parental fault. Similarly, the legal consequences are essentially the same. An adjudication of neglect involves: (1) a determination that the parent or household is unfit or that the child is abandoned, abused, or neglected; (2) a decision that, in the child's best interest, the parent should not have custody or full legal control over the child; and (3) the placement of the child with a court-appointed guardian, a state facility or agency, or, if no immediate harm threatens, placement back with the offending parent, under supervision.

B. CHILD NEGLECT AND ABUSE

1. CIVIL STANDARD
Definitions of child neglect vary from state to state. It is difficult to spell out precise conditions of neglect in a statute. In consequence, judges tend to have broad discretion in finding neglect. "Abuse" tends to involve clearer situations because it slides over into intentional misconduct and usually involves a quite obvious transgression of minimum tolerable standards.

Example: New York's statute (N.Y. Soc. Serv. Law § 371 (4–a) (McKinney 1995)) provides that "neglected child" "means a child less than 18 years of age (i) whose physical, mental or emotional condition has been impaired or is in imminent danger of becoming impaired as a result of the failure of his parent or other person legally responsible for his care to exercise a minimum degree of care (A) in supplying the child with adequate food, clothing, shelter, education, medical or surgical care, though financially able to do so or offered financial or other reasonable means to do so; or (B) in providing the child with proper supervision or guardianship, by unreasonably inflicting or allowing to be inflicted harm, or a substantial risk thereof, including the infliction of excessive corporal punishment; or by misusing a drug or drugs; or by misusing alcoholic beverages to the extent that he loses self- control of his actions; or by any other acts of a similarly serious nature requiring the aid of the court; provided, however, that where the respondent is voluntarily and regularly participating in a rehabilitative program, evidence that the respondent has repeatedly misused a drug or drugs or alcoholic beverages to the extent that he loses self-control of his actions shall not establish that the child is a neglected child in the absence of evidence establishing that the child's physical, mental or emotional condition has been impaired or is in imminent danger of becoming impaired as set forth in paragraph (i) of this subdivision; or (ii) who has been abandoned by his parents or other person legally responsible for his care.''

2. CRIMINAL SANCTIONS

In serious cases of child neglect or abuse, specific statutes apply criminal sanctions separately from the civil proceeding.

Example: C, then fifteen years of age, absented herself from school for part of the day. When she returned home that evening, M, having learned of her daughter's absence from school, struck C on the legs several times with a belt. According to C, F then took the belt and beat her with it, striking her 15 to 20 times on the back, neck, arm and legs. (Result: F was convicted under the state's criminal child abuse law. A parent is not permitted to resort to punishment which would exceed that properly required for disciplinary purposes or which extends beyond the bounds of moderation. Excessive or cruel conduct is prohibited.) *Bowers v. State,* 283 Md. 115, 389 A.2d 341 (1978).

C. CONSTITUTIONAL RIGHTS

1. VAGUENESS OF STATUTORY STANDARDS

Allegedly ''vague'' neglect and dependency statutes have been attacked on constitutional grounds, especially when termination of parental rights was at issue.

Examples: (1) Iowa's statute provided for the termination of parental rights where ''the parents have substantially and continuously or repeatedly refused to give the child * * * care necessary for physical or mental health or morals of the child'' and where ''the parents are unfit by reason of * * * conduct found by the court likely to be detrimental to the physical or mental health or morals of the child.'' (Result: This statute was held to be unconstitutionally vague *both on its face and as applied.*) *Alsager v. District Court of Polk County, Iowa,* 406 F.Supp. 10 (S.D.Iowa 1975). On appeal, 545 F.2d 1137 (8th Cir.1976), the

Circuit Court declined to resolve the important issue of facial unconstitutionality, but affirmed the holding *as applied to the facts of the case.*

(2) An Alabama statute that defined a neglected child as "any child, who, while under sixteen years of age * * * has no proper parental care or guardianship or whose home * * * is an unfit or improper place for such child" was struck down for vagueness. A provision authorized summary seizure of a child if it appears that "the child is in such condition that its welfare requires [seizure]." That provision was held to be an infringement on the fundamental right to family integrity and violating procedural due process, as well as unconstitutionally vague. A provision authorizing termination of parental rights as to a neglected child, defined as any child who has no proper parental care by reason of neglect, was also held unconstitutionally vague. *Roe v. Conn,* 417 F.Supp. 769 (M.D.Ala.1976).

2. RIGHT TO COUNSEL

The U.S. Supreme Court has held that due process does not require that counsel be provided to indigent parents in termination of parental rights proceedings. In *Lassiter v. Department of Social Services of Durham County,* 452 U.S. 18, 101 S.Ct. 2153, 68 L.Ed.2d 640 (1981), William's (C) mother (M) had not provided proper medical care. C was adjudicated neglected and transferred to the custody of the County Department of Social Services. One year later, M was convicted of second degree murder and sentenced to imprisonment for forty years. The Department then petitioned to have M's parental rights terminated on the grounds that she had "willfully failed to maintain concern or responsibility for the welfare of the minor" and because termination was in the latter's best interests. Counsel was not appointed for M. The court concluded that M had had ample opportunity to obtain counsel, but had failed to do so "without just cause." M, however, had not averred that she was indigent. The court terminated her rights. On appeal, M argued that her due process rights were violated by not appointing counsel for her. The U.S. Supreme Court first explained its previous holdings to the effect that an indigent party is entitled to appointed counsel only when he may be deprived of his physical liberty. Applying the three-part *Mathews v. Eldridge* test, 424 U.S. 319, 96 S.Ct. 893, 47 L.Ed.2d 18 (1976), balancing the private interests at stake, the government's interest, and the risk that the procedures used will lead to erroneous decisions, the Court held that counsel did not have to be appointed in *this* case. The Court allowed that "[i]f, in a given case, the parent's interests were at their strongest, the State's interests were at their weakest, and the risks of error were at their peak, it could not be said that the *Eldridge* factors did not overcome the presumption against the right to appointed counsel and that due process did not therefore require the appointment of counsel." The question whether due process calls for the appointment of counsel for indigent parents in termination proceedings was left "to be answered in the first instance by the trial court, subject, of course, to appellate review." The Court added that "[a] wise public policy, however, may require that higher standards be adopted than those minimally tolerable under the Constitution," noting that thirty-four jurisdictions statutorily provide for the appointment of counsel in termination cases.

3. STANDARD OF PROOF

The U.S. Supreme Court has held that, to terminate a parent's rights, the state must meet a "clear and convincing" standard of proof. *Santosky v. Kramer,* 455 U.S. 745, 102 S.Ct. 1388, 71 L.Ed.2d 599 (1982), reviewed a New York statute imposing the "fair preponderance of the evidence" standard. The U.S. Supreme Court looked to the burdens required in other states and noted that "a majority of the States have concluded that a 'clear and convincing evidence' standard of proof strikes a fair balance between the rights of the natural parents and the State's legitimate concerns." The Court went on to hold that New York's lower standard did not satisfy due process requirements. The Court did not consider whether the same "clear and convincing" standard of evidence is required in other adjudications involving intervention, but not involving a termination of parental rights, such as child abuse or neglect cases.

Examples: (1) (Child Abuse). Interpreting *Santosky*, a New York court held that a preponderance of the evidence is sufficient in child abuse cases, because the parent's interest is not entitled to as much weight as in a case alleging neglect. Using the preponderance standard, the trial court found that F had sexually molested his daughter. The finding was based almost entirely on her testimony and her written statement. The court adjudicated the child to be abused and neglected and awarded temporary custody to the county department of social services. F appealed. (Result: Affirmed. "We also cannot ignore that typically, a child abuse (especially in a sexual form) by a parent occurs in circumstances of total secrecy. * * * The trier of the facts is not likely to have a high degree of certainty in resolving such one-on-one testimonial confrontations, between parent and child. Undoubtedly, this is why there are so few criminal prosecutions for incest. Thus, the risk of an erroneous fact finding in favor of the parent would be substantially enhanced by imposing a stricter standard of proof. * * * [I]n In re Winship, 397 U.S. 358, 371, 90 S.Ct. 1068, 1076, 25 L.Ed.2d 368, Justice Harlan aptly described the relevant issue when risk of error is the factor under consideration: 'Because the standard of proof affects the comparative frequency of these two types of erroneous outcomes, the choice of the standard to be applied in a particular kind of litigation should, in a rational world, reflect an assessment of the comparative social disutility of each.' In the instant case, the result of an erroneous fact finding against the parent will, at most, result in his temporary loss of custody for up to 18 months. The result of an erroneous fact finding in favor of the parent, on the other hand, will be the return of the child to the parent's custody, free of any protective State intervention. In a child sex abuse case, the 'social disutility' of such a result approaches the level of absolute abhorrence.'') *In re Linda C.*, 86 A.D.2d 356, 451 N.Y.S.2d 268 (1982).

(2) (Child Neglect and Dependency). M took her six year old son to a hospital emergency room where he was pronounced dead on arrival. An autopsy revealed that the cause of death was "septicemia and peritonitis secondary to perforation of a strangulated inguinal hernia." State caseworkers interviewed M who explained that miracles would safeguard her children and that she would not seek medical help if any of her seven remaining children became ill. The juvenile court had found for M as the children were "apparently well fed, neatly clothed, * * * attend school with some degree of regularity and they have a home which is clean and well kept." (Result: Relying on the fact that a determination of dependency is not irreversible (whereas termination of parental rights is irreversible), the Court distinguished *Santosky* and applied a preponderance of the evidence standard. The Court allowed that although it might be a different case if the children were sick, they seemed to be in good health now and M's statement did not show current dependency. Given the special circumstances, the court would permit state intervention because of something less than what would usually be necessary, such as absence from school, or a report from a neighbor.) *Matter of Appeal in Cochise County, Etc.*, 133 Ariz. 157, 650 P.2d 459 (1982).

4. FREEDOM OF RELIGION

Example: C fell ill and, motivated by her religious belief, M chose to treat the child's illness with prayer rather than medical care. Two weeks later, C died of meningitis. The state charged M with involuntary manslaughter and felony child endangerment, alleging that her negligence was criminal and proximately caused C's death. M's motion to dismiss was denied. M appealed. (Result: Criminal prosecution upheld. "The Legislature has determined that the provision of prayer is sufficient to avert misdemeanor liability for neglecting one's financial responsibility to furnish routine child support. This hardly compels the conclusion that in so doing the Legislature intended to create an unqualified defense to felony manslaughter and child endangerment charges for those parents who continue to furnish prayer alone in the rare instance when a gravely ill child lies dying for want of medical attention. * * * In sum, we reject the proposition that the provision of prayer alone to a seriously ill child cannot constitute criminal negligence as a matter of law.") *Walker v. Superior Court*, 47 Cal.3d 112, 253 Cal.Rptr. 1, 763 P.2d 852 (1988).

5. HOME VISITS AND THE FOURTH AMENDMENT

Recipients of welfare have attacked home visits required for continuing eligibility under the Aid to Families with Dependent Children (AFDC) Program. In *Wyman v. James,* 400 U.S. 309, 91 S.Ct. 381, 27 L.Ed.2d 408 (1971), the U.S. Supreme Court upheld a home visit against a Fourth Amendment challenge. The visit revealed that the child had a "skull fracture, a dent in the head and possible rat bite." The Court noted that the intrusion was reasonable in the circumstances, not an "early morning mass raid upon homes of welfare recipients."

6. **STATE'S RESPONSIBILITY TO INTERVENE—LIABILITY FOR FAILURE TO PRO-TECT?**

Example: F beat five-year-old Joshua (C) into a life-threatening coma. C suffered brain damage so severe that he probably will spend his life in an institution for the profoundly retarded. During the proceeding two-year period, C had been hospitalized three times for suspicious injuries. Although the county caseworker visited the home and dutifully recorded numerous other suspicious injuries, she did nothing more and the Dept. of Social Services (D) took no action. Following C's first hospitalization, D had briefly taken C into its custody but C was returned to F three days later. Thereafter D failed utterly to protect C. C and his mother (M) brought a claim under 42 U.S.C.A. § 1983, alleging that, by failing to intervene to protect him against a risk of violence of which they knew or should have known, D had deprived C of his liberty without due process of law, in violation of his rights under the Fourteenth Amendment. The district court entered summary judgment in favor of D, the court of appeals affirmed, and M appealed. (Held: D had no constitutional duty to protect C from F after receiving reports of possible abuse. "Petitioners concede that the harms Joshua suffered occurred not while he was in the State's custody, but while he was in the custody of his natural father, who was in no sense a state actor. While the State may have been aware of the dangers that Joshua faced in the free world, it played no part in their creation, nor did it do anything to render him any more vulnerable to them. That the State once took temporary custody of Joshua does not alter the analysis, for when it returned him to his father's custody, it placed him in no worse position than that in which he would have been had it not acted at all; the State does not become the permanent guarantor of an individual's safety by having once offered him shelter. Under these circumstances, the State had no constitutional duty to protect Joshua.") *DeShaney v. Winnebago County Dept. of Social Services,* 489 U.S. 189, 109 S.Ct. 998, 103 L.Ed.2d 249 (1989).

D. PARENTAL CONTROL OVER MEDICAL CARE RENDERED THEIR CHILD

1. **PHYSICAL HEALTH**

Generally, parents must consent to any medical treatment given their minor child, except in an emergency. When a child requires medical treatment and the parents deny such treatment, the juvenile court may appoint a guardian for the child and direct the guardian to consent to necessary treatment.

Examples: (1) C was diagnosed as having a type of leukemia. C's parents refused to consent to chemotherapy. (Result: Natural parents do not have the authority of life and death over their children. The parental right to control the child's nurture is akin to a trust, subject to a correlative duty to care for and protect the child. It is terminable by the parents' failure to discharge their obligations. Even though the parents were loving and devoted in all other respects, their refusal to continue with chemotherapy for their child amounted to an unwillingness to provide necessary medical care and warranted an order removing legal custody from them.) *Custody of a Minor*, 375 Mass. 733, 379 N.E.2d 1053 (1978).

(2) F's nonmarital 3½–year-old twins lived with M, who had sole care and custody of them. The custody order obligated M to consult with F on all important matters concerning health, education, and welfare. F's 12–year-old son (S), who had a different mother, had leukemia and would die without a bone marrow transplant. The twins had met S only twice and did not know that he was their half-brother. F asked M to consent to testing the twins as potential bone marrow donors and to harvesting their bone marrow for transplant to S, if they were found to be compatible. M refused both procedures. F's emergency petition was denied, and he appealed. (Result: It was not in the best interest of the *twins* to submit to the bone marrow testing or to the harvesting procedure. "We hold that a parent or guardian may give consent on behalf of a minor * * * child to donate bone marrow to a sibling, only when to do so would be in the minor's best interest. * * * The evidence reveals three critical factors which are necessary to a determination that it will be in the best interests of a child to donate bone marrow to a sibling. First, the parent who consents on behalf of the child must be informed of the risks and benefits inherent in the bone marrow harvesting procedure to the child. Second, there must be emotional support available to the child from the person or persons who take care of the child. * * * Third, there must be an existing, close relationship between the donor and recipient. The evidence clearly shows that there is no physical benefit to a donor child. If there is any benefit to a child who donates bone marrow to a sibling it will be a psychological benefit. * * * The psychological benefit is grounded firmly in the fact that the donor and recipient are known to each other as family. Only where there is an existing relationship between a healthy child and his or her ill sister or brother may a psychological benefit to the child from donating bone marrow to a sibling realistically be found to exist.") *Curran v. Bosze*, 141 Ill.2d 473, 153 Ill.Dec. 213, 566 N.E.2d 1319 (1990).

(3) Instead of seeking conventional therapy, parents took a seven year old child with Hodgkin's disease to Jamaica for nutritional therapy. The court refused to declare the child neglected and noted (1) that several qualified physicians were contributing to the child's care, (2) that great deference must be given a parent's choice as to the mode of medical treatment, (3) that conventional treatment (which would be administered if needed) had toxic effects, and (4) that the nutritional treatment was controlling his condition. *In re Hofbauer*, 47 N.Y.2d 648, 419 N.Y.S.2d 936, 393 N.E.2d 1009 (1979).

2. THE FIRST AMENDMENT ISSUE

Numerous cases illustrate the potential tension and conflict between freedom of religion (typically the parent's) and the child's best interest. Ultimately such cases are resolved by balancing the care required (emergency blood transfusion vs. deferrable care or elective surgery not necessary for survival) against the parent's constitutional right to follow his or her religion in raising the child. The state steps in when the "exercise" of religion by the parent becomes life-threatening to the child. In extreme cases, a criminal prosecution may lie against the parent. (*Walker v. Superior Court*, p. 223).

Examples: (1) A child needed an operation to relieve serious curvature of the spine which threatened that he might become bed-ridden for life. The parent was willing to consent to the operation, but, because of religious beliefs, would not allow blood transfusions necessary for the surgery. Although the court recognized the desirability of the operation, it did not interfere with the parent's decision because the child's life was not in immediate danger. *In re Green*, 448 Pa. 338, 292 A.2d 387 (1972).

(2) A boy suffered from a disease which gave him an appearance the court described as grotesque and repulsive. The mother consented to corrective surgery, but not to blood transfusions. There was no immediate threat to the boy's life. However, he had been exempted from school for several years due to his appearance. The court ordered blood transfusions in the event surgeons, in the exercise of their professional judgment, decided to correct the boy's facial deformity. The court noted "unless some constructive steps are taken to alleviate his condition, his chances for a normal, useful life are virtually nil." *In re Sampson*, 65 Misc.2d 658, 317 N.Y.S.2d 641 (1970) aff'd 37 A.D.2d 668, 323 N.Y.S.2d 253 (1971) aff'd 29 N.Y.2d 900, 328 N.Y.S.2d 686, 278 N.E.2d 918 (1972).

3. MENTAL HEALTH

A Georgia statute allowed a parent or guardian to apply for admission of his or her child to the state's mental hospital. The U.S. Supreme Court held that the risk of error inherent in a parental decision to have a child institutionalized for mental health care is sufficiently great that an inquiry should be made by a "neutral factfinder." It held, however, that Georgia's admission procedures were reasonable and consistent with constitutional guarantees, and that a formal or even quasi-formal hearing was not required. The Court suggested that the inquiry need not be conducted by a law-trained or judicial or administrative officer but must carefully probe the child's background, using all available sources. It is necessary that the decision maker have the authority to refuse to admit a child who does not satisfy medical standards for admission. The child's continuing need for commitment must be reviewed periodically by a similar procedure. *Parham v. J. R.,* 442 U.S. 584, 99 S.Ct. 2493, 61 L.Ed.2d 101 (1979).

4. MINOR'S CONSENT TO MEDICAL TREATMENT

Many states have enacted statutes granting minors the ability to give legal consent to a variety of medical procedures, especially relating to drugs, alcoholism and in the sexual sphere. The U.S. Supreme Court's concern with the minor's right to abortion has paved new inroads in this area.

a. Abortion

The U.S. Supreme Court has held that a "mature" minor may obtain an abortion without parental consent or notification if she establishes her "maturity" in an appropriate "bypass procedure." While numerous cases turn on this issue, the Court has not set a fixed age for "maturity" or provided a clear definition of "maturity." See also pp. 238-239.

Examples: (1) A Missouri abortion statute required the parent's written consent to an abortion requested by an unmarried woman under 18, unless a licensed physician certified that abortion was necessary to preserve the mother's life. (Result: The U.S. Supreme Court held the blanket parental consent requirement unconstitutional. No significant state interests, whether to safeguard family unity or parental authority or otherwise, were found to justify conditioning abortion on parental consent.) *Planned Parenthood of Central Missouri v. Danforth,* 428 U.S. 52, 96 S.Ct. 2831, 49 L.Ed.2d 788 (1976).

(2) A Utah statute required physicians to "notify, if possible," parents or guardians of minors upon whom abortion is to be performed. (Result: "A statute setting a 'mere requirement of parental notice' does not violate the constitutional rights of an immature, dependent minor." As applied here to an unemancipated minor girl living with and dependent upon her parents and making no claim or showing as to her maturity or as to her relations with her parents, the court held that the statute serves important state interests, is narrowly drawn to protect only those interests, and does not violate any guarantees of the Constitution. "We emphasized, however, 'that our holding [in *Danforth*] does not suggest that every minor, regardless of age or

maturity, may give effective consent for termination of her
pregnancy.' [At 75, 96 S.Ct., at 2844, citing *Bellotti I.*] There is
no logical relationship between the capacity to become pregnant
and the capacity for mature judgment concerning the wisdom of
an abortion. In *Bellotti II* [*Bellotti v. Baird,* 443 U.S. 622, 99
S.Ct. 3035, 61 L.Ed.2d 797 (1979)], dealing with a class of
concededly mature pregnant minors, we struck down a
Massachusetts statute requiring parental or judicial consent
before an abortion could be performed on any unmarried minor.
There the State's highest court had construed the statute to allow
a court to overrule the minor's decision even if the court found
that the minor was capable of making, and in fact had made, an
informed and reasonable decision to have an abortion. We held,
among other things, that the statute was unconstitutional for
failure to allow mature minors to decide to undergo abortions
without parental consent"). *H.L. v. Matheson,* 450 U.S. 398, 101
S.Ct. 1164, 67 L.Ed.2d 388 (1981).

(3) A Pennsylvania statute required a minor wishing to obtain an
abortion to obtain the informed consent of one of her parents. A
judicial "bypass" procedure was available. (Held: The one-
parent consent requirement is constitutional. "Except in a
medical emergency, an unemancipated young woman under 18
may not obtain an abortion unless she and one of her parents (or
guardian) provides informed consent * * *. If neither a parent
nor a guardian provides consent, a court may authorize the
performance of an abortion upon a determination that the young
woman is mature and capable of giving informed consent and has
in fact given her informed consent, or that an abortion would be
in her best interests. * * * Our cases establish, and we reaffirm
today, that a State may require a minor seeking an abortion to
obtain the consent of a parent or guardian, provided that there is
an adequate judicial bypass procedure. Under these precedents,
in our view, the one-parent consent requirement and judicial
bypass procedure are constitutional.") *Planned Parenthood v.
Casey,* 505 U.S. 833 112 S.Ct. 2791, 120 L.Ed.2d 674 (1992).

(4) An Ohio statute, with certain exceptions, prohibited any
person from performing an abortion on an unmarried,
unemancipated, minor woman absent *notice* to one of the woman's
parents or a court order of approval. (Held: The statute is
constitutional. "[W]e determine that the statute accords with our
precedents on parental notice and consent in the abortion context
and does not violate the Fourteenth Amendment.") *Ohio v.
Akron Center for Reproductive Health*, 497 U.S. 502, 110 S.Ct.
2972, 111 L.Ed.2d 405 (1990).

(5) A Minnesota statute provided, with certain exceptions, that no abortion could be performed on a woman under age 18 absent notification of *both* of her parents. (Held: The *two*-parent notice requirement is unconstitutional.) *Hodgson v. Minnesota*, 497 U.S. 417, 110 S.Ct. 2926, 111 L.Ed.2d 344 (1990).

b. Birth Control

Since a state may not impose a blanket prohibition on, or a blanket requirement of parental consent to, the choice of a minor to terminate her pregnancy, it follows that the blanket prohibition of distribution of contraceptives to minors is unconstitutional. *Carey v. Population Services*, 431 U.S. 678, 97 S.Ct. 2010, 52 L.Ed.2d 675 (1977). See pp. 238, 280.

E. CHILD ABUSE

1. ABUSE REPORTING STATUTES AND REGISTRIES

Statutes encouraging and facilitating the reporting of child abuse and neglect are universal, but their content is not. Most states specify persons, such as physicians, school teachers and social workers, who are required to report suspected child abuse or neglect. Several states encourage everyone to report such situations. What must be reported is knowledge or suspicion of physical or mental injury, sexual abuse and neglect by a child's parent or immediate family member or any person responsible for the child's welfare or any person living in the same home. However, sanctions for failure to report generally are non-existent or weak.

Example: The Illinois statute provides: "Any [of a vast list of medical, school, social work, counseling professionals or state employees] having reasonable cause to believe a child known to them in their professional or official capacity may be an abused child or a neglected child shall immediately report or cause a report to be made to the Department. * * * The privileged quality of communication between any professional person required to report and his patient or client shall not constitute grounds for failure to report as required by this Act. In addition to the above persons required to report suspected cases of abused or neglected children, any other person may make a report if such person has reasonable cause to believe a child may be an abused child or a neglected child. * * * Any person who knowingly transmits a false report to the Department commits the offense of disorderly conduct * * *. Any person who violates this provision a second or subsequent time shall be guilty of a Class 4 felony. * * * A child whose parent, guardian or custodian in good faith selects and depends upon spiritual means through prayer alone for the treatment or cure of disease or remedial care may be considered neglected or abused, but not for the sole reason that his parent, guardian or custodian accepts and practices such beliefs. A child shall not be considered neglected or abused solely because the child is not attending school in accordance with the requirements of Article 26 of The School Code." (325 ILCS 59.614 § 4).

These registers can be very beneficial, but in practice they may store unsubstantiated rumors and suspicions. Possibly innocent parents have no opportunity to confront their accusers and cannot correct or expunge the record. They may not know that such a record exists.

Example: "This court finds [the central child abuse registry statute] represents an unconstitutional infringement on the rights to privacy and the guarantees of due process. In implementing that section, the State Department of Public Welfare has devised the Child Abuse and Neglect Report and Inquiry System (CANRIS). CANRIS is a computerized system designed to collect and store the confidential information gathered by the state from the inception of an investigation through final disposition. It is clear from the expressed purpose of CANRIS that it goes far beyond the permissible maintenance of investigatory files. The mere filing of a report of child abuse is cause enough for the system to operate. The record in this case indicates that CANRIS places labels of 'perpetrator' on those parents who are ensnarled into this web—a conclusion reached by the state without any judicial determination. Similarly, CANRIS may label the report as 'validated,' which by the terms of its operation manual is appropriate where 'the investigating worker has proved that neglect or abuse exists.' This use of information gathering and dissemination absent a judicial determination of abuse or neglect is an impermissible violation of due process and right to privacy. Of course, the state may maintain investigative files. However, to the extent that CANRIS purports in any way to be a clearinghouse of child-abuse information without a judicial determination thereof, it is an unconstitutional infringement on the rights of the parents." *Sims v. State Dept. of Public Welfare,* 438 F.Supp. 1179, 1192, (S.D.Tex.1977), *rev'd.* on other grounds, 442 U.S. 415, 99 S.Ct. 2371, 60 L.Ed.2d 994 (1979).

2. THE BATTERED CHILD SYNDROME

The "battered child syndrome," *if accepted by the court,* facilitates proof of child abuse in appropriate cases. Evidence of the syndrome is accepted more readily in civil than in criminal cases, but often plays a role in the latter.

Examples: (1) Two-year-old C was admitted to the hospital and placed in intensive care, where she had to be fed intravenously for 2 weeks. She was covered with bruises and abrasions, including an open lesion the size of a nickel under her left eye. She was severely dehydrated and had internal abdominal injuries that were later diagnosed as a fractured spleen, pancreatitis and liver dysfunction. The injuries had occurred approximately one week before C arrived at the hospital. C's medical history, as given by F to the physicians, was inconsistent with C's injuries. F and M were tried for injury to a child and convicted. They appealed, claiming that the trial court erred in admitting evidence of battered child syndrome. (Result: Convictions upheld. "Expert testimony is permitted, in the court's discretion, 'if the witness has a special skill or knowledge, beyond the ken of the average juror, that, as properly applied, would be helpful to the determination of an ultimate issue.' Battered child syndrome has become a well established medical diagnosis. Expert medical testimony that a child suffered from battered child syndrome has consistently been held admissible in other jurisdictions. '[T]he "battered child syndrome" simply indicates that a child found with [certain types of injuries] has not suffered those injuries by accidental means. This conclusion is based upon an extensive study of the subject by medical science.' A diagnosis of battered child syndrome is often indicated when a child's injuries do not jibe with the history given by the parent. A properly qualified expert medical witness, therefore, may appropriately explain the syndrome to the jury and express his opinion that the victim suffers from it.") *State v. Dumlao*, 3 Conn.App. 607, 491 A.2d 404 (1985).

(2) M was convicted for the murder of her infant daughter (C). M had called the police and asked for an ambulance. C appeared to be unconscious. The emergency technicians discovered multiple bruises on C's face, neck, chest and abdomen, and a patch of skin was missing from her neck. One side of C's head was mushy due to blood and fluid under the skin. M said that the child had fallen out of her hands and struck the floor. An autopsy revealed other injuries, including a broken arm and an injured liver. According to a forensic pathologist, these injuries were consistent with battered child syndrome. A clinical psychologist constructed a profile of the typical abusive parent. The profile fitted M's character. M was convicted. The issue on appeal was whether the testimony as to battered child syndrome should have been admitted. (Result: Testimony should *not* have been admitted. "[U]nless a defendant has placed her character in issue or has raised some defense which the battering parent syndrome is relevant to rebut, the state may not introduce evidence of the syndrome, nor may the state introduce character evidence showing a defendant's personality traits and personal history as its foundation for demonstrating that the defendant has the characteristics of a typical battering parent." However, the Court went on to find that the error was harmless due to the overwhelming evidence of M's guilt, and it affirmed the judgment.) *Sanders v. State,* 251 Ga. 70, 303 S.E.2d 13 (1983).

F. DISPOSITION BY THE JUVENILE COURT

After a finding of dependency, neglect or abuse, the court typically (1) appoints a guardian, and (2) may, if appropriate, return the child to the custody of its parents, or (3) put the child in foster care, or (4) institutionalize the child or (5) terminate parental rights.

1. GUARDIANSHIP

An individual, a state agency or a private institution may be appointed guardian. The guardian may be given custody or the child's custody may be given to a third party or agency. In appropriate cases, the child may be returned to the custody of its parent under the supervision of the guardian. The guardian obtains all but complete parental authority in terms of making decisions regarding the child, and only "residual" parental rights and duties (such as the right to reasonable visitation, the duty to support and the right to consent or refuse to consent to adoption) are left with the parent.

2. FOSTER CARE

The child may be placed in (state-licensed) foster care until the home situation has improved. In licensed foster homes, paid foster parents provide substitute family care for a planned period when the child's own family cannot provide appropriate care and when adoption is either not desirable or not possible. The state has the duty to monitor the foster care arrangement to ensure that the child is receiving whatever individual treatment it needs. Since foster parents do not have a constitutional right to procedural protections such as are afforded natural parents, contracts requiring foster parents to relinquish their wards are binding when the decision is made for any reason to transfer the child to another foster home or back to its natural parents.

Example: An organization of foster parents sought declaratory and injunctive relief, alleging that New York's statutory and regulatory procedures for removal of foster children from foster homes violated Due Process and Equal Protection. The foster parents' contention was that "when a child has lived in a foster home for a year or more, a psychological tie is created between the child and the foster parents which constitutes the foster family the true 'psychological family' of the child," and creates "a 'liberty interest' in its survival as a family that is protected by the Fourteenth Amendment." The lower court had concluded that "the pre-removal procedures presently employed by the State are constitutionally defective," and held that "before a foster child can be peremptorily transferred from the foster home in which he has been living, be it to another foster home or to the natural parents who initially placed him in foster care, he is entitled to a hearing at which all concerned parties may present any relevant information to the administrative decisionmaker charged with determining the future placement of the child." (Result: Reversed. Recognizing that "no one would seriously dispute that a deeply loving and interdependent relationship between an adult and child in his or her care may exist even in the absence of blood relationship," the U.S. Supreme Court nevertheless was "persuaded that, even on the assumption that appellees have a protected 'liberty interest,' the District Court erred in holding that the preremoval procedures presently employed by the State are constitutionally defective." The removal procedures were upheld.) *Smith v. Organization of Foster Families for Equality and Reform,* 431 U.S. 816, 97 S.Ct. 2094, 53 L.Ed.2d 14 (1977).

3. INSTITUTIONALIZATION

Following a dependency, neglect or abuse adjudication, the child may be institutionalized in a state home or private institution. The parents' support obligation continues.

Example: S, nearly 15 years of age, left his parents' home and lived with various relatives. A juvenile court found S to be a dependent child. Temporary legal custody was awarded to the state but parental rights were not terminated. When the temporary order was lifted, S returned to his parents' custody. The state then filed a petition seeking reimbursement of monies it expended to support S. Relying on the common law doctrine of emancipation, the parents contested the petition and claimed that their duty to support S had ended when he voluntarily left home to pursue a homosexual lifestyle, of which they disapproved. Declining to apply the doctrine of emancipation, the trial court entered an order requiring repayment. The parents appealed. (Result: The doctrine of emancipation is part of the state's common law; further proceedings were necessary to determine whether S was emancipated and, if so, whether that would relieve parents of their responsibility to support S.) *State, In Interest of R.R. v. C.R. and R.R.,* 797 P.2d 459 (Utah App.1990).

4. TERMINATION OF PARENTAL RIGHTS

Where the possibility of rehabilitation of the parent appears to be remote and the parental neglect or abuse was severe, parental rights may be terminated. With termination, the parent and child legally become "strangers" to each other. However, unless adoption is possible or likely, little may be gained by terminating a parent's rights even in serious cases. The child will lose his or her right to support from the parent and, adrift in the system of institutionalization or foster care, may never regain permanent family ties and legal rights. Termination of parental rights thus is a last resort and is resorted to only in severe cases. Special (constitutional) safeguards apply. (See pp. 221–223).

G. CRIMINAL PROCEDURE

1. HISTORY AND DEVELOPMENT

The "delinquency track" of the juvenile court system developed as a means of protecting children who have committed a crime from being subjected to the same procedures, standards, and punishments applied to adults. The objective was to replace the adversarial nature of criminal proceedings with a "paternalistic" proceeding to determine what is in the best interest of the accused minor. Correction rather than punishment was sought at an age when the child was still impressionable and changeable and, perhaps, bore less than full responsibility for criminal acts. The bulk of delinquency and status offense cases are dealt with by informal supervision or unofficial handling, without an adjudication of delinquent behavior. Incarceration, if imposed, is in a "reform school" or similar institution rather than in a prison.

2. THE NEED FOR REFORM

A major concern was that incarceration could be imposed on a juvenile potentially for a longer period than that for which an adult could have been sentenced for the same offense. Finding that the results in juvenile courts "have not been entirely satisfactory," the U.S. Supreme Court sought to provide more protection for juveniles by mandating that certain procedural rights accorded adult criminal defendants must be granted in the juvenile court system. *In re Gault,* 387 U.S. 1, 87 S.Ct. 1428, 18 L.Ed.2d 527 (1967). These rights include (1) adequate written notice, (2) advice as to right of counsel, (3) confrontation by sworn witnesses, (4) cross-examination of witnesses, and (5) the privilege against self-incrimination, in short, the "essentials of due process and fair treatment." The right to proof beyond a reasonable doubt was granted juveniles in cases involving "adult crimes." *In re Winship,* 397 U.S. 358, 90 S.Ct. 1068, 25 L.Ed.2d 368 (1970). Juveniles, however, do not have a constitutional right to jury trial in a juvenile court delinquency proceeding. *McKeiver v. Pennsylvania,* 403 U.S. 528, 91 S.Ct. 1976, 29 L.Ed.2d 647 (1971).

3. STATUS OFFENSES AND DELINQUENCY

"Status offenses," such as incorrigibility, truancy and running away from home, involve the child's status as a child. They would not be crimes if committed by an adult. Offenders often are referred to as "persons," "minors" or "children" "in need of supervision" (PINS, MINS or CINS). A federal District court held in *Martarella v. Kelley,* 349 F.Supp. 575 (S.D.N.Y.1972) that PINS have a "right to treatment" while in detention, although no similar right has been established for juvenile delinquents.

Example: Following a finding that D had regularly disobeyed her parents, the juvenile court held D to be an undisciplined child in need of the discipline and supervision of the state. D was placed on probation, but she violated probation by keeping late hours, going to places and seeing people forbidden by her parents, and refusing to obey school rules. D was committed to a detention home for juveniles, and she appealed. (Result: "[D's] contention is that [the statute] violates the Equal Protection Clause of the Fourteenth Amendment in that it subjects an undisciplined child to probation and the concomitant risk of incarceration when the child has committed no criminal offense, while adults are subjected to probation and incarceration only for actual criminal offenses. * * * [T]he classification here challenged is based on differences between adults and children; and there are so many valid distinctions that the basis for challenge seems shallow. These differences are 'reasonably related to the purposes of the Act'—that is, to provide children the needed supervision and control. Consequently, the classification does not offend the Equal Protection Clause * * * and even if it be said that the classification here challenged affects 'fundamental interests' or is 'inherently suspect,' it is our view that the desire of the State to exercise its authority as parens patriae and provide for the care and protection of its children supplies a 'compellingly rational' justification for the classification.'') *Matter of Walker*, 282 N.C. 28, 191 S.E.2d 702 (1972).

H. REVIEW QUESTIONS

1. **T or F** Status offenses are acts which, if committed by an adult, would not be a crime.

2. **T or F** In a custody hearing, M, a Jehovah's witness, makes it clear that she would not consent to a blood transfusion for her child. For this reason alone, a court may order C neglected.

3. **T or F** In proceedings to terminate their parental rights, parents have a constitutional right to counsel.

4. **T or F** In proceedings to terminate parental rights, parental neglect or abuse must be proved by clear and convincing evidence.

5. **T or F** Before a minor is committed to a mental institution by his/her parents, the minor is constitutionally entitled to a formal, adversary hearing before a neutral factfinder.

6. **T or F** A judicial determination of child neglect and award of guardianship and custody to someone other than the parents, suspends the parents' support obligation.

7. **T or F** Statutes requiring teachers, physicians and other professionals to report their reasonable suspicion of child abuse, usually carry severe criminal sanctions.

8. **T or F** After foster parents have had custody of a foster child for a "substantial" period of time, they develop a constitutionally protected right to be "first in line" for the adoption of their foster child.

9. **T or F** Under *In re Gault* and numerous U.S. Supreme Court cases that followed, minors being tried in juvenile courts have the same procedural protections that must be accorded adults in criminal prosecutions.

10. **T or F** A parent who, for religious reasons, refuses to seek conventional medical care for his or her ill child may not be criminally prosecuted if the child dies or is harmed.

11. **T or F** When a municipal or state child welfare agency fails to protect a child from serious or fatal child abuse or neglect, the agency is liable to the child of his estate.

12. **T or F** A state's requirement that a minor seeking an abortion *notify* both parents has been held unconstitutional.

13. **T or F** A state's requirement that a minor seeking an abortion obtain *consent* from *one* parent is constitutional.

X

CHILDREN'S RIGHTS

Analysis

A. HISTORY OF PARENTAL CONTROL

"It is basic to our law that the court cannot regulate, by its processes, the internal affairs of the home. As we said more than 30 years ago, '(d)ispute (in the family) when it does not involve anything immoral or harmful to the welfare of the child is beyond the reach of the law. The vast majority of matters concerning the upbringing of children must be left to the conscience, patience and self-restraint of father and mother. No end of difficulties would arise should judges try to tell parents how to bring up their children.' " Jason, J., concurring in *Roe v. Doe,* 29 N.Y.2d 188, 324 N.Y.S.2d 71, 272 N.E.2d 567 (1971).

The old rule was that the father had all but absolute power over his offspring. Today, parents retain significant but not absolute control over their minor children. Limitations are defined by child "neglect," "dependency," "abuse" and compulsory school attendance laws. There is increasing judicial and statutory recognition of minor children as legal entities independent of their parents. Considerable strides have been made by the child in the area of criminal (juvenile delinquency) procedure and in a series of school-related situations. Vis-à-vis their parents, however, the definition of the child's own constitutional rights has not progressed very far, except in the area of sexual rights (*e.g.,* birth control, abortion).

B. CONSTITUTIONAL RIGHTS

Children enjoy some protections under the United States Constitution, but their rights are not equal to or the same as those of adults. The U.S. Supreme Court has noted three reasons why children are treated differently than adults under the Constitution: "[T]he peculiar vulnerability of children; their inability to make critical decisions in an informed manner; and the importance of the parental role in child-rearing." *Bellotti v. Baird,* 443 U.S. 622, 99 S.Ct. 3035, 61 L.Ed.2d 797 (1979).

Examples: (1) A New York statute prohibited the sale or distribution of contraceptives to a minor under the age of sixteen years. (Result: Statute unconstitutional. "The question of the extent of state power to regulate conduct of minors not constitutionally regulable when committed by adults is a vexing one, perhaps not susceptible to precise answer. * * * Certain principles, however, have been recognized. 'Minors, as well as adults, are protected by the Constitution and possess constitutional rights.' '[W]hatever may be their precise impact, neither the Fourteenth Amendment nor the Bill of Rights is for adults alone.' On the other hand, we have held in a variety of contexts that 'the power of the state to control the conduct of children reaches beyond the scope of its authority over adults.' ") *Carey v. Population Services International,* 431 U.S. 678, 97 S.Ct. 2010, 52 L.Ed.2d 675 (1977). (See p. 229).

(2) The U.S. Supreme Court has struck down statutes requiring *parental consent* to a "mature" minor daughter's abortion. *Planned Parenthood of Central Missouri v. Danforth,* 428 U.S. 52, 96 S.Ct. 2831, 49 L.Ed.2d 788

(1976) and *Bellotti v. Baird,* 443 U.S. 622, 99 S.Ct. 3035, 61 L.Ed.2d 797 (1979). (See p. 227).

(3) In *H.L. v. Matheson,* 450 U.S. 398, 101 S.Ct. 1164, 67 L.Ed.2d 388 (1981), a statute requiring *notice* to parents of a minor seeking an abortion was upheld when applied to an unmarried, fifteen-year-old minor, who lived at home and was dependent on her parents. (See p. 227).

(4) In *Planned Parenthood v. Casey,* 505 U.S. 833, 112 S.Ct. 2791, 120 L.Ed.2d 674 (1992), the U.S. Supreme Court held: "Our cases establish, and we reaffirm today, that a State may require a minor seeking an abortion to obtain the consent of a parent or guardian, provided that there is an adequate judicial bypass procedure. Under these precedents, in our view, the one-parent consent requirement and judicial bypass procedure are constitutional.") (See p. 228).

(5) Approximately the same rule (notice to parents permitted but availability of bypass procedure for "mature minors" required) applies to parental *notice* statutes. *Ohio v. Akron Center for Reproductive Health,* 497 U.S. 502, 110 S.Ct. 2972, 111 L.Ed.2d 405 (1990); *Akron II; Hodgson v. Minnesota,* 497 U.S. 417, 110 S.Ct. 2926, 111 L.Ed.2d 344 (1990). (See p. 228-229).

With respect to the parents' authority to commit their child to a psychiatric institution, the U.S. Supreme Court has held that a full, adversary hearing is *not* required under the Due Process clause, so long as certain basic safeguards are in place to prevent parents from "railroading their children into asylums." *Parham v. J.R.,* 442 U.S. 584, 99 S.Ct. 2493, 61 L.Ed.2d 101 (1979). (See p. 226-27).

C. EMANCIPATION

As previously discussed (p. 184), a minor's emancipation terminates the parental support obligation and eliminates minority as a legal defense to contractual obligations. Emancipation also involves the end of parental control over the minor.

D. MINOR'S CAPACITY TO CONTRACT

Contractual obligations incurred by unemancipated minors are voidable. Upon reaching majority, the obligation may be ratified. While it is the parent's duty to provide "necessaries" for a child and, if the parent fails to do so, the parent is liable under the infant's contract, the infant himself is liable on the contract if the parent is unable to provide for the necessaries.

Example: A child received necessary medical attention at a cost of $7,000. The mother (who was on welfare) could not pay the bill. (Result: The child—who had been awarded a judgment compensating for the injury that required the medical attention—was held liable on the contract.) *Gardner v. Flowers*, 529 S.W.2d 708 (Tenn.1975).

E. CHILDREN AND TORT LAW

1. "WRONGFUL LIFE"

Courts disagree whether parents can recover damages from a third party (physician, pharmacist) whose negligent performance or nonperformance of a duty (*e.g.*, sterilization, abortion, supply of medication) results in the conception and birth of an unwanted *healthy* child. (*Caveat*: Distinguish suits on behalf of the child or by the parents directly involving the birth of a "defective" or "deformed" child.)

a. Recovery Allowed

Courts that allow recovery in a "wrongful life" action disagree as to the proper measure of damages. Many courts allow limited recovery for *direct* expenses associated with the pregnancy, sometimes including mental distress caused by the pregnancy. A few courts have allowed more, such as the cost of having and raising the child, reduced by the probable enjoyment the child will bring. The argument that the mother should mitigate damages by having an abortion or by putting the child up for adoption has not been favored.

Example: W and H decided not to have more children, and W underwent an unsuccessful tubal ligation. W became pregnant and delivered a healthy baby. The court held that W and H's damages properly included (1) all expenses associated with the birth, (2) a second sterilization operation, (3) W's lost earnings capacity, (4) day care costs for other children while W was incapacitated, (5) H's loss of consortium, (6) W's pain and suffering in connection with the birth and second surgery, and (7) the expense of raising the child. (Result: Affirmed. The Supreme Judicial Court of Massachusetts held: "The great weight of authority permits the parents of a normal child born as a result of a physician's negligence to recover damages directly associated with the birth (sometimes including damage for the parents' emotional distress), but courts are divided on whether the parents may recover the economic expense of rearing the child. * * * The judicial declaration that the joy and pride in raising a child always outweigh any economic loss the parents may suffer, thus precluding recovery for the cost of raising the child, simply lacks verisimilitude. The very fact that a person has sought medical intervention to prevent him or her from having a child demonstrates that, for that person, the benefits of parenthood did not outweigh the burdens, economic and otherwise, of having a child. The extensive use of contraception and sterilization and the performance of numerous abortions each year show that * * * large numbers of people do not accept parenthood

as a net positive circumstance. We agree with those courts that
have rejected the theory that the birth of a child is for all parents
at all times a net benefit. * * * We conclude that * * * parents
may recover the cost of rearing a normal, healthy but (at least
initially) unwanted child if their reason for seeking sterilization
was founded on economic or financial considerations. In such a
situation, the trier of fact should offset against the cost of rearing
the child the benefit, if any, the parents receive and will receive
from having their child. We discern no reason founded on sound
public policy to immunize a physician from having to pay for a
reasonably foreseeable consequence of his negligence or from a
natural and probable consequence of a breach of his guarantee,
namely, the parents' expenses in rearing the child to adulthood.")
Burke v. Rivo, 406 Mass. 764, 551 N.E.2d 1 (1990).

b. Recovery Denied

Examples: (1) H, W, and their five children brought a malpractice action
against surgeon and hospital, alleging the improper performance
of a sterilization operation on W. (Result: Recovery denied. To
compel the allegedly negligent surgeon to assume financial
responsibility for raising and educating the child would violate
public policy and the law governing provable damages.) *Coleman
v. Garrison,* 349 A.2d 8 (Del.1975).

(2) M and F filed a medical malpractice action against a physician,
alleging that he had negligently performed a tubal ligation after
which M had become pregnant and given birth to a healthy girl.
They sought damages for the expenses of the pregnancy, delivery,
postpartum care, and rearing the child. The trial court dismissed
the part of their claim that asked damages for the expense of
rearing the child. (Result: As a matter of public policy, M and F
have suffered no legally cognizable harm by virtue of the birth of a
healthy child, conceived after an unsuccessful surgical birth
control procedure. Accordingly, there can be no recovery from the
allegedly negligent physician, hospital, and clinic for pecuniary
expenses of raising the healthy, normal, though unplanned, child.)
O'Toole v. Greenberg, 64 N.Y.2d 427, 488 N.Y.S.2d 143, 477
N.E.2d 445 (1985).

c. Contract Actions

When a birth control device failed or a sterilization was unsuccessful, parents
occasionally have sought to claim on a contract or warranty theory. Such
claims generally have not met with success where the recovery sought was in
excess of a refund of payments made.

d. Birth Defects

Where the baby suffered birth defects caused by a physician's negligence,
courts have displayed more sympathy. Some courts term such cases "wrongful

birth". (Note that these cases also may involved the child's *own* "damages" along with medical expenses the parents incur.)

Example: Baby suffered from congenital rubella syndrome. M brought a "wrongful birth" action against her physician, who allegedly had negligently failed to test for and discover that mother had rubella, had failed to advise mother regarding the risks of birth defects in a fetus exposed to rubella, and had thereby deprived mother of information which might have caused her to have an abortion. (Result: Damages for emotional distress and *ordinary* child-raising costs are not recoverable. Extraordinary medical and educational expenses attributable to the child's infirmities may be recovered.) *Smith v. Cote,* 128 N.H. 231, 513 A.2d 341 (1986).

2. WRONGFUL DEATH

A child may recover for pecuniary loss resulting from the wrongful death of a parent. Traditionally, in the absence of pecuniary damage resulting from the death of a minor child, parents could not recover. Today, parents generally may recover for the loss of "society and companionship" of their child, without specific proof of pecuniary damage or economic loss.

3. SUITS BETWEEN PARENT AND CHILD—EROSION OF THE TORT IMMUNITY

Traditional law prohibited tort suits between parents and children. Stated objectives were to preserve family harmony and to prevent collusive suits to collect insurance benefits. (Note: by comparison, the *interspousal* tort immunity rested on the additional notion of the spouses' "oneness.")

Many courts and legislatures have abolished the immunity doctrine, finding the underlying rationale unpersuasive. Other courts have created exceptions, allowing recovery when the child's injury results from the parents' "active" negligence or where the parents negligently entrusted the child with a "dangerous instrumentality." Still others have abrogated the immunity to the extent insurance will pay for the damage, on the assumption that domestic tranquility will not be affected adversely if an insurance company pays.

Examples: (1) A minor child who had no driver's license may be entitled to recover from her parent for injuries received in an automobile accident, when the parents had negligently entrusted the car to the child. *Allstate Ins. Co. v. Reliance Ins. Co.,* 85 Misc.2d 734, 380 N.Y.S.2d 923 (1976).

(2) South Carolina's statutory partial abrogation of the immunity, creating an exception for automobile accidents, was held to violate Equal Protection. The court went on to abolish the immunity completely. *Elam v. Elam,* 275 S.C. 132, 268 S.E.2d 109 (1980).

4. "HEARTBALM" ACTIONS

Children may not recover for "alienation of parental affection" resulting in loss of parental society. Only a few cases have held to the contrary. Conversely, other than in an action for wrongful death, courts do not allow a parent recovery for the loss of a child's society.

Examples: (1) C, a minor, sued D for alienation of affections after D induced M to leave C and F. The trial court dismissed the suit. (Result: The Illinois Appellate court reversed. To maintain an action for alienation of affections under Alienation of Affections Act, C must allege and prove the love and affection of the alienated mother for C, that D willfully or wrongfully alienated the mother's affections by overt acts, conduct, or enticement, and the *actual* damages that were proximately caused by D. "An action by a child for alienation of the affections of one of the child's parents was first recognized in Illinois in [1947]. * * * Four months after [that] decision, the Illinois legislature, presumably aware of the * * * decision, enacted the Alienation of Affections Act. * * * Given this background, we conclude that plaintiff's action falls squarely within the boundaries of the Act. First, the Act expressly applies to 'all actions for alienation of affections begun after the effective date of this act.' The Act draws no distinction between actions for alienation of affections brought by a spouse from those brought by a child. * * * [N]o legislative intent to exclude plaintiff's action from the coverage of the Act can be discerned from the Act's language.") *Rudnick v. Vokaty,* 84 Ill.App.3d 1003, 40 Ill.Dec. 404, 406 N.E.2d 105 (1980).

(2) As a result of complications from a coma arising from the use of a general anesthetic, a sixteen-year-old boy was reduced to the mental age of three, suffered total blindness and severe impairment of his hearing and partial paralysis of his right side. The *parents'* action for loss of their child's "support, comfort, protection, society and pleasure" was denied for policy reasons. Those reasons included the intangible character of the loss, difficulty of measuring damages, as well as the danger of multiple claims and extensive liability. *Baxter v. Superior Court of Los Angeles County,* 138 Cal.Rptr. 315, 19 Cal.3d 461, 563 P.2d 871 (1977).

5. CHILDRENS' TORTS AGAINST THIRD PARTIES—PARENTS' LIABILITY?

In general, parents are not *vicariously* liable for their child's tort against a third party. Exceptions include the "family purpose doctrine" and limited statutory liability. If it has requisite capacity (and money) a child, of course, is liable for its tort, and parents may be liable for their *own* negligence, if they negligently fail to supervise their child and damage results.

Under the "family purpose doctrine," vicarious liability may be imposed on a parent for the negligence of a family member, including a child, while driving the family car. In addition, a majority of states have enacted statutes that hold parents vicariously liable for damage caused by their children's torts, up to a statutory maximum amount, typically in the low thousands. Statutes of this type generally have been upheld against constitutional attack. A New Jersey court has held that a statute imposing *unlimited* strict liability on parents for damage done to school property by their children denied the parents due process. *Board of Education of Piscataway Tp. v. Caffiero,* 159 N.J.Super. 347, 387 A.2d 1263 (1978).

6. PARENTS' CRIMINAL LIABILITY?

Parents are not liable for *criminal* acts of their children.

Examples: (1) A municipal ordinance raised a presumption that a parent is responsible for the misbehavior of a child who twice within one year is adjudged guilty of acts defined as violations of the public peace. (Result: The presumption was held unconstitutional in view of evidence that parental actions are but one factor in the interaction of forces producing juvenile misconduct.) *Doe v. City of Trenton,* 143 N.J.Super. 128, 362 A.2d 1200 (1976).

(2) California Penal Code § 272 punishes "causing, encouraging or contributing to delinquency of persons under 18 years; inducing disobedience to court order" and provides a fine "not exceeding * * * $2,500, or * * * imprisonment in the county jail for not more than one year, or * * * both such fine and imprisonment * * *, or [release] on probation for a period not exceeding five years. *For purposes of this section, a parent or legal guardian or legal guardian to any person under the age of 18 years shall have the duty to exercise reasonable care, supervision, protection, and control over their minor child"* (emphasis added).

F. PROPERTY RIGHTS

Under the common law rule, the minor child's earnings belonged to the father while the child lived with and was maintained by him. Any property acquired by the child in any way other than by its own labor or services (*e.g.,* by gift or inheritance), belonged to the child. In order to provide effective, simple management of gifts to children, forty-six jurisdictions (by 1996) have adopted the Uniform Transfers to Minors Act or a substantially similar statute.

G. EDUCATION: STATE AND PARENTS

State laws require children to attend school for a designated period, typically expressed in terms of age, such as six to sixteen.

1. PRIVATE SCHOOLING

If parents wish to send their children to a private school, a state may not require attendance at a public school. *Pierce v. Society of Sisters,* 268 U.S. 510, 45 S.Ct. 571, 69 L.Ed. 1070 (1925). Many states allow home instruction by parents.

Example: Based on their religious beliefs, M and F decided to educate their children at home and sought a declaratory judgment that their home-school was a qualified nonpublic school under state law. M had attended college for one year and F had graduated from the U.S. Merchant Marine Academy with a degree in maritime science. M and F instructed their children in basic reading and writing, math, and Bible study. The children's standardized test scores were average or above average. (Result: Parent's home instruction met the statutory requirements for compulsory attendance at a nonpublic school. "[O]ur sister jurisdictions, when faced with the question of whether home instruction is prohibited by school attendance statutes which specify various standards for nonpublic schools, have almost always analyzed the question not in terms of any meaning intrinsic to the word 'school' but rather in terms of whether the particular home instruction in question met the statutory standards. In the absence of a clear legislative prohibition of home instruction, we think this is the better approach to the problem.") *Delconte v. State,* 313 N.C. 384, 329 S.E.2d 636 (1985).

2. CONSTITUTIONAL OBJECTIONS TO OBLIGATORY SCHOOLING

In *Wisconsin v. Yoder,* 406 U.S. 205, 92 S.Ct. 1526, 32 L.Ed.2d 15 (1972), the U.S. Supreme Court held that Wisconsin's compulsory school attendance law could not be applied to Amish parents who did not want their children to attend school beyond the eighth grade. The Court balanced the parents' interest in supervising their children's religious training with the state's interest in compulsory school attendance. The Court emphasized that the Amish religion provides a stable environment and noted the economic self-sufficiency of adherents of that religion.

3. PARENTAL CONTROL OVER CLASSROOM CONTENT

Parents continue to voice concerns regarding classroom content, especially in the areas of school prayer, sex education, "creationism vs. evolution," and the required use of certain books.

Examples: (1) The U.S. Supreme Court has decided a series of "school prayer" cases. In one of the more recent cases, the parent of three public school children challenged the constitutionality of an Alabama school prayer and meditation statute. The Court held that an Alabama statute authorizing a daily period of silence in public schools for meditation or voluntary prayer was an endorsement of religion that lacked any clearly secular purpose, and thus was in violation of the

First Amendment. *Wallace v. Jaffree,* 472 U.S. 38, 105 S.Ct. 2479, 86 L.Ed.2d 29 (1985).

(2) School children and their parents objected to the use of certain books and assigned readings. They sought injunctive relief and money damages for alleged violation of their First Amendment right to the free exercise of religion. The Federal district court held that the compulsory use of a textbook series, found offensive to their religious beliefs by fundamentalist Christians, burdened the students' right of free exercise of their religion and was not essential to the state's interests in the education of children and in the literacy of its citizens. (Result: Reversed. "There was no proof that any plaintiff student was ever called upon to say or do anything that required the student to affirm or deny a religious belief or to engage or refrain from engaging in any act either required or forbidden by the students' religious convictions.") *Mozert v. Hawkins County Board of Education,* 827 F.2d 1058 (6th Cir.1987), *cert. den.* 484 U.S. 1066, 108 S.Ct. 1029, 98 L.Ed.2d 993 (1988).

(3) The New York City Board of Education established a two-part AIDS prevention program in the high schools that included (1) classroom instruction on AIDS infection and prevention, and (2) distribution of condoms to students who wanted them. The classroom phase was mandatory, unless parents exercised an "opt-out" provision, whereas condom distribution did not require parental consent, nor could parents opt their children out of this part of the program. Parents of high school students sued to halt the distribution of condoms. (Result: Condom distribution halted because (1) it is a health service which under the public health law requires parental consent, and (2) it violates parental rights to rear children as they see fit.) *Alfonso v. Fernandez,* 195 A.D.2d 46, 606 N.Y.S.2d 259 (1993).

(4) Facing a broader issue than *parental* control, the U.S. Supreme Court has restricted *legislative* control over the school curriculum. The Court struck down a Louisiana statute requiring the teaching of "creation science" alongside evolution, if the latter was to be taught at all. The Court held the law facially invalid because it lacked a clear secular purpose: "The legislative history documents that the Act's primary purpose was to change the science curriculum of public schools in order to provide persuasive advantage to a particular religious doctrine that rejects the factual basis of evolution in its entirety." *Edwards v. Aguillard,* 482 U.S. 578, 107 S.Ct. 2573, 96 L.Ed.2d 510 (1987).

4. DISCIPLINE IN SCHOOLS

Discipline in schools has come under constitutional scrutiny. To illustrate, U.S. Supreme Court cases protect (1) the minor's freedom of political expression (*Tinker v. Des Moines Independent Community School Dist.*, 393 U.S. 503, 511, 89 S.Ct. 733, 739, 21 L.Ed.2d 731 (1969)); (2) the use of lewd and offensive language (*Bethel School District No. 403 v. Fraser,* 478 U.S. 675, 682, 106 S.Ct. 3159, 3164, 92 L.Ed.2d 549 (1986)); (3) censorship of a high school newspaper (*Hazelwood School Dist. v. Kuhlmeier,* 484 U.S. 260, 108 S.Ct. 562, 98 L.Ed.2d 592 (1988)). Further, hearing requirements govern suspensions (*Goss v. Lopez,* 419 U.S. 565, 95 S.Ct. 729, 42 L.Ed.2d 725 (1975)), and students may bring tort suits against school officials for being summarily expelled (*Wood v. Strickland,* 420 U.S. 308, 95 S.Ct. 992, 43 L.Ed.2d 214 (1975)); *cf. Carey v. Piphus,* 435 U.S. 247, 98 S.Ct. 1042, 55 L.Ed.2d 252 (1978).

The U.S. Supreme Court has held that the "cruel and unusual punishment" clause of the Eighth Amendment does not apply to corporal punishment in public schools. Specifically, "[w]e conclude that when public school teachers or administrators impose disciplinary corporal punishment, the Eighth Amendment is inapplicable. The pertinent constitutional question is whether the imposition is consonant with the requirements of due process. * * * We conclude that the Due Process Clause does not require notice and hearing prior to the imposition of corporal punishment in the public schools, as that practice is authorized and limited by the common law," *i.e.,* "to inflict only such corporal punishment as is reasonably necessary for the proper education and discipline of the child; any punishment going beyond the privilege may result in both civil and criminal liability. * * * As long as the schools are open to public scrutiny, there is no reason to believe that the common law constraints will not effectively remedy and deter excesses such as those alleged in this case." *Ingraham v. Wright,* 430 U.S. 651, 97 S.Ct. 1401, 51 L.Ed.2d 711 (1977).

H. REVIEW QUESTIONS

1. **T or F** Unemancipated minors have no constitutional protections in their own right; what protection they have is derived from protections accorded their parents.

2. **T or F** For an emancipated minor, the fact that he or she is under the age of majority is not a legal defense to contractual obligations.

3. **T or F** Parents proving medical negligence that led to the birth of an unwanted healthy child, may collect for the expense of rearing the child in an action for "wrongful life."

4. **T or F** In the case of the wrongful death of their child, parents may recover for the loss of the child's society and companionship.

5. **T or F** To protect "family harmony," children may not sue their parents and parents may not sue their children for torts inflicted on each other.

6. **T or F** A minor may bring an action for alienation of affections against a third party who has caused the break-up of the minor's parents' marriage.

7. **T or F** Parents are not liable for the criminal acts of their dependent children.

8. **T or F** Under certain circumstances, parents may be held liable for torts committed by their minor children.

9. **T or F** The U.S. Supreme Court has upheld the lawfulness of corporal punishment in public schools.

10. **T or F** Parents may prevent a public school from teaching sex education to their child.

XI

LEGITIMACY, ILLEGITIMACY AND PATERNITY

Analysis

A. LEGITIMACY

1. DEFINITION

Legitimacy denotes the status of a child who enjoys a full legal relationship with both parents by virtue of the parents' marriage to each other at the time of the child's birth or conception.

2. PRESUMPTION OF LEGITIMACY

The law presumes that a child born to a married woman is the child of her husband, absent convincing proof of his nonpaternity. This presumption was one of the strongest known to the common law and has become readily rebuttable only with the advent of modern blood tests. However, even if there is (or may be) proof of nonpaternity, estoppel may prevent its use (or production) as evidence.

> ***Example:*** H and W divorced. Custody of three of the four children was given to W. H was ordered to pay support. Attempting to defeat the support order, H alleged that two of the three children in W's custody were not his. H proposed to disprove his paternity with blood tests. (Result: Rules permitting presumption of legitimacy of children to be rebutted by blood tests did not apply so as to permit H to escape liability for support of children whom he had acknowledged as his own for more than fifteen years.) *Watts v. Watts,* 115 N.H. 186, 337 A.2d 350 (1975).

B. ILLEGITIMACY

Illegitimacy denotes the legal status of the child born outside of marriage, or of a child born to a married mother whose husband is not the father if the latter has legally disclaimed the child. In current usage, the term "nonmarital" child is replacing the terms "illegitimate" (unlawful) child or child "born out of wedlock" (archaic).

1. TRADITIONAL ATTITUDES

At early common law, the illegitimate child had no legal rights against either parent. As *filius nullius,* the child was kin to no one and was not entitled to support or inheritance from its parents or other blood relatives. However, the law has long recognized the relationship between a mother and her nonmarital child. Until the U.S. Supreme Court intervened in the late 1960s, most states continued to discriminate against the nonmarital child with regard to the child's legal relationship with its father. Of particular importance were the typical absence of a right of intestate succession, the presence of only a limited, if any, right of support, and limited, if any, eligibility under statutes (*e.g.*, social security, workmen's compensation, wrongful death) requiring proof of descent or specifically limited to legitimate offspring.

2. THE CONSTITUTIONAL MANDATE

Under the Equal Protection and Due Process Clauses, the U.S. Supreme Court has progressively invalidated nearly all forms of legal discrimination involving children born out of wedlock.

a. Standard of Review

The U.S. Supreme Court applies neither the "strict scrutiny" accorded racial classifications, nor the much less stringent "rational basis test," to classifications based upon the status of illegitimacy. Instead, the Court has employed an intermediate standard of review, variously described as requiring a "close and substantial relationship to a permissible governmental interest" *(Califano v. Boles,* 443 U.S. 282, 99 S.Ct. 2767, 61 L.Ed.2d 541 (1979)), Justices Marshall, Brennan, White and Blackmun dissenting, or not being "toothless" *(Mathews v. Lucas,* 427 U.S. 495, 96 S.Ct. 2755, 49 L.Ed.2d 651 (1976)).

b. Relationship to Mother

Levy v. Louisiana, 391 U.S. 68, 88 S.Ct. 1509, 20 L.Ed.2d 436 (1968), was the first U.S. Supreme Court case to apply the Equal Protection Clause to legal discrimination based on illegitimacy. Dealing with an unusual Louisiana law that denied a full legal relationship between the nonmarital child and its *mother,* the case established that a nonmarital child may recover for the wrongful death of its mother. Simultaneously, the Court held that a mother may recover for the wrongful death of her nonmarital child. *Glona v. American Guarantee and Liability Insurance Co.,* 391 U.S. 73, 88 S.Ct. 1515, 20 L.Ed.2d 441 (1968). Since discrimination in the legal relationship between mother and child was very unusual, the significance of these cases lies mainly in their applicability to the father and child relationship.

c. U.S. Supreme Court Cases on the Father and Child Relationship

1) Intestate Succession

Several U.S. Supreme Court cases have directly addressed the right of the nonmarital child to inherit from its deceased intestate father. In *Labine v. Vincent,* 401 U.S. 532, 91 S.Ct. 1017, 28 L.Ed.2d 288 (1971), the Court upheld a Louisiana law denying inheritance to a nonmarital child, even though the father had acknowledged the child during his lifetime. In *Trimble v. Gordon,* 430 U.S. 762, 97 S.Ct. 1459, 52 L.Ed.2d 31 (1977), the Court declared that an Illinois law that did not allow nonmarital offspring to inherit from their intestate fathers denied equal protection. (The Illinois Probate Act allowed nonmarital children to inherit only from their intestate mothers, whereas children born in wedlock could inherit by intestate succession from their mothers and their fathers.) The Court held that a classification based on illegitimacy must bear a rational relationship to a legitimate state purpose, and the provision could not be justified on the ground that it promoted legitimate family relationships. In a footnote, the Court stated that *Labine* had limited value as precedent. In *Lalli v. Lalli,* 439 U.S. 259, 99 S.Ct. 518, 58 L.Ed.2d 503 (1978), the Court held that, for purposes of intestate succession from an unmarried father, New York may require that paternity have been established during the father's lifetime.

2) Right of Support

In *Gomez v. Perez,* 409 U.S. 535, 93 S.Ct. 872, 35 L.Ed.2d 56 (1973), the U.S. Supreme Court held that Texas law could not exclude nonmarital children from a generally enforceable right to paternal support.

3) Wrongful Death

Parham v. Hughes, 441 U.S. 347, 99 S.Ct. 1742, 60 L.Ed.2d 269 (1979), involved a Georgia statute that precluded a father who had not legitimated a child from suing for the child's wrongful death. The statute was upheld on the ground that it provides a rational means of dealing with the problem of proving paternity, and that the father's situation is different from that of the child, in that the father's status is not immutable, and that he could have come forward to claim paternity. Moreover, the statute was found not to discriminate invidiously against a father simply because he is of the male sex.

4) Government Benefits Based on Father and Child Relationship

Examples: (1) A state may not discriminate against nonmarital children in distributing welfare benefits. *New Jersey Welfare Rights Organization v. Cahill,* 411 U.S. 619, 93 S.Ct. 1700, 36 L.Ed.2d 543 (1973).

(2) Nonmarital children, whether or not acknowledged, are eligible to collect workers' compensation benefits occasioned by their father's death. *Weber v. Aetna Cas. and Surety Co.,* 406 U.S. 164, 92 S.Ct. 1400, 31 L.Ed.2d 768 (1972).

(3) Federal law may require that unrecognized nonmarital children prove actual dependency to collect certain social security benefits even while legitimate children and those nonmarital children whose paternity is ascertained need not present such proof. *Mathews v. Lucas,* 427 U.S. 495, 96 S.Ct. 2755, 49 L.Ed.2d 651 (1976).

(4) Statute denying benefits to nonlegitimated nonmarital children who are born after the onset of the father's disability was not reasonably related to the valid governmental interest of preventing spurious claims. *Jimenez v. Weinberger,* 417 U.S. 628, 94 S.Ct. 2496, 41 L.Ed.2d 363 (1974).

(5) In *Fiallo v. Bell,* 430 U.S. 787, 97 S.Ct. 1473, 52 L.Ed.2d 50 (1977), unwed natural fathers and their nonmarital offspring sought to enjoin enforcement of sections of Immigration and Nationality Act that exclude the relationship between nonmarital child and its natural father from the special preference immigration status accorded a "child" or "parent" of a United States citizen or lawful permanent resident, whereas the *mother* and child relationship is covered. The Supreme Court rejected the claim on the grounds that (1)

Congress' power to expel or exclude aliens is largely immune from judicial control (2) no factors in this case warranted more searching judicial scrutiny that generally applied in immigration cases, and (3) it is not for the Court to probe and test the justifications for legislative decisions in this area.

C. ESTABLISHING PATERNITY

1. THE UNIFORM PARENTAGE ACT

About one half of the states have enacted the Uniform Parentage Act or a variation. The Act provides procedures facilitating establishment of paternity. Considerable reliance is placed on improved, modern blood-typing procedures that contribute to certainty and ease of paternity determination.

2. CONSTITUTIONAL REQUIREMENTS

The Supreme Court has not done much to define acceptable procedures for paternity actions.

Examples: (1) In *Rivera v. Minnich,* 483 U.S. 574, 107 S.Ct. 3001, 97 L.Ed.2d 473 (1987), the Court held that Pennsylvania's legislative judgment allowing paternity to be established by a preponderance of the evidence, rather than requiring a higher standard, is entitled to a powerful presumption of validity, when challenged by an alleged father under the Due Process Clause.

(2) In *Lalli v. Lalli,* 439 U.S. 259, 99 S.Ct. 518, 58 L.Ed.2d 503 (1978), the Court did not question New York's imposition of a higher burden of proof (clear and convincing) than that normally required in a civil action (preponderance of the evidence).

(3) In several cases, the Court has struck down, as unduly short, several laws imposing various periods of limitations on paternity actions. *Mills v. Habluetzel,* 456 U.S. 91, 102 S.Ct. 1549, 71 L.Ed.2d 770 (1982), one year, Texas. *Pickett v. Brown,* 462 U.S. 1, 103 S.Ct. 2199, 76 L.Ed.2d 372 (1983) two years, Tennessee. *Clark v. Jeter,* 486 U.S. 456, 108 S.Ct. 1910, 100 L.Ed.2d 465 (1988), six years, Pennsylvania.

3. STATUTES
a. Burden of Proof

Most states impose the civil standard of proof (preponderance of the evidence) in paternity actions. Several states still impose an enhanced burden of proof (such as clear and convincing evidence) that has its roots in the history of the paternity action as a criminal prosecution. The Uniform Probate Code refers to the level of proof required by the Uniform Parentage Act, but for use in states that have not adopted that Act, suggests the enhanced standard (clear and convincing) for a determination of paternity *after* the alleged father's death. UPC § 2–109(2)(ii).

b. Statute of Limitations

The Uniform Parentage Act, in essence, suspends the statute of limitation during the child's minority. Under the federal child support laws, participating states are required to have an 18–year period of limitation. Accordingly, 18 years or longer are now the norm.

4. THE UNMARRIED FATHER'S CUSTODIAL INTERESTS
(See also Adoption, p. 267-270).

Before the U.S. Supreme Court got involved, the nonmarital child's custody, including any decision on adoption, had in most states been wholly under the mother's control. Only a few states heard the unwed father on the question of adoption when he had acknowledged the child in some way, when he had adequately contributed to the support of the child, or when paternity had been established by a court. By now, the U.S. Supreme Court has had a significant effect on adoptions of nonmarital children even while some uncertainty remains concerning the precise meaning in this context of Equal Protection as well as of substantive *and* procedural Due Process.

The U.S. Supreme Court has defined the unmarried father's rights in terms of his *actual relationship* with the child. *Stanley v. Illinois*, 405 U.S. 645, 92 S.Ct. 1208, 31 L.Ed.2d 551 (1972). In *Stanley*, a father who had long lived with the mother and his nonmarital children in a *de facto* family unit was held constitutionally entitled to notice and to a hearing in proceedings involving the custody of his children and, based on a footnote in *Stanley*, numerous states require a *published* notice of the birth of the nonmarital child, addressed "to unknown father" or "to whom it may concern," before an adoption may proceed. However, the "mere existence of a biological link does not merit equivalent constitutional protection." *Lehr v. Robertson*, 463 U.S. 248, 103 S.Ct. 2985, 77 L.Ed.2d 614 (1983).

Examples: (1) In 1978, the U.S. Supreme Court denied an unmarried father a "veto power" over the adoption of his nonmarital child, when for eleven years he had not availed himself of the opportunity under Georgia law to legitimate the child, had supported the child only irregularly and had never lived with the child in a *de facto* family setting. *Quilloin v. Walcott*, 434 U.S. 246, 98 S.Ct. 549, 54 L.Ed.2d 511 (1978).

(2) *Caban v. Mohammed*, 441 U.S. 380, 99 S.Ct. 1760, 60 L.Ed.2d 297 (1979), involved an unmarried father who had lived with the mother and two children for five years, had contributed to the children's support and had seen them frequently after he and the mother separated. The U.S. Supreme Court emphasized the father's *de facto*

relationship with his children and allowed him to block the adoption of his children by the mother's new husband.

(3) An unmarried father had not supported and rarely seen his two-year old child. He sought to invalidate the child's adoption by the mother's husband on the ground that his right to due process was violated when he was not given advance notice of the adoption proceeding nor an opportunity to be heard. The Supreme Court found the distinction between *Caban* and *Stanley* on one side, and this case and *Quilloin* on the other "both clear and significant." "When an unwed father demonstrates a full commitment to the responsibilities of parenthood by 'com[ing] forward to participate in the rearing of his child,' his interest in personal contact with his child acquires substantial protection under the due process clause. * * * But the mere existence of a biological link does not merit equivalent constitutional protection." *Lehr v. Robertson*, cited *supra*.

(4) An unmarried father had briefly enjoyed "the blessings of the parent-child relationship" while he cohabited with the *married* mother. When he sought custodial rights to his daughter, the mother's husband objected. The Supreme Court upheld the traditional presumption of legitimacy that applies to a child born to a married mother and denied the unmarried father any and all rights. *Michael H. v. Gerald D.*, 491 U.S. 110, 109 S.Ct. 2333, 105 L.Ed.2d 91 (1989).

D. CONFLICTS OF LAWS

Legitimacy status generally is respected across state lines as a matter of policy. A *judicial* determination of legitimate status must be accorded "Full Faith and Credit" in sister states.

E. REVIEW QUESTIONS

1. **T or F** A child born to a married woman is presumed to be her husband's child.

2. **T or F** Under traditional American law, a nonmarital child was entitled to inherit from his mother, but not from his father.

3. **T or F** Today, illegitimacy is deemed a suspect classification under the Equal Protection Clause and classifications based on illegitimacy are subject to strict scrutiny.

4. **T or F** A judicial determination of legitimacy is entitled to Full Faith and Credit nationwide.

5. **T or F** States need not afford unwed fathers the same custodial rights vis-à-vis their nonmarital children as married fathers have vis-à-vis their legitimate children.

6. **T or F** Many sources indicate that, at early common law, a nonmarital child was not legally deemed its mother's child.

7. **T or F** For purposes of intestate succession, a state may require that a child's paternity must have been established during the father's life.

8. **T or F** Nonmarital children have a more limited right to paternal support than legitimate children have.

9. **T or F** In terms of providing government derived financial benefits, a statute may not distinguish between nonmarital children who have and those who have not been recognized by the father.

10. **T or F** Once a child meets the definition of legitimacy in the state of its domicile, the Full Faith and Credit Clause requires courts everywhere (in the U.S.) to recognize the child's legitimate status.

XII

ADOPTION

Analysis

A. HISTORY AND DEVELOPMENT

Adoption did not exist under the common law and was established by statute, beginning in the U.S. in the mid-nineteenth century.

B. SOCIAL FUNCTIONS

Adoption (1) serves the adopted child's interest in being raised in a presumably better environment than would be the case without adoption, (2) provides childless couples with children, (3) relieves the natural parent of an unwanted child, and (4) relieves the taxpayer of a potential welfare burden.

C. THE ADOPTION PROCESS

Statutory regulation of the adoption process is detailed and strict. The two main interests are the protection of the child's best interests and the biological parents' rights. The first requires careful scrutiny of where the child goes, and the second ensures that existing parental rights are properly terminated before new parental rights are created in the adoptive parents.

1. AGENCY PLACEMENT
In the majority of adoptions by unrelated persons, state agencies or state-regulated private agencies act as intermediaries between natural and adoptive parents. Advantages of agency placement (as opposed to independent, private placement) typically include: (1) professional investigation and approval of the adoptive parents and their home; (2) continuing supervision of the adoption by the agency for a period of time following the adoption; and (3) maintenance of confidentiality concerning the natural and adoptive parents' identity.

2. INDEPENDENT ADOPTION
Many states prohibit independent adoption by non-relatives and closely regulate independent placement even with relatives. In other states, natural parents may contract to place their children directly with adoptive parents. Proponents of independent adoptions argue that they provide immediate placement for the child with less intrusion into the privacy of the adoptive parents. Critics of independent adoption argue that (1) such adoptions may be challenged more easily than professionally arranged adoptions, (2) there may be inadequate or no professional investigation into the suitability of the adoptive parents, and (3) there may not be the confidentiality typically maintained in agency adoptions. Since court approval to complete the adoption legally is needed in any case, a court may exercise

considerable control over the suitability of any given adoption, depending on the statutes in force and the practices followed.

3. "SALE" OF CHILDREN AND "BLACK MARKET" ADOPTION

Most state laws specifically prohibit and criminalize the payment of consideration in connection with adoption. Prohibited payments include payments to the natural mother or father (with exceptions for out-of-pocket expenses involving the pregnancy) or to middlemen (with exceptions permitting appropriate legal and medical fees). So-called "black market" adoptions involve the "sale" of children. Decreased availability of adoptable children and increased selectivity of adoption agencies (often on religious grounds perceived by some to be discriminatory or arbitrary) have led to an increase in "black market" activity. States have responded to "black market" baby sales in various ways, and some have prohibited independent adoptions altogether.

Examples: (1) Utah St. § 76–7–207 provides: "Any person, while having custody, care, control, or possession of any child, who sells, or disposes of, or attempts to sell or dispose of, any child for and in consideration of the payment of money or other thing of value is guilty of a felony of the third degree. However, this section does not prohibit any person, agency, or corporation from paying the actual and reasonable legal expenses, maternity expenses, related medical or hospital, and necessary living expense of the mother preceding and during confinement as an act of charity, so long as payment is not made for the purpose of inducing the mother, parent, or legal guardian to place the child for adoption, consent to an adoption, or cooperate in the completion of an adoption."

(2) The state charged that A, an attorney, violated Illinois law when he requested $6,500 for placing a child. This was $4,500 more than the reasonable medical and legal expenses. Section 12–1 of the Illinois Adoption Act provides: "No person and no agency, association, corporation, institution, society, or other organization, except a child welfare agency as defined by the 'Child Care Act' * * * shall request, receive or accept any compensation or thing of value, directly or indirectly, for placing out of a child." Section 12–3 of the Act defines "placing out" as meaning "to arrange for the free care of a child in a family other than that of the child's parent, stepparent, grandparent, brother, sister, uncle or aunt or legal guardian, for the purpose of adoption or for the purpose of providing care." (Result: Statute upheld against overbreadth and vagueness attacks, and interpreted to allow legitimate legal and medical fees in adoption cases, so long as none of the money represents payment for "serving as intermediary, go-between, or placing agent; so long as the attorney leaves or refers the placement of children and the arrangements for their placement to agencies duly licensed.") *People v. Schwartz,* 64 Ill.2d 275, 1 Ill.Dec. 8, 356 N.E.2d 8 (1976).

(3) Defendant bought a used car and offered it to the mother of a small child in exchange for the child. The mother gave defendant the child. Defendant pleaded guilty to inducing a mother to part with her child, but reserved the right to challenge the constitutionality of the applicable statute on vagueness grounds. (Result: Statute constitutional. The statute "defines the term 'inducement' to include any direct or indirect financial assistance except 'payment or reimbursement of the medical expenses directly related to the mother's pregnancy and hospitalization for the birth of the child and medical care for the child.' Thus, [the statute] provides clear warning that if a person provides any financial assistance to a parent other than that specifically excluded from the definition set forth in the statute, that person provides an 'inducement' to the parent. * * * Based on the clear language of the statute and assigning the ordinary meaning to the words used in the statute, we hold that the challenged terms have meanings sufficiently precise for a person or ordinary intelligence to understand that offering an automobile to a parent in exchange for physical custody or control of a child is proscribed.") *Douglas v. State*, 263 Ga. 748, 438 S.E.2d 361 (1994).

4. SUBSIDIZED ADOPTION

Many states "subsidize" adoption to assist the placement of children who would be difficult to place without financial subsidy (*e.g.*, older children, physically or mentally handicapped children). The financial aid provided to families who adopt hard-to-place children varies according to the particular circumstances in each case. Aid may be limited to medical costs, or may extend to normal living expenses, or may be limited in duration, though typically aid extends to the age of majority. Federal interest, primarily through subsidies and some regulation (*e.g.*, through the "Adoption Assistance and Child Welfare Act of 1980," as amended), may be waning if current welfare reform trends become permanent.

Example: D.C. Code § 3–115(b) provides: "(1) The Mayor may make adoption subsidy payments to an adoptive family (irrespective of the state of residence of the family), as needed, on behalf of a child with special needs, where such child would in all likelihood go without adoption except for the acceptance of the child as a member of the adoptive family, and where the adoptive family has the capability of providing the permanent family relationships needed by such child in all areas except financial, as determined by the Mayor. * * * (2) For the purpose of this subsection—(A) The term 'child with special needs' includes any child who is difficult to place in adoption because of age, race, or ethnic background, physical or mental condition, or membership in a sibling group which should be placed together. A child for whom an adoptive placement has not been made within six months after he is legally available for adoptive placement shall be considered a child with special needs within the meaning of this section. (B) The term 'adoptive family' includes single persons."

Krause,Family Law 2d —10

5. ADULT ADOPTION

Many states allow adults to be adopted. Since the concerns designed to promote the best interests of children are absent in adult adoption, states impose much less supervision on adult adoptions. Adult adoptions may be accomplished by consent of the parties and entry of a court decree following a simple proceeding.

6. EQUITABLE ADOPTION

Occasionally, persons take a child into their home and, over time, treat the child as their own without formal adoption. In other cases, would-be adoptive parents have agreed to adopt a child and failed to complete the legal formalities needed to finalize the adoption, but they have treated the child as though it had been adopted. In the case of intestate death, the question is whether, for purposes of inheritance, the child should be treated as an adopted child. Most courts refuse to do so, being persuaded that because adoption did not exist at common law, a valid adoption may be accomplished only by compliance with the relevant statute. Some courts have found an express or implied contract to adopt and have held that the "equitable" parents did not perform their part of the contract in that they failed to complete the necessary legal requisites. While the "equitable" adoptee does not acquire the full legal status of an adopted child, inheritance and, less often, support from "equitable" parents has been allowed. Generally, the existence of a contract to adopt must be proved by clear and convincing evidence, and there must be consideration for the promise to adopt, such as the natural parent's surrender of the child and the child's performance of filial obligations.

Examples: (1) H and W told six year old C's natural father of their desire to adopt C. C's natural father delivered C to H and W. H and W changed C's name to their own and raised her as their daughter. Without having formally adopted C, H and W died intestate. (Result: The court concluded there had been an equitable adoption to the extent that C became an heir of H and W.) *Long v. Willey,* 391 S.W.2d 301 (Mo.1965).

(2) H and W took newborn C into their home with the expressed intention of adopting her. The adoption process was never formally completed. Later, W filed for divorce and claimed child support from H. (Result: Child support request upheld. Since H and W had taken C into their home and were the only parents C knew, it was appropriate to impose the obligation of support.) *Wener v. Wener,* 35 A.D.2d 50, 312 N.Y.S.2d 815 (1970).

D. QUALIFICATIONS OF ADOPTIVE PARENTS

Statutes govern the qualifications of adoptive parents. Courts and practice have added detail. The best interests of the child control. Traditional factors include marital status, age, fitness to be a parent, religion, race, and economic status of the prospective adopter(s).

1. SINGLE PARENTS VS. COUPLE

A number of states allow adoption only by married couples. Many states also allow single persons to adopt. Courts recognize that the marital status of prospective adopting parents is a legitimate factor for consideration and prefer adoption by married couples. When a married couple adopts, statutes usually require that *both* parents join in the adoption.

Example: A 42–year-old unmarried woman petitioned to adopt the 13–month-old baby she had been raising. (Result: Petition denied. Although the baby seemed to be developing normally, the court felt that the child's long-term "physical, financial and psychic security as well as his emotional growth would be better met by a younger, married couple.") *In re Adoption of H,* 69 Misc.2d 304, 330 N.Y.S.2d 235 (1972).

2. SEXUAL ORIENTATION

An intending adopter's gay or lesbian sexual orientation has figured as a qualifying factor either on its own or in terms of the intending adopter's single marital status.

Examples: (1) Kaye, Chief Judge: "Under the New York adoption statute, a single person can adopt a child. Equally clear is the right of a single homosexual to adopt. These appeals call upon us to decide if the unmarried partner of a child's biological mother, whether heterosexual or homosexual, who is raising the child together with the biological parent, can become the child's second parent by means of adoption. Because the two adoptions sought—one by an unmarried heterosexual couple, the other by the lesbian partner of the child's mother—are fully consistent with the adoption statute, we answer this question in the affirmative. To rule otherwise would mean that the thousands of New York children actually being raised in homes headed by two unmarried persons could have only one legal parent, not the two who want them." Matter of Jacob, Matter of Dana, 86 N.Y.2d 651, 660 N.E.2d 397 (1995).

(2) M and her female companion (A) decided to have and raise children together. M was artificially inseminated with sperm from an anonymous donor and gave birth to two sons. M and A had taken equal responsibility for raising both children since their births. M and A petitioned to allow A to legally adopt the children while leaving M's parental rights intact. The petitions were uncontested and the state Department of Social and Rehabilitative Services determined that the adoptions were in the children's best interests. The statute provided that adoption of a child deprives the parent(s) of all legal right to the child, unless the adoptive parent is the child's stepparent.

The probate court denied the adoptions, finding that A did not qualify as a stepparent and that A could not adopt the children without terminating M's parental rights. M and A appealed. (Result: Adoption permitted. "Despite the narrow wording of the stepparent exception, we cannot conclude that the legislature ever meant to terminate the parental rights of a biological parent who intended to continue raising a child with the help of a partner. Such a narrow construction would produce the unreasonable and irrational result of defeating adoptions that are otherwise indisputably in the best interests of the children.") *Adoptions of B.L.V.B and E.L.V.B.*, 19 Fam. L. Rptr. (BNA) 1403 (Vt.1993).

3. AGE

Courts consider the age of the adopting parent, both in terms of legal capacity and in relation to the age of the child proposed to be adopted. The adopting parent must be of legal age, although some statutes allow exceptions upon showing of good cause. Many agencies prefer that the age span between adoptive parents and the adopted child approximate a "normal" age span between natural parents and their children. The facts of the particular case control.

Examples: (1) Solely because of their ages, H (aged 68) and W (aged 55) were denied adoption of a 3–year–old who had been a foster child in their home for virtually her whole life. (Result: Reversed. The court looked past the age factor and recognized that to "separate the child from her established home" would invite risk of grave harm to her.) *In re Haun*, 31 Ohio Misc. 9, 277 N.E.2d 258 (1971).

               (2) H and W took newborn C into their home with the stated intent of adopting her. When C was 3 years old, the State Department of Health recommended that H and W's petition for adoption be denied on the sole ground that H was 70 years old and W was 54 years old. (Result: Adoption granted. The court took notice of the fact that C had been living with H and W for three years and that, aside from their ages, H and W had no negative characteristics in relation to the adoption.) *In re Adoption of Michelle Lee T.*, 44 Cal.App.3d 699, 117 Cal.Rptr. 856 (1975).

4. PHYSICAL AND EMOTIONAL DEFECTS

Courts consider physical and emotional handicaps of prospective adoptive parents. If the would-be parents are otherwise qualified, courts typically do not deny an adoption solely on the basis of a handicap that does not directly involve ability to care for the child.

5. RELIGION

It is disputed what role (if any) the religion of the adopting parents and the religion of the child may or should play in the adoption decision. A number of statutes specifically provide that, when practicable or possible, a child should be placed with adoptive parents of the same religious beliefs as the child or natural mother. Such statutes have been defended on the ground that they increase a religious mother's willingness to place her child for adoption. If the child to be adopted is of an age where it has its own religious understanding, religious matching obviously is in the child's best interest.

Examples: (1) H and W were refused permission to file an application as adoptive parents solely because they did not have a religious affiliation. Article VI § 32 of New York's Constitution specified that children be placed *when practicable* in the custody of a person of the same religion as the child. (Result: H and W's right to profess no religion was not violated. H and W would still be eligible, under Article VI, to adopt a child when the natural parents were indifferent to the religious placement of their child or when the child's religious background was unknown.) *Dickens v. Ernesto,* 30 N.Y.2d 61, 330 N.Y.S.2d 346, 281 N.E.2d 153 (1972).

(2) H and W, both Episcopalian, petitioned for the adoption of a Cambodian refugee orphan. The adoption agency denied H and W's request because the agency placed children only with members of evangelical Protestant churches. (Result: Although an agency may attempt to match the religion of the child to the religion of the adoptive parents, the agency may not impose any additional religious requirements on adoptive parents.) *Scott v. Family Ministries,* 65 Cal.App.3d 492, 135 Cal.Rptr. 430 (1976).

(3) H and W petitioned to adopt baby C. Although they were otherwise well qualified as adoptive parents, the trial judge denied H and W's petition solely because they had no religious affiliation. (Result: Reversed. The New Jersey Supreme Court held that, while religion may be considered as a *factor* in determining the suitability of adoptive parents, denial of an adoption solely because the prospective parents have no religious affiliation violates the First Amendment.) *In re Adoption of "E",* 59 N.J. 36, 279 A.2d 785 (1971).

(4) See *Johanson v. Fischer,* p. 44–45.

6. RACE

A statute flatly prohibiting adoption solely because the intending adoptive parents and the child are of different races clearly would be unconstitutional. It is not equally clear that race may not be considered *as a factor* in the determination of whether the best interests of the child will be served by an adoption. It is uncertain what application the U.S. Supreme Court's decision in *Palmore v. Sidoti,* 466 U.S. 429, 104 S.Ct. 1879, 80 L.Ed.2d 421 (1984)(holding that race may not be the *conclusive* determinant of post-divorce custody), should find in this area, although Congress has given some indication: The 1994 "Multiethnic Placement Act" (42 USC § 5115a) prohibits any agency receiving federal assistance from discriminating "in making a placement decision, solely on the basis of the race, color, or national origin of the adoptive or foster parent, or the child," but the agency "may consider the cultural, ethnic, or racial background of the child and the capacity of the prospective foster or adoptive parents to meet the needs of a child of this background as one of a number of factors used to determine the best interests of a child."

Examples: (1) H and W, a white couple, petitioned to adopt their black foster child. The child's natural grandparents filed a competing adoption petition. The trial court found that the two families were equally qualified as adoptive parents, but concluded that race tipped the balance in favor of the natural grandparents. (Result: Upheld. When race is relevant in an adoption contest, the court must make a three-step evaluation: (1) how each family's race is likely to affect the child's development of a sense of identity, including racial identity; (2) how the families compare in this regard; and (3) how significant the racial differences between the families are when all the factors relevant to adoption are considered together.) *Petition of R.M.G.,* 454 A.2d 776 (D.C.App.1982).

(2) M and F were members of the Mississippi Band of Choctaw Indians and residents of the Choctaw reservation. Twin babies were born to M and F in a county 200 miles from the reservation. Because M and F did not want the children to grow up on the reservation, they both consented to the twins' adoption by a non-native-American couple. The county court at the twin's place of birth finalized the adoption. Two months later, the Choctaw Tribe moved to vacate the adoption decree on the ground that under the Indian Child Welfare Act of 1978 (ICWA) the tribal court had exclusive jurisdiction over child custody proceedings involving Indian children domiciled on the reservation. The county court denied the motion. The state supreme court affirmed. (Result: Reversed and remanded to the tribal court. "It remains to give content to the term 'domicile' in the circumstances of the present case. The holding of the Supreme Court of Mississippi that the twin babies were not domiciled on the Choctaw Reservation appears to have rested on two findings of fact by the trial court: (1) that they had never been physically present there, and (2) that they were 'voluntarily surrendered' by their parents. The question before us, therefore, is whether under the ICWA definition of 'domicile' such facts suffice to render the twins nondomiciliaries of the reservation. * * * It is undisputed in this case that the domicile of the mother (as well as the father) has been, at all relevant times, on the Choctaw Reservation. Thus, it is clear that at their birth the twin babies were also domiciled on the reservation, even though they themselves had never been there. * * * The appellees in this case argue strenuously that the twins' mother went to great lengths to give birth off the reservation so that her children could be adopted by the Holyfields. But that was precisely part of the Congress' concern. Permitting

individual members of the tribe to avoid tribal exclusive jurisdiction by the simple expedient of giving birth off the reservation would, to a large extend, nullify the purpose the ICWA was intended to accomplish. * * * We are not unaware that over three years have passed since the twin babies were born and placed in the Holyfield home, and that a court deciding their fate today is not writing on a blank slate in the same way it would have in January 1986. Three years' development of family ties cannot be undone, and a separation at this point would doubtless cause considerable pain. Whatever feelings we might have as to where the twins should live, however, it is not for us to decide that question. We have been asked to decide the legal question of *who* should make the custody determination concerning these children—not what the outcome of that determination should be. The law places that decision in the hands of the Choctaw tribal court.") *Mississippi Band of Choctaw Indians v. Holyfield,* 490 U.S. 30, 109 S.Ct. 1597, 104 L.Ed.2d 29 (1989).

E. CONSENT TO ADOPTION

Proper consent to adoption is essential to accomplish a valid adoption. Consent must be obtained from the biological parents of the child or, if parental rights have been legally terminated, from the agency or guardian entrusted with the care of the child. If the parents are minors, their consent to the adoption typically is valid. If the child is above a certain age, its own consent may be required.

1. CONSENT OF PARENTS

Except where their rights have been legally terminated (or are legally terminated as part of the adoption proceeding), the consent of both biological parents is a universal prerequisite to the adoption of a "legitimate" child. With respect to a nonmarital child, the mother's consent has traditionally sufficed. Importantly, the *unmarried* father has newly gained substantial rights that must be carefully respected if an adoption is to be secure from challenge.

2. CONSENT OF UNMARRIED FATHER

At common law, the mother had custody of a nonmarital child. Under statutes, the unmarried father could be held liable for support, but had no rights to the child. Consequently, he had no right to notice of (or to consent to) the adoption of the child.

a. Judicial (U.S. Supreme Court) Intervention

Since the 1970's, the U.S. Supreme Court has held in a series of landmark cases that the unmarried father has a significant and constitutionally protected interest in the custody and adoption of his nonmarital child. While the unmarried father's interest has not yet been precisely defined, it is clear that he has a right to notice and to be heard and that for constitutional purposes, there is a difference between (1) an unmarried father who has lived with and/or contributed to the support of his child, and (2) one who did not have or was not given that opportunity, and (3) one who did not seize an opportunity that was available to him to show his serious interest in his child. An adjudication that an adoption should not have proceeded without an unmarried fathers's consent does *not* automatically mean that he must be awarded custodial rights.

Examples: (1) M and F lived together intermittently for 18 years and had three children. They were not married. Under Illinois law, children of unwed mothers became wards of the state upon the death of their mother. M died. F sought custody of his children. (Result: F prevails. The U.S. Supreme Court ruled that "all Illinois parents are constitutionally entitled to a hearing on their fitness before their children are removed from their custody." The opinion contained the following footnote: "Extending opportunity for hearing to unwed fathers who desire and claim competence to care for their children creates no constitutional or procedural obstacle to foreclosing those unwed fathers who are not so inclined. Unwed fathers who do not promptly respond cannot complain if their children are declared wards of the State. Those who do respond retain the burden of proving their fatherhood.") *Stanley v. Illinois,* 405 U.S. 645, 92 S.Ct. 1208, 31 L.Ed.2d 551 (1972). (Note: After *Stanley,* courts have disagreed whether *Stanley* requires that notification and an opportunity to be heard be afforded to *all* putative fathers before an adoption can be effectuated. Subsequent U.S. Supreme Court cases have not fully resolved this issue.)

(2) Georgia law provided an unwed father the right to legitimate his child and gain full parental rights with respect to the child's adoption. Here the putative father had not attempted to recognize the child until the adoption process began (eleven years after the child's birth), and the U.S. Supreme Court denied an unwed father the right to veto the adoption of his child. *Quilloin v. Walcott,* 434 U.S. 246, 98 S.Ct. 549, 54 L.Ed.2d 511 (1978).

(3) Where the putative father had lived with the mother for five years, had admitted paternity, and had participated in the raising of the two children, the U.S. Supreme Court allowed him to veto a proposed adoption. *Caban v. Mohammed,* 441 U.S. 380, 99 S.Ct. 1760, 60 L.Ed.2d 297 (1979).

(4) Where, for two years after the birth of his child, the putative father had never contributed to the support of or visited the child, the U.S. Supreme Court denied him the right to veto the child's adoption by the mother's husband. Significantly, the putative father could have gained a voice in the adoption process by adding his name to New York's "putative father registry," but had failed

to do so. The Court held that "[w]hen an unwed father demonstrates a full commitment to the responsibilities of parenthood by 'com[ing] forward to participate in the rearing of his child' [quoting from *Caban*], his interest in personal contact with his child acquires substantial protection under the due process clause * * *. *But the mere existence of a biological link does not merit equivalent constitutional protection.*" (Emphasis added). *Lehr v. Robertson,* 463 U.S. 248, 103 S.Ct. 2985, 77 L.Ed.2d 614 (1983).

(5) An unmarried father sought custodial rights to his daughter by a *married* mother. While the father *had* actually cohabited with the mother and child, the U.S. Supreme Court upheld the traditional presumption of legitimacy and denied the unmarred father's claim. *Michael H. v. Gerald D.*, 491 U.S. 110, 109 S.Ct. 2333, 105 L.Ed.2d 91 (1989).

(6) In "Baby Jessica" and "Baby Richard," the unmarried mother deliberately frustrated the putative father's interest in coming forward. In both cases, the unmarried mothers had surrendered their children for adoption. Baby Jessica's mother had lied about the father's identity. Baby Richard's father had been told that the baby had died. In each case, the father asserted his paternal rights as soon as he found out the truth, and the mother subsequently married the father. While Jessica's adoption had been denied by the trial court, the intending adopters had held Jessica in Michigan for some two years, in defiance of the Iowa court's contempt ruling. In Richard's case, the trial court had ordered the adoption despite the mother's refusal to name the father, and the adopters had retained custody of Richard for more than 3 years. The legal issue in both cases was whether the father's justifiable ignorance of his child's birth was a circumstance that should weigh in his favor when measured against the U.S. Supreme Court's *(Lehr)* standard of giving him at least a chance to "grasp" "the opportunity to develop a relationship with his offspring." Since neither Baby Jessica's nor Baby Richard's father had had any such chance, both cases were ultimately decided in favor of the fathers. (These disputes spawned numerous cases; important citations include: *In Interest of B.G.C.*, 496 N.W.2d 239 (Iowa 1992)(*Jessica*); *Petition of Kirchner*, 164 Ill.2d 468, 208 Ill.Dec. 268, 649 N.E.2d 324 (1995) (*Richard*)).

b. Uniform Parentage Act, Uniform Putative and Unknown Fathers Act, Uniform Adoption Act

The Uniform Parentage Act, the Uniform Putative and Unknown Fathers Act, and the Uniform Adoption Act (§§ 2–401, 2–402) similarly (1) provide for termination of the rights of an *uninterested* putative father, (2) protect the *interested* putative father, and (3) seek to keep interference with the adoption process at a minimum. The UPA provides a procedure by which the court may ascertain the identity of the father and permit speedy termination of his potential rights *if he shows no interest in the child.* If, on the other hand, the natural father or a man representing himself to be the natural father claims custodial rights, the court is given authority to determine custodial rights. It is contemplated that there may be cases in which the man alleging himself to be the father is so clearly unfit to take custody of the child that the court would proceed to terminate his potential parental rights without deciding whether the man actually is the father of the child. If, on the other hand, the man alleging himself to be the father and claiming custody is *prima facie* fit to have custody of the child, an action to ascertain paternity is indicated.

4. UNREASONABLE REFUSAL OF CONSENT

In very exceptional cases, a few courts have held (or appear to have held) that an adoption may proceed without parental consent, if consent is withheld unreasonably in violation of the child's best interest.

Example: At C's birth, M tried to place him for adoption but, for unknown reasons, failed to do so. M never took C home from the hospital, and C spent the next four years in foster homes. When C's foster parents petitioned to adopt him, M refused to consent. M argued that the adoption petition could not be granted without her consent unless she was found to be unfit. (Result: Petition granted. M's consent was withheld unreasonably where C had never known M. In such a case, the test is the best interest of the child.) *In re J.S.R.,* 374 A.2d 860 (D.C.App.1977). (*Caveat*: Quite probably, M's parental rights could have been terminated on the ground of abandonment.)

5. ADOPTION BY STEPPARENT: CONSENT OF THE NONCUSTODIAL PARENT

If adoption is sought by the new spouse of the custodial parent, some courts seem to attach less importance to obtaining the noncustodial parent's consent. If he or she has not substantially contributed to the support of the child or has otherwise "abandoned" the child, his or her consent may not be needed. *In any case, the noncustodial parent is entitled to notice and an opportunity to be heard.*

Examples: (1) When H_1 and W divorced, W received custody of C. W's second husband (H_2) petitioned to adopt C without notifying H_1, on the ground that H_1 had not substantially contributed to C's support for over two years. At the time of the petition, both W and H_2 knew of H_1's whereabouts. H_1 appealed from the granting of the adoption petition. (Result: Adoption set aside on the ground that H_1 had been denied Due Process, *i.e.*, notice and an opportunity to be heard.) *Armstrong v. Manzo,* 380 U.S. 545, 85 S.Ct. 1187, 14 L.Ed.2d 62 (1965).

(2) When H_1 and W divorced, W received custody of the children. For several years, H_1 continued to support and to help care for the children. Following a bitter argument with H_1, W gave information to the police that led to H_1's arrest and incarceration. W then thwarted H_1's attempts to communicate with his children from jail. W's second husband (H_2) petitioned to adopt the children over H_1's objections. W and H_2 claimed that H_1 had failed to substantially contribute to the support of the children or to communicate meaningfully with them. (Result: Adoption denied. Indigency—due here to incarceration—is a valid excuse for non-support, and H_1 had not communicated with his children because he was unable, not unwilling, to do so.) *R.N.T. v. J.R.G.*, 666 P.2d 1036 (Alaska 1983).

6. CONSENT OF AGENCY OR GUARDIAN

The refusal of consent to adoption by an agency or guardian may be overridden more easily than a parent's refusal of consent. If the adoption is determined to be in the best interests of the child, courts tend to permit an adoption over the objection of an agency or guardian.

7. CONSENT OF THE CHILD

Many state statutes provide that if a child is above a certain age (*e.g.*, 10–14 years), the child's consent also is required for adoption.

8. CONSENT OF GRANDPARENTS

Consent of grandparents to adoption is *not* required, unless they are guardians. They may, however, be entitled to notice and to be heard regarding the child's best interests.

Example: M and F, who were not married, had a son (S). F never had contact with S. One year after S was born, M moved in with her parents (G), who provided much of S's care during the next 14 months. Relations between M and G deteriorated. After M (with S) moved out and severed all contact with G, G sought custody and visitation of S. At the same time M selected a couple to adopt S and initiated a petition in another county to terminate her parental rights in conjunction with the proposed adoption. G was not permitted to intervene or to offer evidence as to their relationship with S and any harm to S if their relationship were severed. M and F's parental rights were terminated, S was placed with the prospective adoptive parents, and G appealed. (Result: "Although we agree with the circuit court that for purposes of the [adoption] proceedings the grandparents were not [entitled to intervene], we conclude that they have important, relevant evidence about their longstanding relationship with [S] and the possible harm to the child if the relationship were severed. This is information which

the * * * court should consider in determining [S's] best interests.")
In the Interest of Brandon S. S., 179 Wis.2d 114, 507 N.W.2d 94 (1993).

9. FORMALITIES OF CONSENT

Consent to adoption usually must be written, witnessed, and acknowledged or notarized. Consent to adoption is not binding unless given *after* the child's birth, with statutory requirements ranging from 24 to 72 hours after birth. Many statutes are quite detailed and most courts insist on exact compliance. Properly executed consent papers must be submitted with the adoption petition. If an agency is involved in the adoption, the parent's consent is given to the agency; *i.e.*, the child is "surrendered" to the agency and the agency consents to the specific adoption. Anonymity is thus preserved, and the risk of harm to the child's best interest minimized. In connection with private adoptions, "blank consents" are considered to promote "black market" dealing in babies, and many though not all states prohibit consent to be given in a form that omits indication of the identity of the adoptive parents.

Example: Minnesota law required the signatures of *two* witnesses on the consent. When C was born, M signed two consent forms for adoption. Each form was witnessed by one person. (Result: Adoption set aside. M's consent was legally defective because the two witnesses should have signed the same form.) *In re Alsdurf*, 270 Minn. 236, 133 N.W.2d 479 (1965).

10. FINALITY AND REVOCATION OF CONSENT
a. Natural Parents

If a natural parent has properly consented to the adoption of his or her child, but has a later change of mind, revocation may still be allowed, especially if fraud, duress, or undue influence can be shown. After the final decree has been issued, reversal of the adoption is very narrowly restricted.

Example: A Colombian mother, pregnant by a married Colombian, came to New York for the birth of her child "to minimize the shame of an out-of-wedlock child." Four days after C's birth, M placed C with a reputable adoption agency which, in turn, placed C with intending adopters. A month after C's birth and five days after the prospective adopters had gained provisional custody of C, M sought C's return, because her family had expressed shock at the proposed adoption and offered M support. (Result: The New York Court of Appeals found: "At one extreme, several jurisdictions adhere to the rule that the parent has an absolute right to regain custody of her child prior to the final adoption decree. On the other hand, some jurisdictions adhere to the rule that the parent's surrender is final, absent fraud or duress. The majority of the jurisdictions, however, place the parent's right to regain custody within the discretion of the court—the position which, of course, our Legislature has taken. The discretionary rule allows the court leeway to approve a revocation of the surrender when the facts of the individual case warrant it and avoids the obvious dangers posed by the rigidity of the extreme positions." Sympathizing with the special facts of the case, the court allowed the natural mother to revoke her consent). *People ex rel. Scarpetta v. Spence–Chapin Adoption Service,* 28 N.Y.2d 185, 321 N.Y.S.2d 65, 269 N.E.2d 787 (1971).

b. Reversal of Placement by Agency

Examples: (1) An adoption agency placed 18–month–old C with H and W on the condition that they not file for adoption until C had been with them for a year. During that year, the agency discovered that H was being treated for a drinking problem. In earlier interviews with the agency, H had denied his drinking problem. The agency canceled C's placement on the grounds that H and W had lied. (Result: Revocation of placement must be measured in terms of the best interests of the child, and H and W are entitled to a hearing on this issue.) *C. v. Superior Court for County of Sacramento,* 29 Cal.App.3d 909, 106 Cal.Rptr. 123 (1973).

(2) Shortly after being screened, qualified and accepted as prospective adoptive parents, H and W began experiencing marital difficulties. H and W did not reveal this to the adoption agency, nor did they seek marriage counseling. A child was placed with H and W on a "quasi-adoptive" basis. Within one year of the placement, H and W separated. After being anonymously notified of this separation, the agency determined that the deteriorated family situation was not in C's best interests. "Because of the likelihood that the wife would flee with the minor child," C was removed from the home without advance notice. (Result: Prior notice may be waived only when the child is in "imminent danger." Such imminent danger encompasses the possibility that a prospective parent would flee with the child if notice were given.) *Marten v. Thies,* 99 Cal.App.3d 161, 160 Cal.Rptr. 57 (1979), *cert. denied,* 449 U.S. 831, 101 S.Ct. 99, 66 L.Ed.2d 36 (1980).

F. ANONYMITY

Most states follow the tradition that adoption records are to be sealed in order to secure the relationship between adopter and child. Adopted children generally have no access to names, addresses, or other information concerning their natural parents. Exceptions may be made for good cause, such as medical need, psychological trauma or crisis of religious identity. In several states, adoption is *not* anonymous, *i.e.,* "open." The following interests are in the balance: (1) the adoptee's interest (and curiosity) in knowing his/her origin; (2) the natural parents' interest in privacy; and (3) the adoptive parents' interest in being undisturbed. About one-half of the states now allow adopted children and biological parents who wish information to register. If both sides register, information is exchanged. The Uniform Adoption Act would maintain anonymous adoption and recommends release only of *non*-identifying, typically genetic, information. It also provides a matching registry that is to be available to adopted children over 18 years of age and their former parents. Anonymous adoption has come under—generally unsuccessful—constitutional attack.

Examples: (1) To discover his natural identity, C sought access to his sealed adoption records. C claimed that the Illinois statute that required adoption files to be sealed, and allowed them to be examined only upon court order, violated his constitutional rights. (Result: The Illinois Supreme Court found the statute to be rationally related to the legitimate legislative purpose of protecting the adoption process. C's interest in knowing his origins "should not prevail over the potential infringement of the rights of other parties," such as C's natural and adoptive parents.) *In re Roger B.*, 84 Ill.2d 323, 49 Ill.Dec. 731, 418 N.E.2d 751 (1981).

(2) Invoking the Due Process and Equal Protection clauses, an association of adult adoptees challenged a New York statute that required adoption records to be sealed. The plaintiffs also raised a Thirteenth Amendment argument, claiming that one of the incidents of slavery was the elimination of the parental relation. (Result: The Second Circuit balanced the rights of natural and adopting parents to keep the records sealed against the adoptee's right to know her origins. The court determined that the adoptee's rights were adequately protected by allowing the records to be opened "[u]pon an appropriate showing of psychological trauma, medical need, or of a religious identity crisis." The court ruled that the Thirteenth Amendment argument challenged the adoption laws themselves, not the sealing requirements.) *Alma Society v. Mellon*, 601 F.2d 1225 (2d Cir.1979).

G.   REVOCATION OF ADOPTION

Revocation of adoption challenges the adoption *after* a final decree has been entered. (Distinguish revocation of consent *before* entry of an adoption decree.) Unless there was a defect in the process of adoption (*e.g.*, invalid or absent consent, inadequate notice), courts rarely set aside a final adoption decree. The purpose is to provide stability for the adopted child. Depending on the substance of the challenge, due process questions may arise. Occasionally, adoptive parents have been allowed to revoke an adoption on the ground that they adopted the child without knowledge that the child was seriously "defective," or they may have recourse to tort law to "remedy" a "wrongful adoption." An adoption agency may be allowed to attack an adoption decree on the ground that the adoptive parents had fraudulently misrepresented their qualifications. The overriding policy is to avoid "punishing" the child for a violation of the adoption laws, and many states set specific time frames after which an adoption may no longer be challenged (*e.g.*, Uniform Parentage Act: 6 months).

Examples: (1) C, now an adult, learned that his natural mother had died leaving an estate. Attacking his adoption decree, C was able to show that his natural mother had never formally consented to his adoption. (Result: Since C's mother could have attacked the decree collaterally, the court granted C the same right. Although C was an adult at the time of this proceeding, the statute of limitations did not bar his action since it does not apply to a judgment void upon its face.) *Hughes v. Aetna Casualty & Surety Co.,* 234 Or. 426, 383 P.2d 55 (1963).

(2) Shortly before their adopted C turned two, H and W discovered that C was severely retarded. According to expert medical opinion, C would soon have to be institutionalized. H and W sought to vacate the adoption in order to avoid the financial and emotional burdens that C would present. (Result: Request denied. "[T]he law recognizes no distinction between an adoptive parent and child and a child's relationship to its natural parents.") *In re Adoption of G,* 89 N.J.Super. 276, 214 A.2d 549 (1965).

(3) M was not married to F when their son (S) was born. M agreed to place S for adoption with an attorney associated with a religious cult known as "The Way International." In violation of the adoption statute, both the attorney and the adoptive parents had covered M's personal expenses both before and after the birth. Moreover, the attorney had misrepresented to M a variety of legal aspects governing adoption, and F had not been properly notified. After an interlocutory adoption decree was issued, M saw the Geraldo Rivera show, which exposed "The Way" as a dangerous cult. M and F then moved to set aside the adoption decree. The trial court denied relief, the appellate court affirmed, and M and F appealed. S was now 3 years old. (Result: Adoption vacated. "The procedural safeguards provided in the adoption statutes are not mere window dressing—they serve to protect the interests of the parties, the child, and the public. We hold that the statutory violations, together with numerous other irregularities, under the circumstances of this case require that the interlocutory decree be set aside and the adoption proceeding dismissed.") *In the Matter of the Adoption of P.E.P.,* 329 N.C. 692, 407 S.E.2d 505 (1991).

H. LEGAL EFFECT OF ADOPTION

The legal relationship between adoptive parent and child simulates the legal relationship between parent and biological child. With rare exceptions, adoption terminates all rights and obligations existing between the adopted child and the biological parents.

1. CUSTODY

Adoption gives adoptive parents the same right to custody as if the child were their biological child. Some statutes and courts allow exceptions for visitation by biological grandparents, especially in the case of a stepparent adoption.

Example: Following F's death, a trial court awarded F's parents (G) visitation with F and M's daughter (D). The order was conditional, and was to have no effect if M remarried and M's new husband adopted D. Following M's remarriage and D's adoption by her new stepfather, G appealed the termination of their visitation rights. (Result: Visitation reinstated. "A trial court's authority to grant grandparent visitation * * * continues even after subsequent adoption. The statute allows the trial court, in the best interest of the child, to order grandparental visitation in direct opposition to the wishes of the custodian regardless of who the custodian is. To hold that an adoptive parent has rights to override the [grandparents' visitation statute], would be to apply an exception to the statute that does not exist. To judicially impose such an exception would create rights for an adoptive parent superior to those that exist for a natural parent. Once the grandparents in this case were ordered visitation rights with their minor grandchild, they should not have been deprived of those rights without due process.") *Matter of Visitation of C. G. F.*, 168 Wis.2d 62, 483 N.W.2d 803 (1992).

2. NAME AND BIRTH CERTIFICATE

The adopted child's name ordinarily is changed to that of the adopting parents. Statutes typically provide for the sealing of the original and the issuance of a new birth certificate that designates the adoptive parents as the parents and omits any reference to the biological parents, usually retaining only the actual place and date of the child's birth.

3. INCEST LAWS

Under state incest statutes, for purposes of criminal prosecution and eligibility to marry, both the biological and adoptive families are treated as related to the adopted child.

4. OBLIGATION OF SUPPORT

Adoptive parents incur the same obligation to support the adopted child as if the child were their biological child. A few states may continue to recognize (at least in theory) a subsidiary support obligation on the part of the biological parents that becomes enforceable if the adoptive parents default in their support obligation. As a practical matter, the practice of anonymous adoption makes any such obligation unenforceable. No case has been found where adoption records were unsealed to enforce a biological parent's support obligation.

5. INHERITANCE

a. From Adoptive Parents

The adopted child's right to inherit from an adoptive parent and the latter's family depends upon state adoption and inheritance laws. Today it is virtually universal that the adopted child is treated as "issue" of the adoptive parents for purposes of intestate succession from the latter as well as from the latter's relatives. Similarly, the trend favors interpreting potentially ambiguous terms in wills, such as "child," "issue," and "descendant," to include adopted children.

b. From Kin of Adoptive Parents

While few statutes deal specifically with the right of the adopted child to inherit from the adoptive parent's lineal or collateral kin, the modern rule is to allow such inheritance.

c. From Natural Parents

The right of the adopted child to inherit from its biological parents and their kin typically is terminated by the adoption. In a few states, the child, even though adopted, retains an inheritance relationship with its natural parent, in addition to inheriting from adoptive parents. (Note that the practice of anonymous adoption makes it difficult or often impossible to learn the identity of the natural parents.)

> *Examples:* (1) W's second husband adopted the children of W's first marriage. When the children's natural father died intestate, the children claimed as his heirs. (Result: The court denied the children's right to inherit from the natural father. The court noted that public policy does not favor a system of dual inheritance such as would occur if an adopted child was allowed to inherit from both natural and adopted parents.) *Shehady v. Richards,* 83 N.M. 311, 491 P.2d 528 (1971).
>
> (2) The will of H_1's aunt (T) provided for H_1's share of her estate to go to "the child or children of his * * * body," if H_1 should predecease T. At the time the will was drawn, H_1 had two children and was married to W. Some time later, H_1 and W divorced. W later married H_2 who adopted H_1's two children. H_1 had predeceased T. (Result: Children inherit. Although adoption severs ties between the adopted child and the natural parent, the court found that, for purposes of inheritance, H's children remained identifiable as "children of the body" of H_1). *In re Estate of Zastrow,* 42 Wis.2d 390, 166 N.W.2d 251 (1969).

d. From Adoptee

Adoption statutes and statutes of descent and distribution generally have been construed to allow adoptive parents and often their kin to inherit from their adopted child to the exclusion of the biological parents.

I. REVIEW QUESTIONS

1. The following factor(s) may not be used in evaluating prospective adoptive parents:

    A. Race

    B. Marital status

    C. Religion

    D. Age

2. **T or F** Adoptive parents cannot rescind a completed adoption even if they later discover that, at the time of adoption, the child suffered from an unknown condition, such as insanity or epilepsy.

3. **T or F** Adoption terminates all of the natural parents' rights and responsibilities toward the child.

4. **T or F** Adoption was well established under the common law.

5. **T or F** Court approval is needed to complete the adoption process.

6. **T or F** Adults may be adopted.

7. **T or F** Minor parents are not legally required to consent to the adoption of their child.

8. **T or F** Courts may not consider race in an adoption proceeding.

9. **T or F** If their child has been adjudicated "neglected" or "abused" and a guardian has been appointed for the child, the adoption of their child may proceed without the natural parents' consent.

10. **T or F** A noncustodial parent who has not substantially contributed to the child's support or who has otherwise abandoned the child is subject to having his/her child adopted without consent.

11. **T or F** The minor but "mature" child's consent to its own adoption is required in an adoption proceeding.

12. **T or F** A parent's revocation of consent to a child's adoption will be allowed only if the consent was obtained by fraud, duress, or undue influence.

13. **T or F** The practice of sealing adoption records and allowing neither child nor natural parent access, has been attacked on constitutional grounds.

14. **T or F** The right of an adopted child to inherit from its natural parents terminates with the adoption.

15. **T or F** Subsidized adoption produces a legally incomplete parent and child relationship, only somewhat more secure than foster care.

16. **T or F** The unmarried father has no standing to challenge the mother's decision to place her child for adoption.

17. **T or F** The goal of state adoption statutes is the protection of the rights of adoptive parents.

18. **T or F** Some courts seem to attach less importance to a noncustodial parent's consent to the adoption of his or her child when the prospective adoptive parent is the child's stepparent.

19. **T or F** In a private adoption, parents consent to the adoption of their child by a specific person or persons.

XIII

PROCREATION

Analysis

A. CONSTITUTIONAL UNDERPINNINGS

1. CONTRACEPTION

Since 1965, the U.S. Supreme Court has recognized a protected privacy interest in the use of contraceptives by *married* couples. *Griswold v. Connecticut,* 381 U.S. 479, 85 S.Ct. 1678, 14 L.Ed.2d 510 (1965). *Griswold,* invoking the "penumbras" and "emanations" of and from the 1st, 3rd, 4th, 5th and 9th Amendments, brought marriage under the U.S. Constitution: "We deal with a right of privacy older than the Bill of Rights * * *. Marriage is a coming together for better or for worse, hopefully enduring, and intimate to the degree of being sacred. It is an association that promotes a way of life, not causes; a harmony in living, not political faiths; a bilateral loyalty, not commercial or social projects. Yet it is an association for as noble a purpose as any involved in out prior decisions."

In 1972, the U.S. Supreme Court constitutionally extended access to birth control devices to *unmarried* persons. The Court reasoned that the protected interest in whether or not to conceive a child is an *individual* right: "[W]hatever the rights of the individual to access to contraceptives may be, the rights must be the same for the unmarried and the married alike. If under *Griswold* the distribution of contraceptives to married persons cannot be prohibited, a ban on distribution to unmarried persons would be equally impermissible. It is true that in *Griswold* the right of privacy in question inhered in the marital relationship. Yet the marital couple is not an independent entity with a mind and heart of its own, but an association of two individuals each with a separate intellectual and emotional make-up. If the right of privacy means anything, it is the right of the *individual,* married or single, to be free from unwarranted governmental intrusion into matters so fundamentally affecting a person as the decision whether to bear or beget a child." *Eisenstadt v. Baird,* 405 U.S. 438, 92 S.Ct. 1029, 31 L.Ed.2d 349 (1972).

In 1977, the Court struck down New York legislation criminalizing the distribution of contraceptives to minors under the age of 16 years: "The question of the extent of state power to regulate conduct of minors not constitutionally regulable when committed by adults is a vexing one, perhaps not susceptible to precise answer. * * * Certain principles, however, have been recognized. 'Minors, as well as adults, are protected by the Constitution and possess constitutional rights.' *Planned Parenthood of Central Missouri v. Danforth,* 428 U.S. 52, 96 S.Ct. 2831, 49 L.Ed.2d 788 (1976). '[W]hatever may be their precise impact, neither the Fourteenth Amendment nor the Bill of Rights is for adults alone.' *In re Gault,* 387 U.S. 1, 87 S.Ct. 1428, 18 L.Ed.2d 527 (1967). On the other hand, we have held in a variety of contexts that 'the power of the state to control the conduct of children reaches beyond the scope of its authority over adults.' Of particular significance to the decision of this case, the right to privacy in connection with decisions affecting procreation extends to minors as well as to adults." *Carey v. Population Services International,* 431 U.S. 678, 97 S.Ct. 2010, 52 L.Ed.2d 675 (1977).

2. ABORTION

In the original decision recognizing the woman's right to abortion (*Roe v. Wade,* 410 U.S. 113, 93 S.Ct. 705, 35 L.Ed.2d 147 (1973)), Justice Blackmun summarized the U.S. Supreme Court's majority view:

"A state criminal abortion statute of the current Texas type, that excepts from criminality only a *life saving* procedure on behalf of the mother, without regard to pregnancy stage and without recognition of the other interests involved, is violative of the Due Process Clause of the Fourteenth Amendment.

"(a) For the stage prior to approximately the end of the first trimester, the abortion decision and its effectuation must be left to the medical judgment of the pregnant woman's attending physician.

"(b) For the stage subsequent to approximately the end of the first trimester, the State, in promoting its interest in the health of the mother, may, if it chooses, regulate the abortion procedure in ways that are reasonably related to maternal health.

"(c) For the stage subsequent to viability the State, in promoting its interest in the potentiality of human life, may, if it chooses, regulate, and even proscribe, abortion except where it is necessary, in appropriate medical judgment, for the preservation of the life or health of the mother."

A succession of decisions has emphasized that abortion is very much the *woman's* right. Neither the husband (nor an unmarried would-be father), nor parents of a pregnant minor may be required to consent or even be notified, and thus be put in a position to prevent the exercise of the pregnant female's right to abort. *Planned Parenthood of Missouri v. Danforth,* 428 U.S. 52, 96 S.Ct. 2831, 49 L.Ed.2d 788 (1976); *Planned Parenthood v. Casey,* 505 U.S. 833, 112 S.Ct. 2791, 120 L.Ed.2d 674 (1992). With respect to minors, the U.S. Supreme Court has complicated the picture by limiting autonomy to "mature" minors, without doing much to define a "mature" minor, leaving that to individualized case-by-case determination. See pp. 227-229.

3. STERILIZATION
a. Compulsory Sterilization

In 1927, the U.S. Supreme Court upheld a state statute providing for compulsory sterilization of an insane or retarded person, provided there is notice and a hearing, and the action is not arbitrary or in punishment of a crime. *Buck v. Bell,* 274 U.S. 200, 47 S.Ct. 584, 71 L.Ed. 1000 (1927). If *Buck v. Bell* were challenged today at the U.S. Supreme Court level, change should be expected, at least in the breadth of the holding. However, attempts to litigate such a challenge into the U.S. Supreme Court have not succeeded, and the case still stands. (See *In re Sterilization of Moore,* 289 N.C. 95, 221 S.E.2d 307 (1976)). In *Skinner v. Oklahoma,* 316 U.S. 535, 62 S.Ct. 1110, 86 L.Ed. 1655 (1942), the U.S. Supreme Court held: "We are dealing here with legislation which involves one of the basic civil rights of man. Marriage and procreation are fundamental to the very existence and survival of the race. The power to sterilize, if exercised, may have subtle, far-reaching and devastating effects. In evil or reckless hands it can cause races or types which are inimical to the dominant group to wither and disappear. There is no redemption for the individual whom the law touches. Any experiment which the State conducts is to his irreparable injury. He is forever deprived of a basic liberty. We mention these matters not to reexamine the scope of the police power of the States. We advert to them merely in emphasis of our view that strict scrutiny of the classification which a State makes in a sterilization law is essential, lest unwittingly, or otherwise, invidious discriminations are made against groups or types of individuals in violation of the constitutional guaranty of just and equal laws.''

b. Voluntary Sterilization
Courts have held that a state may not deny elective sterilization.

> *Example:* A city hospital's policy barring use of facilities in connection with consensual sterilization was challenged. (Result: City hospital's prohibition violated the Equal Protection Clause. (1) A fundamental interest was involved, (2) no other surgical procedures were prohibited outright, and (3) other procedures of equal risk and nontherapeutic procedures were permitted.) *Hathaway v. Worcester City Hospital*, 475 F.2d 701 (1st Cir.1973).

B. ARTIFICIAL CONCEPTION

New techniques for noncoital reproduction encompass artificial insemination, ovum donation, *in vitro* fertilization, embryo transfer, and "surrogate motherhood." The availability of these techniques presents legal issues regarding the relationship of a child so conceived to the various "actors" who may be involved. Depending on the facts of the case and the technique used, these actors may include (1) the biological (sperm-supplying) father, (2) the biological father's wife, (3) the biological mother's husband, (4) the biological (ovum-supplying) mother; and (5) the "surrogate mother" who carries (a) another woman's ovum (the sperm donor's wife's or an ovum donor's) or (b) her own ovum/fetus/child to term under an agreement (possibly for hire) calling for the relinquishment of the child upon birth to one or both of the biological parent(s) and/or to an adoptive parent or parents.

1. ARTIFICIAL INSEMINATION
a. Married Couple
Not long ago, courts disagreed as to whether a child conceived by way of artificial insemination was legitimate. (*Gursky v. Gursky*, 39 Misc.2d 1083, 242 N.Y.S.2d 406 (1963)(no), and *People v. Sorensen*, 68 Cal.2d 280, 66 Cal.Rptr. 7, 437 P.2d 495 (1968)(yes)). At the extreme, artificial insemination was held to be adultery. The Uniform Parentage Act, § 5, provides:

"(a) If, under the supervision of a licensed physician and with the consent of her husband, a wife is inseminated artificially with semen donated by a man not her husband, the husband is treated in law as if he were the natural father of a child thereby conceived. The husband's consent must be in writing and signed by him and his wife. The physician shall certify their signatures and the date of the insemination, and file the husband's consent with the [State Department of Health], where it shall be kept confidential and in a sealed file. However, the physician's failure to do so does not affect the father and child relationship. (b) The donor of semen provided to a licensed physician for use in artificial insemination of a married woman other than the donor's wife is treated in law as if he were not the natural father of a child thereby conceived."

This legislation, or legislation patterned after the UPA, now is in effect in most states.

b. Unmarried Woman

The legal situation vis-à-vis the sperm donor of the offspring of an unmarried woman who was artificially inseminated at her request and for her own purposes, remains largely unclear. If the sperm donor can be identified, a paternity action may lie. Conversely, the sperm donor may assert custody or visitation rights.

2. *IN VITRO* FERTILIZATION AND OVUM TRANSPLANTATION

Medical advances have made it possible to extract ova from a woman and fertilize them with male sperm in a so-called Petri dish—*not* the proverbial test tube. The ova thus fertilized may be (1) reimplanted into the woman from whom they came, (2) implanted into another woman (surrogate mother), or (3) frozen, for later use in accordance with (1) or (2) above. The technique (1) enables a fertile woman to bear a child if, for any reason, she cannot conceive naturally; (2) makes it possible for a pregnancy to be "farmed out" to another woman, whether to avoid a medical problem that prevents the ovum-producing woman from successfully completing pregnancy, or simply for reasons of her convenience. In most states there appears to be no serious problem with *in vitro* fertilization in terms of the legality of using the technique. However, potentially applicable laws include (1) restrictions on fetal research, (2) laws forbidding the sale or donation of ova, or (3) prohibitions on experimentation on embryos or discarded fetal material. In some states the legality of *in vitro* fertilization, even as a medical procedure to overcome infertility, may thus be in doubt.

Examples: (1) A Minnesota statute (that may or may not apply to the new techniques) forbids "the use of a living human conceptus for any type of scientific, laboratory research or other experimentation except to protect the life or health of the conceptus." Permitted is "use of a living human conceptus for research or experimentation which verifiable scientific evidence has shown to be harmless to the conceptus." (Minn. Stat. 145.422).

(2) A (now repealed) Illinois law directed that "any person who intentionally causes the fertilization of a human ovum by a human sperm outside the body of a living human female shall, with regard to the human being thereby produced, be deemed to have care and custody of a child for the purposes * * * of the Act to Prevent and Punish Wrongs to children * * * except that nothing in that Section shall be construed to attach any penalty to participation in the performance of a lawful pregnancy termination." Ill.Rev.Stat. ch. 38 § 81–26(7)(1983). The Attorney General of Illinois indicated his unwillingness to apply this statute to *in vitro* fertilization, and a federal court held that the statute did not prohibit *in vitro* fertilization, but applied only to willful endangerment or injury during the period prior to implantation, through willfully destructive laboratory experimentation. *Smith v. Hartigan*, 556 F.Supp. 157 (N.D.Ill.1983). 720 ILCS 510/6 (7) now provides: "No person shall sell or experiment upon a fetus produced by the fertilization of a human ovum by a human sperm unless such experimentation is therapeutic to the fetus thereby procured. * * * Nothing in this subsection (7) is intended to prohibit the performance of in vitro fertilization."

If actors other than husband and wife are involved, legal issues arise regarding the status of offspring conceived by *in vitro* fertilization. Assume now that a husband and wife wish to have a child but cannot have one the usual way:

a. **Husband's Sperm—Wife's Ovum**

If the husband's sperm is used in *in vitro* fertilization of the wife's ovum and the fertilized ovum is re-implanted into her, and they are thereby enabled to have their own child, no question arises regarding their child's legal status: The child is their legitimate child.

b. **Donor's Sperm—Wife's Ovum**

If donor sperm, not the husband's sperm, is used in *in vitro* fertilization of the wife's ovum, and the ovum is reimplanted into the wife, the response should be the same as that given by Uniform Parentage § 5 for artificial insemination: The child should be their legitimate child, provided proper procedures were followed.

c. **Donor's Ovum—Husband's or Donor's Sperm**

If a fertilized donated ovum, not the wife's, is used for implantation into the wife, the response should be analogous to that given under b., above, *i.e.*, the child should be the husband's and wife's legitimate child and any donors should be out of the picture, if proper procedures were followed.

d. **Surrogate Mother—Husband's Sperm and Wife's Ovum**

If a surrogate mother is used to carry a fertilized ovum to term that is genetically the husband's and the wife's, the legal answer should follow the genetic relationship, *i.e.*, the child should legally become the husband and wife's child, after appropriate procedures terminate the potential interests of the surrogate mother and her husband, if she is married.

Example: W and H were unable to conceive a child because W had had a partial hysterectomy. They and a surrogate mother signed a contract providing that an embryo created from the ovum of W and the sperm of H would be implanted in the surrogate, and when the child was born it would live with W and H "as their child." The surrogate mother agreed to relinquish all parental rights. During the pregnancy, the relationship between W and H and the surrogate mother deteriorated, and each woman filed suit seeking a declaratory judgment that she was the legal mother of the unborn child. (Result: The court relied upon California's Uniform Parentage Act and held that, legally, W is, and the surrogate mother is not, the mother of the child. Consequently, the surrogate mother had no claim to visitation or any continued relationship with the child. "We conclude that although the Act recognizes both genetic consanguinity and giving birth as means of establishing a mother and child relationship, when the two means do not coincide in one woman, she who intended to procreate the child—that is, she who intended to bring about the birth of a child that she intended to raise as her own—is the natural mother under California law. * * * The surrogate mother's argument depends on a prior determination that she is indeed the child's mother. Since [W] is the child's mother under California law because she * * * provided the ovum for the *in vitro* fertilization procedure, intending to raise the child as her own, it follows that any constitutional interests [the surrogate mother] possesses in this situation are something less than those of a mother. * * * Moreover, if we were to conclude that [the surrogate mother] enjoys some sort of liberty interest in the companionship of the child, then the liberty interests of [H and W], the child's natural parents, in their procreative choices and their relationship with the child would perforce be infringed.") *Johnson v. Calvert,* 5 Cal.4th 84, 19 Cal.Rptr.2d 494, 851 P.2d 776 (1993).

3. SURROGATE MOTHERHOOD FOR PAY
a. Surrogate Mother and Child
There are two distinct scenarios: (1) The "surrogate mother" is artificially inseminated with the sperm of a man who has contracted with her to have her surrender her rights to the child upon birth, and (2) the "surrogate mother" carries to birth a child that is not genetically hers, *i.e.,* a fertilized ovum (whether or not stemming from the couple contracting with her) was transplanted into her for "carriage and delivery". Note that in (1) nothing is "surrogate" about the mother's biological relationship to her child, whereas in (2) the term seems more appropriate. The second scenario was litigated in

Johnson v. Calvert, above, but "carriage only" surrogacy remains relatively infrequent. Highly publicized litigation has centered, under scenario (1), on the question of the enforceability of a so-called surrogacy contract. The ultimate issue is whether a mother can contract so as to be *compelled* to surrender her genetic child to the father (or to a contractor who instigated the pregnancy by having donated sperm used in the mother's artificial insemination). Statutes against "baby selling" have been drawn upon to strike down such bargains. One difficulty is that where the father himself "purchases" his own biological child, such statutes may not apply.

Examples: (1) Infertile couples and prospective surrogate mothers sought a declaratory judgment that Michigan's Surrogate Parenting Act was not an outright ban on surrogacy contracts for pay. Plaintiffs argued that an outright ban would violate their constitutionally protected privacy rights and the due process and equal protection clauses of the state and federal constitutions. (Result: Only contracts that call for the surrogate's relinquishment of her parental rights to the child are illegal. "Plaintiffs * * * maintain that the state has no compelling interest in intervening in this conduct. We disagree. * * * The first interest is that of preventing children from becoming mere commodities. * * * The best interest of the child is also an interest that is sufficiently compelling to justify government intrusion. * * * A third compelling state interest is that of preventing the exploitation of women. * * * We affirm the lower court's ruling to the extent it holds that the Legislature intended to make void and unenforceable those arrangements that provide both for conception or surrogate gestation services and for the relinquishment of parental rights. The statutory language clearly defines 'a surrogate parentage contract' as consisting of two elements: (1) conception, through either natural or artificial insemination, of, or surrogate gestation by, a female and (2) her voluntary relinquishment of her parental rights to the child. Only a contract, agreement, or arrangement combining these two elements constitutes a 'surrogate parentage contract' that is void and unenforceable under the act. Section 9 of the act provides that a 'surrogate parentage contract' for compensation is unlawful and prohibited. Hence, a contract agreement, or arrangement providing compensation solely for conception or surrogate gestation services is not unlawful and prohibited, because the element of 'relinquishment of parental rights' is lacking.") *Doe v. Attorney General*, 194 Mich.App. 432, 487 N.W.2d 484 (1992).

(2) In 1986, the Kentucky Supreme Court refused to hold that the statute prohibiting the sale of children for adoption applies to surrogate parenting: "The question for us to decide is one of statutory interpretation: Has the legislature spoken? The

fundamental question is whether SPA's involvement in the surrogate parenting procedure should be construed as participation in the buying and selling of babies as prohibited by KRS 199.590(2). We conclude that it does not, that there are fundamental differences between the surrogate parenting procedure in which SPA participates and the buying and selling of children as prohibited by KRS 199.590(2) which place this surrogate parenting procedure beyond the purview of present legislation." *Surrogate Parenting Associates, Inc. v. Commonwealth, ex rel. David Armstrong, , 704 S.W.2d 209 (Ky.1986).*

(3) The famous *"Baby M "*case involved a surrogacy contract under which a married woman had been inseminated with the "purchasing" father's sperm in exchange for a fee of $10,000. Her husband had consented. When the "surrogate" mother refused to give up the child, the trial court ordered it to be turned over to the father and his wife, for adoption by the latter. The trial court held that (1) the "baby selling" law did not apply and (2) the father's right to procreate noncoitally and to contract for surrogacy is constitutionally protected. The contract was held specifically enforceable, the surrogate mother's rights were terminated, custody of the child was awarded to the father, and the latter's wife was allowed to adopt the child. (Result: The New Jersey Supreme Court reversed on all issues except custody. The surrogacy contract was held to violate public policy and the "baby selling" prohibition as well as statutes regulating revocation of consent to adoption and those regulating termination of parental rights. In the child's best interest, however, the court allowed custody of the child to remain with the father and his wife, and remanded the case for appropriate definition of the (surrogate) mother's visitation rights. The court added: "Nowhere, however, do we find any legal prohibition against surrogacy when the surrogate mother volunteers, without any payment, to act as a surrogate and is given the right to change her mind and to assert her parental rights.") *In the Matter of Baby M*, 109 N.J. 396, 537 A.2d 1227 (1988).

b. Legal Relationship Between "Purchaser's" Spouse and Child
Several cases have struggled with the question how the "purchased" child is to be brought into a legal relationship with its biological father and, more importantly, his wife. Paternity and adoption statutes have sometimes been brought into the picture. Generally, the laws on the books are not well suited to this purpose, and the cases point to the need for appropriate legislation.

Examples: (1) In Michigan in 1985, SM gave birth to her third child, C. All parties assumed that C was conceived when SM was artificially inseminated with the plaintiff's (F's) semen. SM had agreed to bear F's child in return for his promise to pay her $10,000 over and above all medical and confinement expenses. F and his wife had physical custody of C. SM and her H had consistently cooperated with F's efforts to obtain a court order acknowledging F's paternity. (Result: The Michigan Supreme Court allowed use of the paternity act to establish F's paternity with a view to bringing the child into his home. "The plaintiff seeks only a paternity act determination that he is the biological father of Teresa Syrkowski. The act was created as a procedural vehicle for determining the paternity of children 'born out of wedlock,' and enforcing the resulting support obligation. The plaintiff is requesting the court to determine the status of the child and his biological paternity. The act allows fathers to seek and receive such determinations.") *Syrkowski v. Appleyard,* 420 Mich. 367, 362 N.W.2d 211 (1985).

(2) The District of Columbia Superior Court referred to the adoption laws to investigate the suitability of a "purchasing" couple, and recommended that the paternity of the "purchasing" husband be verified by blood tests. In a thoughtful opinion, the court raised many serious legal issues in a context involving a $25,000 surrogate mother contract, artificial insemination of the surrogate with the husband's sperm, and a commercial agency. *In Re R.K.S.,* 112 Daily Washington L.Rptr. 1117 (June 6, 1984).

(3) In Kentucky, a surrogate mother and her husband were denied the opportunity to come into court under the law relating to the termination of parental rights and thereby transfer legal custody to the "purchasing" biological father. *In Re Baby Girl,* 9 Fam.L.Rptr. (BNA) 2348 (1983).

c. **Intermediary's Liability**
Intermediaries ("baby brokers"), especially attorneys, run serious risk of civil or criminal liability.

Example: Attorney Keane set up a surrogacy contract between SM (a married surrogate mother), F, (the prospective father) and W (F's wife). SM was artificially inseminated with F's sperm and became pregnant. Later in the pregnancy it was discovered that (1) SM's husband, not F, was the father of the child, and (2) SM carried a virus that can be sexually transmitted. Keane's surrogacy program did not call for any testing. At birth, the child had an active virus infection and, due to that exposure, suffered from multiple birth defects, including mental retardation, hearing loss, and neuro-muscular disorders. SM and F brought a negligence action against Keane and associates, claiming that the source of SM's and the child's exposure was the artificial insemination. SM and F appealed from the district court's dismissal on summary judgment. (Result: Reversed and remanded for a jury trial. "We have noted that this negligence case poses questions of first impression concerning the rights and duties of those involved in surrogacy arrangements. The courts have not yet developed a set of precedents defining these rights and duties. * * * Courts traditionally have imposed an affirmative duty in special relationship cases because the person upon whom the duty to act is imposed has assumed some special task or role and expects a benefit or profit. * * * In addition courts impose a duty to protect in special relationships because one party is in control and the other has entrusted himself to the party in control. * * * Keane and his program fall within the principles found in these negligence cases imposing a duty to act. As the facts make clear, Keane assumed a task and role as a surrogacy broker, and the other professionals participated in the program Keane designed. The group were in this sense joint venturers engaged in an entirely new kind of project. * * * Keane, as well as the doctors and the lawyer, expected to profit from their roles in the program. Keane held out the services of his program. He should not be allowed to wash his hands of responsibility by turning the project over to others, as the dissent argues.") *Stiver v. Parker*, 975 F.2d 261 (6th Cir.1992).

C. REVIEW QUESTIONS

1. **T or F** An individual's decision to use contraceptives constitutionally protected.

2. **T or F** A state may forbid sale of contraceptives to minors.

3. **T or F** A state may constitutionally require that parents of an "immature" minor daughter be notified of her decision to have an abortion.

4. **T or F** A state statute mandating compulsory sterilization of the mentally retarded is constitutional.

5. **T or F** In order to give legal protection to the best interests of the child, modern statutes provide that both the sperm donor and the husband of a woman artificially inseminated legally are fathers of the child.

6. **T or F** There is no question as to the legality of *in vitro* fertilization.

7. Which of the following combinations involving "artificial conception" pose no serious legal question as to the parent and child relationship?

    A. Husband's sperm, wife's ovum, wife carries child to term.

    B. Donor's sperm, wife's ovum, wife carries child to term.

    C. Donor's ovum, husband's sperm, wife carries child to term.

    D.   Husband's sperm, wife's ovum, surrogate mother carries child to term.

    E.   Husband's sperm, surrogate mother's ovum, surrogate mother carries child to term.

    F.   Donor's ovum, donor's sperm, surrogate mother carries child to term.

8. **T** **or** **F**   Statutes forbidding "baby selling" may apply to contracts with a surrogate mother to deliver a child.

9. **T** **or** **F**   Non-coital reproduction is a right protected by the U.S. Supreme Court.

10. **T** **or** **F**   Policy encourages intermediaries to facilitate "surrogacy" for pay.

APPENDIX A

ANSWERS TO REVIEW QUESTIONS

I. THE NATURE OF MARRIAGE

1. ***False.***   The states have established the rights and obligations of marriage primarily by statutes.

2. ***False.***   Although entered by contract, marriage is primarily a status. Courts have held that new laws may redefine rights to (or grounds for) divorce, or realign property and support rights upon divorce, even if reasonable expectations of a party are defeated.

3. ***False.***   The *validity* of a marriage generally is determined under the law of the place of celebration. However, *legal incidents* (rights to property, support, grounds for divorce) generally are determined by the parties' marital domicile.

4. ***True.***   Today's majority view enforces antenuptial agreements if not "unconscionable" when made (UPAA, UMPA). Traditionally, however, courts did not uphold antenuptial agreements that violated traditional "public policies." Today, some jurisdictions still do not enforce an antenuptial agreement if it "encourages" divorce, or alters the "essence" of marriage, such as the marital support obligation. Courts remain wary that there was full disclosure and/or independent legal advice and/or fair provisions for the economically weaker party.

5. ***True.***   Although UPAA permits all manner of contracts regarding "personal rights and obligations not in violation of public policy or a statute imposing a criminal

penalty'' (§ 3 (a) (8)), courts remain loath to involve themselves with day-to-day aspects of marriage, such as requiring certain support levels, or church attendance, or vacation plans. Parties may generally contract freely with regard to property.

6. *False.* Under the UPAA and UMPA, financial provisions are reviewed as of the date of execution of the agreement. Ohio's Supreme Court, in *Gross,* evaluated the fairness of property provisions as of the time of execution of the agreement, but scrutinized support provisions as of the time they are sought to be enforced.

7. *True.* True, although UPAA and UMPA dispense with the consideration requirement. Moreover, the promise of marriage is not effective consideration for federal gift tax purposes.

8. *True.* That may often be the case. However, reconciliation (*e.g.,* withdrawing a divorce petition) or a business relationship may provide sufficient new consideration. Under UPAA and UMPA, consideration is not required for antenuptial or postnuptial agreements nor for the postnuptial modification of antenuptial agreements.

9. *False.* The surrounding circumstances and the donor's intent determine whether a particular gift is so clearly in contemplation of (and thus conditional on) marriage that it must be returned if the marriage is not entered. To illustrate, an engagement ring is generally held to be returnable, whereas a birthday or holiday gift may typically be retained.

10. *True.* These statutes also granted married women numerous other rights, such as contracting and bringing law suits in their own names, and more recently, these statutes abolished or limited interspousal tort immunities.

11. .*True.* UMDA § 207(b) expressly validates a previously invalid marriage once the impediment to the marriage is removed. The previously invalid marriage becomes valid as of the time the impediment is removed.

12. *False.* UPAA § 6(a) allows the spouse against whom enforcement is sought to invalidate the agreement only if the agreement was unconscionable *when made.* In addition, the complaining spouse (1) must not have been provided adequate disclosure, (2) did not waive disclosure, and (3) had no independent knowledge of the other spouse's financial circumstances.

13. *False.* Courts are not bound by provisions that affect children.

14. *True.* Under UMDA § 306(b), provisions that concern support and the disposition of property are binding on the court, unless the court finds that the agreement is unconscionable.

II. MARRIAGE REQUISITES

1. *False.* There are many levels of mental incompetence. (1) Even though a person may not be able to carry on his/her ordinary affairs, if he/she has the capacity to understand the nature of marriage, he/she may give valid consent to marriage. (2) If

the incompetent's difficulties go deeper, a guardian must consent to his/her marriage. (3) At some level, substantive marriage prohibitions against marriage of "feebleminded," *etc.*, persons apply, and even a guardian cannot supply valid consent.

2. ***False.*** Most states require more. The fraud also must go to the "essence of marriage." Misrepresentations as to fertility, pregnancy or important religious beliefs have sufficed to allow annulment; whereas misrepresentations concerning wealth, income or professional position typically have not.

3. ***True.*** Solemnization is not needed in a jurisdiction that recognizes common law marriage. In addition, since many policies coalesce in favor of upholding the parties' expectations or protecting an existing relationship, courts have been lenient in their interpretation of applicable laws. To illustrate: (1) Even a short-term sojourn to another jurisdiction that recognizes common law marriage sometimes has been held to create one; (2) When the parties had *either* a marriage license *or* had undergone a ceremony, a marriage has occasionally been found; (3) Various presumptions regarding the validity of an alleged marriage may uphold what otherwise would be difficult or impossible to prove to be a valid marriage; (4) Where applicable, the putative spouse doctrine protects the innocent party to an invalid marriage, so long as he/she remains in good faith unaware of the defect. Many states, however, specifically (or by interpretation) limit the applicability of the putative spouse doctrine to ceremonial "marriage."

4. ***False.*** If specific requirements are met, some states recognize proxy marriages. In any event, proxy marriages are not considered to be sham marriages.

5. Answer: B

6. ***False.*** The putative spouse doctrine protects a partner to an invalid marriage who has participated in a marriage ceremony only for so long as he/she believes in good faith that the marriage is valid.

7. ***False.*** All states prohibit marriage between a parent and his/her child; most states also prohibit marriage between an aunt and her nephew.

8. ***True.*** Parental consent usually is required up to the age of majority.

9. ***True.*** While adoption simulates the legal relationships created by blood, the genetic argument is inapplicable in the adoption situation. Accordingly, a Colorado Supreme Court decision has allowed siblings by adoption to marry. Generally, however, such marriages remain prohibited.

10. ***False.*** No state allows polygamy. The state has an interest in protecting monogamous relationships, and statutes prohibiting polygamy do not violate the First Amendment.

11. ***False.*** A common law marriage that is valid where entered is generally recognized in all other states, even in those that have abolished common law marriage.

12. ***False***. Only the underage spouse (and in many states his or her parents) may attack the validity of an underage marriage.

III. HUSBAND AND WIFE

1. *False.*   Family law statutes do not govern a non-marital relationship.

2. *True.*   Under *Marvin*, support and property obligations may arise in connection with nonmarital cohabitation on the basis of express or implied agreements, or on the theories of unjust enrichment, quasi-contract, or resulting or constructive trusts.

3. *True.*   However, the marriage would be invalid if Francine's operation had taken place after the marriage.

4. *False.*   Currently, no state grants legal validity to same sex marriages, although in 1996, the issue remained under review in Hawaii.

5. *False.*   Joanne should recover the *quantum meruit* value of her services less the reasonable value of her support.

IV. HUSBAND AND WIFE

1. *False.*   A 1979 U.S. Supreme Court decision (*Orr v. Orr*) invalidated an Alabama statute that restricted alimony to women.   Gender-based classifications may reinforce stereotypes and must be carefully tailored.   A gender-neutral statute based on need would serve legitimate state purposes better than a gender-based statute.

2. *True.*   However, depending on the parties' standard of living, many courts may not consider this item "necessary."   In the alternative, the creditor should proceed on an agency theory (actual or by estoppel).

3. *False.*   So long as the marriage continues, property acquired by each spouse before *or after* marriage is that spouse's separate property.

4. *False.*   Especially where one spouse is financially dependent, courts in most separate property states today recognize marriage as a partnership and "equitably distribute" property without much regard to who acquired it.   The concept of "marital property" is used in many separate property states to define the (divisible) gains of the marriage.

5. *False.*   Today, spouses can take title in any of these forms.

6. *True.*   If *bona fide* transfers are involved, W generally can deplete her estate, so that H takes nothing, if nothing is left.   (The "augmented estate" concept of the Uniform Probate Code seeks to guard against this.)   If property is left in W's estate and her will makes no or inadequate provision for H, H can renounce the will and take a statutory share, usually one-third.

7. *False.*   Separate property typically also includes property acquired after marriage by inheritance, gift, or personal injury recovery.   "Commingling" of property after

marriage may transform separate property into community property. There is a split in authority whether post-marriage income from and/or appreciation of separate property is separate or community property.

8. **True.** Texas, for instance, provides for sole management of community property by the spouse who earned that property. Other states require joint management of community property, with some states excepting business property from joint management. Special exceptions also may govern disposition of community property.

9. **False.** W also can distribute her half of the community property. Since H owns his half of the community property, no provision is made for him to renounce W's will and take a statutory share.

10. **False.** A number of states still allow such actions, even while many states have abolished the actions. Some statutes limit recovery severely.

11. **False.** The husband-wife testimonial privilege has been restricted in many states, abolished altogether in at least one (New Jersey), and is disfavored by influential commentators. In a federal prosecution, the U.S. Supreme Court has held that the witness spouse alone has the right to decide whether or not to testify (*Trammel*).

12. **True.** With few statutory exceptions that (should) no longer apply (*e.g.*, driver's license, voter's registration), a wife has never been *compelled* by law to take the husband's surname. Traditionally she has adopted his name by usage. While the father's name traditionally became the child's (and some cases spoke of this as the father's common law right), cases now hold that parents may give their children any surname they choose. On divorce, and upon her request, the court typically will restore the ex-wife's maiden name (if lost by usage of the husband's name), and may adjust the child's name, if in the latter's best interest.

13. **False.** Unless the parties are separated, courts are unwilling to enforce the spousal support obligation by ordering one spouse to provide support directly to the other. However, in most states a financially dependent spouse may purchase *necessary* items on the other spouse's account.

14. **False.** The 8 original community property states are Arizona, California, Idaho, Louisiana, New Mexico, Nevada, Texas, Washington and their property regimes were derived from or influenced by civil law sources. Wisconsin, however, enacted the Uniform Marital Property Act prepared by the Commissioners on Uniform State Laws who were influenced by the laws of the original 8 community property states.

15. **False.** So far, no state has recognized a cohabitant's right of consortium.

16. **True.** Several states have amended rape statutes, in others the courts have reinterpreted existing statutes or used constitutional arguments to bring down the exemption.

17. **False.** A gift of nonmarital property by one spouse to the other is classified as marital property upon divorce. (Under earlier law, a wife's gift to her husband was subject to the "presumption of advancement" which, unless overcome, returned property W had given to H during the marriage to W on divorce).

18. **True.** Recent amendments to the UPC promulgated by the Uniform Laws Commissioners provide a graduated scale under which the spouse's forced share reaches one-half of the decedent spouse's estate after 15 years of marriage.

V. DIVORCE—STATUS

1. **False.** The *ex parte* divorce decree based on H's domicile is valid and entitled to full faith and credit in all other states. However, the effect of an *ex parte* divorce extends to status only, not to consequences. In short, H's divorce is entitled to full faith and credit, the denial of alimony to W is not.

2. **False.** If an Iowa statute gives the Iowa court jurisdiction ("long-arm" statutes based on maintenance of matrimonial domicile are common and have been upheld against due process challenge), the divorce is valid as to status *and* consequences. In short, the alimony award would be enforceable against H in Wisconsin.

3. *A.*

4. *B.*

5. **True.** Under no-fault divorce statutes in effect in all states a finding of fault is not required. A divorce will be granted on the basis of "incompatibility", or "breakdown of the marriage", or proof of a specified period of time during which the spouses have lived apart.

6. **True.** Despite nominal prohibitions on "collusion", the typical fault-based divorce proceeded by prior arrangements of the parties. Grounds were invented or defenses to existing grounds were not interposed. The courts largely acquiesced. A significant difference between consensual divorce under a fault-based system and a no-fault system was that the "guilty" party or the party desiring a divorce but not having grounds had to make financial or child support and custody concessions to the other spouse in negotiating for consent.

7. **False.** In addition or instead, most states require proof of separation for a specific period of time.

8. **False.** The majority of states continue to provide for fault divorce as an alternative to no-fault divorce. While in some states there has been some change in fault grounds, others continue pretty much on the historical model. Defenses, on the other hand, have been more readily abolished or reduced in relevance. Financial consequences may depend on fault.

9. **False.** Provocation requires a causal connection, recrimination does not. Provocation is a defense and, while recrimination has been converted into a defense in many states, traditionally it constituted a bar to divorce. Provocation need not and recrimination must constitute a ground for divorce.

10. **False.** Desertion requires "fault", *i.e.*, it must be against the will of the other spouse, whereas "living apart" may be consensual.

11. *False.* Traditionally, federal courts have declined jurisdiction in family law matters. This abstention rule was recently reaffirmed by the U.S. Supreme Court. However, under specific statutes, family law matters may be heard (*i.e.*, child support enforcement, interstate child custody).

12. *False.* Personal service does not require minimum contacts. (As reaffirmed in 1990 by the U.S. Supreme Court in *Burnham v. Superior Court.*)

13. *False.* By provoking W's departure, H has constructively deserted W. If H's provocation was adequate, W has not deserted H.

14. *False.* W's specific defense is "connivance."

VI. DIVORCE—FINANCIAL CONSEQUENCES

1. *False.* If the dependent spouse has no realistic employment opportunities or adequate assets and the marriage was of considerable duration, courts still extend alimony payments for indefinite duration, including life.

2–3. *False.* Although all states provide for no-fault divorce in some form, fault grounds are still available as an alternative in a majority of states. If a fault ground is used to litigate the status issue, the consequences may also be affected, although alimony generally is more vulnerable than property division. In addition, in some pure no-fault states, the amount of an alimony award may be reduced by proof of the claimant's severe fault, such as adultery. With regard to property division, the concept of economic fault ("dissipation") is increasingly applied, regardless of the reason for the marital break-up.

4. *False.* H's obligation was contractual, *i.e.*, subject only to contract defenses, until it was incorporated (merged) into the judgment. As an alimony judgment, it would be held generally modifiable in the light of new circumstances. Here, however, H's change in circumstances was voluntary. Worse, H may even have intended to avoid payment of the alimony obligation. In such circumstances, H's obligation will not be modified.

5. *True.* Unless the separation agreement and decree expressly provide otherwise, the alimony obligation terminates at the death of either the payor or payee. Some courts may view the designation as "rehabilitative alimony," along with the six-year limitation, as sufficient to express an intent that death is *not* to terminate the obligation.

6. *Close call.* Remarriage typically terminates an alimony obligation either by operation of law, under the terms of the decree, or based on changed circumstances. Here, because it is paid for a specific purpose, *rehabilitative* alimony may not necessarily be terminated by the recipient's remarriage.

7. *True.* Note, however, that although obligations arising from a property settlement generally remain dischargeable in bankruptcy, new (1990s) federal legislation limits the discharge in bankruptcy of marital property obligations in some circumstances.

8. *True.* The change in circumstances must occur after the alimony decree, and the decree must not expressly or impliedly rule out modifiability.

9. *True.* In a sense, this approach reflects, up to the amount of the alimony paid, the income splitting rationale of the joint return.

10. *True.* The recipient of property in a divorce settlement takes the transferor's adjusted basis for that property. (In 1984, Congress abolished the rule under which the transfer by one spouse to the other of property on divorce was a taxable event, *i.e.*, if the property had appreciated in value, a capital gains tax was due.)

11. *False.* The majority of courts do not classify a professional license or degree as property. Instead, many courts consider one spouse's contribution to the other spouse's education or professional training as an important factor influencing the division of marital and even of separate property or, if there is inadequate property, in the allocation of alimony. Very few courts (prominently in New York) have classified a professional degree or license as a marital asset and "divided" it upon divorce, by awarding to the other spouse *as property* a specific percentage of the "present value" of the degree or license, or even the value of an "enhanced career."

12. *False.* Reconciliation generally terminates a separation agreement. The traditional rationale is that, upon reconciliation, the separation agreement turns into a post-nuptial agreement contemplating divorce and therefore is invalid. A more reasonable rationale is that reconciliation constitutes a change of circumstances amounting to an implied revocation of the separation agreement.

VII. THE PARENTAL CHILD SUPPORT OBLIGATION

1. *False.* A child's independent wealth or income normally does not relieve parents of their support obligation.

2. *True.* Most states impose no support duty on a stepparent who has married the custodial parent, but who has not adopted the child. Several states impose a support duty while the relationship continues.

3. *False.* The Uniform Reciprocal Enforcement of Support Act (URESA) permits a support action to be filed where the dependent resides. The action will be heard and enforced where the obligor resides. Any award collected is sent to the initiating court for disbursement. The newer Uniform Interstate Family Support Act (UIFSA) provides a similar procedure and, in addition, relies heavily on comprehensive long-arm provisions that give a court where the dependent resides exclusive jurisdiction if there is a "significant connection" to the obligor.

4. *True.* Traditionally, the mother had only a secondary child support obligation.

5. *False.* If the "child" cannot care for itself after the age of majority, the obligation of support may be open-ended.

6. *False.* Such statutes have been upheld on the rationale that there is an increased likelihood that a divorced parent will refuse to pay for a college education and that

such legislation therefore bears a rational relationship to the permissible legislative objective of protecting children whose parents are divorced. (*Caveat:* In at least one state, such a statute was held to deny equal protection).

7. *False.* If the state of facts that caused the emancipation ceases to exist, a minor may revert to unemancipated status.

8. *False.* Child support obligations are modifiable if a change of circumstances is proved.

9. *False.* Such statutes have been upheld because they further the legitimate legislative purpose of alleviating some of the state's burden of caring for the indigent.

10. *True.* However, the UMDA and similar statutes allow a support order entered in the context of divorce to continue support payments to the child from the parent's estate or, for higher education, past the child's majority.

11. *False.* Some state guidelines have a built-in cap. In some no-cap states, rather remarkably high amounts of child support have been ordered when the obligated parent's income was very high. In other states, courts have deviated from guidelines and determined a reasonable amount that should be paid for child support.

VIII. CHILD CUSTODY

1. *False.* When the custodial parent dies, the noncustodial parent is next in line for custody, unless there are very special circumstances.

2. *True.* While not binding on the court, absent special circumstances, courts will honor the deceased parents' designation of a guardian. (If one parent predeceased the other, the latter's sole designation will usually be honored.) Note also that the parents' agreement regarding child custody (or support) is not binding on the court even if expressed in a separation agreement or in a premarital agreement.

3. Answer: All except E. Note that in recent cases and under the UMDA the parent's (im)moral conduct matters only if the conduct directly affects his/her relationship to the child. The child's preference is given weight only if it is sufficiently mature to express a reasonable opinion.

4. *True.* A noncustodial parent has a right to visitation which, under the UMDA, may be denied only if it would "endanger seriously the child's physical, mental, moral or emotional health."

5. *False.* Joint custody means shared legal custody, even if one parent is awarded primary physical custody.

6. *True.* If the other parent has custody, typically only a significant, very negative change in the *custodial* parent's circumstances will result in a change of custody.

Stability in the child's environment is viewed as a very important factor in itself. If, however, a third party (*e.g.*, a grandparent) has custody, the natural parent's primary right to custody is given great weight.

7. *False.*   UMDA §407 does not impose a time frame and allows modification of the visitation order if it would be in the best interest of the child.   (See also ##4, 8.)

8. *True.*   Generally, this is correct, although under the UMDA, while it invokes the child's best interests, visitation may be *restricted* only if it would seriously endanger the child's "physical, mental, moral, or emotional health."

9. *True.*   Vis-á-vis third parties, one important (bootstrapping) presumption is that it is in the child's best interest to be in the parent's custody.   For disputes between two parents UMDA §402, quoted in the text, provides detailed standards.

10. *True.*   The parents' right to the custody, care, and control of their child has been held to be a fundamental liberty protected by the Fourteenth Amendment.

11. *True.*   The child may live with one parent permanently or with both parents for alternating periods of time;   however, both parents have legal custody and decisions regarding the child's welfare must be made jointly by both parents.   (See also #5).

12. *False.*   Very few courts enforce grandparental visitation in an *ongoing* marriage. Many statutes and courts distinguish between death and divorce, and most exclude adoption, with exceptions made in the case of adoption by a stepparent.   Statutes and courts often phrase the grandparent's interest in terms of a "privilege," the child's best interest being paramount.

13. *False.*   By that name, the "tender years presumption" no longer has much viability. However, "the primary caretaker presumption," where followed, typically results in young children going to their mothers, not their fathers.

14. *True.*   Parents are *prima facie* entitled to have custody.   (See also ##1, 10).

15. *True.*   The court is guided by the child's best interests and is not bound by the parents' wishes.

16. *False.* The remedy available to F is judicial enforcement of the visitation order.

17. *False.*   F's improved circumstances may be taken into account, but will not eliminate the absent parent's obligation.

18. *True.*   In response to widespread parental "child snatching", Congress legislated Full Faith and Credit protection for custody judgments.

IX. PARENTAL OBLIGATION OF CARE AND CONTROL AND THE JUVENILE COURT SYSTEM

1. *True.*   Such "offenses" involve the child's status as a child and include "incorrigibility", "truancy", running away from home, being beyond the discipline of the parents, *etc.*

2. *False.* A custody order should make the least possible intrusion upon constitutionally protected interests of the parent, in this case First Amendment rights. In similar situations, some courts have required the custodial parent to agree to provide standard medical care, as a condition to custody.

3. *False.* In *Lassiter v. Department of Social Services*, the U.S. Supreme Court did not define an unconditional right to counsel. Instead, it did not rule out the possibility of a constitutional right to counsel if special circumstances combine to make counsel necessary to assure Due Process. The Court also noted that the majority of states statutorily provides the parents counsel in termination of parental rights cases.

4. *True.* In its decision in *Santosky v. Kramer*, the U.S. Supreme Court invalidated on Due Process grounds a New York statute that allowed parental rights to be terminated by a "fair preponderance of the evidence." The court noted that a majority of states imposes a "clear and convincing" standard of evidence and concluded that this standard is called for by the Due Process Clause.

5. *False.* In *Parham v. J.R.*, the U.S. Supreme Court held that a formal or even quasi-formal commitment hearing is not required. However, a determination should be made by a neutral factfinder, who must have the authority to deny admission and who should carefully probe the minor's background.

6. *False.* The child support obligation continues. By contrast, a judicial termination of parental rights would end the support obligation.

7. *False.* The typical child abuse reporting statute carries relatively weak or no criminal sanctions.

8. *False.* The U.S. Supreme Court found in *Smith v. OFFER* that New York procedures for the removal of a foster child from the foster parents' custody were not constitutionally defective, "even on the assumption that the [foster parents] have a protected 'liberty interest.'"

9. *False.* Many but not all constitutional protections have been extended to minors being tried in juvenile courts; prominently missing is the right to jury trial.

10. *False.* Generally, when the physical welfare (especially the life) of a child is jeopardized by a parent's religious belief, the state may intervene to provide conventional medical care and, depending on state statutes, may prosecute the parent if serious harm has come to the child. A tort action may be another option: In 1995, the U.S. Supreme Court let stand a Minnesota decision that upheld a $1.5 million judgment in favor of the father of a child whose custodial mother relied on Christian Science prayer with the result that the child died from untreated diabetes. (*McKown v. Lundman*).

11. *False.* Unless a special duty to protect the specific child can be found, the agency is not responsible for harm done to the child. As demonstrated by the U.S. Supreme Court in *DeShaney v. Winnebago City Department of Social Services*, the burden of finding such a duty is very difficult to meet.

12. *True.* The requirement that she notify *one* parent, however, is constitutional, provided an adequate judicial bypass procedure is available to a mature minor.

13. *True.* However, an adequate judicial bypass option must be available to a mature minor.

X. CHILDREN'S RIGHTS

1. *False.* Increasingly, the U.S. Supreme Court as well as state courts have recognized a broad spectrum of constitutional rights of minors, sometimes (particularly in the context of abortion) in direct opposition to rights asserted by their parents.

2. *True.* This is what emancipation is about. Note also that the contract of an unemancipated minor is ratified when the age of majority is reached without disavowal.

3. *False.* Typically, though with some exceptions, the birth of a healthy child has been held not to give rise to an action by the parents. However, where a baby suffers birth defects caused by a third party's negligence, an action typically is available.

4. *True.* Under older law, only pecuniary harm was compensated. Since in our economy parents do not usually suffer pecuniary harm from the loss of their child, the old rule has been generally abandoned and monetary recovery is allowed for intangible harm.

5. *False.* The traditional immunity doctrine has been generally restricted or abandoned. However, various limitations on tort recovery remain in effect, especially in the area of parental discretion and control, or relating to insurance.

6. *False.* The general rule remains that minors may not bring such actions, even though an occasional court has held to the contrary. (Remember: There is a strong tide running against these cases in the wife/husband context.)

7. *True.* Parents may not be held criminally responsible for the criminal acts of their children. (Note: Under very rare statutes that focus on parental failure to supervise their children, parents may incur some limited criminal liability.)

8. *True.* When the "family purpose doctrine" applies, parents may be held responsible for torts committed by their child while driving the family car. Beyond that, statutes commonly impose liability up to a certain amount on parents for certain torts committed by their children. Finally, parents may be liable for their own negligence in failing to supervise their child.

9. *True.* If appropriate safeguards are followed. (*Ingraham v. Wright*).

10. *False.* Nevertheless, many school systems permit parents to opt their children out of sex education or condom distribution programs.

XI. LEGITIMACY, ILLEGITIMACY, AND PATERNITY

1. *True.* This rule is intended to protect marriage and children. It is rooted in the old common law.

2. *True.* Note, however, that a few states until recently still denied the illegitimate child a right to take by intestate succession from the mother's kin.

3. *False.* The U.S. Supreme Court has called for heightened, but not the strict scrutiny that applies to a "suspect classification," such as race.

4. *True.* Any final judgment is entitled to Full Faith and Credit.

5. *True.* The U.S. Supreme Court has not defined precisely the extent of the unwed father's interest. While it is clear that an unmarried father has significant (Due Process) rights with regard to his child, it also is clear that a distinction is permissible between unmarried fathers who have lived with or supported their child and those who have not.

6. *True.* At common law, an illegitimate child was considered *filius nullius*—the child of no one, and was not entitled to support or inheritance from either parent or other blood relatives.

7. *True.* The U.S. Supreme Court has held that such a requirement does not violate the Equal Protection Clause in that it is substantially related to important state interests, such as preventing fraudulent claims on estates. (*Lalli v. Lalli*).

8. *False.* While the U.S. Supreme Court has not made this completely clear, it is probable that, once paternity is established, an illegitimate child has the same support rights as a legitimate child. (*Gomez v. Perez*). This result also follows from state child support formulas and tables.

9. *False.* The U.S. Supreme Court has upheld such a distinction, because it allows governmental agencies to avoid the burden and expense of case-by-case determination. (*Mathews v. Lucas*, but *cf. Jimenez v. Weinberger*).

10. *False.* Only a *judicial* determination of legitimacy is entitled to Full Faith and Credit. As a matter of conflicts law and good policy, however, once achieved, legitimate status achieved in one state is generally recognized in others.

XII. ADOPTION

1. *False.* All of these factors have been held relevant in determining the best interests of a child in relation to a prospective adopter.

2. *True.* Courts typically do not allow adoptive parents to relieve themselves of responsibility for an adopted child more easily than a natural parent could relieve himself of responsibility for a natural child. A tort action against the adoption agency, however, may be available.

3. ***True.*** In a few states however, the natural parent may retain a subsidiary support obligation, enforceable if the adoptive parents fail to support the child. An inheritance relationship may also subsist.

4. ***False.*** Adoption was established by statute.

5. ***True.*** Court approval for adoption is mandated in all states. Depending upon the statute and court practices, a court may exercise considerable discretion in approving an adoption.

6. ***True.*** Many states allow adult adoption. Such adoptions are subject to little supervision; however, permission has frequently been denied to a gay or lesbian person to adopt a lover, or in other cases in which adoption was attempted to be put to a use not deemed consistent with legislative intent.

7. ***False.*** A minor parent's consent to the adoption of his/her child is required.

8. ***False.*** Race has generally been considered as a *factor* in adoption, but cannot be the sole basis for the determination, except in cases falling under the Indian Child Welfare Act. (The relevance of *Palmore* v. *Sidoti*—the U.S. Supreme Court's interracial custody decision—in regard to interracial adoptions has not been fully determined.)

9. ***False.*** A neglect or abuse adjudication does not terminate parental rights and the parents retain a "residual" legal relationship to their child. Adoption may not proceed without their consent, or without legal termination of the parents' rights.

10. ***True.*** "Abandonment" generally is a ground for terminating parental rights and unexcused failure to render support may constitute abandonment.

11. ***True.*** Typical state statutes require the child's consent if he/she is above a certain age, often set at 14 years.

12. ***False.*** A parent's consent to adoption typically is scrutinized *very* closely. Even seemingly minor formal flaws in the consent may suffice to set aside parental consent.

13. ***True.*** Constitutional challenges on anonymous adoption have been mounted, but they have not succeeded. However, numerous states permit some access to adoption information, some by a "registry matching" process, whereby adopted child and biological parent are brought together if *both* file requests for information.

14. ***True.*** Typically, the adoption or descent and distribution statute explicitly denies or is held implicitly to deny the right of inheritance from natural parents, however, in a few states an inheritance relationship survives the adoption.

15. ***False.*** Subsidized adoptions are available in many states to provide financial assistance to families who adopt a "hard-to-place" child. The legal relationship between the adopter and the adopted child is complete and permanent.

16. *False.* Very false. The *interested* unmarried father may not be ignored, as the prospective adoptive parents of *Baby Jessica* and *Baby Richard* learned to their and, more importantly, to the children's disadvantage.

17. *False.* Statutory regulation of the adoption process is focused primarily on the child's best interests, as well as on the rights of the child's biological parents, specifically that their rights be terminated properly and finally before the adoption takes place.

18. *True.* The noncustodial parent, in any event, is entitled to notice and an opportunity to be heard. Moreover, when he or she has complied with a support obligation and maintained contact with the child, termination of the absent parent's rights is very difficult or impossible.

19. *True.* Unless the child is surrendered to an agency, most states prohibit consent to be given in "blank" or a form that does not identify the identity of the adoptive parent(s).

XIII. PROCREATION

1. *True.* The U.S. Supreme Court has protected the decision not to have a child both as a privacy interest inherent in marriage (*Griswold*)and as an individual right (*Eisenstadt*).

2. *False.* State restrictions inhibiting privacy rights of minors are valid only if they serve a significant state interest (*Carey*). Indeed, some schools now distribute free condoms to students.

3. *True.* The parental right to control an *immature* minor daughter has not been affected by various U.S. Supreme Court decisions striking down statutes interfering with the autonomy of a *mature* minor daughter.

4. *Probably False.* While *Buck* v. *Bell,* the U.S. Supreme Court's 1927 decision upholding a compulsory sterilization statute, has not been overruled, a review by the U.S. Supreme Court of this area probably would result in very substantial restrictions being placed on compulsory sterilization, or outright prohibition.

5. *False.* Under § 5 of the Uniform Parentage Act (that provision or similar legislation has been enacted by a majority of the states), only the woman's husband is treated as the child's legal father provided he has consented to his wife's insemination.

6. *False.* Laws forbidding or restricting fetal research and experimentation on embryos or utilization of discarded fetal material possibly may apply to *in vitro* fertilization.

7. A, and in a majority of states, B, and by analogy to sperm donation, probably C and, under *Johnson v. Calvert*, D. E and F, however, remain fraught with legal uncertainty.

8. ***True.*** However, where the child is the result of inseminating the surrogate mother with the "purchasing" father's sperm, the situation is less clear. Some courts have held that such a transaction is not covered by a "baby selling" statute.

9. ***False.*** The U.S. Supreme Court has not ruled on the constitutional status of "assisted reproduction." Commentators are divided on the applicability of a right to procreate in the context of artificial conception, or the extent of any such right. It seems noteworthy that the U.S. Supreme Court decisions most often cited to support such a right primarily involve protection of decisions *not* to procreate.

10. ***False.*** While intermediaries (*e.g.*, sperm banks) are permitted to act and may be regulated in a number of states, courts and statutes have increasingly disfavored "profiteers" in this sensitive area (*Doe v. Atty. Gen.*).

APPENDIX B

PRACTICE ESSAY QUESTIONS

QUESTION I

George comes to you and requests your legal advice. His story is that, for several years, he had been living with Linda more or less openly in her apartment. During that time, "to keep up appearances", he had not given up his rented room nearby. Eleven months ago, Linda told him that she had become pregnant, that he was not the father and "would [he] please move out immediately". George then moved back to his room. Within weeks, Linda proceeded to marry Bill, an older, rather wealthy local lawyer. When her child was born three months ago, Bill was delighted and raised no questions.

George wants you to file a paternity suit and obtain visitation rights to the child or, preferably, full custody. He is willing to pay child support out of his income of about $20,000/year. He has moved in with his mother who he says is willing to provide day-to-day care for the baby, while George is at his job. He offers you $5,000 (borrowed from his mother) as a cash retainer—and he is the first potential client you have seen in days. Advise George.

QUESTION II

To save taxes on divorce, Ann and Jack agreed in their separation agreement (subsequently incorporated into their divorce decree) that Jack would pay substantial ($5,000/month) combined alimony and child support to Ann, but that essentially all property, consisting primarily of a major real estate investment, would be retained by

Jack, except for Ann's jewelry and personal items. The real property had been purchased for about $50,000 with savings from Jack's earnings as a physician and had appreciated in value substantially, to about $200,000 at the time of the divorce. Ann and Jack had been married seven years and had two children, the custody of whom was awarded to Ann. Ann had been trained as a hamburger helper at McDonald's, but has not worked there or anywhere else for five years.

Now, three years after the divorce, Ann (39 years of age) is cohabiting with Joe (30 years of age), in the apartment Ann rents with the funds received monthly from Jack. Ann and Joe have no jobs and no income, other than the alimony paid by Jack. They do not seem interested in marriage.

Jack consults you regarding his wish to stop paying Ann alimony and child support. He also seeks custody of his two children, a boy of 9 years of age and a girl of 7. His current expenses are high, involving a new wife, their two-year old child and her three children from a previous marriage that had ended with her husband's death. Jack's income situation also has deteriorated since his divorce. While he had earned $100,000/year at the time of divorce, he now is down to $75,000/year, because his group practice was absorbed by an H.M.O. Worst of all, Jack lost all his real estate in a fire two years ago, after forgetting to pay his insurance premiums. (The value of the lots barely paid for the removal of the debris). Advise Jack.

QUESTION III

Conrad Grebel's wife, Anna, wishes to divorce him. Anna declares she has fallen in love with Dr. Jaime Mendoza, a university professor of comparative religion, with no particular religion of his own, whom she met when he came to Amishtown, PA, to buy cheese. She also complains that she has never seen much of Conrad as he works on the farm all day, and every evening he works as a blacksmith, by candlelight. The Grebels have never had electricity, radio, telephone, nor TV.

The Grebels and their extended families have been Old Order Amish since time immemorial, and Conrad and Anna have raised their two children (a girl 10 years old, a boy 12 years old) in that religion. Conrad has always taken a strong interest in his children, somewhat sternly, of course, and both parents have raised the children rather strictly in accordance with the Amish religion.

Before their separation, the Grebels resided in a 5–room farm house on 1000–acres, the latter now worth about $200,000. The house was built by Conrad just before the marriage from materials supplied by his father. It has a current replacement cost of about $40,000. The acreage is composed of 300 acres each spouse inherited from his/her family, 200 acres Conrad purchased during the marriage (from profits earned in the farming operation and savings from his evening job as a blacksmith), plus 200 acres Anna received as a wedding gift from her father when she was married. Their inherited acreage had a tax basis of $1,000 per acre, the wedding gift was then worth $2,000 an acre, and the acreage purchased during the marriage cost $3,000 per acre. All the acreage is now and always was of equal value on a per-acre basis. All the acreage was farmed as one unit by Conrad. No separate operating records were kept, and joint tax returns were filed. Anna has never had a job outside of the home, and did not participate in the operation of the farm in any way. Conrad's net profit is $10,000 per year from his farming (supplementing the ample in kind production from the farm that has always supplied most of the family's food and other daily needs), plus $10,000 cash income per year from his evening work as a blacksmith.

When she moved to Universitytown Anna requested and was awarded temporary alimony, child custody and child support. She now is staying at a motel, along with the children. Recently, the children have become a little more difficult to handle, due perhaps to the excitement of the impending divorce and their change to a wholly secular school in Universitytown. They have now been at that school for one month. Already the boy is talking of becoming an astronaut and the girl an ocean geographer. Her attraction to Dr. Mendoza has solidified into a "steady dating" relationship, but she asserts that she has no intention of marrying him. Specifically, they carry on their "affair"—Conrad admits to uncertainty as to whether adultery has occurred or is occurring—in Dr. Mendoza's home during the day, while the children are in school and Mendoza is between classes. Anna now wants to proceed with a divorce.

Advise Conrad regarding (1) child custody (which both parents desire intensely); (2) his liability for alimony to Anna; (3) Anna's property rights in their home and farm; and (4) his child support obligation should he fail to win custody. (NOTE: Discuss (3) in terms of property law prevailing in (a) typical separate property states and (b) typical community property states. Discuss the other issues (1), (2), (4), in terms of "prevailing" law in the U.S., giving important divisions in authority due play).

QUESTION IV

Your first job after graduation is as law clerk to Chief Justice Lavender of the Oklahoma Supreme Court. The trial court holding excerpted below is up on appeal. The Justice has asked you to write a memorandum discussing the relevant issues and suggesting the proper analysis and disposition of the case. (Do not be concerned how the case got to the Supreme Court from the trial court or whether, in real life, Justice Lavender actually would follow your advice).

In making the award in question, the trial court stated the following: "The Court finds that the plaintiff helped support the defendant and the family by being employed throughout the time the defendant attended pre-medical school and medical school, and has contributed to such support during the defendant's training to be a doctor, and has contributed materially to his medical education. The Court further finds that during the more than twelve years that plaintiff worked and helped defendant obtain this medical degree and train to be a doctor, she could look forward to the time when she would enjoy the prestige and position, as well as the financial comfort, of a doctor's wife. That the granting of a divorce, through no fault of plaintiff, prevents her from reaping those awards. She is relegated to her pre-marital status, except for the acquiring of an insubstantial amount of property, not recompensed for the years she has helped the defendant to attain his professional standing. The Court further finds that the defendant is now on the threshold of a successful professional life, an able-bodied man, and has a present income of some $20,000 annually. That as a medical doctor his reasonable anticipated income will be $80,000 to $120,000 per year. The Court finds that the plaintiff has a vested interest in the defendant's medical profession, which is deemed to be a valuable property right. The only means of awarding her that property right is by alimony in lieu of division of property. *** The Court further finds that the defendant is reasonably expected to earn $1,000,000 over the first twelve years of his beginning practice of medicine, with a net income of not less than $500,000. That the plaintiff is entitled to forty percent (40%) thereof as alimony in lieu of division of property. That plaintiff is therefore entitled to judgment as permanent alimony in lieu of a division of property in the amount of $200,000." (Facts adapted from *Hubbard v. Hubbard*, 603 P.2d 747 (1979)).

QUESTION V

Anna Marie Sappington, who was being paid $750 per month in alimony by her ex-husband, was sharing the former marital home with Lyle Montgomery. They shared the responsibilities of home upkeep, attended social activities together, and occupied the same room when traveling. He had access to the entire house and kept his clothes there. Lyle contended that he originally moved in to protect Anna Marie, as she was afraid of being alone. He argued that he has no interest in women and has been impotent for three or four years. Both parties denied having any sexual interest in the other and denied any sexual conduct toward the other, claiming instead that their relationship was solely that of friends.

This case involves the interpretation and application of the Marriage and Dissolution of Marriage Act which, in pertinent parts, provides: "Unless otherwise agreed by the parties in a written separation agreement set forth in the judgment or otherwise approved by the court, the obligation to pay future maintenance is terminated upon the death of either party, or the remarriage of the party receiving maintenance, or if the party receiving maintenance cohabits with another person on a resident, continuing conjugal basis."

Plaintiff Mr. Sappington has petitioned the court to relieve him of further alimony payments and has brought in Dr. Carol Moy, a professor of psychiatry and family practice at Southern University School of Medicine as his expert witness. She testified at the trial in this case. She counsels couples who are dissatisfied with their relationships and assists people in developing a conjugal relationship, including males who are impotent. She indicated that penile penetration is not the only form of sexual intercourse, that there are verbal and non-verbal ways of expressing sexuality. While indicating that a conjugal relationship does not necessarily involve sexual intercourse or sexual gratification, she defined a conjugal relationship as "a total family relationship *** between a male and a female [is] usually understood to be a relationship of two people living, functioning together in a mutually supportive atmosphere."

1. You are the judge! Decide this case, giving reasons. (Facts from *In re Marriage of Sappington*, 478 N.E.2d 376 (1985)).

2. As a legislative assistant to Representative X, make recommendation as to whether, how and why the statute should be retained, amended or repealed.

QUESTION VI

George and LaVon Feisthamel were married on October 18, 1974. They entered into an antenuptial agreement dated October 5, 1974, prior to the marriage. They separated in July, 1994.

The respondent, LaVon Feisthamel, is a 62 year old woman in fair health. LaVon has had a history of problems relating to high blood pressure, depression, post-menopausal problems, and osteoarthritis. She underwent eye surgery for glaucoma shortly before the trial in this matter and further surgery may be needed. LaVon has not been in the employment market significantly. While she was a registered nurse, she is not currently licensed since her training occurred many years ago and she has never worked in that capacity. LaVon worked as a housewife and homemaker in a previous marriage and, following her first husband's death, was employed for a short time as a secretary/receptionist in a Chiropractic Office. During her marriage to the appellant, she worked as a homemaker and housewife. She has made numerous attempts to obtain full employment and obtained a temporary Vista volunteer job for which she received $357 per month. That job ended in May, 1987.

The appellant, George Feisthamel, is a 59 year old male in generally good health. George has been employed by Long Construction Company and Western Energy for many years as a heavy equipment mechanic. He is a member of the International Union of Operating Engineers. He continues to reside in the family home. LaVon moved from the family home in July, 1994.

Both of the parties owned certain properties, both real and personal, prior to their marriage. The trial court found that the antenuptial agreement dated October 5, 1974, excluded from consideration all real and personal property owned by either party prior to the marriage in determining the issues of maintenance and division of marital assets.

The provision involving the maintenance issue in the October 5, 1974 antenuptial agreement states:

"That in the event, after entering into the marriage, said parties find they cannot live together congenially as husband and wife and decide to separate and/or to secure a divorce, and it is necessary to make an equitable division of their property rights and a determination of the rights, if any, of Second Party to separate maintenance or temporary or permanent alimony, all real and personal property now owned by the parties shall not be taken into consideration. Provided, however, in event of such separation and/or divorce, Second Party shall be entitled to an equitable division of the property accumulated and acquired as a result of and in connection with their marriage. Provided, further when said accumulated property has been equitably divided said parties shall execute and deliver to each other, a release of any and all right, title and interest which they may have or claim in and to the property now owned or hereafter accumulated by either party. Provided, further that in the event a divorce is granted by a Court of competent jurisdiction to either party the terms of this contract shall be binding upon said Court, and at the time of granting said divorce this contract shall be incorporated in said decree."

This provision was honored in the final decree. The trial court divided the net marital assets equally between the parties and awarded LaVon maintenance in the amount of $1,000 per month commencing November 1, 1995, and ending November 30, 1999.

George and LaVon contest the award of maintenance and the property disposition. George claims that the District Court should have considered a certain annuity of $500 as well as other income or benefits LaVon might receive from a trust provided by her deceased first husband. LaVon's position is that the annuity income of $500 per month and any trust benefits are covered by the antenuptial agreement and should not be considered for determining the appropriateness of maintenance. LaVon further argues that the maintenance awarded is too low and for too short a time even if the annuity were to be considered because she lacks sufficient property to provide for her reasonable needs and is unable to support herself through appropriate employment.

Decide on appeal and give reasons. (Facts adapted from *In re Marriage of Feisthamel*, 739 P.2d 474 (1987)).

QUESTION VII

In 1977, Lois Smith and Max Michoff became romantically involved, even though Max was already married. Their relationship continued, and Max divorced his wife. Lois and Max then decided to, and did, live together. At the time, Lois was employed by Max as a prototype technician, working forty hours per week and earning eleven dollars per hour.

In 1979, Lois and Max moved from California to your state. That same year, Lois Smith legally changed her name to Lois Michoff. Max's attorney handled the name change. Lois claimed that she changed her name at Max's request; he believed that if they had a woman-owned construction-type business, they would "fare better in getting jobs." For example, according to Lois, they could bid five percent over the low bid and nevertheless be classified as the low bidder. Moreover, Max wanted Lois to be the sole owner so that his ex-wife could not make a claim against the business. It is uncontroverted that Max had concealed $50,000 from his former wife and the court in which he obtained his divorce. The record, however, does not indicate whether Max had defrauded his former wife out of other assets.

The parties started a construction equipment rental business called L & M Rentals (named for Lois and Max). Lois obtained the business license and paid the licensing fees. The business license listed Lois as the sole owner. When the parties started L & M Rentals, Max transferred all of his assets from a former business to L & M Rentals. Most of the cash was then used to purchase a certificate of deposit in the name of L & M Rentals. Although Max thus had contributed a large portion of the funds to start L & M Rentals and Lois was listed as sole owner, Lois and Max had orally agreed that they really were to be co-equal owners of the business. Consequently, Lois devoted her efforts and time toward running the business, including such integral functions as bookkeeping and maintaining the equipment.

Approximately six months after starting L & M Rentals, Lois and Max discovered that they needed a contractor's license to operate the business. Lois therefore applied for such a license. Lois was listed as the owner of the business and Max was listed as the "qualified employee." Lois testified that they had agreed that it was their company; thus, again, Lois provided much of the skill and labor necessary for the business' success. Her services included doing all of the office work (bookkeeping, payroll, and paperwork) and assisting in the maintenance, service, and running of the equipment. The profits from the business were either invested into the business or retained as savings.

Lois continued to do the bookkeeping, and she also updated the records, reviewed bids, negotiated contracts and labored in the field—performing such jobs as flagging and running heavy equipment. Whenever L & M Rentals sought a license increase, it was Lois who applied for the increase. In order to obtain the necessary contractor's bonds from the Contractor's Board, Lois personally guaranteed the bonds.

During their relationship, Max held Lois out as his wife. In fact, in 1984, Max entered a partnership agreement with Robert Frybarger and requested that Lois sign a consent of spouse. This provision provided: "We, the undersigned, being the respective wives to the parties to the foregoing partnership agreement, have read and understand said agreement executed by our husbands. Each of us hereby approves and consents to the said partnership agreement and agrees to be bound by all of its provisions."

Max and Lois filed joint tax returns as husband and wife commencing in 1980 and continuing through 1995. For the years 1983 through 1995, they also filed tax returns under L & M Rentals, showing Lois as an officer and owner. Moreover, L & M Rentals incorporated and elected to file a sub-chapter S election on March 24, 1983. The election was signed by Lois and Max and designated the holdings of the corporation as jointly owned property.

After Lois and Max terminated their sexual relationship earlier this year (Lois apparently left Max because he had been physically abusing her), she brought this action, seeking a declaration and judgment that she owns one-half of all of the parties' assets, including of course L & M, their home and furnishings and various investments. She also seeks long-term support from Max.

As best you can, decide this case under your state's law, giving reasons. To the extent you do not know your state's law, apply "national" law. To the extent you do know your state's law, compare "national" law. (Facts are adapted from *Western States Construction, Inc. v. Michoff*, 108 Nev. 931, 840 P.2d 1220 (1992)).

*

APPENDIX C

TEXT CORRELATION CHART

	Areen 1995 Supp. 3rd ed.	Clark, Glowinsky 5th ed.	Ellman, Kurtz, Bartlett 2d ed.	Krause 1993 Supp. 3rd ed.	Mnookin & Weisberg 3rd ed.	Schneider, Brinig	Wadlington 3rd ed.	Westfall	Weyrauch, Katz, Olsen
I. THE NATURE OF MARRIAGE									
A. Religious Influence		2–16					21–22	126–146	
B. Contract or Status				82–85		343–354	12–21		
C. Controlling Factors Affecting the Marriage Contract		101–115							
D. Marriage and the Supreme Court of the United States	34–48 126–135	69–88	851–854	324–336			29–61	4–11 189–196	484–496
E. Common Law Marriage	71–77			61–69					
F. Married Women's Property Acts		9		175–176			207–210		
G. The Antenuptial Agreement	158–173	17–48	661–687	92–114	1020–1071	314–315	1140–1168		41–73
H. Agreements During Marriage	78–85	678–687		115–118					
I. Conflicts Aspects of Marital Agreements				114–115					
J./K. Breach of Promise to Marry and Gifts in Contemplation of Marriage				120–122			107–118	180–187	
II. MARRIAGE REQUISITES									
A. Formal Requirements	48–68	88–110	19–74	50–69 74–81 S.17–19		12–16	125–127 140–181	188–208	161–308
B. Substantive Requirements for Valid Marriage	2–33 66–77 S.1–13	124–159		2–49 S.2–14		3–56	127–181	197–205	513–586
C. Conflicts of Laws			74–77	70–73			181–187		
D. Annulment				501–513			118–125	591–611	502–512
III. COHABITATION WITHOUT MARRIAGE									
A. Unmarried Cohabitation	900–908	48–68	799–847	130–167		399–461	70–105	272–294	213–264
B. Same-Sex Relationships	25–26	124–137	46–53	8 1223		563–575	51–70	56–75	307

	Arsen 1995 Supp. 3rd ed.	Clark, Glowinsky 5th ed.	Ellman, Kurtz, Bartlett	Krause 1993 Supp. 3rd ed.	Mnookin & Weisberg 3rd ed.	Schneider, Brinig	Wadlington 3rd ed.	Westfall	Weyrauch, Katz, Olsen
IV. HUSBAND & WIFE									
A. Support Obligations During Marriage	285–290	514–518	84–94	183–192		234–245	210–221	100–104 239	
B. Property Rights	290–293			202–233			221–232	231–239	92–156
C. Torts and the Family	238–255 272–278 1106–1112 1122–1129 1310–1323	699–727	121–144	233–247		175–181	233–238 262–267 640–644	239–248 256–270 255–309 485–500	317–324
D. Marriage and Criminal Law	255–272 278–284		121–144	256–292			238–263	248–256	466–477
E. Family Names	122–124 1158–1165	673–678		176–182 1134–1191			191–207		
V. DIVORCE—STATUS									
A. Access to and Jurisdiction of Courts	392–416	728–754	613–660	470–491 S. 58–62			944–948 974–1019	545–589	987–1039
B. Traditional Grounds and Defenses	317–340	755–757 772–773	161–165	403–429			940–944	611–621	
C. Divorce Reform	340–355	757–772	165–212	430–451		59–117	948–973	687–694	
D. Separation				492–500					
VI. DIVORCE—FINANCIAL CONSEQUENCES									
A. Alimony on Divorce	724–728	797–805 873–925	261–301 338–354	514–580 S. 63–67		256–306	1030–1060	694–697 851–916	623–644
B. Property Division on Divorce	716–724 728–750	806–873	213–260 321–331	581–676 S. 70–85		256–306	1104–1140	702–844	589–612
C. Separation Agreements	816–842	1002–1032	688–756	691–709		316–317	1168–1191	1077–1119	
VII. THE PARENTAL CHILD SUPPORT OBLIGATION									
A. Historical Development	514–518	514–518	355	1023–1029	216–229			445–449	
B. Duration of the Obligation	518–523	518–523	356–367	1075–1081					
C. Criteria for Awarding Support	760–770 S. 88–125	925–966	368–402	1045–1062	246–252 256–277	970–1001	1060–1077	464–479 989–1010	896–907
D. Stepparent's Duty to Support		524–527	362–363	1029–1037	253–256		1077–1090	208–211 981–989	

	Areen 1995 Supp. 3rd ed.	Clark, Glowinsky 5th ed.	Ellman, Kurtz, Bartlett	Krause 1993 Supp. 3rd ed.	Mnookin & Weisberg 3rd ed.	Schneider, Brinig	Wadlington 3rd ed.	Westfall	Weyrauch, Katz, Olsen
F. Disposition of the Juvenile Court	1429–1505	382–389 1614–1649			1079–1203		728–741	179–180	
G. Criminal Procedure									
X. CHILDREN'S RIGHTS									
A. Constitutional Rights	1523–1552		1069–1111	1196–1222 S. 181–197					
B. History of Parental Control	1074–1082	657–665		1117–1121					661–671
C. Emancipation	1358–1375	668–669		1133–1134			644–646		
D. Minor's Capacity to Contract	1323–1330	665–668							
E. Children and Tort Law					347–348				
F. Property Rights									
G. Education: State and Parents	1165–1199		1049–1064	1142–1152	59–102	1046–1072	466–494	146–157	646–661
XI. LEGITIMACY, ILLEGITIMACY, AND PATERNITY									
A. Legitimacy		254–257		884–918 S. 124–129			269–282		
B. Illegitimacy	1246–1267	257–288		919–932	229–231 238–242 287–300			18–20	
C. Establishing Paternity	207–217	288–307 314–345	881–965	932–992 S. 130–133	231–237 242–245 745–776		289–343	381–410	
D. Conflicts of Laws		307–314					343–344		
XII. ADOPTION									
A. History and Development	1552–1581	420–477					826–828		953–958
B. Social Function						1073–1109	828–847		
C. The Adoption Process	1582–1589			1097–1105					
D. Qualifications of Adoptive Parents	1553–1567			1290–1308					

	Areen 1995 Supp. 3rd ed.	Clark, Glowinsky 5th ed.	Ellman, Kurtz, Bartlett	Krause 1993 Supp. 3rd ed.	Mnookin & Weisberg 3rd ed.	Schneider, Brinig	Wadlington 3rd ed.	Westfall	Weyrauch, Katz, Olsen
E. Consent to Adoption	195–207 S. 216–234 S. 257–266	347–382 389–400	1219–1231	993–1022 1309–1322 S. 134–157	735–745		282–289 768–782 847–891	411–428	743–822
F. Anonymity	1596–1602			1282–1289			925–934	431–435	
G. Revocation of Adoption	1589–1595	469–477	1232–1252	1327–1332	779–782		920–921	440–442	
H. Legal Effect of Adoption	1609–1613 S. 266–275	477–479	1332–1345	1323–1326			907–920 934–939		
XIII. PROCREATION									
A. Contraception and the U.S. Supreme Court	217–222 S. 136–171	69–79	848–859	324–332	983–1006	477–494	29–51		350–352
B. Abortion	222–253 909–929 937–960	160–228	969–1018 1086–1111	337–374 S. 35–57	4–59	497–561	345–346 355–367	21–56	353–394 684–718
C. Sterilization	960–962 978–1017	228–254	1018–1022	1165–1171			346–355	314–325	
D. Artificial Conception	1026–1073 S. 181–210	480–514	1300–1331	1372–1433 S. 205–240	677–695 901–914		367–465	333–381	823–830

APPENDIX D

GLOSSARY*

* Based on Black's Law Dictionary.

A

Adoption Legal process pursuant to which a child's legal rights and duties toward his natural parents are terminated and similar rights and duties toward his adoptive parents are substituted. The procedure is entirely statutory and has no historical basis in common law.

Affinity Relation which one spouse because of marriage has to blood relatives of the other. The connection existing, in consequence of marriage, between each of the married persons and the kindred of the other. Degrees of relationship by affinity are computed as are degrees of relationship by consanguinity. The doctrine of affinity grew out of the canonical maxim that marriage makes husband and wife one. The husband has the same relation, by affinity, to his wife's blood relatives as she has to them by consanguinity and vice versa. Affinity is distinguished into three kinds: (1) Direct, or that subsisting between the husband and his wife's relations by blood, or between the wife and the husband's relations by blood; (2) secondary, or that which subsists between the husband and his wife's relations by marriage; (3) collateral, or that which subsists between the husband and the relations of his wife's relations.

Alienation of Affections "Alienation of affections" is a tort based upon willful and malicious interference with marriage relation by third party, without justification or excuse. The elements constituting the cause of action are wrongful conduct of defendant, plaintiff's loss of affection or consortium of spouse and causal connection between such conduct and such loss. See also Consortium; Heartbalm Statutes.

Alimony Comes from Latin "alimonia" meaning sustenance, and means, therefore, the sustenance or support of the wife by her divorced husband and stems from the common-law right of the wife to support by her husband. Allowances which husband or wife by court order pays other spouse for maintenance while they

321

are separated, or after they are divorced (permanent alimony), or temporarily, pending a suit for divorce (pendente lite). Generally, it is restricted to money unless otherwise authorized by statute. But it may be an allowance out of the spouse's estate.

Alimony in Gross Alimony in a lump sum, is in the nature of a final property settlement, and hence in some jurisdictions is not included in the term "alimony," which in its strict or technical sense contemplates money payments at regular intervals. Refers to those alimony arrangements where entire award is a vested and determined amount and not subject to change.

Alimony Pendente Lite An allowance for temporary alimony made pending a suit for divorce or separate maintenance including a reasonable allowance for preparation of the suit as well as for support.

Annulment To nullify, to abolish, to make void an attempted or purported marriage by competent authority. An "annulment" differs conceptually from a divorce in that a divorce terminates a legal status, whereas an annulment establishes that a marital status never existed.

Antenuptial Agreement A contract between spouses made before and in contemplation of marriage. Antenuptial agreements are generally entered into by people about to enter marriage in an attempt to resolve issues of support, distribution of wealth and division of property in the event of the death of either or the failure of the proposed marriage resulting in either separation or divorce. Commonly, the statute of frauds requires a writing and signing to be enforceable.

Arbitration The reference of a dispute to an impartial (third) person chosen by the parties to the dispute who agree in advance to abide by the arbitrator's award issued after a hearing at which both parties have an opportunity to be heard. See also Conciliation; Mediation.

Augmented Estate Estate reduced by funeral and administration expenses, homestead allowance, family allowances, exemptions, and enforceable claims to which is added value of property transferred to anyone other than bona fide purchaser and value of property owned by surviving spouse at decedent's death. This concept is used in the Uniform Probate Code.

B

Banns of Matrimony Public notice or proclamation of a matrimonial contract, and the intended celebration of the marriage of the parties in pursuance of such contract. Such announcement is required by certain religions to be made in a church or chapel, during service, on three consecutive Sundays before the marriage is celebrated. The object is to afford an opportunity for any person to interpose an objection if he knows of any impediment or other just cause why the marriage should not take place.

Bigamy The criminal offense of willfully and knowingly contracting a second marriage (or going through the form of a second marriage) while the first marriage, to the knowledge of the offender, is still subsisting and undissolved. The state of a man who has two wives, or of a woman who has two husbands, living at the same time. A married person is guilty of bigamy, a misdemeanor, if he contracts or purports to contract another marriage, unless at the time of the subsequent marriage: (a) the actor believes that the prior spouse is dead; or (b) the actor and the prior spouse have been living apart for five consecutive years throughout which the prior spouse was not known by the actor to be alive; or (c) a court has entered a judgment purporting to terminate or annul any prior disqualifying marriage, and the actor does not know that judgment to be invalid; or (d) the actor reasonably believes that he is legally eligible to remarry. Model Penal Code, § 230.1. See also polygamy.

C

Capacity Legal qualification (i.e. legal age), competency, power or fitness. Ability to understand the nature and effects of one's acts. The ability of a particular individual or entity to use, or to be brought into, the courts of a forum.

Cohabitation To live together as husband and wife. The mutual assumption of those marital rights, duties and obligations which are usually manifested by married people, including but not necessarily dependent on sexual relations. See also "Palimony."

Collusion In divorce proceedings, collusion is an agreement between husband and wife that one of them shall commit, or appear to have committed, or be represented in court as having committed, acts constituting a cause of divorce, for the purpose of enabling the other to obtain a divorce. But it also means connivance or conspiracy in initiating or prosecuting the suit, as where there is a compact for mutual aid in carrying it through to a decree.

Comity Recognition that one sovereignty allows within its territory to the legislative, executive, or judicial act of another sovereignty, having due regard to rights of its own citizens. In general, principle of "comity" is that courts of one state or jurisdiction will give effect to laws and judicial decisions of another state or jurisdiction, not as a matter of obligation but out of deference and mutual respect.

Common–Law Marriage One not solemnized in the ordinary way (i.e. non-ceremonial) but created by an agreement to marry, followed by cohabitation. A consummated agreement to marry, between persons legally capable of making marriage contract, *per verba de praesenti,* followed by cohabitation. Such marriage requires a positive mutual agreement, permanent and exclusive of all others, to enter into a marriage relationship, cohabitation sufficient to warrant a fulfillment of necessary relationship of man and wife, holding out to the public as such, and an assumption of marital duties and obligations.

Community Property Property owned in common by husband and wife each having an undivided one-half interest by reason of their marital status. Nine states have community property systems. The rest of the states are classified as common law jurisdictions. The difference between common law and community property systems centers around the property rights possessed by married persons. In a common law system, each spouse owns whatever he or she earns. Under a community property system, one-half of the earnings of each spouse is considered "earned" by the other spouse.

Conciliation The adjustment and settlement of a dispute in a friendly, unantagonistic manner. See also Arbitration; Mediation.

Condonation The conditional remission or forgiveness, by means of continuance or resumption of marital cohabitation, by one of the married parties, of a known matrimonial offense committed by the other, that would constitute a cause of divorce; the condition being that the offense shall not be repeated. Condonation to constitute valid defense in divorce action, must be free, voluntary, and not induced by duress or fraud.

Conjugal Of or belonging to marriage or the married state; suitable or appropriate to the married state or to married persons; matrimonial; connubial.

Connivance The secret or indirect consent or permission of one person to the commission of an unlawful or criminal act by another. As constituting defense in divorce action, is plaintiff's corrupt consent, express or implied, to offense charged against defendant.

Consanguinity Kinship; blood relationship; the connection or relation of persons descended from the same stock or common ancestor. Consanguinity is distinguished from "affinity," which is the connection existing in consequence of a marriage, between each of the married persons and the kindred of the other. Lineal consanguinity is that which subsists between persons of whom one is descended in a direct line from the other, as between son, father, grandfather, great-grandfather, and so upwards in the direct ascending line; or between son, grandson, great-grandson, and so downwards in the direct descending line. Collateral consanguinity is that which subsists between persons who have the same ancestors, but who do not descend (or ascend) one from the other. Thus, father and son are related by lineal consanguinity, uncle and nephew by collateral consanguinity.

Consortium Conjugal fellowship of husband and wife, and the right of each to the company, society, cooperation, affection, and aid of the other in every conjugal relation. Damages for loss of consortium are commonly sought in wrongful death actions, or when spouse has been seriously injured through negligence of another, or by spouse against third person alleging that he or she has caused breaking-up of marriage. "Loss of consortium" means loss of society, affection, assistance and conjugal fellowship, and includes loss or impairment of sexual relations. Cause of action for "consortium" occasioned by injury to marriage partner, is a separate cause of action belonging to the spouse of the injured married partner and though derivative in the sense of being occasioned by injury to spouse, is a direct injury to the spouse who has lost the consortium.

Criminal Conversation Sexual intercourse of an outsider with husband or wife. Tort action based on adultery, considered in its aspect of a civil injury to the husband or wife entitling him or her to damages; the tort of debauching or seducing of a wife or husband. See also Alienation of Affections; Heartbalm statutes.

Curtesy The estate to which by common law a man was entitled, on the death of his wife, in the lands or tenements of which she was seised in possession in fee-simple or in tail during her coverture, provided they have had lawful issue born alive which might have been capable of inheriting the estate. It was a freehold estate for the term of his natural life. In some jurisdictions, there was no requirement that issue have been born of the union. The estate has gradually lost much of its former value.

D

Desertion As used in statute providing that parental consent to adoption is not required when parent has wilfully deserted child evinces settled purpose to forego, abandon, or desert all parental duties and parental rights in child. Constructive desertion: That arising where an existing cohabitation is put an end to by misconduct of one of the parties, provided such misconduct is itself a ground for divorce. For example, where one spouse, by his or her words, conduct, demeanor, and attitude produces an intolerable condition which forces the other spouse to withdraw from the joint habitation to a more peaceful one. Divorce law: As a ground for divorce, an actual abandonment or breaking off of matrimonial cohabitation, by either of the parties, and a renouncing or refusal of the duties and obligations of the relation, with an intent to abandon or forsake entirely and not to return to or resume marital relations, occurring without legal justification either in the consent or the wrongful conduct of the other party. The elements of offense of "desertion" as grounds for divorce are a voluntary intentional abandonment of one party by the other, without cause or justification and without consent of party abandoned.

Dissolution of Marriage (See Divorce, Annulment).

Divisible Divorce Decree of divorce may be divided as between provisions for support and alimony and provisions dissolving the marriage. Doctrine applied in cases under Full Faith and Credit Clause in connection with effect of foreign divorce on support provisions.

Divorce The legal separation of husband and wife, effected by the judgment or decree of a court, and either totally dissolving the marriage relation, or suspending its effects so far as concerns the cohabitation of the parties.

Divorce *a Mensa et Thoro* A divorce from table and bed, or from bed and board. A partial or qualified divorce, by which the parties are separated and forbidden to live or cohabit together, without affecting the marriage itself.

Divorce *a Vinculo Matrimonii* A divorce from the bond of marriage (annulment). A total divorce of husband and wife, dissolving the marriage tie, and releasing the parties wholly from their matrimonial obligations.

Domicile That place where a man has his true, fixed, and permanent home and principal establishment, and to which whenever he is absent he has the intention of returning. The permanent residence of a person or the place to which he intends to return even though he may actually reside elsewhere. A person may have more than one residence but only one domicile. Matrimonial domicile: The place where a husband and wife have established a home, in which they reside in the relation of husband and wife, and where the matrimonial contract is being performed.

Dower The provision which the law makes for a widow out of the lands or tenements of her husband, for her support and the nurture of her children. A species of life-estate which a woman is, by law, entitled to claim on the death of her husband, in the lands and tenements of which he was seised in fee during the marriage, and which her issue, if any, might by possibility have inherited. The life estate to which every married woman is entitled on death of her husband, intestate, or, in case she dissents from his will one-third in value of all lands of which husband was beneficially seized in law or in fact, at any time during coverture. Dower has been abolished in the majority of the states and materially altered in most of the others.

E

Equitable Adoption "Equitable adoption" refers to situation involving oral contract to adopt child, fully performed except that there was no statutory adoption, and in which rule is applied for benefit of child in determination of heirship upon death of person contracting to adopt.

Emancipation The term is principally used with reference to the emancipation of a minor child by its parents, which involves an entire surrender of the right to the care, custody, and earnings of such child as well as a renunciation of parental duties. The emancipation may be express, as by voluntary agreement of parent and child, or implied from such acts and conduct as import consent, and it may be conditional or absolute, complete or partial. Complete emancipation is entire surrender of care, custody, and earnings of child, as well as renunciation of parental duties. A "partial emancipation" frees a child for only a part of the period

of minority, or from only a part of the parent's rights, or for some purposes, and not for others.

Estoppel "Estoppel" means that party is prevented by his own acts from claiming a right to detriment of other party who was entitled to rely on such conduct and has acted accordingly. An inconsistent position, attitude or course of conduct may not be adopted to loss or injury of another. Estoppel is a bar or impediment which precludes allegation or denial of a certain fact or state of facts, in consequence of previous allegation or denial or conduct or admission, or in consequence of a final adjudication of the matter in a court of law. It operates to put party entitled to its benefits in same position as if thing represented were true.

Estover An allowance (more commonly called "alimony") granted to a woman divorced a mensa et thoro, for her support out of her husband's estate.

***Ex Parte* Divorce** Divorce proceeding in which only one spouse participates or one in which the other spouse does not appear.

F

Fornication Unlawful sexual intercourse between two unmarried persons. Further, if one of the persons be married and the other not, it is fornication on the part of the latter, though adultery for the former. In some jurisdictions, however, by statute, it is adultery on the part of both persons if the woman is married, whether the man is married or not.

Forum Non Conveniens Term refers to discretionary power of court to decline jurisdiction when convenience of parties and ends of justice would be better served if action were brought and tried in another forum. The doctrine is patterned upon the right of the court in the exercise of its powers to refuse the imposition upon its jurisdiction of the trial of cases even though the venue is properly laid if it appears that for the convenience of litigants and witnesses and in the interest of justice the action should be instituted in another forum where the action might have been brought. The doctrine presupposes at least two forums in which the defendant is amenable to process and furnishes criteria for choice between such forums.

Full Faith and Credit Clause   The clause of the U.S. Constitution (Art. IV, Sec. 1) which provides that the various states must recognize legislative acts, public records, and judicial decisions of the other states within the United States. There are exceptions to this, a major one being that a state need not recognize a divorce decree of a state where neither spouse was a legal resident. Doctrine means that a state must accord the judgment of a court of another state the same credit that it is entitled to in the courts of that state. See also Comity.

H

Heartbalm Statutes   State statutes abolishing or restricting common law right of action for alienation of affections, breach of promise to marry, criminal conversation, and seduction of person over legal age of consent.

I

Illegitimate Child   Child who is born to parents who are not married to each other.

Incest   The crime of sexual intercourse or cohabitation between a man and woman who are related to each other within the degrees wherein marriage is prohibited by law. A person is guilty of incest, a felony of the third degree, if he knowingly marries or cohabits or has sexual intercourse with an ancestor or descendant, a brother or sister of the whole or half blood (or an uncle, aunt, nephew or niece of the whole blood). "Cohabit" means to live together under the representation or appearance of being married. The relationships referred to herein includes blood relationships without regard to legitimacy, and relationship of parent and child by adoption. Model Penal Code, § 230.2.

Intestacy   The state or condition of dying without having made a valid will, or without having disposed by will of a part of his property.

J

Joint Tenancy   An estate in fee-simple, fee-tail, for life, for years, or at will, arising by purchase or grant to two or more persons. Joint tenants have one and the same interest, accruing by one and the same conveyance, commencing at one and the same time, and held by one and the same undivided possession. The primary incident of joint tenancy is survivorship, by which the entire tenancy on the decease of any joint tenant remains to the survivors, and at length to the last survivor. Type of ownership of real or personal property by two or more persons in which each owns an undivided interest in the whole and attached to which is the right of survivorship. Single estate in property owned by two or more persons under one instrument or act.

L

Legal Separation   (See Separate Maintenance; Divorce *a mensa et thoro*).

Legitimacy   Lawful birth; the condition of being born in wedlock; the opposite of illegitimacy or bastardy.

"Long Arm" Statute   Various state legislative acts which provide for personal jurisdiction over persons who are nonresidents of the state and who have contacts within the state deemed sufficiently significant (measured under the due process clause) to have them brought before the courts of the state for litigation.

M

Maintenance   The furnishing by one person to another, for his support, of the means of living, or food, clothing, shelter, etc., particularly where the legal relation of the parties is such that one is bound to support the other, as between father and child, or husband and wife. The supplying of the necessaries of life. Term "maintenance" means primarily food, clothing and shelter.

Marriage   Legal union of one man and one woman as husband and wife. Marriage, as distinguished from the agreement to marry and from the act of becoming married, is the legal status, condition, or relation of one man and one woman united in law for life, or until divorced, for the discharge to each other and the community of the duties legally incumbent on those whose association is founded on the distinction of sex. A contract, according to the form prescribed by law, by which a man and woman capable of entering into such contract, mutually engage with each other to live their whole lives (or until divorced) together in the state of union which ought to exist between a husband and wife. The word also signifies the act, ceremony, or formal proceeding by which persons take each other for husband and wife. Marriage which follows all the statutory requirements of blood tests, license, waiting period, and which has been solemnized before an official (religious or civil) capable of presiding at the marriage. See also Voidable Marriage; Void Marriage.

Mediation Intervention; interposition; the act of a third person in intermediating between two contending parties with a view to persuading them to adjust or settle their dispute. Settlement of dispute by action of intermediary (neutral party). See also Arbitration; Conciliation.

Meretricious Of the nature of unlawful sexual connection.

Migratory Divorce Term used to describe a divorce secured by a spouse or spouses who leave(s) his/their domicile and move(s) to, or reside(s) temporarily in, another state or country for purpose of securing the divorce. See also *Ex parte* divorce.

Miscegenation Term formerly applied to marriage between persons of different races.

Monogamy The marriage of one spouse only, or the state of such as are restrained to a single spouse. The term is used in opposition to "bigamy" and "polygamy".

N

Necessaries An article which a party actually needs. Things indispensable, or things proper and useful, for the sustenance of human life. The word has no hard and fast meaning, but varies with the accustomed manner of living of the parties. Necessaries consist of food, drink, clothing, medical attention, and a suitable place of residence, and they are regarded as necessaries in the absolute sense of the word. However, liability for necessaries is not limited to articles required to sustain life; it extends to articles which would ordinarily be necessary and suitable, in view of the rank, position, fortune, earning capacity, and mode of living of the household.

Neglected Child A child is "neglected" when his parent or custodian, by reason of cruelty, mental incapacity, immorality or depravity, is unfit properly to care for him, or neglects or refuses to provide necessary physical, affectional, medical, surgical, or institutional or hospital care for him, or he is in such condition of want or suffering, or is under such improper care or control as to endanger his morals or health.

Non-marital Child See "Illegitimate Child".

P

"Palimony" Slang term with meaning similar to "alimony" except that award, settlement or agreement arises out of nonmarital relationship of parties (*i.e.*, nonmarital partners). *Marvin v. Marvin* held that courts should enforce express contracts between nonmarital partners except to the extent the contract is explicitly founded on the consideration of meretricious sexual services, despite contention that such contracts violate public policy; that in the absence of express contract, the court should inquire into the conduct of the parties to determine whether that conduct demonstrates implied contract, agreement of partnership or joint venture, or some other tacit understanding between the parties, and may also employ the doctrine of quantum meruit or equitable remedies such as constructive or resulting trust, when warranted by the facts of the case.

Paternity The state or condition of a father; the relationship of a father.

Peonage A condition of servitude (prohibited by 13th Amendment) compelling persons to perform labor in order to pay off a debt.

Per Verba de Futuro By words of the future (tense). A phrase applied to contracts of marriage.

Per Verba de Praesenti By words of the present (tense). A phrase applied to contracts of marriage.

Plural Marriage In general, any bigamous or polygamous union, but particularly, a second or subsequent marriage of a man who already has one wife living under system of polygamy.

Polygamy The offense of having several wives or husbands at the same time, or more than one wife or husband at the same time. Bigamy literally means a second marriage distinguished from a third or other; while polygamy means many marriages. See also monogamy.

Postnuptial After marriage.

Prenuptial Before marriage.

Pretermitted Heir A child or other descendant omitted by a testator. Where a testator unintentionally fails to mention in his will, or make provision for, a child, either living at the date of the execution of the will or born thereafter, a statute may provide that such child, or the issue of a deceased child, shall share in the estate as though the testator had died intestate.

Putative Marriage A marriage contracted in good faith and in ignorance (on one or both sides) that impediments exist which render it unlawful.

Putative Spouse One, in an invalid marriage, believing, in good faith, to be the spouse of another.

Proxy Marriage A marriage contracted or celebrated through agents acting on behalf of one or both parties. A proxy marriage differs from the more conventional ceremony only in that one or both of the contracting parties are represented by an agent; all the other requirements having been met.

R

Reconciliation The renewal of amicable relations between two persons who had been at variance; usually implying forgiveness on one or both sides. In law of domestic relations, a voluntary resumption of marital relations in the fullest sense.

Recrimination A charge made by an accused person against the accuser; in particular a counter-charge of adultery or cruelty made by one charged with the same offense in a suit for divorce, against the person who has charged him or her. Under doctrine of "recrimination", if conduct of both husband and wife has been such as to furnish grounds for divorce neither is entitled to relief.

Res Judicata A matter adjudged; a thing judicially acted upon or decided; a thing or matter settled by judgment. Rule that a final judgment rendered by a court of competent jurisdiction on the merits is conclusive as to the rights of the parties and their privies, and, as to them, constitutes an absolute bar to a subsequent action involving the same claim, demand or cause of action. And to be applicable, requires identity in thing sued for as well as identity of cause of action, of persons and parties to action, and of quality in persons for or against whom claim is made. The sum and substance of the whole rule is that a matter once judicially decided is finally decided.

S

Separate Maintenance Money paid by one married person to the other for support if they are no longer living as husband and wife, but are not divorced. See also Alimony.

Separate Property Property owned by married person in his or her own right during marriage.

Solemnization To enter marriage publicly before witnesses in contrast to a clandestine or common law marriage.

Sua Sponte Of his or its own will or motion; voluntarily; without prompting or suggestion.

T

Tenancy by the Entirety A tenancy which is created between a husband and wife and by which together they hold title to the whole with right of survivorship so that, upon death of either, other takes whole to exclusion of deceased heirs. It is essentially a "joint tenancy," modified by the common-law theory that husband and wife are one person, and survivorship is the predominant and distinguishing feature of each.

V

Voidable Marriage One which is not void when entered into and which remains valid until either party secures lawful court order dissolving the marital relationship. A voidable marriage is one where there is an imperfection which can be inquired into only during the lives of both of the parties in a proceeding to obtain a judgment declaring it void.

Void Marriage One not good for any legal purpose, the invalidity of which may be maintained in any proceeding between any parties. Such marriage is invalid from its inception, and parties thereto may simply separate without benefit of court order of divorce or annulment.

APPENDIX E

TABLE OF CASES

APPENDIX F

INDEX

References are to Text and do not include the "Capsule Summary"

335

†